Slow Philosophy

Slow Philosophy

Reading against the Institution

MICHELLE BOULOUS WALKER

Bloomsbury Academic
An imprint of Bloomsbury Publishing Plc

B L O O M S B U R Y
LONDON • OXFORD • NEW YORK • NEW DELHI • SYDNEY

Bloomsbury Academic
An imprint of Bloomsbury Publishing Plc

50 Bedford Square	1385 Broadway
London	New York
WC1B 3DP	NY 10018
UK	USA

www.bloomsbury.com

BLOOMSBURY and the Diana logo are trademarks of Bloomsbury Publishing Plc

First published 2017
Reprinted 2017 (twice), 2018

© Michelle Boulous Walker, 2017

Michelle Boulous Walker has asserted her right under the Copyright, Designs and Patents Act, 1988, to be identified as Author of this work.

All rights reserved. No part of this publication may be reproduced or transmitted in any form or by any means, electronic or mechanical, including photocopying, recording, or any information storage or retrieval system, without prior permission in writing from the publishers.

No responsibility for loss caused to any individual or organization acting on or refraining from action as a result of the material in this publication can be accepted by Bloomsbury or the author.

British Library Cataloguing-in-Publication Data
A catalogue record for this book is available from the British Library.

ISBN: HB: 9781474279918
PB: 9781474279925
ePDF: 9781474279901
ePub: 9781474279932

Library of Congress Cataloging-in-Publication Data
A catalog record for this book is available from the Library of Congress.

Typeset by RefineCatch Limited, Bungay, Suffolk
Printed and bound in Great Britain

For Christian and for Solomon

CONTENTS

Acknowledgements x
Preface: Why Slow Reading Today xii
    Posing the Question: What is it to Read xii
    About the Chapters xvii

Introduction: On Being Slow and Doing Philosophy 1
The Love of Wisdom and the Desire to Know 1
The Play between the Instituting and the Instituted in Philosophy 5
Philosophy as a Way of Life: Slow Reading – Slow Philosophy 8
Resisting Institutional Reading 32

1 Habits of Reading: Le Dœuff's Future Philosophy 35
Philosophy as Discipline 36
Philosophy's Old Habits of Reading 37
How Men and Women Read 41
Teaching Reading: Sadism, Collaboration? 46
Le Dœuff's Habits of Reading 48
A Philosophy Still to Come: Open-ended Work 51
Habits of Slow Reading 52

2 Reading Essayistically: Levinas and Adorno 55
Emmanuel Levinas: An Ethics of Reading? 56
Institution and Instrumental Reason 61

Theodor W. Adorno: The Essay as Form 62
Luiz Costa Lima: Criticity and the Essay 66
Hans Ulrich Gumbrecht: Reading for *Stimmung* 69
Robert Musil: Essay, Ethics, Aesthetics 71

3 Rereading: Irigaray on Love and Wonder 75
   Psychoanalysis, Listening, Attention 76
   Irigaray's Diotima: The Arts of Philosophy, Reading and Love 78
   Descartes's *Passions of the Soul*: Irigaray's Wondrous Reading 90
   Love and Wonder: Reading 98

4 The Present of Reading: Irigaray's Attentive Listening 103
   The Nobility of Sight: Hans Jonas 104
   Listening-to: Luce Irigaray's Way of Love 108
   The Present of Reading: Friedrich Nietzsche and Others 121

5 Romance and Authenticity: Beauvoir's Lesson in Reading 127
   Romantic and Authentic Love 128
   Reading and Love 135
   Authenticity as Ethics? 142
   Returning to Beauvoir: How Does She Read? 143
   Le Dœuff's Rereading of Beauvoir's Reading of Sartre: Operative Philosophy 144
   Rethinking Operative Philosophy with the Help of Beauvoir's Own Categories of Romance and Authenticity 148
   Beauvoir Reading the Couple: 'Sartre and Beauvoir' 149

6 Intimate Reading: Cixous's Approach 155
   A Desire Resonant with Love 156
   Cixous Writing: *Entredeux* 158

Writing as Gift and Generosity 162
Generosity, Love, Abandon 164
Cixous Reading: Intimacy, Giving 168
The Approach: A Slow Passage between the Self and the
    Strangeness of the Other 169
Cixous and Irigaray: Extreme Proximity? 171
The Gifts of Abandon and Grace: An Ethics of Reading 174

Conclusion: The Attentive Work of Grace 177

Simone Weil: Attention to Gravity and Grace 180
Martin Heidegger: Rapture (*Rausch*) and Meditative
    Thinking 182
Reading as an Aesthetic Experience 184
Hans Ulrich Gumbrecht: Reading for Intensity 186

Notes 191
References 275
Index 295

ACKNOWLEDGEMENTS

Writing is a thoroughly collaborate practice, despite our intuitions and prejudices to the contrary. In acknowledging this, I acknowledge the collaborative work that I have undertaken with Matthew Lamb, who has been a (slow) reader of extraordinary care and grace in relation to this work. I thank him most warmly for the ongoing opportunity to engage in dialogue and to experience the rare pleasure of thinking with another. I thank him, too, for his generosity and openness in an age where a competitive atmosphere haunts the modern institution, and all too often threatens the very fragile nature of intellectual collegiality. In addition, I thank Costica Bradatan for his intellectual belief in this work and his strategic genius in helping me to publish it. Working with Costica and Matthew constitutes one of the sustaining joys of my academic life. Another of these is the privileged relation of working with graduate students – and I thank the many young philosophers I have worked closely with over the years. They continue to inspire and sustain me. I thank them – past and present – most warmly, especially Laura Roberts, Emma Wilson, Mark Cutler, Marco Motta and Bryan Mukandi. I thank, additionally, the generosity and insight of colleagues who have worked with me, encouraged me, and – in some cases – commented on various drafts. I am greatly indebted to them for ongoing conversation and intellectual support. In particular I thank Fred D'Agostino, Anne Freadman, Caitlin Goss, Max Deutscher, Julie Kelso, Martin Lloyd, Nick Trakakis, Carole Ramsey, Ruth Hagengruber and Louis du Toit. I thank, too, my colleagues in the School of Historical and Philosophical Inquiry, especially – though not exclusively, in philosophy. I thank particularly Clive Moore, Marguerite La Caze and Gilbert Burgh. I thank the following people who in various and diverse ways have supported me throughout the writing of this work: Anthony Ashbolt, Christine Barron, Sandi Black, Angela Hirst, Michelle

ACKNOWLEDGEMENTS

Irving, Margi Jones, Hilma af Klint, Thomas Kreutzer, David McMillan, Silvia Menjivar, Nyla Pusinsky and my beloved family. Importantly, I acknowledge and thank my Berlin connection, the scholars, writers and journalists who continue to nourish me intellectually and spiritually. I thank Sabine Sielke, Anne Haubek, Riikka Ala-Harja and Laurel Fulkerson. Finally, I thank Ellie Gleeson at *le mot juste* and my publishers and editors, Liza Thompson, Frankie Mace, Merv Honeywood and Carole Pearce at Bloomsbury for the care and attention they have brought to the publication of this work.

Thanks and acknowledgement to the following journals and publishing houses for permission to reprint revised versions of early work: Early versions of parts of chapter two and chapter three first appeared in different form as "An Ethics of Reading: Adorno, Levinas and Irigaray" in *Philosophy Today* 50(2) 2006: 223–38, "Becoming Slow: Philosophy, Reading, and the Essay" in *Antipodean Philosopher: Public Lectures on Philosophy in Australia and New Zealand* edited by Graham Oppy and N.N. Trakakis Copyright © 2011 (used by permission of Roman & Littlefield Publishing Group. All rights reserved), and "Imagining Happiness: Literature and the Essay" in *Culture, Theory and Critique* 54(2) 2013: 194–208 (reprinted by permission of Taylor & Francis Ltd, www.tandfonline.com). An early version of part of chapter five first appeared in different form as "Love, Ethics and Authenticity: Beauvoir's Lesson in what it means to Read" in *Hypatia* 25(2) Spring 2010: 334–56 (reprinted by permission of John Wiley and Sons Inc).

Special thanks to Richard Flanagan and Vintage for permission to publish passages from *Gould's Book of Fish* (Sydney: Vintage 2012). These passages appear as epigraphs to each of the chapters in this book serving a purpose that is partially revealed in the conclusion.

PREFACE: WHY SLOW READING TODAY?

> *. . . an infinitely slow process of metamorphosis.*
> RICHARD FLANAGAN, *GOULD'S BOOK OF FISH*: 342

I venture to suggest that our age threatens one day to appear in the history of human culture as marked by the most dramatic and difficult trial of all, the discovery of and training in the meaning of the 'simplest' acts of existence: seeing, listening, speaking, reading.[1]

Posing the question: what is it to read?

In his now notorious reading of *Das Kapital,* Louis Althusser, following what he sees to be Marx's lead, asks, 'what is it to read?' We may think of this as an innocent question, but in this same piece Althusser warns us that any philosophical reading must be distinguished from an innocent reading: '[A]s there is no such thing as an innocent reading', he writes, 'we must say what reading we are guilty of' (Althusser 1979: 14). It is not my concern here to follow the contours of the guilty reading that Althusser goes on to elaborate.[2] I merely suggest that his question, read in a certain way, makes it possible to explore some preliminary thoughts concerning the ethics of how we philosophers read. There is, indeed, no innocent reading – and by this I mean that how we read, how we approach and respond to a text, is more than casually significant. This ought to be a friendly warning for those philosophers who think of reading as, at best, a kind of neutral activity. It isn't, and I aim in this book to demonstrate why.[3]

In a film about the philosopher Hannah Arendt by the German director Margarethe von Trotta (Trotta 2012), Arendt is pictured lying on a sofa, smoking. Nothing appears to be happening. Arendt, it seems, is thinking. The length of this scene is unusual when compared to contemporary mainstream cinema; a cinema characterized by 'activity' and 'action', narrowly defined. What is it about this image that unsettles? Time passes – and it does so slowly. In fact, temporality and its unique relation with thinking is a theme von Trotta weaves throughout the entire narrative of the film. Arendt is slow (painfully slow, from the perspective of those editing *The New Yorker*), in delivering what will to the larger reading public become her most controversial work – her report on the trial of Adolf Eichmann in Jerusalem (Arendt 1963). From the perspective of those working at *The New Yorker*, Arendt's work is infuriatingly slow. For those with weekly, or even monthly, deadlines the reality of having to wait for Arendt's 'judgement' to arrive is a burden that positions those of us viewing the film between the seemingly everyday world of journalistic reality – with its deadlines and quick analyses – and the slow world of philosophical thought and judgement. Arendt's report arrives 'late' because her work – her thinking, willing and judging – is work that takes time. It is work that slows one, makes one slow.

I am interested to explore the interconnections between philosophy and slowness, and there are various reasons for this; reasons I discuss as the work unfolds. In essence, though, I am motivated to explore the ground between philosophy and slowness because it provides us with one way of asking questions about what philosophy is today. Within the modern institutional context, the nexus between philosophy and slowness has been seriously compromised. The pressing demands of time, efficiency and productivity make it more and more difficult to adopt a contemplative or intense attitude toward our work. So, in what follows, I explore how slow reading allows philosophy to embrace complexity within an institutional context dominated by speed and efficiency. I explore what it means to read slowly. To read carefully, to reread, and return to what one reads. I consider what philosophical reading is, and what we philosophers do when we read – how we read – because I believe these questions to be of importance to us all, and not only when we are reading philosophy. Why? Because reading is fundamental to the process not only of sound philosophical work and thought, but to the important work that a good many of us do, both inside and outside the university. For academic or professional readers, it is *what* we do, and when our institutional structures make it less likely that we will do this well, problems follow. In the institutional context, such problems take the form of our reduced ability to encounter and work with complexity. Under situations of high time pressure, it becomes more and more difficult to engage with the complex and difficult in substantial and intense ways. Given that the encounter with complexity is one of the fundamental ways we think about philosophical work, then our diminished abilities to cope with this encounter are troubling, to say the least.

Another way of thinking about the problems that follow from our reduced opportunities to read slowly and to engage with complexity is to turn to Martin Heidegger's work on thinking and its relation with technology. Heidegger's insights into modern technological society have a bearing, I think, on what we could call the creeping technological nature of today's institutions. One of Heidegger's main observations is that our modern ways of being or existing are impacted upon by that aspect of technological life that reduces everything in its wake to a resource. Our understanding and our ways of being in the world are in danger of becoming technological themselves. Our very understanding is in danger of reducing the world in which we exist to nothing other than resource, or to what Heidegger refers to as 'standing reserve'. To reduce the world and our understanding of it in this way is to fail, in Heidegger's terms, to 'stay with things', to engage with the world in meaningful, non-utilitarian ways (Heidegger 1977: 3–35, 36–49). By striving for ever more speed, efficiency and interchangeability, this technological world-view makes objects or resources out of the things that have previously had meaning for us.

I think the malaise Heidegger identifies here echoes in many of our modern institutions, and that speed, efficiency and interchangeability characterize the dominant atmosphere or mood (*Stimmung*, Heidegger would say) of our contemporary universities. Indeed, we seem no longer to hear the danger (and irony) in expressions such as 'Human Resources'; and in our ever more futile attempts to 'stay afloat' in an age of 'Progress Reports' and 'Outcomes' both our teaching and our research suffer. This is, of course, intimately linked with what this means for our opportunities simply to think. Under conditions of time stress, it is harder for our work and our thinking to retain its ability to take new paths, to innovate, to question and to challenge. Heidegger's response to this technological reduction of our being-in-the-world to 'resource' is to return to the things of the world. In his later work, he refers to this as 'dwelling' (Heidegger 2013: 141–59). We can think of dwelling as the philosophical attitude that involves 'staying with things', a receptive attitude of 'being-with' that makes authentic existence possible. This, like all good philosophy, takes time.

One of the ways that we can honour the kind of philosophical dwelling that Heidegger calls forth is to honour the temporality in which our everyday work occurs. The image of Hannah Arendt smoking,[4] immersed in thought, unproductive to the technological eye, may then serve as a (slow) call to arms. Honouring the rhythms and temporality of deep and careful thought – thought that is threatened by speed, efficiency and interchangeability – means, perhaps, honouring the importance of a slow engagement with the work that we do. In light of this, my call for slow reading is a political gesture as much as it is an aesthetic one. By engaging slowly, carefully and locally with the complex works that we read, by resisting the lure of 'institutional' readings, ones that reduce thought to information extraction or mining, we refuse or, at the very least, frustrate the modern technological drive that pillages thinking as a productive resource. Reading slowly and rereading, returning time and time again to read anew, we return, similarly, to the things in the world anew. Our slow and very local readings resist the all too familiar tone of those technological or instrumental readings that no longer share a relation with thought.

If philosophy involves the patience of 'sitting with' the world, then Heidegger is right to urge us to dwell, to stop, to reflect – to slow down. The slow and contemplative attitude that Virginia Woolf urges us towards, serves, too, to remind us to steep ourselves in the long and complicated process that reading ought to be. In this sense, slow reading would not simply mean always reading slowly, but would, rather, involve a preparedness to return time and time again to what we read. To attend to reading. We must, Woolf claims, 'wait for the dust of reading to settle; for the conflict and questioning to die down; walk, talk, pull the dead petals from a rose, or fall asleep' (Woolf 1925: 266). In the process of this slow and careful waiting (or attention) our dwelling with the world and with what we read returns. 'Then suddenly without our willing it, for it is that Nature undertakes these transitions, the book will return, but differently' (Woolf 1925: 266). Slow reading is, then, this waiting, this attention, this dwelling that allows the world (and the book) to return to us differently – as thing, Heidegger would say, rather than as resource.

My interest in the intensity of slow reading comes out of a larger concern to re-engage with the instituting moments of a love of wisdom and philosophy as a way of life. As I explain in the Introduction, these moments sit in a complex relation with the instituted structure of philosophy reduced to the desire to know. Together, they comprise the institution of philosophy, the sedimented rules, regulations and habits that, over time, orient philosophical work towards established codes and behaviours – well-worn paths. My argument is that slow reading restores the relevance that the instituting moments no longer hold. Slow reading offers alternatives to the institutional readings that today occur within a culture largely dominated by efficiency, speed and haste.

Accordingly, I ask questions about what it means for philosophers to read. In a certain sense, I explore what philosophy is, and what philosophers do, by asking questions about the kind of reading or approaches to reading we undertake when we read works of philosophy, or when we read philosophically. In the process, I explore what might be termed 'an ethics of reading'. I look into the consequences of dominant institutional practices on the way that philosophers learn to read, suggesting that a contemporary 'corporate' orientation can compromise or undermine our otherwise positive engagement with the processes that structure our work. My work aims to provoke philosophers to think, in a more focused way, about the practice of reading. Given that reading is so central to the work that we as theorists and writers do, my hope is to open the question of reading out to the scrutiny of the ethical domain. In this sense, the study has relevance well beyond the sphere of philosophical discussion and debate. It will be of interest to all who read.

Throughout the work I explore reading in strategic and practical ways, engaging with the thought of some key philosophers and theorists. Friedrich Nietzsche, Ludwig Wittgenstein, Emmanuel Levinas, Theodor W. Adorno, Luiz Costa Lima, Hans Ulrich Gumbrecht, Simon Critchley, Robert Musil, Simone de Beauvoir, Luce Irigaray, Kristof Ziarek, Michèle Le Dœuff, Hélène Cixous, Teresa Brennan and Simone Weil serve as inspiration for developing practices or habits of slow reading, ones that engage the philosopher ethically. In focusing on an ethics of reading that manifests as 'slow reading' or slow philosophy, I offer a pedagogy, exploring how we can facilitate open, engaged and unhurried readings of complex texts and how this can be used both to initiate and invite others into an ethical community of readers. I argue that the significance of slow reading is linked to our desire to be changed or even transformed by our encounter with complex and demanding works.

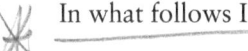
In what follows I offer:

1. An account of how slow reading re-engages the instituting moments of philosophy as a love of wisdom and a way of life, rather than simply as a desire (or a need) to know.
2. An exploration of slow reading as a transformation of the philosopher from one existential state to another.
3. An alternative, more contemplative and ethical way of doing philosophy in an age of speed and haste.
4. An exploration of the importance of unhurried time in establishing our institutional encounters with complex and demanding works.

About the chapters

In the Introduction I offer a series of preliminary thoughts that serve to frame the work on ethics and slow reading that the book undertakes. As I have briefly mentioned, it is here that I explore the complex interplay between the instituting moment of philosophy as a love of wisdom and the instituted structure of philosophy as a desire or a need to know. I argue that by re-engaging the instituting moments or guiding idea of philosophy, slow reading reminds us that a love of wisdom ought be more than, in Wlad Godzich's terms, 'curiously irrelevant to immediate concerns' (Godzich 1994. 237). I explore Pierre Hadot's argument that a love of wisdom is transformative, propelling the philosopher from one existential state to another. I make a case for a modern reclaiming of the term 'slowness', placing my philosophical discussion alongside popular research emerging between the specialist discourses of neuroscience and psychology (Kahnemann, McGilchrist, Wolf) and educational research exploring reading in contemporary institutional contexts

(Bauerlein, Kamuf). From here I discuss slow reading in terms of how philosophers read, engaging briefly with Ludwig Wittgenstein's 'slow cure'. I explore what makes slow reading ethical. To this end I draw on Virginia Woolf's essay 'How to Read a Book', noting with interest the three phases of reading she describes. I raise preliminary questions concerning the reduction of reading to crude scientific accounts of information extraction, asking what this means for reading in relation to the institution. Here I bring the work of Simon Critchley and Hans Ulrich Gumbrecht into play. I consider Critchley's plea for reconnecting with the pleasures and intensities of teaching in order to resist the instrumental modes of exchange that threaten to dominate the institutional practice of philosophy. In Gumbrecht's work I explore the importance of unhurried time in setting up our institutional encounters with complex and demanding works. Following his association of complex encounters with aesthetic experience, I explore the pedagogical importance of Friedrich Nietzsche's untimely reading – his desire 'to read slowly, deeply, looking cautiously before and aft, with reservations, with doors left open, with delicate eyes and fingers' (Nietzsche 1982: 5).

In Chapter One I return to the complex relation between the instituting moments and instituted structure of philosophy, arguing that we can see the transformative work of wisdom at play in what I refer to as Michèle Le Dœuff's 'habits' of reading. I argue that her approach to philosophy as 'work', and her belief that this involves shifting thinking from one stage to another, helps us to appreciate the transformation that propels the philosopher from one existential state to another. Additionally, it helps us to think about what slow reading achieves. I explore Le Dœuff's work on philosophy as discipline in order to identify the dual aspects of the tradition. On the one hand, those aspects of the institution that work to hurriedly close down our engagement with complexity (old habits), and on the other, those moments where an open and engaged thought is evident (new habits). I argue that in her own practice, Le Dœuff demonstrates a reading that we can think of as slow. Her tendency to patiently return, reassess, reconsider and re-engage with texts is a 'habit' of reading – or a practice of reading – that serves her well. These habits effectively slow down reading. Alongside these habits, I explore Le Dœuff's work on the gendered nature of reading in the history of philosophy. Le Dœuff's observation that: 'Men treat the text familiarly and knock it about happily' while 'women treat it with a politeness' is the starting point for new ways of thinking about a future philosophy: new, more modest and less pretentious approaches to thought. Attentive politeness, if not swamped by a 'timidity' or a 'desire to flatter', can lead, Le Dœuff claims, to a form of reading that can 'produce great successes' (Le Dœuff 1989: 124). The fact that these successes are often overlooked by a philosophical discipline that privileges the masculinity of authoritative interpretation over the femininity of receptive reading is a cause for concern. I explore the links between Le Doeuff's work on politeness and my own work on slow reading, suggesting that slow reading cultivates, in the first instance, a receptive attitude of respect that begins by politely listening to the other's point of view. From here I pose the question of how we might unpick old habits of authoritative reading to create new habits that evolve out of, and yet go beyond, polite respect. Le Dœuff's work on an open and incomplete philosophical practice, still to come, helps in this regard. Her future philosophy, at ease with its incompleteness, no longer in need of a defence mechanism involving the exclusion or marginalization of women and others, bypasses a neurotic desire to know and, as such, revives the instituting moments of a love of wisdom and philosophy as a way of life.

In Chapter Two I continue this exploration of a future philosophy in the work of Theodor W. Adorno. I explore the open and open-ended nature of his work on the essay, using this as a starting point for developing a practice of slow reading I call 'essayistic reading'. This essayistic reading links with the instituting moments of philosophy by thwarting our modern preoccupations with system, speed and haste. In place of an efficient or institutional reading (one motivated to extract or to capture information), it offers an open-ended rumination, a reading that meanders in non-systematic ways. This meandering pursues paths largely undetermined. By resisting the containing and limiting gesture that often accompanies the philosophical desire to know, I explain why essayistic reading forgoes absolute comprehension and certainty. To this end, I engage Emmanuel Levinas's work on patience and its centrality to ethics in order to outline the problems that essayistic reading seeks to avoid. Levinas claims that there are many ways in which our dominant philosophical practices in the West fall short of the kind of patient attitude towards the other that makes ethics possible, and I use this to think more specifically about our philosophical practices of reading. I investigate Levinas's claim that philosophy assimilates or domesticates the other into the Same, and argue that many of our current institutional practices of reading are responsible for closing off the strangeness and challenge that the other (text) represents. This leads to a discussion of how reading might manage the difficult task of remaining open to this strangeness. For Levinas this openness or goodness grounds an ethics of response and responsibility that helps us to think of reading in different ways. Drawing on the work of Robert Bernasconi and Simon Critchley, I investigate an ethical structure of reading in terms of Levinas's work. Having done this, I return to Adorno to read his important though little-discussed piece, 'The Essay as Form'. Here, Adorno explores the idea of an open-ended and slowly meandering philosophy that takes its cue from the open-ended form of the essay, and I connect this with Levinas's concerns for ethics. Adorno's call to resist completeness, system and closure is useful, I think, for thinking through what a slow reading or an ethics of reading might possibly entail, and I explore these possibilities by outlining my approach to reading essayistically. In support of this, I draw on work from Luiz Costa Lima (on criticity) and Hans Ulrich Gumbrecht (on reading for *Stimmung*). I conclude with a brief discussion of Robert Musil's work on the essay and its links to both ethics and aesthetics. Throughout this chapter, I explore ways in which ethics can be thought in terms of temporality; that is, how the slow reading of essayistic reading can help to establish an ethical relation of openness with the otherness, ambiguity and strangeness of the text, and how this openness to intensity and intimacy can be transformative.

In Chapter Three I build on the slow and open-ended work of essayistic reading by exploring Luce Irigaray's transformative work on love and wonder. I argue that these terms provide us with practical strategies and attitudes supporting the open and attentive reader. I show how Irigaray's open readings (of Diotima and Descartes) offer us alternative philosophical responses, ones that help us to rethink the future of philosophy in ethical terms. In the process, I develop practices of loving and wondrous readings aimed at re-engaging the instituting moments of a love of wisdom and philosophy as a way of life. I demonstrate how both love and wonder open us to otherness, by opening us to a strangeness that we might otherwise read around. By slowing us and helping us to pause, attitudes of love and wonder open us to a contemplative relation with what we read. However, I argue that love and wonder open us out in subtly different ways. Wonder initiates us into the realm of the other, providing us with an attentive awareness to what is rare and new. This occurs before (and after) any relation between ourselves and the other (subject/world, subject/object, subject/text). Wonder is the passion of moving towards, but it is not yet a relation. Love, on the other hand, is an enveloping; it is the passion that connects us and places us in relation with the other. I explore desire as the arc between the awe of wonder and the enveloping of love, arguing that this understanding of desire contrasts with the desire to know, which is no longer the bridge from wonder to love, but rather a need to know in the service of some anxiety, some utility, some instrumental end. I conclude the chapter by arguing that both love and wonder, in their own ways, have the ability to open our everyday institutional intersubjective relations in a more generous manner, thus orienting us toward a future philosophy that re-engages the instituting moments of philosophy in practical ways.

In Chapter Four I return to Irigaray, this time to engage with her work on listening to explore what it means to think of slow reading as a form of attentive listening. Listening, I claim, builds a bridge with the instituting moments of a love of wisdom and philosophy as a way of life. Listening patiently provides a context of proximity and nearness by bypassing the instituted structure of a pressing desire to know. I argue that Irigaray's desire to 'make something exist', to 'stage an encounter', 'to prepare a place of proximity' and 'to search for gestures' helps to orient philosophy toward slow reading as an open and engaged ethics of reading. Her practice of listening, 'listening-to' and 'listening-with' is preparation for what she refers to as a 'wisdom of love between us' (Irigaray 2002). In support of my intuition – that listening provides the foundation for an engaged ethical reading – I detour via Hans Jonas's essay 'The Nobility of Sight' to explore the hierarchy of the senses that in the West places sight in a pre-eminent position. I do this to raise questions about how we can challenge this hierarchy. I ask what it would mean to think of reading as a kind of listening. We do, naturally, tend to equate reading with seeing, but I suggest that any simple or exclusive coupling of reading with vision 'overlooks' the possibility of exploring reading as an activity that involves more of the body, in more complex ways. I suggest that reading, in the slow or ethical mode that I am exploring, has much in common with an active and engaged form of listening that pre-eminently establishes a relation with the other or text. Listening, perhaps more so than looking, captures what is ethical in the practice of slow reading, and I explore the implications of this for our pedagogical practices and relations. Listening-to preserves the singularity of teacher and of student (or of reader and of text) while simultaneously enabling their being-in-relation. I conclude that within the restraints and structures of our institutions we are still capable of placing the pedagogical relation – between teacher and student – at the centre of an ethical revival of the instituting moments in philosophy that pursue a love of wisdom and a wisdom of love. Such a revival, I note, is something other than a romantic gesture or a return to a golden past. It is, on the contrary, a look toward the future by revising how philosophy can function within the existing institution in new and provocative ways.

In Chapter Five I return to the link between slow reading and love by looking at Simone de Beauvoir's work in *The Second Sex* (1949). I argue that by distinguishing two types of love, Beauvoir helps us to think of two different approaches to reading, and how these are both opposed and interconnected. By accepting Beauvoir's account of romantic love as a flawed, dependent mode of being, and her suggestion that an authentic love – one that engages maturely and openly with the other – is possible, I suggest that we can take the risk of thinking of reading in these terms. I argue that a romantic reading demonstrates an immature dependence in relation to the (other) text, or an equally immature expectation of completeness in relation to the text, whereas an authentic reading offers the possibility of a mature and open-ended approach. I claim that a mature reading accepts both the text's possibilities and its limitations, leading us toward an open and ongoing reading. I maintain that Beauvoir's notion of authentic love can be reworked to develop the idea of an authentic reading as a kind of slow reading or an ethical encounter. The ethical domain of this encounter exists along a continuum over space and time. What I call 'authentic reading' is a reading that resists the certainty and containment of institutional forms of reading; those professional practices that occur without the time required to allow the dust to settle or for impressions to be received (Woolf 1932). Returning to reading by slowly rereading provides us with the discerning quality of attention that allows for a transformation from romance to authenticity to unfold. In this sense, I claim that authentic reading is a slow practice or exercise of attention that builds toward maturity. This process of maturity will not be hurried; it takes time to establish, and it occurs by building on the spontaneity of the first force of romantic love. I conclude that authentic reading works through the problems inherent in institutional forms of reading by re-engaging with the instituting moments of a love of wisdom and philosophy as a way of life. In reading Beauvoir's work in the light of this discussion I am able to raise the question of what kind of reader she is. Specifically, it allows me to ask how Beauvoir reads Sartre – the Sartre of *Being and Nothingness*. I argue that Michèle Le Dœuff's immensely influential reading of Beauvoir's reading of Sartre (in terms of an operative philosophy) can be rethought in terms of Beauvoir's own categories of romance and authenticity, and it is in this sense that we can think of Beauvoir's work on love as a lesson in what it means to read.

In Chapter Six I explore Hélène Cixous's practice of reading in order to think of slow reading as an approach of intimacy, tenderness and love. I argue that an unhurried approach towards the other allows us to think of reading as a process of transformation: one that literally transforms us from one existential state to another. I claim that Cixous's approach takes us from the heaviness of the subject who desires to know and to fix, toward the weightless, attentive and receptive space of the ethical encounter. I explore Cixous's particular practice of reading by first encountering the central place writing holds in her work. Cixous's writing is motivated by a slow and respectful approach toward the other – rather than by any desire for appropriation, mastery, or knowledge of the other – and I maintain that this approach guides her reading too. The ethical dimension evident in Cixous's approach to reading is very much grounded in the attentive intimacy she seeks to establish with the other. To read is to be attentive to the trace of the other, and this attention takes time. Additionally, and perhaps paradoxically, it calls for an emptying of the self to prepare for the other, an abandon that allows the other to gleam. Accompanying attention is patience, and Cixous demonstrates this in the slow and considered waiting that forms the approach, which is nothing other than the imperceptible movement toward the other in passion and in grace. Grace, as we see in the conclusion, is the patient work of ethics that opens us to a love of wisdom and philosophy as a practical way of life.

I conclude the book by tying together various themes that have emerged throughout the work, and by suggesting that ethics and aesthetics meet in the work of attention that best characterizes the kind of slow reading I have been exploring. To this end I touch briefly upon Simone Weil's work on gravity and grace, Teresa Brennan's work on discernment, Martin Heidegger's work on rapture (*Rausch*) and meditative thought, and Hans Ulrich Gumbrecht's work on intensity. What I show is that slow reading involves an intensity of reading, or a quality of attention, that keeps the question of ethics both open and alive. I maintain that slow reading matters because it develops practices aimed at reviving the instituting moments of philosophy. Slow reading engages the guiding idea of a love of wisdom in order to restore the transformative potential of philosophy, ensuring that it becomes something more than curiously irrelevant to immediate concerns. In 'an age of "work", that is to say, of hurry, of indecent and perspiring haste, which wants to get "everything done" at once . . . this art does not so easily get anything done, it teaches to read well, that is to say, to read slowly, deeply, looking cautiously before and aft, with reservations, with doors left open, with delicate eyes and fingers' (Nietzsche 1982: 5).

Introduction: On Being Slow and Doing Philosophy

Perhaps reading . . . is one of the last defences human dignity has left, because in the end [it] remind[s] us . . . that we are more than ourselves; that we have souls. And more, moreover.

RICHARD FLANAGAN, *GOULD'S BOOK OF FISH*: 33

The love of wisdom and the desire to know

Philosophy in the West bears within its practice two different approaches to thought. To simplify matters we can think of these as, on the one hand, a love of wisdom and, on the other, a particular form of the desire to know. To understand the complex relations between these approaches we need to think about philosophy as an institution. By doing so, we can appreciate how a love of wisdom has, over time, come to be dominated by a very distinctive desire – or better still, a need – to know. However, rather than simply being opposed to this desire to know, a love of wisdom inhabits the institutional space that philosophy has become. This habitation is anything but straightforward; it signals a subterranean presence that has the ability to challenge the forensic desire for knowledge that philosophy, over time, has become.

My argument in this book is that it is timely for the love of wisdom, the instituting moment of Western philosophy, to retrieve its pre-eminent place in philosophical work. To this end, I develop a philosophical practice of slow reading to counter the effects of containment and mastery that the institutionalized practice of philosophy has to a large extent become. As such, I seek to revitalize the institution, rather than to do away with it. By extending the range of legitimate philosophical practice and by reintroducing modes of attentive contemplation, my aim is to work toward a future philosophy realized in the here and now – a slow philosophy.

We can think of the love of wisdom as a kind of guiding idea that precedes the institutionalization of philosophy. In the figure of Socrates we find an embodiment of this guiding idea. Pierre Hadot's work on the history of philosophy from Ancient Greece to the present focuses on Socrates as the *philo-sopher* – the lover of wisdom. This love of wisdom takes the form of what Hadot refers to as spiritual exercises, 'an invitation to a new way of life, active reflection, and living consciousness' (Hadot 1995: 157), where justice (and the like) can never be understood without us living it (155). 'Such a fully just existence is that of the sage, who is not *sophos*, but *philo-sophos*: not a wise man, but one who desires wisdom, precisely because he lacks it' (157).[1] Like the *daimon* Eros, Socrates desires wisdom in the form of a journey toward his own perfection, an 'opening up onto something beyond himself' (162). As a spiritual exercise (love of wisdom), Plato's dialogues exceed pure philosophical system in order to perform the experience of love. Here the love of wisdom merges with a wisdom of love. This experience is transformative, propelling the philosopher from one existential state to another. Philosophy here is very much a way of life: 'Yet the dialogue itself, qua event and spiritual activity, already constitutes a moral and existential experience, for Socratic philosophy is not the solitary elaboration of a system, but the awakening of consciousness, and accession to a level of being which can only be reached in a person-to-person relationship' (Hadot 1995: 163).

If the love of wisdom inaugurates a transformative relation – a way of life that binds philosopher to philosophy – what can be said of the forensic desire to know? Hadot argues that while philosophy as a way of life, guided by the love of wisdom and the desire for transformation, is embodied in the spiritual practices of ancient

Greek philosophy, over time this succumbs to philosophy reconceived as an exclusively scholarly discourse. We can think of this scholarly orientation toward philosophy as the motivation behind a forensic desire for knowledge that stands in place of any direct experience of philosophy as a love of wisdom and a personally transformative experience. From Socrates to Plato and on to Aristotle we note a shift in the definition and practice of philosophy.[2] The love of wisdom gives way to a particular form of the desire to know and this desire dominates the gradual institutionalization or sedimentation of scholarly philosophical inquiry as we know it today. Aristotle, in Book I of the *Metaphysics*, writes:

> All men by nature desire to know. An indication of this is the delight we take in our senses; for even apart from their usefulness they are loved for themselves; and above all others the sense of sight. For not only with a view to action, but even when we are not going to do anything, we prefer seeing (one might say) to everything else. The reason is that this, most of all the senses, makes us know and brings to light many differences between things.
>
> ARISTOTLE 1971: A, 980 a25

From Aristotle on, this form of the desire to know is inscribed in the practice of Western philosophy. Knowledge replaces the love of wisdom with the result that system and certainty become, over time, dominating principles. By the time we reach Descartes, we encounter a desire to know so exhaustive and forensic in its practice that only absolute certainty will prevail. Philosophy and science merge in the discovery of not only our ignorance but more importantly in the conviction that we must, at all costs, dispel this ignorance. We must know. In the opening pages of *A Discourse on Method*, Descartes outlines his four principles, the rules that establish his methodology:

> The *first* was never to accept anything for true which I did not clearly know to be such; that is to say, carefully to avoid precipitancy and prejudice, and to comprise nothing more in my judgment than what was presented to my mind so clearly and distinctly as to exclude all ground of doubt.
>
> The *second*, to divide each of the difficulties under examination into as many parts as possible, and as might be necessary for its adequate solution.

The *third*, to conduct my thoughts in such order that, by commencing with objects the simplest and easiest to know, I might ascend by little and little, and yet, as it were, step by step, to the knowledge of the more complex; assigning in thought a certain order to those objects which in their own nature do not stand in a relation of antecedence and sequence.

And the *last*, in every case to make enumerations so complete, and reviews so general, that I might be assured that **nothing was omitted**.

DESCARTES 1912: 15–16 emphasis in bold added

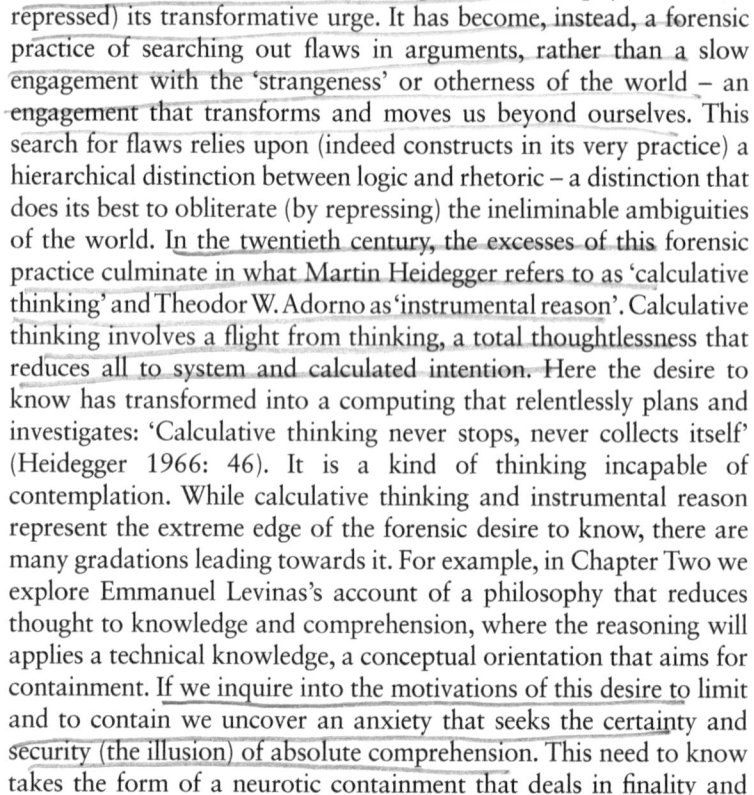

We are a long way here from Socrates's love of wisdom. Descartes's goals of certainty and exhaustiveness sit uncomfortably with Socrates's claim that he knows nothing at all. Philosophy has lost (or repressed) its transformative urge. It has become, instead, a forensic practice of searching out flaws in arguments, rather than a slow engagement with the 'strangeness' or otherness of the world – an engagement that transforms and moves us beyond ourselves. This search for flaws relies upon (indeed constructs in its very practice) a hierarchical distinction between logic and rhetoric – a distinction that does its best to obliterate (by repressing) the ineliminable ambiguities of the world. In the twentieth century, the excesses of this forensic practice culminate in what Martin Heidegger refers to as 'calculative thinking' and Theodor W. Adorno as 'instrumental reason'. Calculative thinking involves a flight from thinking, a total thoughtlessness that reduces all to system and calculated intention. Here the desire to know has transformed into a computing that relentlessly plans and investigates: 'Calculative thinking never stops, never collects itself' (Heidegger 1966: 46). It is a kind of thinking incapable of contemplation. While calculative thinking and instrumental reason represent the extreme edge of the forensic desire to know, there are many gradations leading towards it. For example, in Chapter Two we explore Emmanuel Levinas's account of a philosophy that reduces thought to knowledge and comprehension, where the reasoning will applies a technical knowledge, a conceptual orientation that aims for containment. If we inquire into the motivations of this desire to limit and to contain we uncover an anxiety that seeks the certainty and security (the illusion) of absolute comprehension. This need to know takes the form of a neurotic containment that deals in finality and verdict, rather than in the openness of an ongoing questioning.

My argument throughout is that philosophical practices guided by this desire or need to know result all too often in closed and systematic accounts.[3] By establishing the rules, regulations and demands of systematic thought this kind of philosophy loses its way as a love of wisdom – an open questioning that transforms the philosopher from one existential state to another – and becomes, instead, an institution. As we will see, in founding philosophy as institution, and later still as corporation, we set a path towards the speed and efficiency that will eventually displace the slow, reflective and meditative tradition from which philosophy as a love of wisdom emerges. So, while the desire to know is the impetus behind philosophy as an institution, the love of wisdom retains, nonetheless, a subterranean relation with it. In what ways, then, can we understand these practices as more than simply opposed?

The play between the instituting and the instituted in philosophy

Whenever the codes and conditions that have assured the consensus necessary for communication begin to change radically or to break down, attention is inevitably drawn to the question of institutions.

WEBER 1987: 33

I mentioned earlier that we can think of the love of wisdom as a kind of guiding idea that precedes the institutionalization of philosophy. It is time now to think more carefully about what this entails. To think of philosophy as an institution or as an institutionalized discourse is to ask questions about how this institution comes into being and what tensions constitute it once it exists. While our initial impulse is to equate the institution with the status quo, there are good reasons to resist doing so. Certainly, academic institutions work to maintain what are deemed acceptable scholarly procedures and behaviours, and yet to focus exclusively on this conservative function of discipline is to overlook the internal tensions that constitute the act of founding the institution. In Merleau-Ponty's (2010) lectures on 'Institution and Passivity' he explores the ambivalent nature of the institution, differentiating between what is already 'instituted' and what is 'instituting', innovative or coming into being. Temporality, he argues, can be understood philosophically as the unfolding of the new within the familiar. In a similar vein, the work of the French sociologist René Lourau is helpful for thinking about the transformative aspect of the institution, distinguishing, as does Merleau-Ponty, between the *instituting* process and the *instituted* structure of the institution. In *L'Analyse institutionelle* (1970) Lourau argues that the conservative, disciplinary aspect of the institution

> has been increasingly used to designate what I and others before me have called the *instituted* (*l'institué*), the established order, the already existing norms, the state of fact thereby being confounded with the state of right (*l'état de droit*). By contrast, the *instituting* aspect (*l'instituant*) . . . has been increasingly obscured. The political implication of the sociological theories appears clearly here. By emptying the concept of institution of one of its primordial components (that of instituting, in the sense of founding, creating, breaking with an old order and creating a new one), sociology has finally come to identify the institution with the status quo.
>
> LOURAU 1970: 137, cited in Weber 1987: xv

In *Institution and Interpretation* (1987), Samuel Weber takes up Lourau's distinction between the instituting process and the instituted organization in order to explore the ambivalent relation between the dynamic, transformative moment and the determinant structure of the disciplinary norm. Weber refers to the 'intrinsic and violent instability' (17) of the institution, and in so doing urges us to appreciate the complexity underlying the processes of institutionalization. In *The Culture of Literacy* (1994) Wlad Godzich pursues Weber's discussion, first by outlining the three conditions for the process of institutionalization: a guiding idea, prescribed behaviour and set procedures. Like Weber, and Lourau and Merleau-Ponty before him, Godzich reminds us of the tension inherent in the institution – simultaneously towards policing on the one hand, and exploring on the other:

> We tend to think of institutions as apparatuses, that is, as constituted bodies with their internal procedures and delimited

field of intervention. But an institution is first and foremost a guiding idea, the idea of some determined goal to be reached for the common weal; it is this goal that is sought according to prescribed behavior and by the application of set procedures. This idea itself is adopted by a group of individuals who become its public possessors and implementers. This group then becomes the institution as a result of the combining of the guiding idea with the set procedures. The members of the group are shaped by the guiding idea they seek to implement and the procedures they apply; they adopt common behavior, develop similar attitudes, all of which tend to unify them into a determinate and identifiable group and give the institution its distinct unity.

GODZICH 1994: 236

Unlike the others, however, Godzich points to the underlying significance of the guiding idea and how it combines with the set procedures that will come to define the discipline or institution. What is most relevant for our discussion is that he goes on to position the guiding idea along with the instituting moment – the dynamic, transformative process that exists in a complex relation with the instituted or established order. The guiding idea is the flash of inspiration and imagination that avoids the established paths of acceptable thought and practice, and yet it is somewhat paradoxically incorporated into the newly emerging discipline or institution. Once there, the guiding idea or instituting moment becomes 'curiously irrelevant to immediate concerns':

In short, the insightful path [of the guiding idea] is turned into a beaten one, with the subsequent development of procedures within and by the institution being akin to road-improvement. The trailblazing ... the instituting, becomes a moment of odd standing in the now constituted institution. Its necessity is acknowledged, for without it the institution would not exist, but *it no longer really matters* except insofar as the marking out of the line that brought point of departure and point of arrival together is concerned. In other words, the instituting moment, which endows the entire institution with signification and meaning, is held within the institution as *both proper to it and yet alien: it is its other, valued to be sure yet curiously irrelevant to immediate concerns.*

GODZICH 1994: 237, emphasis added

The guiding idea remains in a somewhat subterranean relation with the institution as 'both proper to it and yet alien' and this is, I think, a useful way of thinking about the relation between the love of wisdom and the contemporary institution of philosophy. For the institution of philosophy, the love of wisdom no longer really matters, though it has at one time endowed the entire institution with signification and meaning. It is now paradoxically both proper to it and yet nonetheless alien. It is valued, to be sure, and yet curiously irrelevant to immediate concerns. My argument throughout this book is that slow reading, a practice that takes its cue from the love of wisdom, is about restoring the relevance that the instituting moment no longer holds. As such, slow reading is a revitalization of a love of wisdom and philosophy as a way of life (instituting moments) in the face of the dominance of the desire to know and philosophy as a scholarly discourse (instituted order).

Philosophy as a way of life: slow reading – slow philosophy

It is to him [the *flâneur*], aimlessly strolling through the crowds in the big cities in studied contrast to their hurried, purposeful activity, that things reveal themselves in their secret meaning: 'The true picture of the past *flits* by' ('Philosophy of History'), and only the *flâneur* who idly strolls by receives the message … the *flâneur*, through the *gestus* of purposeless strolling, turns his back to the crowd, even as he is propelled and swept by it.

ARENDT 1969: 12–13[4]

The instituting moment of philosophy as a love of wisdom involves the patient work of thought. It is, first and foremost, the patience involved in 'sitting with' the world and of being open to it; not merely for the sake of being patient but, rather, for engagement with the complexity of the world that this slow and open process of thought permits. Philosophy, at its best, involves judgement, but not the fast and furious judgement of a final verdict. Rather, it is the judgement that comes from suspending certainty, from hesitating, deliberating and taking time. Philosophy's patience goes

INTRODUCTION: ON BEING SLOW AND DOING PHILOSOPHY 9

hand-in-hand with slowing down – a slowing that allows thought to emerge and respectfully engage with the world. In certain respects this kind of philosophical work follows the purposeless strolling of Walter Benjamin's *flâneur*; turning its back on everyday hurried, purposeful activity (even while it is propelled and swept by it); philosophy sinks into the world. In some significant ways, it resembles serious works of art. Art, too, takes time and patience.[5] Of course, Heidegger writes at length about this relation between art, philosophy and time. When he writes 'art breaks open an open space, in whose openness everything is other than usual' (Heidegger 1971: 75) and (echoing Hölderlin) 'poetically, man dwells', he acknowledges that good art and good philosophy urge us to stop, to reconsider, to rethink everything we think we know. Philosophy and art provide us with different ways of dwelling on the things of our world. We see evidence of this slow, patient work in the photography of Alfred Stieglitz, an artist who understands the importance of a meditative relation with the world. Stieglitz's art can be seen as a slow and repeated return to the world, one that quite literally takes its own time. In his perceptive essay on Stieglitz's Lake George years, Peter Conrad captures this well:

> The art he [Stieglitz] practiced was meditative, a prolonged reverie, not the quick seizure of instants. He was happy to spend 20 years photographing the same stand of poplars, the same configurations of clouds overhead or the same barn ... In 1925, he told novelist Sherwood Anderson, 'I have been looking for years – 50 upwards – at a particular skyline of simple hills ... I'd love to get down what "that" line has done for me – may be I have – somewhat – in those snapshots I've been doing the past few years'.
>
> CONRAD 2010: 68[6]

I think of Stieglitz's photographic art – his patient 'looking' and returning – as a kind of reading, a slow and meditative openness that shares affinity with the kind of reading that underpins the slow philosophy I am interested in. So, what follows are a series of thoughts on how to frame the work on ethics, aesthetics and reading that this book explores. These ideas announce my interest in a reading that comfortably returns, time and time again, to the same terrain – the same book, the same passage, the same title – to ponder its significance with all the benefit of unhurried time, the passage of time and the silence and space this time affords. I think of this reading as an unfinished reading, an inconclusive reading, a wondrous reading that manages to remain open and engaged (present) with what it reads – ready for transformation and ready, too, for the possibility of revelation. By revelation I mean access to what often remains hidden from our everyday awareness, or our everyday, casual, quick and hasty modes of reading and being. This revelatory reading is what helps to bring something into existence, not simply to uncover it.

Slow reading suggests a positive kind of reading; an engaged and open reading that gains much by taking its time. However, it is prudent, at the outset, to draw attention to the various connotations that the word 'slow' has in the English language. If we turn to a dictionary definition we are bombarded with a host of negative meanings: sluggish, not quick, not clever, blunt, uninteresting, dull, dull-witted, stupid.[7] It seems that 'slow' used as a term for 'dull' and 'tedious' dates from around 1841, and while this is mere speculation, it is possible that this and other pejorative connotations arise within the context of early industrialized society and the theories of progress and efficiency that accompany it.[8] Associations of slowness with sloth (*acedia*), one of the deadly sins, bring to the fore slow physical movement, inertia and, in extreme cases, paralysis. These associations surface earlier and date from medieval times.[9] Consequently, my use of the term 'slow' necessities a modern reframing and reconsideration of its various negative connotations.[10] Such a reframing, though, does not deny the senses in which slowness can, in various circumstances, be problematic. For example, slowness can, in some political contexts, be equated with inaction and prevarication.[11] In Europe in the twentieth century, the fallout from the Munich Pact suggests that a slowness to act can be a political evil. While there is strong reason to support this claim, my argument is that when it comes to reading, a slow and reflective approach is necessary to counter a speed and haste that threatens the very culture of intense thought today.

It is clear that in everyday life there are countless instances where speed is both necessary and desirable. Problems begin, though, when speed encroaches more and more on those practices that comprise the academic institution. In the context of academic research and reflection, I argue that the cult of speed and haste is both misplaced and undesirable. If we understand our work in terms of the critical processes involved in engaging with complexity, then speed and haste represent dangers that threaten to derail our reflective work. Overcoming historical prejudices against slowness means simultaneously uncovering the often unconscious – or barely conscious – associations we make with speed. One way of thinking about this is to look towards the philosophical research on complexity that Paul Cilliers undertakes. In an article 'On the Importance of a Certain Slowness' (2006), he argues that the positive and common equation of speed with efficiency is a destructive one founded upon current distortions in our understanding of time. These distortions, in turn, rest upon the interconnection between instrumental theories we hold concerning the modern world and the effects of certain computer and communications technologies. Cilliers supports his case by reference to the temporal nature of complex systems, specifically to the relation between memory and anticipation, and the importance of delay and iteration in building complex systems (Cilliers 2006: 107). He is keen to explain that the argument for slowness is most certainly not a conservative one: 'It is not merely backward looking nor a glorification of what has been' (107). On the contrary, it concerns our present and our future. We could say that it concerns our ability to embrace the challenges that an increasingly complex world throws forth. An equation of slowness with delay, from the perspective of an uncritical valuation of speed, serves to distance us further from the reflective work that thinking is.[12] Relatedly, the case for slowness is not an argument against speed or fastness in appropriate contexts and at appropriate times. It is, rather, a reminder that speed is not a virtue in itself, and that efficiency (even the kind that speed is said to produce) is not necessarily helpful in our attempts to encounter complexity in more meaningful and creative ways. As Cilliers points out: 'The argument is against unreflective speed, speed at all costs, or, more precisely, against speed as a virtue in itself: against the alignment of "speed" with notions like efficiency, success, quality, and importance' (107).[13]

The common opposition between fast and slow is possibly not the most helpful for thinking about slow reading. Reading or rereading can at times be fast. What it should ideally not be, however, is hurried or rushed. Perhaps when it comes to reading philosophy, 'rushing' or 'haste' are terms that unsettle any neat binary between fast and slow. Being fast becomes problematic when it is a matter of rushing or hurrying.

My own modern reframing and reclaiming of slowness resonates with some of the popular research emerging in between the specialist discourses of neuroscience and psychology.[14] One relatively recent work in this field demonstrates an interest in questions of temporality, and while this research has little direct relation to what I am exploring here, it nonetheless suggests possibilities for future thought. Iain McGilchrist's study, *The Master and His Emissary: The Divided Brain and the Making of the Western World* (2009), explores the implications of the difference between the cerebral hemispheres, suggesting that it is not what each hemisphere does that is important in figuring this difference but, rather, how each goes about doing what it does. Gilchrist's observation, that the most fundamental difference between the hemispheres is the quality of *attention* each gives to the world, is intriguing, and more so when he goes on to link this to our ability (or not) to relate reciprocally with whatever exists apart from (or other to) ourselves. He writes: 'The kind of attention we pay actually alters the world: we are, literally, partners in creation. This means we have a grave *responsibility*, a word that captures the reciprocal nature of the dialogue we have with whatever it is that exists apart from ourselves' (McGilchrist 2009: 5). McGilchrist distinguishes two very different sets of values and priorities linked to these differing forms of attention: on the one hand, a largely conceptual, hierarchical and bureaucratic attention (associated with left hemispheric processes); and on the other, a deeper, relational and contextual attention (associated with the right hemisphere). He contends that these attentive modes exist in between creative tension and open warfare, and that the 'battles between them are recorded in the history of philosophy, and played out in the seismic shifts that characterize the history of Western culture' (14). (We might think of these as a love of wisdom and a forensic desire to know). While there are dangers aplenty in adopting a bihemispheric account of the brain (let alone the mind) – and McGilchrist certainly cautions against doing so uncritically – it is tempting to think of his deeper, relational and contextual attention as resonating with the account of slow reading that I am developing here. This is not, however, to suggest there is a neuroscientific basis for the slow and open reading I am calling for. Rather, it is to point to the central role that attention plays in contemporary accounts of our intellectual ways of being in the world (McGilchrist 2009).

Attention is the focus of a number of recent studies that delve into the superficiality of contemporary online reading. In *Proust and the Squid: The Story and Science of the Reading Brain* (2007), Maryanne Wolf suggests that superficial skimming techniques developed online are finding their way back to our complex everyday reading encounters, with the result that our reading abilities are impaired (Wolf 2007). Michael Rosenwald, in his discussion of this contemporary research, reports that cognitive neuroscientists (such as Wolf) warn that we 'seem to be developing digital brains with new circuits for skimming through the torrent of information online' and that these circuits are in competition with 'traditional deep reading circuitry developed over several millennia' (Rosenwald 2014). Given 'our' increasing tendency to become restless with reading material, Rosenwald wonders whether scanning and skimming are able to impair the development of deep reading skills. He reports that the pace and different spatiality of online reading, what is sometimes referred to as 'non-linear reading', is considered troubling: 'The Internet is different. With so much information, hyperlinked text, videos alongside words and interactivity everywhere, our brains form shortcuts to deal with it all – scanning, searching for key words, scrolling up and down quickly' (Rosenwald 2014). What the effects of these skimming techniques are on more traditional linear forms of reading is a question Wolf and others are keen to engage.

In a paper devoted to the inadequacies of contemporary North American teenage reading skills, Mark Bauerlein argues that students used to multitasking and online nonlinear skimming are increasingly unprepared for the demands of university reading.[15] Engaging with complex texts demands skills that 'screenagers' are ill-equipped to undertake. For Bauerlein, the basic skills of concentrated attention, uninterrupted thinking and receptivity are lacking in an alarmingly large proportion of first-year students. In an effort to counter this trend Bauerlein makes the case for developing habits of slow reading aimed to accustom high school students to the attentive mode that complex material demands:

> This is not to say that schools should go Luddite. We should continue to experiment with educational technology, but we

should also preserve a crucial place for unwired, unplugged, and unconnected learning. One hour a day of slow reading with print matter, an occasional research assignment completed without Google – any such practices that slow down and intensify the reading of complex texts will help. The more high school teachers place complex texts on the syllabus and concoct slow, deliberate reading exercises for students to complete, the more they will inculcate the habit. The key is to regularize the instruction and make slow reading exercises a standard part of the curriculum. Such practices may do more to boost college readiness than 300 shiny laptops down the hall – and for a fraction of the price.

BAUERLEIN 2011: 33

Our educational institutions ought to resist the trends Bauerlein reports on, not facilitate or give in to them. Of course, there are institutional pressures related to funding and resources, and this is related to the practice of linking funding to student numbers. There are no easy solutions here, and yet philosophy can arguably play a key role in raising the issues and engaging in critical ways with these.

My interest in the need for slow reading (raised in Bauerlein's work), and with what it means to do philosophy slowly and patiently, sits rather uncomfortably with what it means for many of us to do philosophy today; that is, to undertake philosophy within an institutional context of speed and haste.[16] What are the implications of this institutional practice for the quality of attention we are able to sustain and the reading practices that come from this? Does the institution impact on our ability to read well? One way of thinking about these questions is to turn to the definition of philosophy and philosophical practice that emerges in the work of Ludwig Wittgenstein.[17] Wittgenstein describes philosophy as a slow way of living; he writes: '[the] slow cure is all important' (Wittgenstein 1967: 69).[18] In his lectures on the foundation of mathematics he adds: 'I am trying to recommend a certain sort of investigation ... [T]his investigation is immensely important and very much *against the grain* of some of you' (Wittgenstein 1976: 103). Wittgenstein's investigation is, above all, protracted. His philosophy is essentially a slow process – one in which the philosopher comes 'by degrees to a new understanding of the nature of the problems that trouble him [or her]' (McGinn 1997: 23).[19] Wittgenstein's 'therapeutic' philosophy celebrates a slow and engaged mode of thinking. Indeed, we need to appreciate this point in order to better appreciate why it is that he writes in the ways that he does. Wittgenstein's later challenge to strictly argumentative modes of thought is part of the 'protracted' nature of his project. In *Über Gewissheit* he writes 'Meine Sätze sind alle *langsam* zu lessen' (Wittgenstein 1984: 531) and this calls us to read his work in a particular way. Not only does this philosophy need time to emerge, but it must be received slowly as well. *Meine Sätze sind alle langsam zu lessen* (My sentences are to be read slowly) – we must read Wittgenstein slowly if 'philosophy' is to be done at all.

In his discussion of the intensity with which Wittgenstein engaged philosophy, Raimond Gaita draws our attention to the devastating effects of the instrumentalization of those institutions we still call universities. By bringing to mind the intensity this instrumental conception has displaced, Gaita celebrates the slow and attentive mode of philosophy that Wittgenstein embraced:

> Wittgenstein suggested that philosophers should greet one another by saying, 'Take your time'. One needs time to muse, to meditate. Meditative reflectiveness does not issue quickly in publications and is often not sure of itself. It is seldom impressive on its feet. Yet for those of us who are not geniuses, it nourishes critical reflection, enabling one sufficient space and time to step back and to examine assumptions one might not have noticed.
>
> GAITA 2012

Philosophy here is clearly philosophy as a way of life.[20]

Both Wittgenstein's writing and his philosophical method frustrate attempts to systematize thought in crudely 'scientific' ways. They frustrate the reduction of philosophy to a restricted form of the desire to know. In many respects, Wittgenstein's work calls forth our imagination rather than our argumentative faculties. As Ray Monk points out, Wittgenstein was fond of drawing attention to the links between his approach and Freud's. Both works are therapeutic in the sense that they aim to produce 'the kind of understanding that consists in seeing connections' (Wittgenstein, cited in Monk 2005: 72).[21] Given what Wittgenstein has to say about a slow approach to philosophy we can think of this understanding – one that creates connections and interrelations – as a slow and careful reading open to the world around us. For Wittgenstein, this openness and the sensibility that arises along with it is evident in works of art where experience trumps calculation as a mode of engaged being. The kind of understanding that emerges from really good art is the kind that cannot be 'evaluated, weighed, pondered, by appeal to any system of general principles or universal laws' (Monk 2005: 104).[22] So too, I argue, with slow reading: an approach to reading that cannot be determined in advance by systematic principles or laws. In slow reading we move beyond calculation to thought.

Wittgenstein's exhortation to read slowly fits rather nicely with something that Virginia Woolf writes. In her essay 'How Should One Read a Book?' (1925), Woolf encourages a slow and meditative attitude, urging us to open to what we read, to steep ourselves in the long and complicated process that reading is (Woolf 1925: 259).[23] Having established the importance of this, she reminds us of the 'true complexity of reading' (266), suggesting that there are two different phases and that both these benefit from a slow and careful approach. The first phase involves reading slowly, in order to open to and receive impressions; this is a kind of mindful 'sitting-with' what we read,[24] while the second phase works on these impressions, passing judgements and making comparisons. The weight of inevitability of this second phase of (hard and lasting) judgement is significantly lightened, though, by Woolf's insistence that a slow and careful waiting 'for the dust to settle' must precede any account. We must decide, but 'not directly':[25]

> The first process, to receive impressions with the utmost understanding, is only half the process of reading; it must be completed, if we are to get the whole pleasure from a book, by another. We must pass judgment upon these multitudinous impressions; we must make of these fleeting shapes one that is hard and lasting. *But not directly*. Wait for the dust of reading to settle; for the conflict and questioning to die down; walk, talk, pull the dead petals from a rose, or fall asleep. Then suddenly without our willing it, for it is thus that Nature undertakes these transitions, *the book will return, but differently. It will float to*

the top of the mind as a whole. And the book as a whole is different from the book received currently in separate phrases.
WOOLF 1925: 266, emphasis added[26]

Woolf's 'not directly' interests me here, and if we couple this to what she later hints at as a phase beyond judgement[27] (or 'verdict' – which is so final), then what emerges is a practice of reading that takes its own time, a reading capable of perceiving the 'signs and hints of almost imperceptible fineness, from the twist and turn of the first sentences' (259). Woolf's suggestion that another reading lies beyond judgement links her discussion with imagination, rather than with comparison or discrimination.[28] This far 'rarer pleasure' (269) comes only with time: 'as time goes on perhaps we can train our taste ... we shall find that it is changing a little; it is not so greedy, it is more reflective. It will begin to bring us not merely judgements on particular books, but it will tell us that there is a quality common to certain books' (268). This imaginative reading brings insights that come from a continual questioning, a bringing of questions that arise from the slow and repeated reading and rereading that time allows.[29]

And yet, this rarified imagination that gives birth to an almost transcendental mode[30] of reading is eclipsed on the final page of Woolf's essay. By way of conclusion, she returns to the everyday reader she addresses in the opening pages. Here she urges us to read slowly and unprofessionally: 'reading for the love of reading' (270), refusing the speed and haste of the journalistic literary critic and the circumstances that lead to *him* having 'only one second in which to load and aim and shoot' so that *he* 'may well be pardoned if he mistakes rabbits for tigers, eagles for barndoor fowls, or misses altogether and wastes his shot upon some peaceful cow grazing in a further field (270).[31]

We will return to this cow and its slow, ruminant grazing, but allow me to say now, in response to Woolf's work, that her call to read slowly and unprofessionally links us back to Wittgenstein's earlier insistence. Woolf's 'unprofessional' reading can productively be thought of as a kind of non-institutional reading, a reading that refuses the speed and haste required by the corporate nature of today's institutional demands – demands dominated by a need to know. To read professionally or institutionally would thus mean to read without the time required to allow the dust to settle, or for impressions to be received. It would mean to read 'directly', without the necessary and essential element of time that makes the world of difference. With Wittgenstein, we can condemn an institutional context that reduces philosophical reading to a mode that occurs primarily as immediate and hasty judgement [verdict], a reading that occurs without the time taken for impressions to be received and, more often than not, without waiting for the dust of reading to settle.

This kind of hasty reading is sometimes aligned, for better or worse, with a 'scientific' or 'technological' model that has, over the past century or so, constructed links between reading and information. In the context of institutional trends that have seen 'science' emerge as the model for all intellectual work, a normative idea of reading has taken hold, one that stresses an almost exclusive intimacy between reading and 'information extraction' or 'mining'. In 'The End of Reading' (2000), a paper commenting on this disconcerting trend, Peggy Kamuf discusses how this impoverished idea of reading is reproduced in the modern university:

> Reading is or is read as technique for capturing information. Thus according to the scientific model . . . reading is essentially information technology. We can suppose, therefore, that this model of reading will be increasingly reinforced by the general network of information technologies as they continue to replace reading's traditional support, for now some seventeen or eighteen hundred years, the book. The book ends, but this model of reading, at least, will not. On the contrary, it will become the vastly dominant way in which something still called reading continues. It is not just as an abstract moment of definition that we must deal with this scientific and dominant model of reading. That model of reading is also getting produced and reproduced in reading practices. The common notion of reading as information-extraction sets the principles, and thus institutes the laws and the institutions through which reading practices are maintained, that is, reintroduced, reproduced, and reinforced in each new generation of readers, as we like to think of them.
>
> KAMUF 2000[32]

Wittgenstein's ideal of philosophy as a 'slow cure', so much against the grain for institutional practices today, is an important counter to reading as 'information-extraction' that Kamuf warns against. In what we might think of as a modern take on Wittgenstein's call, Hans Ulrich Gumbrecht returns to the 'slow cure' by celebrating the potential that the institution has within it to enact this cure. In this sense we can say that Gumbrecht works with the 'instituting' process of the institution – ever alive and open to innovation. In three works, *The Powers of Philology* (2003), *Production of Presence* (2004) and *Our Broad Present* (2014) Gumbrecht writes about the importance of time, and how this relates to an entirely different way of thinking about what reading is. To begin with, Gumbrecht makes a positive link between reading and complexity, arguing that a certain slow and careful reading, without immediate institutional demands, makes it possible for us to confront – I would say 'encounter' – high levels of complexity, thus resisting the temptation to reduce and simplify the issues at hand. Alternative modes of reading would engage this complexity, rather than reduce it by 'mining' or 'extracting' manageable chunks. Slow reading would inhabit a space between the pain and joy of losing and regaining intellectual orientation:

> This formula, exposing oneself to high intellectual complexity without having an immediate need to reduce this complexity, is probably close to a new and highly auratic[33] concept of 'reading' that humanists today increasingly use as a positive self-reference. *Reading* here is clearly not synonymous with *deciphering* (as was the case in the heyday of semiotics). Rather, the word seems to refer to both a joyful and painful oscillation between losing and regaining intellectual control or orientation.
> GUMBRECHT 2003: 85

Gumbrecht is working here with an idea of complexity that owes something to Niklas Luhmann's now classical discussion of the university as an institution of teaching as well as of research. Famously, Luhmann depicts the university as a 'secondary social system' whose primary identifying function ought ideally be the production of complexity, 'in distinction from and in reaction to most other social systems' (Gumbrecht 2004: 128, 129).[34] Supporting this definition, Gumbrecht claims that our primary pedagogical task should be identifying instances of complexity and then staging 'our students' encounters' with the inevitable oscillations these instances entail.[35] Reading is thus re-figured in his work as a kind of bitter-sweet exposure or openness to complexity, one that inevitably takes its time. Precisely because it takes its time, Gumbrecht's reading positions itself as kin to the domain of art. He writes: 'This would mean that any academic work that fits the formula of being a confrontation with complexity in a situation of low time-pressure; academic work in all its different dimensions, whether learning, teaching, or doing research . . . all this would be close to aesthetic experience' (Gumbrecht 2003: 86).[36]

This important link to aesthetic experience occurs if and only if the institution provides a context of 'low time-pressure' or, more simply, time. What Gumbrecht says here makes sense, especially if we think of Stieglitz's aesthetic experience as work carried out over long periods of time. Stieglitz's photographic art is possible *because* of this time. For Gumbrecht, the possibility for real philosophical or critical work (in the academy) is enhanced when one is exposed to complexity within an institutional context that both recognizes and safeguards (we might say 'cares for') the importance of 'excess' time:

> The condition of the possibility for lived experience and for *Bildung* to happen is time – more precisely, the academic and ivory tower-like privilege of being allowed to expose oneself to an intellectual challenge without the obligation to come up with a quick reaction or even with a quick 'solution' . . . We need institutions of higher education to produce and to protect excess time against the mostly pressing temporalities of the everyday . . . the academic institution is [or should be] all about such untimeliness.
> GUMBRECHT 2003: 87[37]

Once again, philosophy here returns to philosophy as a way of life.

For Gumbrecht, this Nietzschean untimeliness involves 'the intense quietness of presence' (Gumbrecht 2004: 137) that severs us from the demands of productivity and meaning that have paradoxically and problematically become usual for so many of us working in contemporary universities.[38] Gumbrecht's vision of untimeliness would enhance the possibility of academic work once again resembling aesthetic experience, precisely by providing the time for 'intensity' to emerge.[39] If aesthetic experience is partially defined by an intensity that disrupts our everyday view of the world, then philosophy becomes intense when the institution provides the possibility of what Gumbrecht refers to as 'riskful thinking' or a slow 'thinking [of] what cannot be thought in our everyday worlds' (Gumbrecht 2004: 126).[40] This intense kind of work both accompanies and is enabled by the reading that Gumbrecht applauds, the reading that sees us hover slowly and hesitatingly between 'losing and regaining intellectual control and orientation' (Gumbrecht 2004: 128). This type of reading emerges from stopping; it comes out of our 'being quiet for a moment' (142–3), and this is possible only when time is not an issue. Gumbrecht calls us 'to be quiet for a moment from time to time amid the technological and epistemological noise of our general mobilization' (141) and, by way of example, he points us towards the practice of Japanese No theatre, suggesting that herein lies one instance of slowing and opening to the intensity of the world:

> No pieces ... and their music are breathtakingly slow and repetitive. But ... if you have enough patience to let the slowness of emerging and vanishing of form and unformed presence grow on you, then after three or four hours, No can make you realize how your rapport to the things of the world has changed ... [through composure] you ever so slowly begin to let things emerge, you become part of them.
> GUMBRECHT 2004: 150–1

By allowing things to emerge and becoming part of them, we open ourselves to the world in new and important ways.

If Gumbrecht's celebration of the slowness of No theatre seems worrying to the Western (or specifically, the North American) mind, then it may be worth reminding ourselves of what philosophy, as a practice – at its best – embodies. Philosophy, in its ideal form, *is* a slow and repetitive art. In doing philosophy well we return time after time to similar passages, similar problems and similar writers. We patiently absorb ourselves in questions that can engage us for a lifetime. We sit quietly and immerse ourselves in contemplative thought, and we do so in order to gain a perspective or 'intensity' that our everyday lives do not readily afford. We compose ourselves so that the world returns to us anew. Seen from an imaginary 'outside', philosophy is a slow business indeed; it is hardly a gripping spectator sport. And yet, this very manner of doing philosophy is under threat in the modern university, where a desire to know and to produce so often outweighs a love of wisdom and of exploration. Gumbrecht's earlier claim – that our primary pedagogical task should be identifying instances of complexity and then exposing our students to these so that they may encounter the joy of sinking deeply into a slow and careful engagement with the complexities of thought – reminds us of the positive role that teaching can – and ought to – still play in the institution.[41] It seems to me that teaching is the future of the kind of slow reading and slow philosophy that I am interested in nurturing. Are there ways, then, that we can, as teachers of philosophy, welcome our students into an ethical community of readers? I certainly think so, and it is my hope that this book provides a step in that direction. In essence, though, the very act of valuing the teaching that we do is a way of reclaiming the instituting moment of the institution as our own; a first step towards a future philosophy. Simon Critchley has some helpful things to say about this in his paper 'What is the Institutional Form for Thinking?' (Critchley 2010).[42] Here he invites us to become more attentive to the practice of teaching, imagining alternatives to dominant institutional modes; alternatives that move us away from the increasingly corporate models that have come to dominate the academy. This overlay of a corporate mentality carries with it an instrumental approach to 'output' and 'production'[43] that, I think, inevitably places time restrictions on thought and reading alike. By reclaiming the pleasures of teaching, learning and thinking, Critchley argues in his paper that we can, to a large extent, resist the pressures that threaten the very possibility of thought. It is precisely here, in this reconnection with the pleasures of teaching, that a slow reading can gradually take root. Though slow reading is not Critchley's focus, what he has to say about thought and its relation with pleasure nonetheless supports my case. His call for 'a better, collaborative, institutional form for thinking' based on the enjoyment of teaching (Critchley 2010: 24) is one that has much in common with the idea of the teaching of a reading that opens us patiently to the otherness of the world. When Critchley refers to 'the delicate tact of teaching' and its involvement in 'the formation of human beings' (26), I think of this in terms of the ethical work that the teaching of slow reading can do. Importantly, Critchley locates the pleasures and joys of such a teaching within the ethos of familiarity and trust – an ethos that 'is fragile, at times obscure, and that cannot be reduced to the bean-counting methods of measuring research quality' (22).[44] Philosophy as a way of life triumphs here over any desire to calculate and simply to know.

Critchley's determination to reconnect with the pleasures of teaching and Gumbrecht's desire to enhance the possibilities for intensity rest largely on the institution's ability to provide the space and time for real thought to emerge. Both sit well with approaches to teaching philosophy that recognize the importance of reading slowly, and both challenge institutionalized models of reading or doing philosophy reduced to 'information-extraction' or 'mining'. Critchley argues that, at its best, philosophy doesn't offer knowledge conceived as information. In fact, it doesn't even offer wisdom. What it does offer, though, is a disposition *towards* wisdom: 'a disposition toward thinking and thoughtfulness' (Critchley 2010: 29), 'an orientation of the soul toward the true' (25).[45] By challenging the discourse on knowledge and offering in its place 'a nonknowledge where the object of philosophical investigation is not conceptualized, compartmentalized, or neatly defined' (26), philosophy, we can argue, becomes again a love of wisdom and a way of life. Gumbrecht's intense reading and Critchley's pleasurable teaching move us well beyond 'information' and a forensic desire to know. Now I think that Wittgenstein's 'slow cure' returns to us in the patient and intense reading that we have seen Gumbrecht invoke. In saying so, I am suggesting that Wittgenstein can be thought of as a silent interlocutor in Gumbrecht's contemporary discussion. And yet, there is another voice that needs to be included in this conversation. I have already indicated that Gumbrecht frames what he says about the institution in terms of Friedrich Nietzsche's idea of an untimely philosophy.

It is time now to consider what Nietzsche has to say about reading. Throughout his work, Nietzsche writes eloquently on the need for us to become slow, and much of what he says sits well with Gumbrecht's celebration of intensity. In the Preface to *Daybreak*, Nietzsche describes the reading that accompanies this art of slowing – this slow philosophy:

> That venerable art which demands of its votaries one thing above all: to go aside, to take time, to become still, to become slow . . . But for precisely this reason it is more necessary than ever today

> ... in the midst of an age of 'work', that is to say, of hurry, of indecent and perspiring haste, which wants to get 'everything done' at once ... this art does not so easily get anything done, it teaches to read well, that is to say, to read slowly, deeply, looking cautiously before and aft, with reservations, with doors left open, with delicate eyes and fingers.
>
> NIETZSCHE 1982: 5[46]

Nietzsche's description of a reading 'with doors left open, with delicate eyes and fingers' is a marvellous counter to an anxiety that needs 'to get "everything done" at once' and to the modern university that seeks comprehension and certainty with 'indecent haste'. It is a reminder, too, that teaching matters. In addition, Nietzsche's reading counters a certain kind of philosophy that reduces reading to a conflict or struggle, a battle where what we read is to be ultimately contained, determined – pinned down, known. As Nietzsche himself reminds us, 'the worst readers are those who behave like plundering troops: they take away a few things they can use, dirty and confound the remainder, and revile the whole' (Nietzsche 1996: 137).[47] In place of this combative reading, Nietzsche offers us a slow reading that partakes of an almost bovine sensibility. For example, he provides the following rather striking image: 'I admit that you need one thing above all in order to practice the requisite art of reading ... you almost need to be a cow for this one thing and certainly not a "modern man": [and what is this thing?] it is rumination' (Nietzsche 1965: 9–11).

Making good on my earlier promise to return to our cow, we can, with Nietzsche's help, think of slow reading as a kind of rumination, a slow chewing over of thought. Rumination gives us ample time to engage with what we read.[48] We allow impressions to form. We allow the dust of our reading to settle. We patiently take our time. It is possible to think of slow reading in terms of the slow movement generally,[49] which acknowledges that 'speed has helped to remake our world in ways that are wonderful and liberating' but that our current addiction to haste is now verging on the catastrophic (Honoré 2004: 4). The slow food movement, part of this slow movement, consciously promotes the idea of rumination that I am celebrating here, and to juxtapose these two – slow reading with slow food – is to bring reading and eating into a potentially fruitful dialogue.[50]

In what follows I touch briefly upon moments in contemporary philosophical practice that bear traces of Nietzsche's call to slowness, linking reading with – and thereby renewing – the instituting moment of philosophy as a love of wisdom and a way of life.

We find traces of Nietzsche's call to slowness in the work of the French philosopher Jean-François Lyotard. In his later work, Lyotard sees critique (along with theory and interpretation) as part of a restricted judicial process, in that it remains tied to the adversary's position. In order to work philosophically in new ways, he avoids the finality of verdict by developing an approach characterized by an indeterminate judgement. Bill Readings, following Lyotard's lead, frames this new approach to judgement in terms of reading. Lyotard's 'reading', he says can be understood as 'a performance which should be judged in ethical terms' (Readings 1991: xxiii),[51] involving, as it does, invention rather than fidelity. In *Libidinal Economy*, Lyotard writes: 'We do not interpret, we read, and we effect by writing' (Lyotard 1993: 94). So the work of philosophy is for Lyotard the work of reading, and I would add to this that his particular form of reading is ethical in that it is characterized by an openness to otherness that occurs in slow and unhurried ways. For example, in *Driftworks*, Lyotard speaks of 'drifting' as an alternative to the adversary's position of critique (Lyotard 1984). Lyotard's drifting is a slow reading that turns its back on the hurried judgement of critique and verdict.

In indeterminate judgement Lyotard is referring to situations or events where something occurs, with the result that our pre-existing understanding is radically disrupted – leaving us with no obvious way to think through what has happened. In such a context, Lyotard urges us to experiment with new ways of engaging with the event, ones that imaginatively open us to what has happened, rather than prematurely resolving and thus containing and ultimately losing the event. Indeterminate judgement involves inventing new understanding, and this process of experimentation and invention takes time. Here, the philosopher engages slowly, so as to avoid a hasty and reductive conceptualization. This 'paralogical experimentation'[52] resists the lure of a judgement that both limits and contains.[53] As it moves it hesitates, ever careful not to resolve the event in some convenient and prematurely finished form.[54] Imagination takes the place of conceptualization here and in this, and other respects, Lyotard's work connects with Wittgenstein's philosophical project (Lyotard 1985).

The philosophical and political, not to mention juridical, implications of Lyotard's important work on indeterminate judgement bring us, if we continue with the imaginary genealogy I am proposing, to the equally significant work of the Brazilian intellectual, Luiz Costa Lima whose work we will consider in Chapter Two. Costa Lima's work on 'criticity' – a questioning that does not lead to the finality of judgement – evokes a similarly slow and open engagement that requires imagination in the place of conceptual rigour and system (Costa Lima 1996).[55] His point, that the 'reasonable' quality of (philosophical or theoretical) thought too often threatens to drown the voice of imagination, to tame it in order to better control and regulate it, sits nicely alongside the concerns that Lyotard has for judgement in general. Costa Lima's work, more consciously oriented towards questions of reading than Lyotard's, highlights the fate of imagination and its links with fiction (broadly interpreted) in modern times. Throughout his many works, Costa Lima explores the mechanisms of control that work to institutionalize both reading and thought,[56] and in doing so he gestures towards other possibilities – other ways of reading and engaging that promise to salvage the great potential of thought. Costa Lima's work is particularly important reading for those of us who are institutionally based, as it challenges us to think through the implications of a specialized academic or professional reading (critique) that departs from reading perhaps more commonly practiced.[57] And while he does not say so himself, the reading that Costa Lima both gestures towards and performs in his own work is slow – precisely in the sense of Nietzsche's reading 'with doors left open, with delicate eyes and fingers'.

This slow reading finds quite another inflection in the work of Luce Irigaray. Irigaray's readings of some of the major philosophical texts of the Western tradition provide us with models of engaged and ethical encounter (Irigaray 1993). Starting from a love of wisdom and moving towards a wisdom of love, Irigaray challenges the institution to face its instituting moment. In her encounter with Descartes's *Passions of the Soul* she provides us with a reading that offsets the dangers of speed and haste with the slowness of a wonder that constantly stops to encounter difference.[58] (Nietzsche surfaces momentarily in Irigaray's essay as a luminous guide whose own thought inspires a patient return to wonder.)[59] Wonder, the first of the passions, stops us, stills and quietens us long enough to be in proximity with the other, to slowly appreciate the strangeness or newness of the other, rather than hurriedly moving on. Wonder opens us to the element of surprise, exposing us to the other's uniqueness and difference, suspending us between flux and certitude. Wonder provides the basis for an open and optimistic engagement with the other – 'doors left open ... delicate eyes and fingers'. No anxious search for certainty and containment, but rather an infinite response that patiently reaches out time and time again. The implications for an open and engaged reading seem clear to me here.[60]

I have suggested that Nietzsche's call to read slowly, to become slow, to avoid haste, to read 'with doors left open, with delicate eyes and fingers' finds sympathetic expression in the work of writers as diverse as Lyotard, Costa Lima and Irigaray.[61] I have hinted – all too briefly in an Introduction savouring the delights of slow reading – how I see this to be the case, and I have reframed their work in order to emphasize the links I see with Nietzsche's call. But what precisely is the nature of this call? What is it in Nietzsche's work that separates him from the haste of a largely modern philosophy? Is Nietzsche's call an ancient one? One way of exploring these questions is to think, at the same time, about Hadot's suggestion that in the modern era only a few rare exceptions (Nietzsche included) challenge the legacy of the scholastic tradition by returning to something of the ancients.[62] He writes:

> The idea of philosophy reduced to its conceptual content has survived to our own time ... We encounter it every day in our university courses and in textbooks at every level; one could say that it is the classical, scholastic, university conception of philosophy. Consciously or unconsciously, our universities are still heirs of the 'School' – in other words, of the Scholastic tradition.
>
> HADOT 2002: 258

And in an earlier work:

> From now on, with few rare exceptions like Schopenhauer or Nietzsche, philosophy would be indissolubly linked to the university ... This fact is not without its importance.

Philosophy – reduced ... to philosophical discourse – develops from this point on in a different atmosphere and environment from that of ancient philosophy. In modern university philosophy, philosophy is obviously no longer a way of life or a form of life – unless it be the form of life of a professor of philosophy ... modern philosophy is first and foremost a discourse developed in the classroom, and then consigned to books.

HADOT 1995: 271[63]

Hadot is concerned to distinguish ancient philosophy from the discourse-bound tradition of scholasticism – to distinguish philosophy as a way of life from philosophy as a written discourse. Philosophy 'today', he claims, emerges out of a scholasticism that abstracts itself from life: 'philosophy in the Middle Ages had become a purely theoretical and abstract reality. It was no longer a way of life' (Hadot 1995: 270):

If ancient philosophy established an intimate link between philosophical discourse and the form of life, why is it that today, given the way the history of philosophy is usually taught, philosophy is presented as above all a discourse, which may be theoretical and systematic, or critical, but in any case lacks a direct relationship to the philosopher's way of life?

HADOT 2002: 253

Hadot charts stages in what he sees as this gradual deformation of philosophy, and he concludes this with a discussion of Descartes – a philosopher he sees as best embodying this 'new' philosophy that disengages with life.[64]

The fact that Hadot identifies Nietzsche in this story is interesting; interesting because it suggests that Nietzsche manages to escape the stranglehold of scholasticism by retaining ties (complex as these may be) to an ancient philosophy that remains, above all, a way of life.[65] Might pace have something to do with the invisible thread that connects Nietzsche back to the ancients? While Hadot's understanding of the problem is the focus on discourse that emerges from scholasticism, I suggest that contemplation and the slow pace required for contemplation to occur is also an issue here.[66] We need to ask whether there is something in the scholastic tradition that works against a slow practice of philosophy – one that ties us back to the world. Does the abstraction of scholasticism ultimately undermine contemplation of one's place *in* the world? Does scholasticism initiate a way of doing philosophy – a methodology – that separates us from philosophy practised as a *way* of life?[67] Clearly the answer to these questions from Hadot's point of view is a resounding yes!

Another way of thinking about this is to separate slow reading from a formulaic version of close reading. We can distinguish slow reading from this kind of close reading in the following ways. Slow reading follows an anti-systematic trajectory and has questioning as its major motivation. It is an open-ended reading that has ethics as its core – ethics here denoting an openness to the other. In certain kinds of close reading the temporality of slow reading is replaced with a spatiality of being close, rather than proximate. This somewhat suffocating closeness interrogates at close quarters, providing a microscopic examination of the other. This version of close reading is systematic and formal; it draws its inspiration from the needs of the system – to read systematically and thoroughly. To confirm what is already known. It is exhaustive, and all too often works to contain what it reads by producing a systematic or coherent commentary, one that at times smoothes over ambiguities and irregularities. This form of close reading interprets and attributes meaning, while slow reading takes the opportunity to engage in open-ended thought. In this sense, scholasticism – and its modern institutional philosophical counterpart – involves a version of close reading that is, at its worst, devoid of contact with the world or the philosopher's life. This abstract, internal, disengaged reading fails to return us *to* the world. Slow reading, on the other hand, is a practice that grounds thought in the body, in experience – it is both external and open-ended. It is a reading that encourages us to take our time, to pause, to look up from the page; taking the time to do so, rather than remaining with one's head buried in the page, as is so often the case in formulaic forms of close reading. Of course, having said all this, we need to distinguish systematic and formula-driven versions of close reading from those that are both slow and problematizing.[68]

If philosophy is to regain something of the weight or gravity of its ancient practice, to be once more a love of wisdom, we need to reinstate a pace that permits it to become, again, a way of life.[69] In the light of this, I suggest we practise a philosophy and a reading that is both slow and meditative; a careful and concerned practice that patiently connects us both with what we read and with how we live. Such a reading involves a slow engagement capable of attention to what we have seen Gumbrecht refer to as the complexity of the world.[70] This reading challenges contemporary philosophy to be more than 'activity' and 'mobilization',[71] something more than production – perhaps a slow sinking into the world[72] that allows thought its time.[73] Indeed, Hadot himself points us in this direction when at the end of a section entitled 'Learning How to Read', he writes:

> And yet we have forgotten *how* to read: how to pause, liberate ourselves from our worries, return into ourselves, and leave aside our search for subtlety and originality, in order to meditate calmly, ruminate, and let the texts speak to us. This, too, is a spiritual exercise, and one of the most difficult. As Goethe said: 'Ordinary people don't know how much time and effort it takes to learn how to read. I've spent eighty years at it, and I still can't say that I've reached my goal'.
>
> HADOT 1995: 109[74]

The eighty patient years that Goethe spends learning how to read echo the fifty slow and meditative years we saw Stieglitz devote to his photographic art of 'reading' early in this Introduction. Both invest time and effort in learning how to read well, and given the connotations of the term 'reading', this may not be as surprising as it seems. *Chambers Dictionary of Etymology* suggests that in English from roughly 1175 *reden* comes to mean to consider, discern, read (writing), and that it is influenced by the word *rǣdan* in Old English (West Saxon), meaning to explain, read, rule, advise (before 899). Associations of reading with advising, counselling, considering or explaining something complex or difficult to understand, come to English via the Germanic languages where such associations are common. However, later associations of reading with the deciphering of written symbols appears to be unique to English and Old Icelandic. In addition, reading has historic associations with 'considering' in Old Irish (*immrādim*), 'minding' in Old Welsh (*amraud*) and 'caring for' in Old Slavic (*raditi*) (Barnhart 2010: 891).[75] Perhaps this subterranean sense of reading as 'caring for' helps us to better appreciate the kind of slow and careful (ethical) effort that reading is for Goethe and Stieglitz. Slow reading comes out of the practice of both caring for what we read and for how we go about it.

This sense of reading as 'caring for' allows us to ask precisely what it is that slow reading permits. Of course, we have been discussing this throughout the Introduction and yet it is worth returning to this one more time. It seems to me that what slow reading allows is an open relation to the complexity of the world we inhabit. In this it partakes of a love of wisdom and philosophy as a way of life. By granting us unhurried time, we are able to open out to the world. It is this openness that permits us what is ultimately an ethical relation with our world. Openness to otherness, to strangeness, to complexity is what *constitutes* ethics. And slowness, in this sense, is what *enables* this openness. Now it may well be that slowness takes various forms. Indeed, we need only look to musical notation and tempo to discover that slowness exists along a continuum from moderately to very slow. Between the moderate walking pace of *andante* and the very, very slow gait of *larghissimo*, there exists the possibilities of *andante moderato*, *adagietto*, *adagio*, *larghetto*, *largo*, *lento* and *grave*. In addition, there are *ritardando* and *rallentando*, both of which indicate a gradual slowing down. It may be useful to think of slow reading along this continuum, or even along the entire continuum of tempo. What I mean by this is that at any given time the openness we seek, in order to connect with the otherness, strangeness or complexity of the world, may be accessible in a variety of ways. Slowness may be our first and necessary encounter with the world in order that we read in engaged, open and ethical ways, and yet successive readings or rereadings (whether slow or not) may occur in quite different ways. For example, slow and open approaches to reading may build over time to a sudden burst of insight where, however fleetingly, we engage the world in entirely different ways. The moment of '*Aha-Erlebnis*'[76] is one way of thinking about the culmination of slow and ruminant thought in a moment of instant gestalt. Throughout this book, I will argue that the practice of returning to what we read – of rereading and being willing to reread (at whatever speed) – is fundamental to any ethical engagement with complexity.

In a similar vein, it is also worth considering the importance of space in any discussion of what slow reading might possibly entail. The tempo of a slow or meandering reading arguably requires space or room for such a reading to move around in; that is, room for the reading to occur. References in musical tempo to 'walking pace' are not incidental. They indicate the spatial location of tempo *in* the world; between the body *and* the world. Slow reading proceeds at a meandering walking pace and, as such, is a reading that arguably fits the body's rhythms.

What ultimately makes a slow and meditative reading worthwhile is not only that it hesitates or suspends judgement, that it deliberates before it takes a stance or compares one work with another. Rather, what makes such a reading worthwhile is that these eventual acts of judgement or comparison emerge out of a process of slow, careful and open immersion *in* the work – in the reading. Slow reading is an open reading that delights in taking its time, in sitting with the text, waiting for the dust of reading to settle before gathering itself to respond to the text and to engage fully with it. With Nietzsche, Wittgenstein, Woolf and Gumbrecht, I am calling for a slow, open and considered reading, a careful reading that is concerned more with raising questions than with determining answers. An open reading that ignores the demands of system and structure for the sheer pleasure and intensity of allowing thought its time. This reading allows us 'to go aside, to take time, to become still, to become slow' so that we resist the hurry of 'indecent and perspiring haste, which wants to get "everything done" at once'. This reading does 'not so readily get anything done' but rather 'teach[es us] to read well, that is to say, to read slowly, deeply ... with reservations, with doors left open, with delicate eyes and fingers'.

Resisting institutional reading

By framing this investigation in terms of the complex interplay between the love of wisdom (the instituting moment) and the forensic desire to know (the instituted structure), I am working with a series of oppositions that follow from this division. Accordingly, slow reading restores the relevance that the instituting moment no longer holds by gathering a set of practices that resist the dominance of institutional forms of reading. For example, in the following chapters I explore slow reading as an attentive rereading rather than a speed reading; as a common or unprofessional reading rather than a professional one; as an open or open-ended reading rather

INTRODUCTION: ON BEING SLOW AND DOING PHILOSOPHY 33

than a closed or finite one; as an exploration of ambiguity and contradiction rather than a need to know; as an imaginative engagement rather than a disciplined approach; as an experimental gesture rather than a rigorous one; as a fascination rather than a final interpretation; as an intellectual curiosity rather than a deferential account; as a questioning rather than an explanation; as an incomplete reading rather than a final one; as a partial account rather than an exhaustive one; as a suspended judgement rather than a verdict; as an essayistic reading rather than a systematic one; as a loving relation or wondrous appreciation rather than an authoritative account; as an attentive listening rather than a closed mind; as a careful engagement rather than a reductive response; as an authentic reading rather than a romantic or a deferential one; as a slow and intimate approach rather than a hasty reduction; as a generosity and a giving rather than a plundering; as a polite respect rather than a pretentious or an authoritative interpretation; as a discerning reading rather than a self-interested one; as an intense encounter, an extreme proximity or an *entredeux* rather than an objective account; as a meandering, an unhurried reception, a reflection, a rumination, a meditative relation, a patience, a receptive attitude rather than an activity, a mastery or a mobilization; as a feeling, an atmosphere or a mood rather than an academic exercise; as an attention, rapture, felicity, surrender or grace rather than the gravity of a calculation; as a future philosophy rather than a moribund one; as an ethical engagement rather than an adversarial one; as an ethics of reading rather than a desire to know.

By institutional reading I mean the kind of reading that comes to dominate the modern institutional context. In philosophy this means the largely professional reading undertaken in the university that occurs within a culture of speed and haste – of publish or perish. Reading institutionally means to read without the time required to allow the dust to settle, or for impressions to be received. It means reading directly, without the necessary and essential element of time. It means reading so as to produce immediate (and often hasty) judgements (verdicts). It means reading 'scientifically' or 'technologically' (as 'information technology') – for information and for information extraction. It means reading to mine resources. It means reading to construct coherence by radical simplification and jumping hastily to conclusions. It means reading closely in the sense of an exhaustive, systematic or formal reading that draws inspiration solely from the needs of the system. It means reading purely to interpret rather than to engage. It means reading in an abstract, disengaged manner, in place of a relation with the world. It means reading in order simply to know. Each of these faces of institutional reading limit our potential to pursue a love of wisdom, whether this be in our research, our teaching, our collegiality or our interactions with other traditions and other disciplines.[77]

In offering alternatives to institutional reading I look towards slow reading as the work involved in transformation that philosophy as a way of life should be. This transformation comes about through the quality of attention that underpins and ties together each of the slow reading practices I explore. My aim is to offer these instances of slow reading as counters to the institutional readings that unconsciously support the dominant scholarly context of speed and haste. In doing so, I seek to reclaim or release what is best in our Western tradition – the instituting moments – by formulating contemporary philosophical practices that engage with the Socratic orientation of philosophy as a love of wisdom rather than as simply a desire to know. In effect, my work introduces a necessary reversal in practice, aimed to challenge and eventually undo aspects of this institutionalization. Having said this, though, I should be clear that my project is not a return to some ideal past or prior position, which would of course be a kind of romantic gesture, but rather it offers a way of rethinking how philosophy within its current institutional context can operate. It works with the institution to revitalize it, acknowledging that the guiding principal of the love of wisdom can and ought to be more than curiously irrelevant to immediate concerns.

CHAPTER ONE

Habits of Reading: Le Dœuff's Future Philosophy

Resolving to read
RICHARD FLANAGAN, *GOULD'S BOOK OF FISH*: 373

In the Introduction I outlined two very different aspects of philosophical work: the *instituting* moments of a love of wisdom and philosophy as a way of life, and the *instituted* structure of a desire to know. These tendencies come together in complex ways to form the *institution* of philosophy as we know it today. I argued that the guiding principle – the love of wisdom – is responsible for instituting an orientation towards philosophy as transformative, propelling the philosopher from one existential state to another. In this chapter, I continue this exploration, looking to Michèle Le Dœuff's work to focus on what I refer to as her 'habits' of reading. I argue that Le Dœuff's approach to philosophy as 'work' and her belief that this involves shifting thinking from one stage to another is an excellent way of thinking about the transformation that propels the philosopher from one existential state to another. As such, Le Dœuff's work brings us back to the instituting moments of a love of wisdom and philosophy as a way of life, offering us sites of resistance to the institutional reading I seek to avoid.

Philosophy as discipline

Before proceeding to Le Dœuff's habits of reading, I want to take a moment to engage with what she has to say about the institution of philosophy, as this has direct bearing on the argument I develop in this book. Put simply, Le Dœuff's exploration of contemporary philosophy as a discipline offers us a helpful way of thinking about how and why the guiding idea of a love of wisdom recedes in the institutional context – and how a desire to know and to limit comes to the fore. Additionally, Le Dœuff's understanding of the disciplinary nature of contemporary philosophy has implications for the kind of future philosophy she works towards: a future that allows us to challenge the institutional culture of philosophy.

In an early work, *The Philosophical Imaginary* (1989), Le Dœuff explores the various limits and borders that accompany philosophy when it is practised as a discipline. She claims that philosophy works to repress, exclude and dissolve an otherness that it sets itself against: 'For philosophical discourse is a discipline, that is to say a discourse obeying (or claiming to obey) a finite number of rules, procedures or operations, and as such it represents a closure, a delimitation which denies the (actually or potentially) indefinite character of modes of thought; it is a barrage restraining the number of possible (acceptable) statements' (Le Dœuff 1989: 114). Le Dœuff's argument is a complex one, engaging with the paradox of philosophy's relation with its interminable otherness. Philosophy creates itself precisely by opposing itself to an outside or exterior that it largely creates: 'For in defining itself through negation, the philosophical creates its Other: it engenders an opposite which, from now on, will play the role of hostile principle, the more hostile because there is no question of dispensing with it' (115). Philosophy's hallucinated and persecuting other (its internal enemy) haunts its borders, and surfaces in philosophy's clashes with other discourses and modes of thought. Philosophy as discipline does its best to exclude the otherness that exists paradoxically at its inner imaginary core.[1] In this sense, its disciplinary nature is constructed as a general form of exclusion, and this works to minimize philosophy's contact with an otherness that inhabits the world. When experienced as discipline, philosophy is a closing down that seeks a restricted and managerial relation with the world. This specific form of philosophy is equated, in Le Dœuff's account, with closure, delimitation, exclusion, restraint and control, and we can recognize in these terms a depiction of the instituted and institutional nature of philosophy.

Given this, we can ask why Le Dœuff situates her own work within the domain of philosophy. We can ask, too, how she understands her relation with its disciplinary or institutional practice. If philosophy has historically worked towards closure, how can it help us to engage openly today? Old habits die hard and the disciplinary nature of philosophy is certainly cause for concern, and yet Le Dœuff's work is aimed squarely at identifying and transforming those aspects of philosophical work that close down our engagement with the complexity of the world. At the same time, she affirms a positive history, a history that we can equate with the instituting moments of philosophy – a love of wisdom and philosophy as a way of life. In this positive mode, Le Dœuff looks in two directions at once; she identifies moments in the history of philosophy where open and engaged thought is evident, while simultaneously looking towards a future philosophy that is not defined by discipline, one that – as we will see later in the chapter – resembles other modes of thought. Indeed, she writes: 'Personally, if I did not stop halfway on the path to identification [as many other aspiring women philosophers have done], it was because I thought I saw the possibility of a fork in the path ahead, and thus of throwing in my lot with a philosophical practice which was still to come' (Le Dœuff 1991: 79).

Philosophy's old habits of reading

If philosophy has functioned to a large extent as discipline and exclusion what are the implications of this institutional structure for reading? Although reading is not Le Dœuff's obvious focus, there are many observations scattered throughout her work that help us to respond to this question. Reading carefully through her œuvre, we can piece together a series of insights that help us to identify (i) old habits of reading; (ii) engaged and open modes of reading; and (iii) questions concerning the gendered nature of reading more generally.

In a section of the 'Third Notebook' of *Hipparchia's Choice*, which begins appropriately with a reference to 'the ethics of the trade', Le Dœuff identifies three ways to characterize the relations between philosophy and the history of philosophy (Le Dœuff 1991:

166). What she says here can usefully be thought in terms of three different approaches to reading the history of philosophy, or simply as three ways that philosophers read. Genevieve Lloyd's depiction of these three relations, although not referring to them as readings, offers a helpful way to engage with and extend the categories Le Dœuff constructs, and I will refer to it here. The first approach involves reading as a kind of clear articulation of the truth or knowledge previous philosophers have written: reading as a desire to know what is already known. It is a somewhat ahistorical reading or commentary that positions the great work as 'monument'. The assumption is that an absolute transparency allows past philosophers to know and to write in ways that admit no 'unthought' to inhabit the text. The key to this kind of reading is a faithful rendering that, as Lloyd notes, positions the commentator 'at the speaking position of the author, stripping away the misinterpretations that have preceded her, to offer a clear articulation of what the author really said' (Lloyd 2000: 33). This approach to reading shares something of the commitment that Le Dœuff elsewhere refers to as fidelity (Le Dœuff 1989: 125). The faithful reader Le Dœuff identifies in *Hipparchia's Choice* is committed to the work of uncovering a truth that is self-evidently there.[2]

The second approach to reading that Le Dœuff identifies places truth or knowledge with the contemporary reader. Here reading targets the philosopher's 'unthought', aiming to identify and shame those points of tension that structure the philosophical work. With hindsight the reader uncovers what is hidden in the text, demonstrating that 'the exegete understands a work better than its author, since the former knows both the work, its outside and what links it to its outside' (Le Dœuff 1989: 167). There are links, here, with aspects of Le Dœuff's early approach to reading in *The Philosophical Imaginary*, and Lloyd identifies two versions of this second approach: in the weaker version 'the interpretation of imagery in philosophical texts goes together with a search for points of tension in a work: The imagery is seen as inseparable from the difficulties, the "sensitive points" of an intellectual venture', while in the stronger version 'the interpretation of the philosopher's imagery involves a deeper tension – approaching a contradiction – in the workings of the text' (Lloyd 2000: 34).

Le Dœuff's third approach equates reading with 'work' and here a different practice comes into play. A sense of movement frames reading as dynamic: neither as 'a monument' (complete/finished), nor as 'an effect which is blind to its origins' (incomplete/lacking), but rather as 'an effort to shift thinking from one stage to another' (reading as a love of wisdom). Reading as work would be neither completion nor beginning; more properly it would be 'impulse and movement' (Le Dœuff 1989: 168). This effort to shift thinking from one stage to another is one good way of thinking about reading in ethical terms, and we will return to this in due course. For now, though, let us make some preliminary observations that will help us later to think more carefully about the relation of this third approach and Le Dœuff's own reading practices. This third approach moves beyond uncovering the tensions structuring the philosophical text (as with the second approach Le Dœuff identifies), establishing a more collaborative relation with what it reads. Creativity and imagination are brought into play, stretching the original intentions of the author in new and unexpected ways. As Lloyd observes, the reader opens philosophy out to wider concerns:

> The contemporary reader of philosophical texts becomes not the superior judge of the author's pretensions, but rather a constructive, though tough-minded, appropriator. The difference is one of tone and spirit. The task is collaborative rather than antagonistic (or adversarial): not so much to confront the author with what has been repressed or evaded, but rather to rethink in a new context what the author said.
>
> LLOYD 2000: 37

Contemporary concerns and issues can revitalize earlier philosophical discussions, and earlier discussions can help to open contemporary concerns in new and sometimes unexpected ways. Le Dœuff's approach to reading as work shares something with the reading Nietzsche celebrates when he writes: 'We honor the great artists of the past less through that unfruitful awe which allows every word, every note, to lie where it has been put than we do through active endeavors to help them to come repeatedly to life again' (Nietzsche 1996: 126).[3]

Le Dœuff's third approach to reading shifts philosophy away from its old habits, and orients reading towards practices that prefigure a future philosophy. In doing so, it expands the possibilities of philosophical discourse, bringing it into both relation and collaboration with discourses other than its own. Philosophy moves towards an interdisciplinarity that undoes the closure, exclusion and anxious concern for borders that have historically characterized its methods and, more generally, its self-definitions. As such, Le Dœuff's attempt to think of philosophy or reading as 'work' is an important contribution to our ongoing efforts to keep the question of what philosophy is alive.[4] Indeed, speaking with Bergson and Deleuze, Le Dœuff underlines the importance of replacing 'the notion of philosophy as a monumental system with that of thinking-on-the-move' (Le Dœuff 1991: 168). Le Dœuff's depiction of philosophy as thinking-on-the-move demonstrates how challenging the desire to know does not need to return us to some kind of past and static conception of philosophy, but rather that it can orient us towards new and future practices that nonetheless have their roots in the love of wisdom that comes down to us from the ancients. Thinking or reading-on-the-move helps us to counter the neurotic fears that historically attach to philosophy's borders, allowing us to think more openly about how philosophical concerns can both be launched from elsewhere and, in turn, how these concerns can relaunch investigations in other fields.

> By seeking a model of this type in Bergson, 'I am sorting things out for myself'. Indeed, if we adopt the conception of philosophical thought as something ever-changing, which started elsewhere in several places at once and is moving towards an elsewhere or elsewheres which cannot be foreseen, the boundary between what is 'philosophy' and what is not loses its clarity. This seems to me important for more than one reason ... 'In wanting to enclose a vast domain, one ends up by demolishing one's finances' said Democritus; the full meaning of these words merits contemplation. The enclosure of the field of philosophy could, in practice, lead to its greater exhaustion, from all points of view.
>
> LE DŒUFF 1991: 169

By way of countering or better still preventing the exhaustion Le Dœuff identifies, her third reading reaches out towards other discourses to open philosophy to the strangeness of the world, and in this it prefigures a future philosophy within a contemporary 'now'. There are connections to be made between this open-ended approach to reading and Le Dœuff's own practice, but before going on to explore these I want to return to Le Dœuff's observations concerning the first approach to reading: the one she identifies as commentary. My reasons for doing so are related to the distinction Le Dœuff makes elsewhere regarding two types of commentary and how we can think of these as gendered reading practices.

How men and women read

> Everyone knows that the more of a philosopher one is, the more distorted one's reading of other philosophers. Think of Leibniz's reading of Malebranche.
> LE DŒUFF 1989: 125

In *Hipparchia's Choice*, Le Dœuff identifies an approach to reading characterized by a faithful rendering or commentary of the great philosophical work. In an essay 'Long Hair, Short Ideas' in *The Philosophical Imaginary*, Le Dœuff engages with the complexities of commentary, noting that there are at least two variations of this form of reading: one marked by fidelity, the other by violation. There are different approaches to commentary and historically these approaches have aligned with a gendered division of masculinity and femininity. This is important for a number of reasons: one of these being that commentary has been one of the few avenues where women have been able to participate philosophically. We recall that in *Hipparchia's Choice*, Le Dœuff speaks of the dangers women face in being marginalized philosophically by strategies of permissiveness, amateurism and fidelity, and how she insists that being relegated to commentary is one of these dangers.[5] However, there are two forms of commentary and the 'masculine' approach to the form attracts a great deal more philosophical kudos than its 'feminine' counterpart. So-called 'strong readings' are the effects of a type of commentary that violates the great philosophical work by creatively reworking it.[6] Back in 'Long Hair, Short Ideas', Le Dœuff observes that while we are all, to a great extent, 'imprisoned in this phantasmagoria of the commentary' we are so in different ways. Trapped between the alternatives of violation and fidelity, women routinely assign themselves the subordinate (feminine) position 'in the distribution of theoretical tasks' (Le Dœuff 1989: 38):[7]

Who better than a woman to show fidelity, respect and remembrance? A woman can be trusted to perpetuate the words of the Great Discourse: she will add none of her own. Everyone knows the more of a philosopher one is, the more distorted one's reading of other philosophers. Think of Leibniz's reading of Malebranche, or Hegel's reading of Kant! They cannot respect the thought of the other: they are too engrossed in their own. Nietzsche said that a scientist's objectivity indicated his lack of instinct. How could a woman manhandle a text, or violate a discourse? The vestal of a discourse which time threatens to eclipse, the nurse of dismembered texts, the healer of works battered by false editions, the housewife whom one hopes will dust off grey film successive readings have left on the fine object, she takes on the upkeep of the monuments, the forms which the mind has deserted. A god's priestess, dedicated to a great dead man. This phantasmagoria of the commentary has to some extent enabled women to find a place for themselves in philosophical work. A minor one, however: as in cooking, so in commentary – the high-class works are always reserved for a Hyppolite or a Bocuse.

LE DŒUFF 1989: 125[8]

There are questions, of course, concerning the status of commentary in English-speaking philosophical circles and how this equates with its role in the French context Le Dœuff evokes, but this aside, she makes an important point in bringing to our attention the question of how women and men read.[9] The distinction Le Dœuff draws between weak and strong commentary (faithful reading or violation) – or between commentary and 'philosophy proper' – has implications for how we think about reading and the various habits it involves.[10] Indeed, Le Dœuff draws our attention to the gendered nature of these habits in her questions: 'Is it true that "to read is to write" and to rewrite what one thinks one is reading? And if that is the case, does the "same" book cease to be the same, depending on whether it is read by a man or a woman?' (Le Dœuff 1991: 65).[11] Although Le Dœuff thinks it likely that a woman (especially a feminist woman) will bring a different set of priorities and orientations to any reading,[12] she does not feel there is any need to transform these differences 'into a radical and definitive difference', suggesting instead that 'we would do better to assume that any way of [reading] someone else's work can be analysed and should be examined' (Le Dœuff 1991: 66). This examination ought to, of course, involve an assessment of the social and political context within which any reading is embedded.

From Le Dœuff's perspective, commentary has been one of the few places where women have been able to feel somewhat at home in philosophy. Penelope Deutscher takes up this question of 'being at home', observing that for Le Dœuff it occurs by first identifying with and then separating from our philosophical mentors and their work (Deutscher 2000: 199–220). In separating from our teachers and the authority of the discipline over time, we develop an independent relation with philosophy that allows us finally to be at home in our own right. For many women, this process is not straightforward and Le Dœuff explores the various structural and institutional conditions that make it less likely for them (us) to complete a separation beyond an initial (and possibly tentative) identification. Despite this, she thinks optimistically about the ways in which women philosophers can make a positive force out of being 'not quite at home'.[13] Le Dœuff's discussion of identification and separation to some extent parallel the types of love and reading that we will go on to explore in relation to Beauvoir's work in Chapter Five. Identification has much in common with a romantic relation with the other, and separation is part of what underpins and makes possible any authentic relation. The value of Le Dœuff's discussion is that it provides a nuanced understanding of how the two moments, identification *and* separation, work together and how both are integral to our ability to be 'at home'.

In the context of university examinations in philosophy, Le Dœuff makes observations that connect with the few things she has said regarding men and women and their relation to commentary. She suggests that there are two identifiable approaches to reading evident in student responses. On the one hand, there is a tendency towards authoritative interpretation, while on the other there is evidence of a polite receptivity. Writing in 1980 she notes:

> [A] paper can be identified as masculine by its authoritative tone, by the way interpretation dominates over receptivity to the text, resulting in a decisive and profound reading or in fantastic misinterpretation. Women, on the other hand, are all receptivity, and their papers are characterized by a kind of polite respect for the fragmentation of the other's discourse (this is called

'acuteness in detailed commentary but lack of overview'), by a great timidity (it is as though they left it to the text to explain itself), and also by a talent for what one might call the 'flattering comparison' . . .

Men treat the text familiarly and knock it about happily; women treat it with a politeness for which girls' education has its share of responsibility. If the timidity and desire to flatter are not too strong this form of reading can, I think, produce great successes, a distanced kind of reading which enables one to see what is implicit in the text or to pick out the 'gaps' in a theorization.

LE DŒUFF 1989: 124

It is perhaps not overly surprising that those marking university examinations in the 1980s would routinely (if unconsciously) map masculinity with authority and femininity with receptivity. However, the distinction between these two approaches remains interesting for us today and is worth some further consideration.[14] We learn from Le Dœuff that decisive and profound readings are ones demonstrating an authoritative style that lacks deference towards the text; these readings exhibit a certain violence and familiarity (are these connected?) and are happy to knock the text about; in these approaches interpretation dominates over receptivity (a desire to know over a wisdom of love?). Politely receptive readings, on the other hand, present an attentiveness to detail that is undercut by timidity,[15] a tendency towards flattering comparison, and a general lack of overview.[16] What Le Dœuff observes here we may refer to as culturally embedded gendered habits of reading, habits that are passed down institutionally from generation to generation.[17] In this context philosophy perpetuates dominant modes of reading, granting the greater spoils to those aggressive and authoritative approaches that serve to make their mark – or at the very least, to leave an impression.[18] While we associate habit with settled tendency or customary behaviour, Le Dœuff's strategy is to unmask the complacency behind these approaches so that we might think about them in new and different ways. Le Dœuff begins this process of reassessment when she states that '[i]f the timidity and desire to flatter are not too strong [the politely receptive] form of reading' can 'produce great successes, a distanced kind of reading which enables one to see what is implicit in the text or to pick out the "gaps" in a theorization' (Le Dœuff 1989: 124). This positive (though qualified) account of politely receptive reading gives us pause to reconsider our own cultural biases in order to think through the advantages of reading in non-authoritative ways.[19] (It may also help us to think a little differently about the role of the romantic reading that we will discuss in Chapter Five.)

One way of thinking through the advantages of reading in non-authoritative ways may be to reread the faithful and detailed commentaries of women philosophers; that is, to attend to this work in ways that we have failed to do in the past, possibly in our haste to consume the definitive interpretation by the latest, greatest and most fashionable philosopher of the day. Clearly, the French tradition values these commentaries, and Le Dœuff certainly acknowledges this.[20] However, we usually think of these readings as supporting existing philosophical values, thus reinforcing the hegemony of great texts by great men. If, however, we return attentively to these commentaries and reread them, we may discover something more than fidelity and respect. Perhaps we have been guilty of under-reading these works; of finding within them little other than what our expectations (and prejudices) support. If so, then the 'faithful' commentary requires another look. It may be the case, for example, that a polite demeanour hides something altogether more provocative and engaged.[21] Is it really true that these women have perpetuated the words of the Great Discourse and added *none* of their own? (Le Dœuff 1989: 125). This suggests some important recuperative work needs to be done in rereading these significant historical works by women.

However, if Le Dœuff is correct, and these commentaries by women are as faithful as she suggests, then we ought to return to the question of reading in order to think through the strategies involved in moving loving (or romantic) commentary towards more ethically engaged forms. We need to move, as Le Dœuff so rightly claims, beyond the false alternatives of fidelity and violation, for I am not suggesting that the way forward for women (or others) in philosophy is to mimic the violations of the past. There are, indeed, alternatives to reading too politely and paying no attention at all, alternatives Le Dœuff identifies as 'work'. How are we to think further about these alternatives? How are we to unpick the habits of authoritative reading, creating new habits that evolve out of and yet go beyond polite respect? In short, how are we to challenge the institutional or disciplinary culture of philosophy? The alternatives we seek are evident in Le Dœuff's own work. Her own particular engagements with the history of philosophy offer us attentive readings that help us to develop new 'habits' – habits that prefigure a future philosophy that she works toward. This future philosophy, while pointing us forwards, has roots in the instituting moment of the Socratic tradition that orients philosophy towards a love of wisdom. As such, it challenges the reduction of philosophy to the limited practice of a desire to know.

Teaching reading: sadism, collaboration?

If we are concerned to develop new habits of reading, ones that move us beyond an authoritative relation with our tradition, then teaching, as we have seen from our discussion in the Introduction, is an important place to begin. Le Dœuff has something to say about this in her essay 'Red Ink in the Margin' (Le Dœuff 1989: 57–99) where she draws our attention to our disciplinary incapacity to deal effectively with contradiction and how this failure underpins negative responses to a certain genre of student commentary. A sadistic streak infiltrates our desire to banish what is deemed vague in student readings, ensuring obedience to dogma, and Le Dœuff questions the somewhat brutal manner in which this is enacted:

> [P]edagogy is not unrelated to sadism. For the point of this correction [red ink in the margin] is, rather, for the master to confirm his mastery – that is, in the first place, his difference relative to the pupil, who lives only off a philosophical subculture, whereas the master 'knows his texts' otherwise than through second-hand sources ... This does not only happen in the pedagogical relation between teachers and their students; it operates also, in a brutal manner, in examinations. The charge of 'hearsay knowledge of the great philosophical texts', of 'vague knowledge of the most classical works' is too insistent in the examiners' reports to be ignored. I would gladly wager that what is called 'vague' is not always devoid of sense, and that one might learn a good deal by giving a hearing to the failed scripts. At any rate, the incapacity which we perhaps all share to handle the category of contradiction in what pertains to the history of

philosophy is not a result of simple logical infirmity: having once recognized the non-univocal nature of philosophical texts, how can one correct an essay, mark a commentary? The maintenance of a hierarchy of readings is a necessary corollary of the use of texts in school and university. What are the implicit criteria of this hierarchization? Their exploration remains to be undertaken.

LE DŒUFF 1989: 98–9

Given the many difficulties of justifying a clear hierarchy of readings, Le Dœuff's suggestion to give failed (or 'vague') examination scripts a hearing acts as both a challenge and a provocation to institutional forms of teaching that defer to authority in habitual and unquestioned ways. Here, engaged and open thought is sacrificed to discipline narrowly defined – obedience to dogma, or red ink in the margin as a sign of the master's superior status. If much of our teaching is technically sadistic, then what alternatives remain? Le Dœuff's response to this would be, I think, to exchange the model of master and pupil for something more collaborative. Collaborative work features centrally in her vision of a future philosophy open to a shared and more communal intellectual space. In collaboration I am open to the other, inclined towards the other in potentially creative ways. I am more likely to pay attention to the other, to listen attentively, and to learn from what the other has to say. As a teacher, I can model a polite respect that engages without deferring. (In other words, I can give my students' readings a hearing.) Polite respect can be a starting point for a reciprocity that builds in the process of collaborative work. Reciprocity is, too, the key to an ethical relation between me and the other. Between the master 'who knows' and the pupil 'who does not yet know', Le Dœuff seeks a ground for collaborative work that goes beyond a limited sense of personal initiative: 'it is hard to describe the revolution that would be effected by a collective form of philosophical work *and* by a recognition of the fact that, in any case, the enterprise cannot be reduced to personal initiatives'. She finds inspiration for this in Pascal's recognition that '"I do not do everything on my own", that I am a tributary to a collective discourse and knowledge, which have done more towards producing me than I shall contribute in continuing to produce them' (Le Dœuff 1989: 127).[22] Of course, what Le Dœuff says here fits well with Simon Critchley's account of the need to reclaim the pleasures of teaching we discussed in the Introduction. Both Le Dœuff and Critchley look towards teaching as a way of undoing the sadistic (and masochistic) qualities that infiltrate philosophy in its institutional forms. Both offer us alternatives that revitalize the instituting moments of a love of wisdom and philosophy as a way of life.

Le Dœuff reminds us of the importance of recognizing 'the necessarily incomplete character of all theorization' (Le Dœuff 1989: 127) and I think this relates to something we saw in Hans Ulrich Gumbrecht's work in the Introduction. Recall that Gumbrecht speaks of the importance of our teaching and research in producing *Bildung*, claiming that we can take positive and practical steps in this direction by 'confronting ourselves and our students with any object of a complexity that defies easy structuring, conceptualization, and interpretation'. By exposing our students and ourselves to 'high intellectual complexity without having an immediate need [time pressure] to reduce this complexity' we encourage thought to be slow, open and engaged (Gumbrecht 2003: 84, 85). The reading that accompanies this complexity allows for an engagement with ambiguity and contradiction that Le Dœuff believes certain modes of philosophical instruction are unmotivated to nurture. By taking our time and sinking into the complexity and intensity of a philosophical work, by identifying and exploring its contradictions, reading becomes much more than obedience to dogma or a faithfully reiterated commentary on a great text.[23] It can literally be a labour of love.

Le Dœuff's habits of reading

Throughout this chapter, I have moved back and forwards between positive and negative accounts of habit. I have suggested, on the one hand, that philosophy clings to old habits of reading, and, on the other, that we can establish new habits – ones that open our reading in attentive and ethical ways. For the French phenomenological philosopher, Maurice Merleau-Ponty, habit is a knowledge the body cultivates in the process of habitual activity (Merleau-Ponty 1962). This is an interesting way of thinking about habit in relation to reading, because it reminds us of the bodily context of our intellectual work. For Siri Hustvedt, 'The act of reading takes place in human time; in the time of the body, and it partakes of the body's rhythms, of heartbeat and breath, of the movement of our eyes, and of our fingers that turn the pages, but we do not pay particular attention to any of this' (Hustvedt 2012: 134). We might respond to Hustvedt that we do not pay attention because the work of reading has become habitual. Habit is activity that becomes something like a second nature, an activity from which 'we' consciously withdraw. In this, I think that habit has something in common with our institutional ways of doing things, for institutional or disciplinary activities are carried out in largely unconscious ways. Indeed, we can think of institutions (or even traditions) as structures supported by unacknowledged habits. Changing habits is, by definition, a difficult thing to undertake. Yet this is what I think Le Dœuff sets out to do. Le Dœuff's way of doing philosophy is to unmask the habitual activities of certain ways of thinking and reading so that a future philosophy can be something other than what it is today. To do this, she makes conscious the habits that sustain the more obvious pretensions of philosophy so that we may address them in our attempts to do better work. (We can read her work in *The Philosophical Imaginary* in this way.) In effect, Le Dœuff exchanges old habits for new, understanding that habit orients us towards the world whether for better or for worse.

Le Dœuff's habits of reading have been honed over years of careful attention to a history of philosophy that she cares a great deal about. Perhaps it is her real affection for the works that comprise this history that allows her to engage in such productive ways. By carefully unpicking the worst of the habits supporting the pretentious aspects of this tradition, she is able to tailor a set of new, open and engaged approaches to reading. In part, these approaches begin with, and yet go well beyond, the polite receptivity we have seen her identify. Attentiveness to detail is one of the hallmarks of Le Dœuff's reading practice, and yet this attention, however polite and engaged, is something quite different from the faithful commentary she has reservations about. Max Deutscher puts it well when he writes: 'Though Le Dœuff will make unparalleled [readings] of the "great texts", this is not out of awed respect for them . . . She keeps her distance from its entirety, however close her readings of its details' (Deutscher 2000: 11). This attentive quality of her reading originates in generosity and in a real intellectual curiosity rather than in the deference of a devoted approach.

Thinking back to the third approach to reading that Le Dœuff identifies – the transformative reading that shifts thinking from one stage to another – we see how this helps us to elucidate what is distinctive in her own reading habits. This approach equates reading with work, and is helpful for framing the collaborative relation that Le Dœuff establishes with what she reads.[24] The methods she employs in her readings are oriented towards the kind of work that gets things done; they are strategies aimed at particular problems and in this sense can be gauged in terms of their 'sufficiency to their tasks'.[25] This approach to reading involves attention to both detail and context. It intervenes in a particular place for a particular purpose, not setting out to provide an overarching critique or systematic account.[26] Its goals are less ambitious or, in Le Dœuff's own terms, less pretentious. This is, to use another of her terms, an operative approach to philosophy, a particular or temporary intervention that opens reading out towards other works and other disciplines exterior to philosophy.

One of the practices that supports Le Dœuff's approach to reading as work is her habit of rereading. Le Dœuff returns to the history of philosophy, reading and rereading its works, the better to reassess and reconsider her relation with these. In Chapter Five we witness an example of this in her readiness to reread Simone de Beauvoir's work. By re-engaging with Beauvoir's thought, Le Dœuff's successive readings explore new and challenging ways of understanding the real difference Beauvoir's political and ethical thought makes. While Le Dœuff's early readings are insightful, it is her successive returns that open Beauvoir's work to us in really radical ways. Revisiting a field that one feels one has explored well can uncover surprising and unexpected results.[27] If openness is an ability to be changed by what we read, then Le Dœuff's habit of rereading results in a more open, engaged and dynamic approach.

Returning to the question of Le Dœuff's relation with philosophy, I suggest that her strategic approaches to reading provide her with an identification that changes from context to context. Does this suggest a nomadic sense of being everywhere at home?[28] Whatever the case, Le Dœuff's current 'home' in philosophy emerges somewhat paradoxically out of her work on the future of philosophy, a future that is by definition an as yet unrealized home. In order to appreciate the full import of Le Dœuff's reading we need to engage with the plans for her future home – the future philosophy she points us toward.

A philosophy still to come: open-ended work

Le Dœuff commits herself to a new form of philosophy, one unmotivated by a desire for absolute knowledge or theoretical omnipotence, and it is noteworthy that she connects this with a future in which the 'feminine' will no longer be required as the inferior marker that a hegemonic rationality compares itself against. In *The Philosophical Imaginary*, she writes:

> Since for the last twenty-five centuries philosophers have been comparing the world to a theatre and philosophy to a tragedy, relating this metaphor to the close of the performance that makes a well-finished whole of the play, I would say that the future of a philosophy that is no longer anti-feminist is being performed somewhere in the region of Brechtian drama, which . . . produces unfinished plays which always have a missing act and are consequently left wide open to history.
>
> LE DŒUFF 1989: 118

The openness of Le Dœuff's future philosophy is a philosophy at ease with its incompleteness,[29] one no longer in need of a 'defence mechanism involving the exclusion of women' and others. This brings forth 'the idea of an unfinished philosophical discourse, never closed and never concluded', disconnected from any 'totalizing aim' (Le Dœuff 1989: 126). Given the close connections in Le Dœuff's work between approaches to philosophy and ways we read, we can revise her depiction slightly to reveal an incomplete reading, wide open to the otherness it engages. Le Dœuff's future reading disconnects from any totalizing aim. In this, its ethical qualities rest partially on the fact that it 'no longer considers its incompleteness a tragedy' (Le Dœuff 1989: 126). From tragedy to Brechtian drama,[30] Le Dœuff moves us towards a reading that embraces the incomplete nature of philosophy and understanding, one that resists the temptation to reconstruct the theatre of the other as a fantasized whole.[31]

It occurs to me that the primary way that Le Dœuff explores this unworried, incomplete approach is in the written form of the essay. Indeed, she introduces *The Philosophical Imaginary* as a collection of essays aimed at exploring hunches in philosophy in open and experimental ways: 'a series of essays, perhaps the only format allowing one not to close a question reductively before it has even been posed' (Le Dœuff 1989: 2). Le Dœuff adopts the essay as an unhurried form of questioning that follows no predetermined path. In the essay we can return to rework and reconsider our positions in relation to thought. We can constantly reframe the boundaries of our research in open and open-ended ways. In addition, we can engage and disengage with other disciplines, moving across intellectual terrain in unencumbered ways. In certain senses, the essay allows us to be at home (or at the very least at ease) in unfamiliar and nomadic territory. In this, the essay is the precursor to a future, more open philosophical form.

The essay's modesty undoes those lingering pretensions within philosophy towards a complete and total knowledge (a desire to know). Like the fragment and the notebook (both of which Le Dœuff employs), the essay announces an unfinished and incomplete work. This announcement occurs without the customary anxiety that certain approaches to reading and writing philosophy entail. In this, the essay, and the future hopes Le Dœuff attaches to new and incomplete forms of doing philosophy are signs of an ethical openness to the world. They are signs, too, of new habits orienting us towards reading as a process of mediation in a future philosophy which – for the time being – remains difficult to conceptualize. To return to Le Dœuff's earlier observation, and to reframe it, we can suggest tentatively that the ethical nature of a future philosophy is evident in it no longer considering its incompleteness a tragedy.[32]

Habits of slow reading

Towards the close of the Introduction, I outlined the dominant characteristics of institutional reading. I pointed to the problems inherent in allowing this form of reading to dominate contemporary philosophical work. I described the reduction of reading to information extraction and mining – undertaken within a context of high time pressure, and I suggested that this form of reading supports the instituted structure of philosophy as a desire to know. Le Dœuff's approach to philosophy as 'work' and her belief that this involves shifting thinking from one stage to another sets in motion a transformation that propels the philosopher from one existential state to another. Le Dœuff's work on re-figuring habits of reading provides us with ways of reintroducing the instituting moments of a love of wisdom and a philosophy as a way of life.

In what specific ways are the habits of reading we have identified in Le Dœuff's work connected with the slow reading we are exploring in this book? Earlier in this chapter, I mentioned that Le Dœuff's third approach to reading – the effort to shift thinking from one stage to another – is one way to think about reading in ethical terms. These two things are related. Slow reading is the philosophical practice that enables an unhurried openness to otherness; it involves a desire to be transformed in this open encounter. In our efforts to shift thinking and reading from one stage to another we undertake the work of this transformation. We embrace openness as the beginnings of a reciprocal relation with the other and the world. In this sense we can think of Le Dœuff's focus on the future as ushering in a new reader capable of transforming philosophy from what we know of it today. Whatever form or forms it takes, a future philosophy will engage with complexity and the unthought, demanding an attentiveness to ambiguity and contradiction. It will be, once again, a love of wisdom and philosophy as a way of life.

Le Dœuff's habits of reading demonstrate an ongoing patience, a willingness to return to texts to reread them and to re-engage with them. This return, or looking back,[33] slows reading in ways that permit careful thought to emerge. Similarly, her fine-tuned attention to detail and her attentiveness in general are qualities that slow down thought. In this regard, Le Dœuff's ability to stage reading as a conversation with her texts is the source of an attentiveness that opens to the play of imagination at work in what she reads. This may be, as we see in *The Philosophical Imaginary*, an attentiveness to the unacknowledged imagery structuring philosophical argument and reason, or it may be an attentiveness to imagination more generally defined. Whatever the case, Le Dœuff's reading opens to the infinite possibilities that imagination heralds, prefiguring the outline of a philosophy still to come. In this it partakes of the wondrous openness of philosophy as a love of wisdom rather than a neurotic desire to know. By drawing on the best of the Socratic tradition, Le Dœuff's philosophy looks forward rather than (simply) back, ensuring that philosophy remain a present and future engagement with life.

CHAPTER TWO

Reading Essayistically: Levinas and Adorno

> *... this question of roads marks the fundamental divide between the ancient Greek & Roman civilizations. You make a straight road like the Romans & you are lucky to get three words:* Veni, vidi, vici. *You have a crooked goat path like the Greeks all over the Acropolis & what do you get? The entire damn* Odyssey *&* Oedipus Rex, *that's what.*
>
> RICHARD FLANAGAN, *GOULD'S BOOK OF FISH*: 187–8

Essay (noun): A trial, a test; an experiment. Assay. A trial specimen, a sample; an example; a rehearsal. An attempt, an endeavour. A short prose composition on any subject. A first tentative attempt at learning, composition, etc; a first draft.

Essay (verb): Assay. Attempt to accomplish or perform (a deed, task, etc.): make an attempt (at); undertake or try to do.

Essayist: A writer of essays. A person who carries out tests or trials.

Essayistic: Discursive, informal.

Esse: Be (Latin) essential nature, essence.[1]

Towards the close of the previous chapter, we looked at Michèle Le Dœuff's hopes for a future philosophy. There I argued that the open and unfinished nature of this future links us back to the instituting moments of a love of wisdom and philosophy as a way of life. This openness avoids the totalizing aim of a desire to know. Le Dœuff embraces the incomplete nature of philosophy in the current form that her philosophical work takes, and I suggested that the essay is the form that conjures her future in the here and now. The essay allows us the time and space to reconsider our work in open and open-ended ways. In this chapter, I return to these themes in order to develop a form of slow reading that takes its cue from the essay. I develop a practice of reading I refer to as 'essayistic', one that I find embedded in the philosophical work of Theodor W. Adorno. This essayistic reading links with the instituting moments of philosophy by thwarting our modern preoccupation with speed and haste. In place of an efficient or institutional reading (one motivated to extract or to capture information), it offers an open-ended rumination that meanders in non-systematic ways – a meandering thought that, as we will see, pursues paths largely undetermined.

The essayistic reading I pursue in this chapter is one that resists the instituted structure of philosophy's desire to know. It resists the containing and limiting gesture that so often accompanies this desire. Additionally, it resists the desire for absolute comprehension, for the certainty and security of knowledge that accompanies the anxiety of needing, at all costs, to know. The problems inherent in this containing aspect of instituted philosophy are explored by Emmanuel Levinas in his work on ethics, and I draw on it here as a way of outlining the problem or problems that an essayistic reading seeks to address.

Emmanuel Levinas: an ethics of reading?

> In conformity with the whole tradition of the West, knowing, in its thirst and its gratification, remains the norm of the spiritual.
> LEVINAS 1998: 96

One of the starting points for my inquiry into reading, and reading well, has been the work of the Lithuanian-born French philosopher

Emmanuel Levinas. Levinas's work in and on philosophy is carried out in the context of his broader examination of ethical responsibility and obligation, and it is this context that encourages me to place the question of ethics at the centre of my investigation.[2] By doing so, I draw on the instituting moments of a love of wisdom and philosophy as a way of life that I see as fundamental to Levinas's philosophical approach.

Levinas's work on patience and its centrality to the ethical relation outlines a slow encounter with the other (or strangeness of the other) that does not rush to reduce the other back to what I already know or can understand. Patience involves exposing and subjecting myself to the other; coming near, in order that a relation be established and the work of ethics done.[3] Throughout his work, Levinas points to the many ways that our dominant philosophical practice in the West falls short of the kind of patience that he refers to here. For example, he points to the philosophical tendency to reduce the world to pre-existing categories or understandings. This reductive tendency has implications for how philosophers read, and I shall explore these in the course of this discussion.

To begin with, Levinas suggests that in the production of certain kinds of philosophical knowledge there is a tendency to comprehend the other or object in terms of seizing or grasping it. There is, he writes:

> [T]he notion of an intellectual activity or of a reasoning will – a way of doing something which consists precisely of thinking through knowing, of seizing something and making it one's own ... an activity which *appropriates* and *grasps* the otherness of the known. A certain grasp ... Knowledge as perception, concept, comprehension, refers back to an act of grasping. The metaphor should be taken literally: even before any technical application of knowledge, it expresses the principle rather than the result of the future technological and industrial order of which every civilization bears at least the seed ... that unit of knowledge in which *Auffassen (understanding)* is also, and always has been, a *Fassen (gripping)*. The mode of thought known as knowledge involves man's concrete existence in the world he inhabits, in which he moves and works and possesses.
>
> LEVINAS 1989: 76[4]

Levinas is clearly describing the instituted structure of the desire to know in his account here. According to him, philosophy has certain ways of doing things, and its dominant (institutional) mode – the reasoning will – cultivates a kind of understanding (or knowing) that readily grips or grasps what it encounters.[5] We can both see and hear the direct connection between this theoretical understanding and the literal act of gripping in the German language, where *fassen* (gripping) provides the base and ground for *Auffassen* (understanding).[6] Levinas's point here is not minor. He implicates certain philosophical modes of understanding in acts of seizure. The philosopher 'seizes' the world and this has the effect of containing experience; in effect, leaving little to no trace of what has been encountered. Philosophy grasps and contains the world through the force of conceptual or logical argument, reducing it to what can already be understood. But what is the motivation for this kind of containment? For Levinas, this containment occurs in order to establish the certainty and security of knowledge – of (absolute) comprehension; the certainty and security of the ground of the reasoning will.

While we can argue that this is something of a caricature of philosophical practice, a great deal of what we academic philosophers do is motivated by a need or anxiety to know, and to know fully (in the manner of the neurotic),[7] and this need finds expression in a certain institutional way of going about reading. Some of the more extreme readings that accompany this anxiety seek to grasp or contain in ways that result in a kind of stand-over technique. This mode of philosophical reading (extracting/mining) intimidates by reduction (and 'knock-down arguments'), by demanding that what is read deliver up, yield or surrender its goods in such a way that 'knowledge' is subsequently confirmed. Other versions of reading in this reductive mode proceed by trivializing or simplifying existing work for the sake of creating a strategic space for their own ideas. In such readings there is little engagement with the complexity (or otherness) of what is being read.[8] At times, there is no engagement at all. Indeed, these reductive modes of reading are, at other times, a form of containment via assimilation. Simon Critchley, ever the careful reader of Levinas's work, picks up on this in the following account: 'For Levinas, the ontological event which defines and distinguishes the entire philosophical tradition from Parmenides to Heidegger, consists in suppressing all forms of otherness [*L'Autrui* – the singular other] and transmuting alterity into the Same (*le Même*).

Philosophy is the assimilation of the other into the Same, where the other's otherness is assimilated and digested like food and drink' (Critchley 1989: 100).[9]

Here the other (or text) is hastily consumed, appropriated and assimilated back to ourselves and our own existing knowledge. The reductive tendencies that Levinas uncovers bear something in common with Sigmund Freud's remarks about the technical process of secondary revision in the dream-work. Freud claims that the absolute otherness of the unconscious – although this is not his exact term – is forcefully reduced back to the logical structures and meanings of rational thought. He characterizes secondary revision in intentional terms, arguing that its purpose is to clean up what registers as the messy incoherence that, if left intact, challenges the pretensions of rational thought. Freud writes:

> The thing that distinguishes and at the same time reveals this part of the dream-work is its purpose. This function behaves in the manner which the poet maliciously ascribes to philosophers: it fills up the gaps in dream-structure with shreds and patches. As a result of its efforts, the dream loses its appearance of absurdity and disconnectedness and approximates to the model of an intelligible experience.
>   FREUD 1965 [1900]: 528

Freud's intelligible experience brings us back to the desire to know. In likening secondary revision to the 'shreds and patches'[10] that the philosopher employs in order to fabricate a rational meaning, Freud alludes here, albeit playfully and somewhat indirectly, to the force of philosophical reading, the sense in which the philosopher obliterates the otherness that confronts 'him' in 'his' attempt to impose clarity and meaning.[11] In a not dissimilar fashion, Levinas wants to show how philosophy's meanings are like Freud's manifest dream – fabricated events. And in doing so, he urges us to confront, in ethical terms, the effects of this fabrication. While meaning may emerge from the work (secondary revision?) that philosophy does, it is, Levinas contends, at the expense of the otherness philosophy hopes to domesticate. At best we might say that philosophy misses the other in its ardour to found truth. At worst – and this is certainly Levinas's point – we have to face the fact that this kind of philosophical practice obliterates the very alterity (or foreignness) of the other, what makes it distinct and different in the first place. In desiring at all costs to know, philosophy loses its way.

If the grasp of assimilation and containment that Levinas identifies in the reasoning will is as problematic as he suggests, what other ways are left open for philosophy? What other ways are there to read? And what might mark such other readings as ethical? Levinas offers us a way of engaging with these questions, at least indirectly, in the sense that he distinguishes between a dominant philosophical approach that imagines that it can finalize and complete a topic (*le Dit* – the Said), and another philosophical response, one that touches upon a theme in such a way as to leave the terrain of understanding both open and open-ended (*le Dire* – the Saying) (Levinas [1961] 1969).[12] We can, of course, think of these in terms of the instituting moment (*le Dire*) and the instituted structure (*le Dit*). Additionally, we can think of Levinas's open and open-ended approach in terms of Le Dœuff's future philosophy. Levinas's open-ended approach (*le Dire*) involves an attitude of respect that recognizes the strangeness of what is there to read. It involves encounter and engagement, rather than containment and finality; it reorients the philosopher toward, alongside, or 'near to' what he or she reads, rather than positioning him or her over and above it (Levinas 1998: 142–3).[13] Now, I am glossing Levinas a little here, as what he has to say speaks more directly to an alternative approach to writing philosophy, but this can – and ought to, I think – allow us to think, as well, of reading in new and specifically ethical ways.

The kind of reading I am hinting at here involves the risk of exposure or nearness to the other that Levinas equates with sincerity. This exposure or proximity *is* precisely ethics.[14] It is an attitude of openness, or we might even say goodness, that occurs despite oneself. Over and above a philosophy that presents itself as finished and complete, 'impervious to critique', a reading influenced by Levinas's approach would offer 'the sort of talk that enters into genuine sociality by opening itself to the critique and justification of others' (Smith 1986: 64). We can reorient what Levinas has to say about this other way of doing philosophy quite directly towards our question of reading. By doing so, we can say that the very act of reading opens the possibility of an ethical space or encounter, one that signals our willingness to be changed or transformed by what we read.[15] Here we reconnect with the instituting moment of philosophy. Such a reading opens and exposes the one who reads. Indeed, this exposure, encounter or nearness challenges a reading that all too hastily grasps and contains, that finalizes and neatly settles a matter.[16] Such a reading is characterized by a slowness, a preparedness to return to the text and to reread, not prematurely to have done with the text and finalize it in *a* reading (a definitive interpretation or 'knowledge').[17] Such a reading remains open (proximate, near) to the text.[18] Such a reading opens philosophy – and thought – to an indeterminate space from which the ethics of a 'receptive attitude' or 'patient attention to the other' may emerge. As such, philosophy can be enticed to relax its anxiety to know and to know fully, and come that bit closer to being an open, slow and wondrous engagement with life.

Institution and instrumental reason

The effects of the instituted structure of philosophy are such that philosophy ceases to be a way of life. Philosophy ceases to be an open, slow and wondrous engagement with life. It becomes, rather, a desire to know where thought is reduced to a mere instrument – a means for knowing, and gathering information. Institution and instrument are thus in close proximity, and we see this clearly in Adorno's work on identity thinking and instrumental reason. 'Identity thinking' is Adorno's term that links with what we are calling the 'instituted moment of philosophy'. It refers to reductive modes of thought whereby a kind of bureaucratic reasoning dominates the specificity and individuality of phenomena. Identity thinking facilitates the manipulation and domination of the material phenomena of the world by subsuming difference under abstract classifications and categories. Identity thinking makes instrumental reason possible. Instrumental reason is Adorno's (and Horkheimer's) term for understanding how thought reduces to facts, and how this supremacy of facts comes to dominate our ways of being in the world. In *Dialectic of Enlightenment* (1979), Adorno and Horkheimer argue that human suffering and the domination of nature issue from the instrumentalizion of reason. By reducing thought to system and measurement, reality becomes quantifiable, calculable, known. Reason – along with our abilities to think, to read, and to write – is reduced to a mere tool for identifying and accumulating facts – for systematizing what we know. If philosophy succumbs to instrumental reason, it becomes simply a form of identity thinking, incapable of resisting the instituting structure of the desire to know. If, on the other hand, philosophy resists the modern slide towards instrumental reason and calculation, if it resists the institution, then thought is free to think in non-instrumental ways (Boulous Walker 1993b). Adorno gestures towards philosophy in this non-instrumental mode, arguing for a critical philosophy that re-establishes a relation with what we have been calling the instituting moments of philosophy. In so doing, Adorno offers alternatives beyond the containing gestures that we have seen outlined in Levinas's account.

Theodor W. Adorno: the essay as form

Adorno's important essay 'The Essay as Form' (Adorno [1958] 2000: 91–111) provides an alternative to instrumental or institutional accounts. Written in 1958, it can be seen as one of Adorno's many important contributions to the question of how we can do philosophy differently – hints towards a future philosophy, if you like (both in content and in form).[19] Here, he calls for an alternative approach, one that imagines new ways of writing philosophy and new ways of honouring thought. Paradoxically, this approach is characterized by a form that resists form. Adorno claims that the essay resists all attempts to pre-structure and predetermine thought, to orient and domesticate it towards predetermined ends. By refusing to rely on criteria established prior to writing, the essay celebrates an open inquiry, an open-endedness not often found in philosophical work.[20] This open inquiry is expressed in the very heart of the essay, the slow and persistent questioning that propels inquiry on. Questioning *is* the essay, and it is this that releases writing and thought from any *systematic* demands.[21] The essay form, nowadays seen as a non-academic mode of writing, is concerned more with raising questions than with answering them. It is perhaps concerned with questions that, at times, we can only wonder at.

Of course, Adorno is working with a very particular – we might even say idiosyncratic – idea of what the essay is,[22] and we see this in his claim that the essay refrains from reduction to a principle, and that it does so, in part, by exploring the fragmentary and partial rather than the (imaginary and closed) whole; it deals with what remains unfinished, incomplete.[23] The essay 'does not strive for closed, deductive or inductive, construction. It revolts above all against the doctrine – deeply rooted since Plato – that the changing and ephemeral is unworthy of philosophy' (Adorno 2000: 98). Free from the violence of dogma, the essay is deaf to the usual reproach that the fragmentary, the ephemeral, and the random lie somehow outside legitimate thought. By embracing the fragmentary[24] and the inconclusive, the essay suspends traditional philosophical method in favour of a *meandering* thought that pursues a path or paths always largely undetermined.[25] This openness 'takes the anti-systematic impulse into its own procedure' (Adorno 2000: 100), and recognizes as delusion 'the longing for strict definitions' that promises to eliminate 'the irritating and dangerous elements of things that live within concepts' (Adorno 2000: 101).[26] As such, the essay resists both identity thinking and instrumental thought. By engaging with singularity and difference it refuses to reduce the instance of the specific under the law of the general. While the institution beats a familiar path towards knowledge and truth narrowly defined, the essay meanders its way along branching tributaries, without concern for where it is supposed to be.

For Adorno, the essay is evidence that 'thought does not advance in a single direction',[27] but rather that 'aspects of the argument interweave as in a carpet' (Adorno 2000: 101). This interweaving or 'density of texture' speaks to the layering inherent in the essay – the careful return to a theme in order to texture it again and again. Never quite done, the essay celebrates patiently, attentively the demands of thought. 'In the essay discreetly separated elements enter into a readable context; it erects no scaffolding, no edifice. Through their own movement the elements crystallize into a configuration' (Adorno 2000: 102).[28]

Above all, the essay resists the rule-bound tradition of philosophy that Adorno sees inaugurated in 1637 with Descartes's *Discourse on Method* (Descartes 1912).[29] Here, as we have seen in the Introduction, absolute certainty guides the earliest gestures of modern Western theory and science, setting the tone for a method of inquiry that comes to resemble an exhaustive quest for the final word. Philosophy, henceforth, will be the certainty that nothing is omitted.[30] As an antidote to this quest, Adorno sees the essay as a kind of unmethodical method that resists the demand (and delusion) of completeness:

> The essay . . . does not permit its domain to be prescribed . . . it says what is at issue and stops where it feels itself complete – not where nothing is left to say. Therefore it is classed among the oddities. Its concepts are neither deduced from any first principle nor do they come full circle and arrive at a final principle.
> ADORNO 2000: 93

Due to its experimental and open nature the essay is without ground and without security, 'it must pay for its affinity with open intellectual experience by the lack of security, a lack which the norm of established thought fears like death' (Adorno 2000: 101). This insecurity is, at least in part, presumed in Adorno's notion of the configuration. Here the structure, hierarchy and organization of the traditional philosophical mode (of conceptuality) is challenged by the essay's open weave. The configuration marks the work of the essay or, we might even say, of thought. The insecurity that is constitutive of the essay and its configuration is, Adorno says, melded to a kind of positive guilt – a guilt that arises from the essay's refusal to conclude, or to speak definitively.[31] We can think of this refusal as the essay's open-endedness, its interest in 'establishing internal cross-connections' (Adorno 2000: 108–9), of coordinating elements 'rather than subordinating them' (Adorno 2000: 109). In practice, these combine to fuel the ongoing work of thought. Above all, the essay is non-institutional; it disrupts all attempts at grounding thought – of structuring, organizing, reducing, establishing, calculating, dominating.

Towards the close of his essay, Adorno cautions that in an age of technological rationality the essay's time is uncertain:

> The relevance of the essay is that of anachronism. The hour is more unfavorable to it than ever. It is being crushed between an organized science, on one side, in which everyone presumes to control everyone and everything else . . . and on the other side, by a philosophy that makes do with the empty and abstract residues left aside by the scientific apparatus . . . The essay, however, has to do with that which is blind in its objects . . . Therefore the law of the innermost form of the essay is heresy. By transgressing the

orthodoxy of thought, something becomes visible in the object which it is orthodoxy's secret purpose to keep invisible.

ADORNO 2000: 110

According to Adorno, it is precisely the essay's unfashionable or untimely nature that speaks to its urgency. In an age of increasing technocracy our need for the essay and its anti-systematic (and anti-institutional) resistance is ever more crucial. The essay resists thought's reduction to what we have seen Adorno elsewhere refer to as 'instrumental rationality' (Adorno and Horkheimer 1979). The law of the innermost form of the essay is heresy and this heresy lies (paradoxically) in the attitude of respect that the essay demonstrates towards thought. By refusing too hurriedly to seize the world, to understand it by containing it, to speak definitively, to summarize, or assimilate it, the essay offers us a future philosophy – one that holds out the hope for a slow engagement with the complexity, ambiguity and strangeness of the world.[32]

Now, all that Adorno has to say here relates to the essay as a kind of writing, but I want to extend the radical nature of Adorno's insights considerably by rethinking the essay in terms of reading.[33] Reading essayistically – or in the mode of the essay – would be a kind of open-ended reading subordinated to no agenda other than thought itself. It would be a non-institutional reading that risks the uncertainty of not knowing where it might lead, of not relying parasitically on a system that limits the imagination. Indeed, reading essayistically would be precisely imagination.[34] It would be a slow, open-ended rumination[35] that takes its time and returns, time and time again, to the matter at hand. Such a reading would thwart our modern preoccupation with speed and haste, and open us to the wondrous space of a slow and unhurried engagement that welcomes thought, rather than shutting it out. Just as the essay engages its topic in ways that meander luxuriously through time and space, so too would reading essayistically open philosophy – or thought – to an indeterminate space from which the ethics of a 'receptive attitude' or 'patient attention to the other' may emerge.[36] This receptive attitude announces a (special) kind of passivity that may seem out of place in modern philosophical practice. At this moment, Adorno's work on the essay merges with ideas on 'the enlarging concentration', 'the patience for its matter', and the 'long and unforced gaze upon the object', and in doing so challenges philosophy to be more than activity and mobilization.[37] What emerges, I think, is a kind of meditative work – the work of thought that sinks into its relation with the world. This idea of meditative work brings us back to philosophy as a slow way of life, philosophy as a slow sinking into the world – a patient engagement that allows thought its time.

We can see something of this meditative work in what Martin Seel refers to as Adorno's ethic of contemplation, a praxis by which one is open to the other while allowing the other to be (Seel 2004: 264).[38] In *Negative Dialectics*, Adorno defends this non-instrumental receptiveness, distinguishing it from a self-sufficient or instrumental contemplation, one indifferent 'to the task of changing the world'. It is possible, he claims, to have 'contemplation without inhumanity' (Adorno 1979: 244). The very non-instrumental quality of the contemplative ethic Adorno champions is its unhurried receptiveness to the other, marking the self as open to change and transformation. In this sense, contemplation comes close to the tenderness that Adorno sees as 'nothing other than awareness of the possibility of relations without purpose' (Adorno 1974: 41). The tender work of openness is the basis of our ethical relation with the other and the world. In opening us tenderly towards the other, Adorno's work reinvigorates the instituting moments of a love of wisdom and philosophy as a way of life. Non-instrumental modes merge with non-institutional ones, creating relations without purpose or intent.

Luiz Costa Lima: criticity and the essay

The importance of a slow, more open-ended approach to reading, one that allows thought its time, finds expression, too, in Luiz Costa Lima's work on *criticity*, which is his term distinguishing 'the act of questioning from both the act of judging ("critique") and the activity by means of which the act of judging is effected ("criticism")'.[39] Criticity is the idea Costa Lima develops to explore the critical thread that escapes from Kant's ambiguous attempt to define aesthetic judgement. Criticity and aestheticization are two modalities of aesthetic experience and in 'The Subject and the Law: A Kantian Heritage', the second chapter to *The Limits of Voice* (Costa Lima 1996), Costa Lima distinguishes these in the following manner. Criticity, or the critical orientation, embodies an openness, a questioning against the grain and a refusal to be systematized: it is a 'form of investigation that eschews both dogmatism and scepticism, seeking the limits of reason and trying to locate them in the object it experiences and considers' (Costa Lima 1996: 129). Criticity avoids the Law (and the instituted structure of the institution). Aestheticization, on the other hand, is systematic, establishing a law of its own in the absence of a universal law (God). It is 'the reduction, in actual practice, of any and all value to the aesthetic dimension' (Costa Lima 1996: 129).[40] Criticity is an approach that engages with works (and the world) as unique, rather than 'present[ing] them as examples or illustrations of something that precedes them' (Costa Lima 1996: 149).[41] It is a 'progressive, experimental drive that does not aim at a predetermined point of arrival' (Costa Lima 1996: 176).

From this, it is not surprising to learn that Costa Lima's work on *criticity* engages with work on the essay, and in order to highlight the questioning that both *criticity* and the essay share, he turns to Georg Lukács's seminal work, *Soul and Form*, to read the introductory piece 'On the Nature and Form of the Essay' (Lukács 1974) (Adorno refers to this work four times throughout his own essay).[42] Lukács's essay is influential, and it is worth pausing a moment to consider it here. He begins his discussion by focusing on the essay as an ambiguous form, one hovering between art and science: 'Science affects us' he writes, 'by its contents, art by its forms: science offers us facts and relations between facts, but art offers us souls and destinies' (Lukács 1974: 3). Somewhere in between lies the essay, and while it is neither one nor the other, the essay veers towards art in some important ways. Questioning frames the essay, gives it a kind of form, and this questioning (which seeks no 'solutions') serves to bind it in a familiar way to the art it comes so closely to resemble.[43] In the essay '[t]he question is posed immediately: what is life, what is man, what is destiny? But posed as a question only; for the answer, here, does not supply a "solution" like one of the answers of science or, at purer heights, those of philosophy. Rather, as in poetry of every kind, it is symbol, destiny and tragedy' (Lukács 1974: 7). The essay is an errant 'form', 'the genre of problematization par excellence, its own richness ... not allow[ing] it to assume a form: it [thus] remains protean, formless'.[44] For Costa Lima, it will be this process of problematization that comes to the fore. The essay judges, but this is a special form of judgement that refuses the finality of the Law's verdict in order to continue questioning. The essay is neither truth, nor system; the essay is not Law, and Costa Lima establishes his case for believing this in the presentation of four related points:

> First, the essay has an 'elective affinity' with the fragment:[45] both emphasize what is unfinished or does not seek justification by previously established systems. Second, the essay's very unfinishedness makes it inadequate as a vehicle for the conveying of contents, information, instrumental schemes, so that it tends to focus on its own structure – that is, on its form. Third, the essay is not form in the absolute, but belongs in what is previously occupied *by* form, so that what singularizes it is the interval where it remains. The essay is the genre that occupies the interval between the discourse for which form is the principle – poetical or fictional discourse – and those for which questions about meaning are the principle, above all, philosophical discourse. It is less a medium for the circulation of ideas than a medium for questions ... [And finally] fourth, treating the essay as a genre makes it easier to draw attention to its varieties. The essay may either be an antisystematic discussion of ideas or, in its constant antisystematicity, keep close to the writing subject's life.
>
> COSTA LIMA 1996: 64

The essay does not desire to know. It has affinity with the fragment and the unfinished, is inadequate for the conveying of mere information, is a medium for questions, and is by its nature antisystematic. In addition, the essay occupies the interval between poetry and philosophy, positing it as proximate and near to both. The essay, as Costa Lima appears to describe it here, embodies an ethical approach that provides us with alternative non-institutional ways of doing philosophy. Now, Costa Lima's task is, among other things, to investigate the challenge that questioning, or criticity, presents to the prevailing order. For him, the essay embodies this challenge, taking up an important position *vis-a-vis* the Law,[46] one that positions it in proximity to (though not in identification with) literary experience:

> It is precisely because of its affinity with criticity (questioning, reading) that the essay is marked more by the forcefulness of its questioning than by the unerringness of its answers. That is why the essay is the form that, though not identified with the literary

experience, is closest to it. This closeness becomes more visible when we see literature as the discourse that questions and puts into perspective what a society considers to be true.

COSTA LIMA 1996: 63

Costa Lima's work on criticity and the essay provides us another way of thinking about what reading might entail. Via the meandering[47] path of the essay's questions, we are able to build a slow and careful approach to what so often remains hidden or silent. Indeed, in his discussion of Michel de Montaigne's famous *Essais*, Costa Lima makes several references to this idiosyncratic approach in the rambling or meandering pace of his writing (Costa Lima 1996: 37, 40, 55), noting that Montaigne searched for a new flexible form (the essay) to bear witness (56), one that accommodated his condemnation of fixed positions, codification, and 'the exultation of the factual as an index of truth' (52). Montaigne invents 'a floating, unsystematic punctual, personalized meditation . . . [which addresses] the strangeness of what is unknown to reason' (Costa Lima 1996: 34). For Costa Lima, this first and most famous of essayists provides us with a model of a slow and engaged approach.[48]

So while the essay is a judgement (or series of judgements), it is not a verdict; in this, the essay is arguably near to Lyotard's indeterminate judgement.[49] For Costa Lima, the essay is antisystematic, though not against method; it is, more specifically, against the totalizing pretensions of method[50] and for this reason it is possible, Costa Lima hints, to think of the essay as something other than 'a melancholy guerilla fighter who knows from the outset that the system is certain to win in the end' (Costa Lima 1996: 63). Does Costa Lima mean here that it is possible to think of the essay as a nascent form of some future philosophy? Some new non-totalizing method? Some future philosophical approach? Let us, for the time being, assume this to be so.

Hans Ulrich Gumbrecht: reading for *Stimmung*

If we are to imagine a different approach to reading, one that takes the liberties of the essay to its heart, we can turn to Hans Ulrich

Gumbrecht and his recent work on *Stimmung*,[51] which provides an ideal starting point for our inquiries. While Gumbrecht's work comes out of literary theoretical discussions, I think that what he has to say about reading can be thought through to great advantage in the philosophical domain. Like Adorno and Costa Lima before him, Gumbrecht engages with Lukács's work on the essay in *Soul and Form*, noting with pleasure his demand that the essay deviate from a limited 'scientific' search for truth in order that the essayist 'find, at the end of his way, what he has not sought: life itself' (Lukács, cited in Gumbrecht 2012: 17). The meanderings of the essay, the various detours and pauses it takes, permit the essayist to counter the limited ambitions of interpretation and systematic method, in favour of following the hunches or hints that counterintuitive thought permits. For Gumbrecht, 'Following a hunch means trusting an implicit promise for a while and making a step towards describing a phenomenon that remains unknown – one that has aroused our curiosity and, in the case of atmospheres and moods, often envelops and even enshrouds us' (Gumbrecht 2012: 17).[52] Gumbrecht's approach of reading for *Stimmung* is 'to follow configurations of atmosphere and mood in order to encounter otherness in intense and intimate ways' (12–13). Now this description of an intense and intimate encounter with otherness is a good way of thinking about the traces of the instituting moments that comprise the ethical dimensions of slow reading that I am developing throughout this book. Reading for *Stimmung* provides one approach, among many, for reading in different and more open ways. I am seduced by Gumbrecht's work, particularly because of its stress on intensity and intimacy, and its orientation towards what Lukács identifies as 'life'. Gumbrecht's approach mobilizes the body[53] and its affects for reading in vital and energetic ways:

> Reading for *Stimmung* cannot mean 'deciphering' atmospheres and moods, for they have no fixed signification. Equally little does reading for *Stimmungen* mean reconstructing or analyzing their historical or cultural genesis. Instead, it means discovering sources of energy in artifacts and giving oneself over to them affectively and bodily – yielding to them and gesturing toward them ... [Reading for *Stimmung* is] an experiment, where certainties and conventions of how to write [and read] are still undefined.
> GUMBRECHT 2012: 18

Reading for *Stimmung* is thus an experimental mode of reading[54] – a trial, an attempt – that takes its cue from the essay's engaging form. Here, interpretation and meaning occupy a back seat in relation to an intimate engagement with atmosphere and mood.[55] Gumbrecht speaks of the 'intensified aesthetic fascination that *Stimmung* now holds' (Gumbrecht 2012: 20),[56] and we might ponder this fascination and its resonance for contemporary philosophical work.

Robert Musil: essay, ethics, aesthetics

What Adorno, Costa Lima and Gumbrecht have to say here can be placed alongside a short essay by Robert Musil written in 1914, three years after Lukács's *Soul and Form*. In this piece, Musil (writing in German) begins by linking the word 'essay' with the words 'ethics' and 'aesthetics', noting (as does the *Shorter Oxford English Dictionary*) its connections with weighing (assay) and attempting (Musil 1990: 48). For Musil, the essay mediates between epistemology as the science of knowledge on the one hand, and life, art, and feeling on the other; thus, allowing it a form of judgement that refuses to succumb to the finality of a verdict. 'There is no total solution, but only a series of particular ones', writes Musil (Musil 1990: 49). The essay mediates, too, between morality on the one hand and life on the other. It lies between the moral realm of duty, obligation and intention and the experience of feelings such as love and anger. In expressing this point, Musil comes close to articulating something akin to Gumbrecht's notion of *Stimmung*. He writes: 'As people belonging to a moral circle, with duties, obligations, and intentions, *we read a poem and, as we read, all this changes a little in a fashion that can be pinned down almost only by feelings*, which quickly dissipate' (Musil 1990: 49, emphasis added).

Musil's work in this essay is to draw attention to the kind of reading and writing that can connect thought ethically and aesthetically with life, and in this there are connections with Lukács's work. There are connections, too, with Nietzsche's approach. Indeed, Musil mentions Nietzsche, along with Emerson, Maeterlinck, Epicurus and the Stoics, as belonging 'in the circle of the essay' (Musil 1990: 51), a circle characterized by 'the constant movement of essayistic thought' aimed at 'the reshaping of what is human' (50). Musil concludes this piece with the prescient observation that we are now confronting a new division in intellectual work. On the one hand, thought is directed towards knowledge; while on the other, it is directed towards a transformation of man. Musil's distinction echoes the distinction we have been working with between instituted and instituting moments in philosophy. Clearly, the essay's work is of the transformative kind. We can link what Musil says here with Gumbrecht's description of reading for *Stimmung* as an intense and intricate encounter with otherness, and in doing so we highlight both the ethical and aesthetic quality of working in this transformative essayistic mode. Indeed, when we think of the time that Musil is writing, his tone appears (to our contemporary ears) strangely optimistic, noting: 'New kinds of relationships among people are showing up' (51).

What attracts me to the essay (as Musil and the others describe it) as a way of thinking about reading is its open and uncertain nature; its relaxed and confident exploration that permits – indeed, encourages – experimentation and imagination. This helps us to think about reading in significantly different ways. The essay makes possible the kind of thought carried out (as Nietzsche says) 'with doors left open, with delicate eyes and fingers'. It is a slow and sometimes hesitant reading (or weighing) that cannot be otherwise. The essay, anachronistic – and yet all the more necessary – in a time of speed and haste, opens the space of reading to ethics by allowing us the time and leisure to engage – to question and to continue questioning 'in the midst of an age of "work"' (Nietzsche 1982: 5). The essay opens us to the intensity and intimacy of the other, thus establishing its ethical credentials.

This is why I am calling for an essayistic reading – a slow and considered reading, one that is concerned more with raising questions than with finalizing answers. A reading that ignores the demands of system and structure for the sheer pleasure of allowing thought its time. Like the essay, this reading would allow us 'to go aside, to take time, to become still, to become slow', so that we might resist the hurry of 'indecent and perspiring haste, which wants to get "everything done" at once'. Like the essay, this reading would 'not so readily get anything done' but rather would 'teach [us] to read well, that is to say, to read slowly, deeply . . . with reservations, with doors left open, with delicate eyes and fingers' – and ears (Nietzsche 1982: 5).

To conclude, Levinas's challenge to the containing tendency in philosophy that reduces thought to a desire for certainty and knowledge, alongside his call for an alternative approach, one that responds ethically to the otherness and strangeness of the world, when read alongside Adorno's, Costa Lima's, Gumbrecht's and Musil's celebration of the essay as form, tempts us to return to our initial question: what is it to read? I think that the open,[57] somewhat tentative, nature that emerges from their particular approaches to and attitudes about philosophy are useful for rethinking the question of how we read. Indeed, Levinas's own practice, characterized by a readiness to reread, along with Adorno's call for an open-ended essayistic writing that resists the demands of a totalizing and instrumental discourse, Costa Lima's *criticity*, Gumbrecht's reading for *Stimmung* and Musil's insistence on life, motivate us to seek examples of philosophical readings that hint towards an ethical future in their present forms. Such readings can, I think, be found in the work of Luce Irigaray. It is not accidentally that I choose Irigaray, as her own carefully crafted readings, developed now over decades, have been intimately influenced by Levinas's account of philosophy and his ethical agenda. To say this is not to reduce, in any simple sense, Irigaray's work to Levinasian themes – her own readings of Levinas would not, in any case, permit this – but rather to acknowledge the connection between Levinas's thought and her own. Having said this, it is important to note fundamental differences in their approaches. Briefly put, we might summarize these as follows. While Levinas is concerned to chart the ethical responsibility that we face as a result of our asymmetrical and yet proximate relations with the other, Irigaray's ethical relation charts a reciprocity and love that might be possible between those who recognize and celebrate sexual difference. Irigaray speaks about the possibility of an amorous exchange, while Levinas is concerned with the face-to-face encounter. Irigaray's intimate and intense readings of Levinas's work offer rich and subtle examples of what we might think of as ethical readings (or even as readings for *Stimmung*). Indeed, it is noteworthy that her readings of Levinas take the form of questions posed. The question arguably provides a way to approach the other (text) in a way that opens out any reading towards a space of encounter or dialogue. Rather than offering a final verdict on Levinas, Irigaray's questions open out her reading towards this possible encounter.[58] Her readings of Plato and of Descartes take a similar form, in that they both pose questions, questions that, as we will see in the following chapter, Irigaray keeps returning to in order to reread and reconsider them anew.

CHAPTER THREE

Rereading: Irigaray on Love and Wonder

And if we kept on taking & plundering & killing, if the world kept on becoming ever more impoverished of love & wonder & beauty in consequence, what, in the end, would be left?

RICHARD FLANAGAN, *GOULD'S BOOK OF FISH*: 227–8

. . . we approach the other in a state of wonder and grace.[1]

In the previous chapter, I outlined an essayistic form of reading to counter the effects of institutional reading within the modern academy. I argued that essayistic reading offers an open-ended rumination that takes its time, meandering in non-systematic ways. In this chapter, I explore Luce Irigaray's work on love and wonder, arguing that these terms provide us with practical strategies or attitudes supporting the open and attentive reader. From this I develop practices of loving and wondrous readings aimed at re-engaging with the instituting moments of a love of wisdom and philosophy as a way of life. Irigaray's focus on love and wonder serves to orient my discussion of reading (as proximate, near and open) towards the figure of love, and this theme continues in subsequent chapters.

In this chapter, Levinas's ethical concern with rereading and Adorno's practice of an open-ended philosophy find expression in the form and content of Irigaray's readings. In her work on love – in relation to Diotima's speech in Plato's *Symposium* – and wonder – in relation to Descartes's *The Passions of the Soul* – we find a slow and careful engagement structured around questioning and the patient return of rereading. Reading is thought here through the figures of love, wonder, and the slow encounter – approaches that demonstrate an ongoing preparedness to return to the text. This open-ended reading gestures towards an alternative philosophical response, one that makes it possible (with Levinas) to rethink the task of philosophy in ethical terms.

Psychoanalysis, listening, attention

It is important to begin any discussion of Irigaray's reading practices by noting the centrality of psychoanalytic practice to her early and ongoing philosophical work. Irigaray's open and attentive mode towards the other[2] is arguably a mature response to the training she received as an analyst, where an attentive ear and a willingness always to return to and reconsider what has been said marks the ethical mode of analytic *Mitsein*. Her commitment to, and training in, psychoanalytic practice frames the encounter she *performs* in her philosophical work.[3] The idea of the unconscious as a challenge to 'truth', 'verification' and 'objectivity' provides Irigaray an attentive way of listening to the repressions and denials of philosophy (and psychoanalytic theory itself). Indeed, in 'The Power of Discourse and the Subordination of the Feminine' (1975), Irigaray states:

> This process of ... rereading has always been a psychoanalytic undertaking ... That is why we need to pay attention to the way the unconscious works in each philosophy, and perhaps in philosophy in general. We need to listen (psycho)analytically to its procedures of repression, to the structuration of language that shores up its repressions, separating the true from the false, the meaningful from the meaningless, and so forth.
> IRIGARAY 1985c: 75[4]

In addition, she writes: 'We need to proceed in such a way that linear reading is no longer possible (Irigaray 1991: 80).[5]

The practical centrality of listening to the psychoanalytic enterprise means that it provides an excellent apprenticeship in attentive reading. Such a reading positions Irigaray as 'all ears', attentively open to what unfolds;[6] not deciding in advance what she will discover.[7] What I show in this chapter is how the attentive reading that Irigaray perfects in her early psychoanalytic encounters informs the themes of love and wonder that she goes on to enact in her later philosophical work.[8] Irigaray's philosophical reading is the internalization of this attention. Accordingly, love and wonder are, I contend, attitudes held by the open and attentive reader.

We need to stress that Irigaray's attentive listening is not in any simple sense a passive or wholly receptive reading. From her psychoanalytic practice, Irigaray appreciates the difference between two different modes of reading: a reading that interprets or attempts to master what it reads (desiring to know), and a more open-ended approach, one that recognizes elements of transference in the process of reading. This second kind of reading, as Margaret Whitford explains, 'does not attempt to assume a position of mastery and recognizes that the presumption of coherence is an illusion produced by the transference'.[9] This alternative, open-ended reading positions one in a relation of non-mastery to what one reads, and it does so by avoiding the position of critique.[10] By working with the transference, such a reading works with the other/text in a creative process of transformation.

One more point before moving on to Irigaray's readings. There is a decidedly European sensibility to her work, one at odds with the haste of much North American culture. Freud helps us to understand how a positive attitude towards slowness distinguishes the European sensibility from that founding the New World. In his 1937 essay on psychoanalytic practice, 'Analysis Terminable and Interminable', Freud famously sums up what he sees as both the potential and the limitations of psychoanalytic practice, making reference to the time analysis takes: 'Experience has taught us that psycho-analytic therapy . . . is a time consuming business. Hence, from the very first, attempts have been made to shorten [it] . . . But there was probably still at work in [these attempts] some trace of . . . impatient contempt' (Freud 1974: 216). Interestingly, Freud goes on to ground these impatient attempts in 'the stress of the contrast between the post-War misery of Europe and the "prosperity" of America', suggesting that this impatience was 'designed to accelerate the tempo of analytic therapy to suit the haste of American life' (Freud 1974: 216). Freud's reservations (anxieties?) regarding the future of psychoanalytic practice in the context of the impatient demands of American life are worth noting, and echo something of Nietzsche's concerns that we have seen in the Introduction to this book regarding the 'indecent and perspiring haste, which wants to get "everything done" at once'. Nietzsche calls us away from such haste 'in the midst of an age of "work"' and towards that 'venerable art' that demands we 'go aside', 'take time' and 'become still' in order to 'become slow'. 'This art', Nietzsche reminds us, 'does not so easily get anything done, it teaches to read, that is to say, to read slowly, deeply, looking cautiously before and aft, with reservations, with doors left open, with delicate eyes and fingers' (Nietzsche 1982: 5). Freud's admission that analytic reading is and must be a slow reading,[11] one that literally takes its time, partakes, I think, of the particularly European sensibility that we hear in Nietzsche's work. It is towards an expression of this European sensibility in the work of Luce Irigaray that we now turn.

Irigaray's Diotima: the arts of philosophy, reading and love

In 'Sorcerer Love' (Irigaray 1993: 20–33) Irigaray revisits the source of myriad Western interpretations and analyses of love – Plato's *Symposium* (Plato 1967).[12] In doing so she engages with a foundational moment in Western culture, as far as love is concerned. In her reading she chooses to focus on the person of Diotima whose words are reported by Socrates in her absence – faithfully or unfaithfully, we do not know. I think she does this, in part, in order to engage with Plato's work in a more attentive and careful way. By focusing on Diotima, Irigaray is able to avoid engaging simply with Platonism; that is, a reductive reading of Plato's work that has, in the Western tradition, tended to homogenize, reduce or even domesticate the otherness of Plato's challenging works. By listening attentively to Diotima's voice, Irigaray is better able to hear the nuance and open-endedness in those moments where Diotima's views exceed Platonism.

Irigaray briefly sets the scene for her encounter with Diotima by hinting at the significance of Diotima's womanly absence – her body and voice – from this defining moment in the tradition of Western thought.[13] The reading that Irigaray goes on to offer is subtle, open and attentive to nuance. She carefully teases out the layers of Diotima's 'speech', showing how two different voices emerge. Irigaray is not concerned to rush to a conclusion or verdict on Diotima. Rather, she begins by complimenting Diotima's teaching which is, she says, dialectical, though dialectical in a way different from Hegel's. Diotima's dialectical method or approach to doing philosophy establishes an intermediary space that is not abandoned in a later movement towards a newly synthesized truth:

> In effect, it doesn't use opposition to make the first term pass into the second in order to achieve a synthesis of the two, as Hegel does. From the outset, she establishes an *intermediary* that will never be abandoned as a means or path. Her method, then, is not a propaedeutic of the *destruction* or the *destructuration* of the two terms in order to establish a synthesis that is neither one nor the other. She presents, uncovers, unveils the insistence of a third term that is already there and that permits progression: from poverty to wealth, from ignorance to wisdom, from mortality to immortality. Which, for her, always comes to a greater perfection of and in love.
>
> IRIGARAY 1993: 20–1[14]

Progression always leads to a greater perfection of and in love: here Irigaray emphasizes the transformative nature of philosophy as a way of life. By bringing our attention to Diotima's method she reminds us, later in her reading, of the importance, philosophically, of establishing and maintaining an intermediary space, and we will return to this in good time. But for now we focus on Irigaray's important observation that Diotima equates love, and the movement of love, with this intermediary space. 'It is love that leads to knowledge, whether in art or more metaphysical learning. It is love that both leads the way and is the path. A mediator par excellence' (Irigaray 1993: 21).[15] Diotima's dialectic is, then, the enactment of this intermediary space of love which 'stands between' (21).[16] From Diotima, Irigaray learns the lessons of a philosophical thinking or a reading that hovers; one that remains in constant movement or becoming, never fixed, never finished, never complete. The movement of thought or reading, what keeps it open-ended and incomplete, is, then, precisely what makes it ethical. Ethics, here, is thought of as an open movement or arc towards the other, one that is never complete, and Diotima's dialectic provides Irigaray with a model of this becoming:

> Diotima's dialectic is in at least *four terms*: the here, the two poles of the encounter, and the beyond – but a beyond that never abolishes the here. And so on, indefinitely. The mediator is never abolished in an infallible knowledge. Everything is always in movement, in a state of becoming. And the mediator of all this is, among other things, or exemplarily, *love*. Never fulfilled, always becoming.
>
> IRIGARAY 1993: 21

Never fulfilled, always becoming. This is to be the slow and open-ended gesture of Irigaray's own reading, and this is how she will engage with Diotima and the complexity – indeed, the uncertainty and ambiguity – of her speech.

According to Irigaray, Diotima's teaching involves a questioning of Socrates's own positions;[17] it is a questioning that renounces the masterly attitude of positing established or fixed truths. In and through this questioning, Diotima calls certainty – Socrates's certainty, at least – into question. Diotima's philosophical method or mode of teaching is certainly worthy of mention. Rather than refuting or opposing Socrates, she playfully undoes his assurance by unsettling his convictions. She mocks Socrates, but in the playful and good-natured manner that one might interact with a child. In doing so she sets up an encounter or ethical exchange with Socrates that is somewhat at odds with the more oppositional (or even adversarial) mode of interaction between the male participants present at Plato's *Symposium*. Just as love is the movement or tension between two terms that will transform each of these, so too is Diotima's mode of address. In teaching, she sets up a loving relation between the two, and this relation is largely established in and through her questions to Socrates.[18]

An important example of Diotima's questioning occurs when she enquires into the nature of love (*eros*). This good-natured exchange eventually leads Socrates to reconsider his earlier conviction – that love is a god – opening the way for Diotima to suggest to Socrates the demonic nature of love; that is, the sense in which love mediates between the divine and the mortal, thus negating its status as a god. Love is 'in a state that can be qualified as daimonic: love is a *daimon*. His function is to transmit to the gods what comes from men and to men what comes from the gods. Like all that is daimonic, love is complementary to gods and to men in such a way as to put everything in touch with itself' (Irigaray 1993: 22–3).[19] This demonic nature of love is what places it as an intermediary between opposites. Love mediates not only between the Gods and men, but between poverty and plenty, ignorance and wisdom, ugliness and beauty, and so on.[20] This observation is important because it is at this same point that Diotima suggests to Socrates the tie between philosophy and love. 'Wisdom is one of the most beautiful of things, and Love is love of beauty, so it follows that Love must be a lover of wisdom, and consequently in a state half-way between wisdom and ignorance'.[21] Love is not to be confused, however, with a desire to know. Love does not respond to its appreciation of ignorance with needing to know. It does not fill its emptiness with knowledge. Rather, it responds by taking an alternative path, by becoming a love of wisdom and a way of life. Philosophy is a love of wisdom. Philosophy occupies the intermediary space between wisdom and ignorance; it is the movement between these opposites. And in this, Diotima shows, it is a kind of love itself. Irigaray interprets this passage in the following way: 'love is a philosopher and a philosophy. Philosophy is not a formal learning, fixed and rigid, abstracted from all feeling. It is a quest for love, love of beauty, love of wisdom, which is one of the most beautiful things' (24).[22] Irigaray gathers here what we have been calling the 'instituting moments' of a love of wisdom and philosophy as a way of life. Now I shall, in due course, return to this statement – that love is philosophy – but for the moment let us stay with the progression or movement of Irigaray's reading of Diotima's speech.

Irigaray moves on to Diotima's discussion of the engendering in beauty of the body and soul, and she suggests that a certain passage here has never really been understood. When Diotima says: 'The union of a man and woman is, in fact, a generation; this is a thing divine; in a living creature that is mortal, it is an element of immortality, this fecundity and generation' (Diotima, cited in Irigaray 1993: 25),[23] Irigaray responds by suggesting that Diotima points, however fleetingly, to 'the presence of immortality in the living mortal' (25); that is, to the dialectical relation or intermediate space that passionate love holds. According to Irigaray, Diotima will momentarily celebrate the ambiguous unity of the meeting between divine and mortal:

> All love is seen as creation and potentially divine, a path between the condition of the mortal and that of the immortal. Love is fecund prior to any procreation. And its fecundity is *mediumlike*, *daimonic*, the guarantee for all, male and female, of the immortal becoming of the living . . . Love's aim is to realize the immortal in the mortal between lovers.
>
> IRIGARAY 1993: 25–6

What is deeply significant for Irigaray, at this point in Diotima's speech, is that this momentary celebration of love as an intermediary or bridge between the divine and the mortal, the physical and the metaphysical, is cut short by what appears (at least for Irigaray) as a surprising, almost brutal reduction in her approach. When Diotima moves to ground her discourse on love in procreation, Irigaray laments that love loses the demonic quality that she has previously attributed to it. Irigaray refers to this as the moment at which Diotima's method 'miscarries'[24] and because the passage is crucial to her reading, I shall repeat it in its entirety here:

> Diotima's method miscarries here. From this point on, she leads love into a split between mortality and immortality, and love loses its daimonic character. Is this the foundational act of metaphysics? There will be lovers in body, lovers in soul. But the perpetual passage from mortal to immortal that lovers confer on each other is blurred. Love has lost its divinity, its mediumistic, alchemical qualities between couples of opposites. Since love is no longer the intermediary, the child plays this role. Occupying the space of love, the child can no longer be a lover and is put in the place of love's incessant movement. It is beloved, no doubt. But how can one be loved without being a lover? And isn't love trapped there *in the beloved*, contrary to what Diotima wanted in the first place? A beloved who is an *end* is substituted for love between men and women. A beloved who is a *will*, even a *duty*, and a *means* of attaining immortality, which the lovers can neither attain nor aspire to between themselves. This is the failure of love, for the child as well. If the pair of lovers cannot safeguard the place for love as a third term between them, they can neither

remain lovers nor give birth to lovers. Something becomes frozen in space-time, with the loss of a vital intermediary and of an accessible transcendental that remains alive. A sort of teleological triangle is put into place instead of a perpetual journey, a perpetual transvaluation, a permanent becoming. For this, love was the vehicle. But, if procreation becomes its goal, it risks losing its internal motivation, its 'inner' fecundity, its slow and constant generation, regeneration.

IRIGARAY 1993: 27[25]

The fecundity and transformative potential of Diotima's teachings on love has been lost. The perpetual movement that underlies the openness, searching, and incessant questioning of a love of wisdom has also been lost. Love is no longer the intermediary space that communicates between the divine and the mortal, and it is no longer the slow and constant act of regeneration. In Diotima's terms, the intermediary of the dialectic has been abandoned. Love has been sacrificed to immortality. Love has become a 'means', a teleological quest. It is no longer demonic. Diotima has forgotten her own lesson, and as a consequence her method miscarries. Irigaray wonders whether this moment may be the founding act of the metaphysical – the falling into two irreconcilable worlds of body and spirit. At this moment, Diotima seems lost to Irigaray.[26] Nonetheless, she is prepared to return to Diotima's speech to continue reading (and to reread), and in returning she finds, to her delight, that Diotima returns to her 'becoming' – to her depiction of love as a perpetual increase that makes no reference to the finality of procreation or the child. Diotima's discussion of 'the losses caused by age' being 'repaired by new acquisitions of a similar kind' leads her to suggest that this process 'enables the mortal to partake of immortality, physically as well as in other ways'.[27] And here Irigaray is pleased to read a re inscription of the demonic nature of love in Diotima's account: 'we are a "regrowth" of ourselves, in perpetual increase. No more searching for immortality through the child. But in ourselves, ceaselessly. Diotima returns to a progression that admits love as it has been defined before she evoked procreation: as an intermediate terrain, a mediator, a space-time of permanent *passage* between mortal and immortal' (28). The movement and the transformative nature of love have been returned.

Irigaray rediscovers the Diotima of fecund inspiration, but she laments that it is only to lose her once again. This time Diotima places the stake of love beyond the self, not simply in the sense of the child-product, but rather in terms of the (related) quest for immortality through fame or renown. While such goals might, indeed, be sought in the begetting of children, Diotima notes that a superior path leads to the begetting of children of the soul, the spiritual progeny of wisdom and virtue. According to this Diotima:

> Those whose creative instinct is physical have recourse to women, and show their love in this way, believing that by begetting children they can secure for themselves an immortal and blessed memory hereafter for ever; but there are some whose creative desire is of the soul, and who long to beget spiritually, not physically, the progeny which it is the nature of the soul to create and bring to birth. If you ask what that progeny is, it is wisdom and virtue in general . . . Everyone would prefer children such as these to children after the flesh.
> *Symposium* 208, 209 PLATO 1967: 90, 91[28]

Irigaray mourns the fact that Diotima's demonic love dissolves under the weight of an immortality to be conferred. It is no longer a becoming, but now an end (a finality, a verdict). Love serves as servant to the master of immortal reknown. The ephemeral nature of being must at all costs be denied, kept at bay by the promise of life eternal, and in her reading Irigaray laments this passing:

> What seemed to me to be original in Diotima's method has disappeared once again. This intermediary milieu of love, which is irreducible, is resplit between a 'subject' (an inadequate word in Plato) and a 'beloved reality'. Falling in love no longer constitutes a becoming of the lover himself, of love in the lover (male or female), or between the lovers, but is now the teleological quest for what is deemed a higher reality and often situated in a transcendence inaccessible to our mortal condition. Immortality has already been put off until death and does not figure as one of our constant tasks as mortals, a transmutation that is endlessly incumbent upon us here, now – its possibility having been

inscribed in the body, which is capable of becoming divine. Beauty of body and of soul are hierarchized, and the love of women becomes the lot of those who, incapable of being creators in soul, are fecund of body and expect the immortality of their name to be perpetuated through their offspring.

IRIGARAY 1993: 29

What is interesting here is that it is this moment in Diotima's speech that has often been the (exclusive) focus of many feminist readings.[29] This Diotima, the woman who elevates the spiritual love and begetting of men over the physical love that women inspire, is often portrayed as Plato's (or even Socrates's) mouthpiece, and there is, indeed, considerable debate as to what 'her' motives in this passage really are.[30] Such readings reduce the ambiguity of Diotima's speech by fixing and determining it as one consistent and unambiguous statement. For Irigaray, though, this passage is only one of many in Diotima's speech. Certainly it provides cause for feminist concern, but Irigaray's manner of reading is to read this passage alongside those others that we have already seen. To be sure, Irigaray laments the disappearance of Diotima's demonic method. She mourns the reduction of love to a teleological quest, and is critical of the hierarchy that displaces love's intermediary sense. For Irigaray, the demonic function of love dies in the face of an intention and teleology of the human will. Love, she notes regretfully, now becomes

> political wisdom, the wisdom of order in the city, not the intermediary state that inhabits lovers and transports them from the condition of mortals to that of immortals. Love becomes a kind of raison d'état. It founds a family, takes care of children, and of all those children who are the citizens. The more its objective is distanced from individual becoming, the more valuable it is. Its stake gets lost in the immortal good and beautiful seen as collective goods. The family is preferable to the generating of lovers, between lovers. Adopted children are preferable to others. It is in this way, moreover, that it comes to pass that love between men is superior to love between man and woman. Carnal procreation is subordinated to the engendering of beautiful and good things. Immortal things. This, surprisingly enough, is the view of Diotima. At least as translated through the words of Socrates.

IRIGARAY 1993: 30–1[31]

Diotima reduces love to a means, but Irigaray does not dwell on this moment. She does not use it to define the entirety of Diotima's teachings on love. She does not reduce the complexity of Diotima's thought to this one instance. While she regrets what Diotima has done, she goes back to restate the strength of Diotima's early method and in doing so points to the ambivalence of Diotima's speech, an ambivalence she refuses to reduce to the demand of a certain logical thought. It is because Irigaray is able to suspend these contradictory moments within Diotima's discourse that she is able to offer us an open reading, one that refuses to totalize its encounter with the otherness and ambiguity of Diotima's speech. Irigaray's reading remains – up until the very last sentence – open and ready to reread. Indeed, she notes towards the end that, were she to return to Diotima's speech with the question of beauty to the fore, an entirely different voice might well emerge. It is possible, she says, that Diotima's understanding of beauty might ultimately work to confuse the opposition between immanence and transcendence. Like love, beauty, too, might move as intermediary between the sensible and transcendental realms '[u]nless what she proposes to contemplate, beauty itself, is seen as that which confounds the opposition between immanence and transcendence. As an always already sensible horizon on the basis of which everything would appear. But one would have to go back over everything to discover it in its enchantment' (Irigaray 1993: 33).

The ambivalent and open-ended conclusion that Irigaray proffers suggests her readiness to challenge her own assumption that Diotima has abandoned love as an intermediary; it suggests her readiness to move on from what might have been the fixed terrain of her own thought. In this, Irigaray's reading is a kind of love or beauty in action, it is an intermediary that moves constantly between what appear to be the opposed poles of Diotima's speech. Irigaray's reading does the work of bringing into communication the seemingly severed realms of Diotima's possibility. The sensible and the transcendental are no longer alternatives but meet here in the midst of Irigaray's response.[32] The coda to Irigaray's response (we can think of Irigaray's reading aesthetically as a fugue)[33] introduces an uncertainty to her reading, a hesitation that allows it to become an intermediary between both the moods of her enthusiasm and her disappointment in relation to Diotima's speech; it takes us back to the beginning of her speech. Diotima is thus transformed from a destination into the 'already sensible horizon' that Irigaray's reading slowly arcs towards. Irigaray has offered us what we might think of as an ethical reading of Diotima's speech;[34] an open and open-ended encounter that leaves space for much still to be considered. There is no reduction in her reading of Diotima to preconceived accounts. There is no attempt to complete her discourse, to have it finished once and for all. What is really ethical in her reading is that it allows for the complex otherness of Diotima's speech to slowly emerge. This otherness is typified in the real ambiguity and tensions that structure Diotima's speech. These ambiguities and tensions are maintained; they are not swept away in a hurried attempt to homogenize Diotima's 'message'. In the unfolding of Irigaray's encounter with Diotima we learn what are arguably important lessons. We learn about a way of doing philosophy – thought through the image of love – that moves us beyond the attitude of appropriation towards that of encounter. Irigaray's reading is, indeed, a reading of Diotima on love, but it is also at the same time a lesson in what philosophy and philosophers might be or become. To put this another way, we might say that Irigaray's readers – touched by this experience of love – learn alternative philosophical responses, ones characterized by a preparedness to encounter the other, to read, and to reread again.[35] In the process, Irigaray's readers are reacquainted with the instituting moments of a love of wisdom and philosophy as a way of life. In love we journey towards wisdom in a way that is 'never fulfilled, always becoming' (Irigaray 1993: 21).

In the light of this we need to think about what it has meant for us to read Irigaray from the perspective of the slow reading I am developing here. In what way or ways has it enabled us to contact the lesson in love that Irigaray's reading offers? By reading Irigaray slowly and attentively I have attempted to keep the ethical gesture of Irigaray's reading alive. By demonstrating how Irigaray's work not only thematizes love but, more importantly, performs it, I have re-presented it as an alternative to the reductive institutional readings I have sought to avoid. By performing the intermediary nature of love by repeatedly moving between opposing terms, Irigaray's reading performs simultaneously a love of wisdom and a wisdom of love, rather than simply a desire to know. In so doing, my reading suggests that Irigaray's reading offers an alternative way of doing philosophy – a future philosophy, in Le Dœuff's terms.

We can understand better what slow reading permits if we juxtapose this with other more familiar ways of reading Irigaray's work. Andrea Nye's reading of Irigaray's reading of Diotima provides us with one such example (Nye 1992: 77–93). I have concerns with Nye's reading, concerns that touch upon the dangers inherent in institutional readings. While Nye's reading provides moments of great insight offering us, in places, a subtle account of Diotima's distance or difference from Platonism, it arguably does so at the expense of what I am calling here an ethical, slow, or loving reading of Irigaray's text.[36] To begin with, Nye uses her criticisms of Irigaray's reading as a point from which to launch her own reading of Diotima. While this is a fairly standard philosophical mode, we need to ask whether it is, in all truth, necessary. Nye accuses Irigaray of misreading or misunderstanding Diotima and ultimately of inappropriately reducing her to Platonism. Now, such a reading of Irigaray's text is, I think, a disappointing one in that it reduces Irigaray's reading to a definitive and closed account that, as I have argued in this chapter, is difficult to sustain. The beauty (the 'force', if you like) of Irigaray's reading lies precisely in the ambiguity it sustains in relation to Diotima's voice. As we have seen, Irigaray does not decide, definitively, about Diotima's teachings; she leaves open the question of Diotima's lapse into Platonism, precisely in order to return to the importance of her teachings on love. Irigaray celebrates both the thematic content and procedure of Diotima's method. And the fact that she does so makes it possible for her to provide us with an open-ended conclusion; indeed, one that I have demonstrated refuses to conclude at all. Irigaray's conclusion is, as we have seen, the possibility of a new beginning – a call to return to Diotima's speech in order to read it again.

In her desire to offer us her own Diotima, I think that Nye misses the subtlety of Irigaray's gesture. She misses, too, the opportunities that Irigaray's reading opens up. Nye accuses Irigaray of reducing or denying Diotima's actual authority in the *Symposium* (Nye 1992: 78). This is, I think, once again a poor reading (or an unhelpful one), as Irigaray refuses to decide on the authority or presence of Diotima, offering us ambiguous messages throughout. Nye contends that Irigaray reduces Diotima's concerns to those of a French feminist – and a lapsed French feminist at that: 'Irigaray *judges* Diotima as a lapsed French feminist struggling to maintain the "correct method" against philosophical orthodoxy. Although Diotima begins well with an ironic onslaught on dualistic, hierarchical categories, she soon reverts to an orthodoxy of her own. Instead of continuing to derail Socratic logic, Diotima becomes a Platonist' (Nye 1992: 79, emphasis added). The implication of Nye's account of Irigaray's reading here seems to be that Irigaray's Diotima partakes of a marginal feminist critique before succumbing to the inevitable logic of (a masculine) Platonism. Now, even if we were to grant that there is such a thing as a French feminist (as if the rich and complex feminist work carried out in France could be reduced to such an identity) we would, nonetheless, be left with certain hesitations regarding Nye's argument here. Nye's reading of Irigaray's reading of Diotima's speech is reductive (too impulsive, too fast). It glosses over the ambiguities that Irigaray, I think ethically, announces. There is, simply, no singular Diotima for Irigaray, and thus no Diotima who can be read definitively in terms of a dominant male text – in this case, in terms of Plato's *Symposium*. Diotima's teachings and method are significant for Irigaray *precisely because* they unsettle the question of Platonism and its authority. The ethical nature of Irigaray's reading lies in its questioning, its attention to detail, its slowness, its willingness to wait and to listen, to pause before returning to the text: this, in the place of a too hasty response.

Interestingly, Nye goes on to claim that we can understand Irigaray's reduction of Diotima to Platonism through Irigaray's relation to Derridean deconstruction:

> The source of [Irigaray's] strategy is, of course, Jacques Derrida ... Like other French feminists, Irigaray [finds] in these strategies both a possible antidote for the paralyzing realization that sexism can be built into semantic structure, and a flattering reversal of the proverbial sexist claim that women are inferior because they are illogical and incapable of consistency. Derrida seems to suggest a way in which women, excluded from and degraded in male culture, can still undermine, if not overcome, that culture.
>
> NYE 1992: 81, 82

This is an odd gesture on Nye's part as it repeats the same sin that she so vehemently criticizes in Irigaray. Nye reduces the complexity of Irigaray's reading to what is arguably a questionable account of Derrida's method. She silences the ambiguous and ethical encounter that Irigaray constructs in relation to Diotima by reducing her reading to the logic of a supposedly dominant male text. While Platonism, here, gives way to Derridean deconstruction, the sin of reduction remains essentially the same.

Nye's reading, then, provides an example of how *not* to read Irigaray. It is a reading lacking the 'love' that makes it possible to return to Irigaray; a reading that is always a 'readiness to re-read'. It is not too much to say that it is an example of the misreadings, ungenerous accounts or even unethical readings that are all too often perpetuated both in and as philosophy. What, precisely, is the ethic supporting Nye's reading? Has she 'under-read' Irigaray? Read her poorly? Ah, but what if we were to return to Nye's reading ourself? What if we were to rethink Nye's gesture here, in terms of another, as yet undecided, category? To offer a slower, more loving or generous, or ethical reading of our own? It would seem that Irigaray's lesson is, indeed, one that we each have to learn over and over again.

Descartes's *Passions of the Soul*: Irigaray's wondrous reading

We have already seen the force of Descartes's four principles and the significance they hold for Adorno, whose task it is to set the meandering uncertainty of the essay as an antidote to Cartesian certainty. And yet, in the work of this seventeenth-century French philosopher we can find what appear to be two different philosophical attitudes or approaches; two different ideas of what it means to do philosophy. While Descartes is typically characterized as the 'chief architect of the seventeenth-century intellectual revolution which destabilized the traditional doctrines of medieval and Renaissance scholasticism ... [laying] down the philosophical foundations for what we think of as the "modern" scientific age' (Cottingham 1995: 188),[37] this is not, as we will see, the whole story. His early ambition, outlined in *A Discourse on Method*, is an attempt 'to replace the "speculative" philosophy of scholasticism with a practical philosophy' that will 'improve the human lot' (191). To this end Descartes sets out to provide philosophical inquiry with 'the methods and reasoning of mathematics' in order to ensure 'the kind of precision and certainty which traditional philosophy lacked' (189). Indeed, much of Descartes's early work can better be described by what we would now think of as science rather than philosophy. In this it marks a key moment in the development of the desire to know.

In *A Discourse on Method* (1637) Descartes famously discusses 'the foundations of knowledge, the existence of God, and the distinction between mind and body. The metaphysical arguments contained here, and greatly expanded in [his] philosophical masterpiece, the *Meditations on First Philosophy* (1641), constitute [what most consider to be] the philosophical core of the Cartesian system' (189). Depictions of Descartes as the one who inaugurates 'modern philosophy by making questions about the validation of knowledge the first [and primary] questions' (189) are well grounded if we take these two texts as our major, or even sole guides, to understanding his thought. However, the picture appears somewhat different if we read his last work, *The Passions of the Soul* (1649–1650), alongside the earlier systematic works. We will stay momentarily, though, with the earlier work in order to understand something of Descartes's methodology; that is, his way of doing philosophy and the various attitudes this entails. It will become clear why doing this helps us to return to the question of reading and philosophy's often poor record in relation to it. By reducing reading to a desire to know, philosophy sabotages its earlier love of wisdom.

If we return to the opening pages of Descartes's *Discourse*, we find that they provide us with a certain caricature of philosophy and philosophical method – one that allows us to see the problems inherent in an overly systematic philosophical attitude. Here Descartes outlines his four principles, the rules that establish his methodology, which become the attitudes and orientations for much modern Western philosophy and science. As we have already seen in the Introduction, an overarching desire for absolute certainty and finality drives these principles:

> The *first* was never to accept anything for true which I did not clearly know to be such; that is to say, carefully to avoid precipitancy and prejudice, and to comprise nothing more in my judgment than what was presented to my mind so clearly and distinctly as to exclude all ground of doubt.

The *second*, to divide each of the difficulties under examination into as many parts as possible, and as might be necessary for its adequate solution.

The *third*, to conduct my thoughts in such order that, by commencing with objects the simplest and easiest to know, I might ascend by little and little, and yet, as it were, step by step, to the knowledge of the more complex; assigning in thought a certain order to those objects which in their own nature do not stand in a relation of antecedence and sequence.

And the *last*, in every case to make enumerations so complete, and reviews so general, that I might be assured that nothing was omitted.

DESCARTES 1912: 15–16

The cherished goals of certainty and exhaustiveness that Descartes's rules strive to achieve are highly problematic from the perspective of the slow or ethical reading that we are pursuing here. In Descartes's methodology philosophy works by way of a kind of clinical decomposition or dismembering of whatever it sets out to read. Descartes establishes here the ground for an ultimate principle of systematic thought – one that breaks the object (of inquiry) 'into as many parts as possible', leaving nothing unsaid, nothing unthought – nothing in reserve. This exhaustive approach dissects the object, leaving the world literally in bits and pieces.[38] This moment of Descartes's thought inaugurates (or more properly, reinforces) a philosophical tendency – a desire to know – that stifles ambiguity and uncertainty (otherness) beneath layers of knowledge. As Adorno writes, Descartes's method or frame of reference 'becomes an *axiomatic doctrine* that is being set up as the *gateway* to thought' (Adorno 2000: 103, emphasis added).[39] In effect, this gateway provides no hesitation or pause, no interval between ourselves and the other.

Perhaps another way of saying this is to suggest that the philosophical method that Descartes's principles embody leave us with no point of contact with the other; or, more specifically for our purpose here, with no possibility of contact with the otherness or strangeness of what we read. By contact I mean ethical contact – an engagement that permits an openness and a preparedness to be transformed by the encounter with the other. There is no sense in which the delicate or strange otherness of the text can survive the onslaught of Descartes's exhaustiveness. And this goes to the heart of my concern. What we need, philosophically speaking, is an attitude or approach that engages with the text – not one that contains it by summing it up or weighing it – the better to bury it under the weight of systematic rigour. Strangely, ever so strangely, we find the trace of such an attitude or approach in Descartes's final work, the *Passions*.

The Passions of the Soul is Descartes's last work, written shortly before his visit to Sweden in 1649–1650. Here Descartes, as J. Cottingham points out

> examines the physiological basis for our feelings and sensations. Although the mechanisms of the body are [for him] no part of our nature as 'thinking beings', Descartes none the less maintains that there is a 'naturally ordained' relationship whereby physiological events automatically generate certain psychological responses; learning about these responses, and about the conditioning process which can allow us to modify them in certain cases, is the key to controlling the passions 'so that the evils they cause become bearable and even a source of joy'.
> *Passions*, art. 212, COTTINGHAM 1995: 191

It is within this complex context that Descartes offers us his philosophical exploration of one of the great passions: wonder; and it is this that, perhaps surprisingly, provides us with another way to move ethically towards the strangeness of the other. We can rework some aspects of Descartes's discussion of wonder to provide an attitude or approach towards reading that is both open and ethical.[40]

Wonder (*l'admiration*)[41] is, according to Descartes, the first of the passions.[42] It is a state of surprise that exists fleetingly. In the *Passions* he refers to the 'rare' or the 'new' sources of wonder that provide an otherness that haunts by refusing to be tied back to the immediacy and stilling predictability of the mundane or the known. Wonder resists the desire to know by suspending judgement. Wonder provides the space or interval between ourselves and the world, so that we can momentarily rediscover it as new. We might say that wonder is the movement of a thought – of all thought – that has not yet congealed into the inflexibility of rigour, which is, of course, the inflexibility of the institution:

> When the first encounter with some object surprises us, and we judge it to be new or very different from what we formerly knew, or from what we supposed that it ought to be, that causes us to wonder and be surprised; and because that may happen before we in any way know whether this object is agreeable to us or is not so, it appears to me that wonder is the first of all the passions; and it has no opposite, because if the object which presents itself has nothing in it that surprises us, we are in no wise moved regarding it, and we consider it without passion.
> DESCARTES 1931: art. 53, 358

Suspended in a state of wonder, we short-circuit the desire to definitely know and contain the world which offers itself to us in this passionate and unfamiliar guise. We refrain from deciding about the world or judging it.[43] We suspend the desire to know. For Descartes, 'Wonder is a sudden surprise of the soul which causes it to apply itself to consider with attention the objects which seem to it rare and extraordinary' (Descartes 1931: art. 70, 362). It is, to borrow Sigmund Freud's use of the term, an *unheimlich* encounter that repositions the familiar in literally a wondrous or disconcerting way: 'for we shall only wonder', writes Descartes, 'at that which appears rare and extraordinary to us, and nothing can so appear excepting because we have been ignorant of it, or also because it is different from the thing we have known; for it is this difference which causes it to be called extraordinary' (Descartes 1931: art. 75, 364). This first encounter troubles the certainty of our knowledge of the world, and in doing so opens us out, even if fleetingly, to the possibility of the other as unknown – the other that moves us beyond conventional modes.[44] Wonder is first and foremost movement; a movement towards. And this is precisely where Irigaray's reading of Descartes comes in.

Not content with reducing Descartes's thought to the homogeneity of 'Cartesianism', Irigaray returns to and rereads his *Passions* in order to engage with the strangeness of the text. Her reading of Descartes occurs, of course, in the context of her rereadings of key texts in the Western philosophical tradition, and these are collected in *An Ethics of Sexual Difference* (Irigaray 1993).[45] Irigaray's reading of Diotima's speech also appears here. What Irigaray achieves in this book is a series of engaged readings that listen attentively to moments in the history that escape many of the familiar interpretations we have of these works. While some are content to reduce Descartes to the Cartesianism they expect to find in his work, or Plato to his Platonism, Irigaray's readings are much more ambitious. Irigaray patiently follows the path or paths these philosophers take, in order to address them on their own terrain. Her readings are rereadings that pose questions which open up and unsettle any certainty or consistency that we may hope to find there.

In her encounter with Descartes's work, Irigaray undergoes a series of responses that we might think of in terms of 'attitudes', 'passions' or even 'moods'. Indeed, it is possible to chart something like an emotional distribution or map of the terrain of her reading, which moves between moments of exhilaration and moments of disappointment as she follows the contours of Descartes's thought. This collection of discrete attitudes (*Stimmungen* in Gumbrecht's terms) alternate throughout the text, while never resolving into any whole. Irigaray begins by noting that 'We need to reread Descartes a little and remember or learn about the movement of the passions' (Irigaray 1993: 72).[46] In this introductory section she employs the language and metaphors of physics, echoing Descartes's own physical language. She laments the scission between the physical sciences and thought, questioning whether this 'threatens thought itself' (72).[47] Are we to think of her reading as a remedy to this scission, a kind of sensible transcendental that brings thought back to the body and to the world? For Irigaray, the effects of this scission are seen in the closing down of our relation with the other, in our lack of wonder: 'And there is no *window*, no sense remaining open on, or with, the world, the Other, the other. In order to dwell within it, transform it. What is lacking there in terms of the passions is *wonder*' (73).[48]

Having established the importance of the movement of the passions and of our openness to the other, Irigaray moves on to celebrate the moment when Descartes first describes the encounter that causes us to stop and wonder. In this passage Descartes positions wonder as the first of the passions: 'wonder is the first of the passions; and it has no opposite, because if the object which presents itself has nothing in it that surprises us, we are in no wise moved regarding it, and we consider it without passion' (Descartes 1931: art. 53, 358). In response, Irigaray ponders the contemplative nature of wonder, what we might think of as the slowness of wonder: 'it matters for "man" . . . to know how to stop in order to rest, to leave an interval between himself and the other, to look toward, to contemplate – *to wonder*' (73). Wonder involves rest and contemplation, a kind of temporary withdrawal that is simultaneously active and passive. It is an interval that allows us to contemplate the otherness of our encounter, and to resist the 'speed of [the machine's] acceleration' (74). The dangers of speed and acceleration (of a calculation and a desire to know) are thus offset by wonder, the first of the passions which is 'indispensable not only to life but also or still to the creation of an ethics' (74). An ethics of wonder allows us to experience the other as new and different from how we imagine them to be. It helps us to avoid reducing or assimilating the other to ourselves. Wonder does not partake of rejection, and thus does not involve itself with opposites or contradictory positions. 'Before and after appropriation, there is wonder' (74), Irigaray writes.[49] Wonder is the surprise of the new that is not yet assimilated, the curiosity or interval that keeps us from missing the other, the passage or bridge between two closed worlds. It is a nearness or proximity which is not a coincidence. In short, wonder is 'the advent of the other' (75), and as such it provides us with an ethical orientation towards our world.

However, when Descartes writes that 'To wonder is united esteem or disdain according as it is at the greatness of an object or its smallness that we wonder' (Descartes 1931: art. 54, 358), Irigaray fears that he is in danger of losing wonder. By quantifying wonder, he enters the realm of opposites – great/small, esteem/disdain – and risks losing the unique space-time of wonder of which Irigaray reminds us. And yet, Descartes returns to wonder in his discussion of desire which Irigaray claims (despite Descartes's 'confusions') is 'the spaces of freedom between the subject and the world ... the moment[s] of illumination – already and still contemplative – between the subject and the world' (76–7). Here we have the first movement towards the other that 'is not yet frozen in a predicate that would split the world in two' (76). Irigaray rethinks Descartes's account of desire – grouped as it is together with the secondary passions – as the attraction that survives the first encounter by establishing a relation or conversation between the two.

Irigaray welcomes Descartes's observation that '[w]onder is a sudden surprise of the soul which causes it to apply itself to consider with attention the objects which seem to it rare and extraordinary' (Descartes 1931: art. 70, 362), and yet she laments the fact that he situates this attentive wonder solely in the brain: 'It is thus primarily caused by the impression we have in the brain which represents the object as rare, and as consequently worthy of much consideration' (Descartes 1931: art. 70, 362). For Descartes, wonder, being the first of the passions (the primary passion), is distinct from those which follow – Love, Hatred, Joy, Sadness and Desire – in the sense that its effects are caused by impressions in the brain, while the remaining passions are located in the heart and blood, thus mobilizing various parts of the body. The danger inherent in Descartes's inscription of wonder in the brain is, according to Irigaray, that 'It would remain a purely cerebral striving towards the answer to the question of *who* or *what* is the object of wonder' (78).

And yet Descartes redeems himself to a point when he returns to the question of what is rare and extraordinary: 'for we shall only wonder at that which appears rare and extraordinary to us, and nothing can so appear excepting because we have been ignorant of it, or also because it is different from the thing we have known; for it is this difference which causes it to be called extraordinary' (Descartes 1931: art. 75, 364). For Irigaray, Descartes here introduces difference as stimulating and attracting. Wonder emerges out of and guides us towards difference. And while sexual difference could be situated at this point in Descartes's discussion, Irigaray simply notes that he fails to think of this. Nonetheless, wonder affirms difference and this leads her to ponder the separation of wonder and love: 'The question of wonder and love remains. Why would these passions be separated? Do we love with the heart and blood and not through thought? Do we wonder with the head and not with the heart? ... would [Descartes] differentiate between men and women on this point?' (79–80).[50]

How, then to think of wonder?[51] In the closing paragraphs, Irigaray gathers together what she has discovered in her rereading of Descartes and tells us that wonder is the passion that maintains a path between physics and metaphysics, a movement towards the other and possibly through, a bridge between the instant and eternity, and an attraction around the unexplored; '[t]he point of passage between two closed worlds' (75). Wonder is the space-time of encounter before judgement (or relation) occurs: 'Before and after acts of opposition, there would still be wonder: pure inscription, pure movement, pure memory' (80). Wonder offers the passion of the first encounter, 'an *opening* prior to and following that which surrounds, enlaces' (81–2).[52] Wonder is the complete openness of an engagement with difference: 'An *excess* resists: the other's existence and becoming as a place that permits union and/through resistance to assimilation or reduction to sameness' (74). Wonder is the force that stops us, slows us, opens us. Accordingly, wonder is the possibility of an ethical opening towards the other (a humility). Indeed, it is the possibility of ethics in any general sense, and Irigaray's descriptions of wonder here provide us with a helpful way of thinking about what an ethical reading might look like. The attentiveness that characterizes wonder allows us to think of it in terms of the kind of slow engagement that slow reading is. Wonder provides us with a way to pace our reading in an engaged and ethical manner. It releases us from the anxiety of Descartes's four principles, freeing us to suspend judgement, to withhold it, while maintaining an attentive ear and yielding to the difference that surfaces in what we read. In helping us to ruminate and to rest, wonder provides us with the resources we require to return to what we read, to reread yet again.

Irigaray's reading of Descartes is wondrous in its own right, in the sense that – full of questions – it causes us to pause in front of his work; her reading moves wondrously between the disparate moments of his thought, bridging the various positions he takes, and opening his work to the ethical possibilities that wonder entails. Irigaray's exploration literally wanders from place to place, resisting the temptation to take *a* position on Descartes's thought, to finalize and judge what it has achieved. Her reading creates spaces in Descartes's work where he is able to wonder at himself. Irigaray's questions make these spaces possible. Along with Descartes, we wonder too.

Love and wonder: reading

Irigaray's rereadings of Diotima and Descartes provide us with discussions of love and wonder that help us to think differently about how we might read. Both love and wonder open us to otherness and, in doing so, open us to the strangeness that we might otherwise read around. By slowing us down and helping us to pause, attitudes of love and wonder open us to a contemplative relation with what we read. And yet love and wonder open us in subtly different ways. Wonder arguably initiates us into the realm of the other, providing us an attentive awareness to what is rare and new. It occurs before (and after) any relation between ourselves and the other: between subject and world, or subject and object. Wonder is, Irigaray writes: 'Our attraction to that which is not yet (en)coded, our curiosity . . . vis-à-vis that which we have not yet encountered or made ours' (75). Wonder is our attraction, our not-yet-relation with the other that we experience in a contemplative mode: 'Wonder being the moment of illumination – already and still contemplative – between the subject and the world' (77). It is the 'passion of moving toward' (80), but it is not yet a relation. It is a being-with or being-in-proximity-to rather than a coupling. Wonder, unlike love, is not an enveloping: 'It corresponds to time, to space-time before and after that which can delimit, go round, encircle' (81). Wonder is 'not yet reenveloped in love' because, Irigaray tells us, it is the 'passion that inaugurates love' (82).

Love, on the other hand, is the passion that envelopes, connects us and places us in relation with the other. In love I am now fully subject, able to face and respond to the other who is distinct from me. In love I am able to go beyond a movement towards the other in order to touch and welcome its otherness. But how might wonder become love? This question, I think, returns us to Irigaray's comments on desire. Desire survives the original and wondrous encounter, providing the force of attraction that draws me to the other: 'Desire would be . . . the first movement *toward*, not yet qualified. Taking as its momentum the subject's passion or the object's irresistible attraction' (76). Desire is a bridge between the awe of wonder and the enveloping of love. It permits a communion between myself and the other, and makes possible a conversation that love will eventually become. Desire spans the distance between myself and the other left open in awe. Between love and wonder, Irigaray's desire reminds us how philosophy loses its way. In becoming a desire *to know*, desire is no longer the bridge from wonder to love (the movement towards) but rather a need to know in the service of some anxiety, some utility, some instrumental end.

Awe can be thought of in terms of the deferred judgement that wonder is: a 'movement that precedes even desire?' (81). While love, as we learn from Diotima, occurs between two fixed points as an incessant movement between the two, wonder moves in less terrestrial ways, and Irigaray's evocation of Nietzsche serves to demonstrate this well:

> Could Nietzsche's *Beyond Good and Evil* signify something of a return to wonder? To a passion of pure knowledge, pure *light*? . . . Before and after acts of opposition, there would still be wonder: pure inscription, pure movement, pure memory. Even pure thought? . . . A wonder that lasts. A bridge between the instant and eternity. An attraction and return all around the unexplored, all barriers down, beyond every coast, every port. Navigating at the centre of infinity, weightless. A movement lighter than the necessities of the heart, of the affect? A movement of dance or flight? Leaving the earth, its security, to navigate through fluids – marine, aerial, celestial. The passion of movement toward. Through? Which would never stop.
>
> IRIGARAY 1993: 80

Irigaray's reference to a wonder that would never stop speaks to the anxiety that Descartes has in relation to excessive wonder. While wonder is good in that it opens us in curious and passionate ways to the new and the rare, if it continues unabated Descartes warns that it risks turning into astonishment that 'causes the whole body to remain as immobile as a statue, and prevents our perceiving more of the object than the first face which is presented, or consequently of acquiring a more particular knowledge of it. That is what we commonly call being astonished, and astonishment is an excess of wonder which can never be otherwise than bad' (Descartes 1931: art. LXXIII, 364). Descartes further warns against the malady of blind curiosity where one is given over to wonder in such a way that they 'seek out things that are rare solely to wonder at them, and not for the purpose of *really knowing them*' at all (Descartes 1931: art. LXXVIII, 366, emphasis added). Here Descartes betrays the moment of utility[53] that finds its way into his discussion of wonder, where the purpose of really knowing things serves as an end point or destination for the awestruck or curious philosopher. '[T]here is no other remedy to prevent our wondering to excess', writes Descartes, 'than that of *acquiring a knowledge* of various matters and exercising ourselves in the consideration of all those which may appear the most rare and strange' (Descartes 1931: art. LXXVI, 365, emphasis added). Knowing calms the anxiety that wonders may literally never cease. Or is it love that stops wonder from becoming astonishment?

Perhaps Descartes's anxiety in the face of an excessive wonder comes out of the uncertainty of an encounter with what is not only new and rare, but wholly unknown (unable to be really known). Does this bring us back to the *Discourse*? If so, then it is Irigaray's wonder, not Descartes's, that we follow in our attempt to think of reading in wondrous terms.[54] Both love and wonder, as Irigaray imagines them, provide us ways of opening to otherness in order that we might really read. Beyond this, love and wonder, in their own ways, have the ability to open our everyday institutional intersubjective relations in more generous ways. As such, we open towards a future philosophy by re-engaging the instituting moments of a love of wisdom and philosophy as a way of life.

CHAPTER FOUR

The Present of Reading: Irigaray's Attentive Listening

I am but the reader, I tried to plead with them. But they did not listen, could not listen, would never listen, & seemed intent only on making me the instrument of their vengeance.

RICHARD FLANAGAN, *GOULD'S BOOK OF FISH*: 326

When we think how philosophy is communicated, we usually think about reading, writing, and speaking. One philosophical activity that has not been reflected on much is that of listening, and even more so, that of being listened to.[1]

Isn't the philosopher someone who always hears (and who hears everything), but who cannot listen, or who, more precisely, neutralizes listening within himself, so that he can philosophize?[2]

I ask the reader of the text to accept the invitation to listen-to in the present, to enter into dialogue with a thought, with a way of speaking, and to give up appropriating only a content of discourse in order to integrate it among knowledge already gained.[3]

Reading is creative listening that alters the reader.[4]

In this chapter, I explore what it means to think of reading as a kind of attentive listening. I suggest that reading, in the ethical mode I am investigating here, has much in common with an active and engaged form of listening that pre-eminently establishes a relation with the other or text. Listening, perhaps more so than looking, captures what is ethical in the practice of reading.[5] Listening, as we will see, builds a bridge with the instituting moments of a love of wisdom and philosophy as a way of life.[6] It bypasses the instituted structure of a desire to know by providing a context of proximity, gesture and nearness. In this regard, Luce Irigaray's work is exemplary. Her insistence on the centrality of love to the philosophical enterprise provides a useful frame for reconnecting with the guiding idea of a love of wisdom, helping us to think differently about how philosophers read. Her desire to 'make something exist', to 'stage an encounter', 'to prepare a place of proximity' and 'to search for gestures' helps orient philosophy towards a slow reading that pays attention to the other and allows otherness to be. Before engaging with Irigaray's work, though, I begin by taking a brief detour through what the phenomenologist Hans Jonas has to say on the question of the senses. I do this in order to raise questions about what it means to think of reading as a kind of listening. We tend to equate reading with seeing, but any simple or exclusive coupling of reading with vision 'overlooks' or misses the possibility of exploring reading as an activity that involves more of the body, in more complex ways.

The nobility of sight: Hans Jonas

While Jonas never raises the question of reading in his phenomenological work, there is nevertheless much that we can draw on in order to follow the important gesture he makes of bringing the *corporeality* of perception into play. Perception is Jonas's primary interest in his important essay 'The Nobility of Sight' (Jonas 1953: 135–55), and here he begins his discussion with a short historical overview of the hierarchy of the senses that emerges from classical Greek philosophy, a hierarchy that works to position sight alongside the noblest activity of the mind – *theoria*. In this 'partiality of classical philosophy for one of the bodily senses' (152) sight furnishes 'the analogues for the intellectual upperstructure' serving as the model of perception in general and thus as 'the measure of the other senses' (135). As the 'most excellent of the senses', the distinct qualities of sight[7] come to provide the very ground, not only of *theoria*, but of 'some basic concept of philosophy' (152). In this, vision and sight ground the desire to know:

> *Simultaneity of presentation* furnishes the idea of enduring present, the contrast between change and the unchanging, between time and eternity. *Dynamic neutralization* furnishes form as distinct from matter, essence as distinct from existence, and the difference of theory and practice. *Distance* furnishes the idea of infinity. Thus the mind has gone where vision pointed.
> JONAS 1953: 152

In his section on 'Seeing and time', Jonas makes a case for the three unique qualities of sight – simultaneity, neutralization and distance – arguing that they determine the *objectivity* or objective nature of the noble sense.[8] 'Only the simultaneity of image allows the beholder to compare and interrelate: it not only offers many things at once, but offers them in their mutual proportion, and thus objectivity emerges preeminently from sight' (144). The 'wandering glance of attention' is able to hold numerous things at once in order to relate and compare them. In the process, it remains detached and distanced from the things it surveys. This 'image-function' of sight (146) permits objectivity by ensuring a distance between 'the thing as it is in itself' and 'the thing as it affects me', and this is how vision comes to be linked with *theoria*, theoretical truth, abstraction and 'all free thought' (147):[9]

> The object, staying in its bounds, faces the subject across the gap which the evanescence of the force context has created. Distance of appearance yields neutral 'image' which, unlike 'effect', can be looked at and compared, in memory retained and recalled, in imagination varied and freely composed. Thus becomes essence separable from existence and therewith theory possible. It is but the basic freedom of vision, and the element of abstraction inherent in it, which are carried further in conceptual thought; and from visual perception, concept and idea inherit that ontological pattern of objectivity which vision has first created.
> JONAS 1953: 148–9

However, this abstraction, that begins in vision and ends in theory, carries with it a loss in 'the cognitive economy of man', who Jonas dubs 'the pre-eminently seeing creature' (147). (We might add here that the pre-eminently seeing creature is simultaneously a pre-eminently knowing creature.) The visual process eliminates any causal connection between this seeing creature and 'his' world. The seeing creature is 'not yet engaged by the seen object' and in this sense, writes Jonas, 'sight differs decisively from touch and hearing' (145). As a consequence, the 'self-contained object' emerges independently from the 'self-contained subject' (148). Sight foregoes the embedded security of the 'lower' senses and in so doing discovers itself to be the 'least "realistic" of the senses' (147). Objectivity has been gained, but at what cost? A love of wisdom, a way of life? 'Thus vision secures that standing back from the aggressiveness of the world which frees for observation and opens a horizon for elective attention. But it does so at the price of offering a becalmed abstract of reality denuded of its raw power' (Jonas 1953: 148).

It is clear from his writing that Jonas subscribes to a particular tradition in Western thought that asserts the superiority of sight; however, he simultaneously unsettles this wisdom by claiming that while sight remains a special sense – the noblest of the senses – it does so only in virtue of its largely unacknowledged dependence upon the other senses. Sight 'is incomplete by itself; it requires the complement of other senses and functions for its cognitive office; its highest virtues are also its essential insufficiencies. Its very nobility calls for the support of more vulgar modes of commerce with the importunity of things'. All eminence, he writes, 'pays for itself [with] the price of increased dependence' (135–6). Sight needs the 'lower' senses; it depends on hearing and touch.[10] Sight's nobility is the crowning glory of a sense that benefits from the work carried out by its subjects – the subjugated senses. Thus, hearing and touch play crucial though largely unacknowledged roles in the so-called abstract, higher order cognitive functions, and 'truth' ignores these senses at its peril:

> Vision . . . is not the primary but the most sublime case of sense perception and rests on the understructure of more elementary functions in which the world is maintained on far more elementary terms. A king with no subjects to rule over ceases to be a king. The evidence of sight does not falsify reality when supplemented by that of the underlying strata of experience, notably of motility and touch: when arrogantly rejecting it sight becomes barren of truth.
> JONAS 1953: 149

The more elementary functions of hearing and touch emerge as the essential ground of all knowing.[11] And yet this *ground* remains largely invisible – silent, unfelt. From this vantage point, another philosophy emerges, one concerned to gather the riches of all the senses, to put the entire body into play. Here philosophy renews itself with a pre-Platonic elemental encounter with hearing and touch – the body animated with rhythm, gesture and sound. Interestingly, in the Appendix to his chapter on 'The Nobility of Sight', Jonas claims that we can trace the origins of this separation of perception and sensation – of theory and practice (or the *vita contemplativa* and the *vita activa*) – to our forgetting of the body and its motility.[12] Conscious, abstract thought does its best to erase the obvious traces of our bodily being. By focusing on vision and sight, and abstracting and aggrandizing this bodily dimension into a purely cognitive domain, the body and its rich elementary resources are covered over and forgotten. And yet, as Jonas points out, 'the *motility of our body* generally, is not called in *post hoc* only but is already a factor in the very constitution of seeing and the seen world themselves, much as this genesis is forgotten in the conscious result' (152). For Jonas, this philosophical trend is typified in Immanuel Kant's separation of the idea of a theoretical subject from *praxis*. This idea of the passive or receptive nature of mere sense and sense knowledge determines the entire orientation of Western epistemological thought:[13]

> Kant posed the question of the cognitive organization of our percepts as the question of the relative shares of 'receptivity' and 'spontaneity,' of the passive and active components of our being. But by 'activity' in this context he understood mental activity alone (the formal articulation of the sense material through the categories of the understanding), not bodily action of the psychophysical person in his practical dealings with the world. It is strange how little the command of our limbs entered into the long history of the problem.
>
> JONAS 1953: 152–3

While certain philosophers since this time have challenged the bias of Kant's theoretical subject – notably Georg Hegel in *Phenomenology of Spirit* (Hegel 1977) – Jonas cautions that such challenges have tended to swing too far, thus finding themselves in 'the natural danger of being provoked into opposite partisanship' (153). In order to avoid either danger – a disavowal of bodily action or a hypostatization of the body – Jonas simply draws our attention to bodily action and the command of our limbs in order to invite us to think about the role of the body in the everyday intellectual activities of thinking and understanding. This is interesting because it gives us pause to think about the role or roles of the body in reading, and of the relation between reading and listening more specifically. In general, a certain philosophy tends to forget that *bodies* read.[14] It forgets what complex roles the body plays in acts of reading and understanding. Without thinking, it reduces reading to its purely cognitive dimensions, and often goes on to imagine the cognitive as an immaterial domain. Given this, a turn towards listening might be the jolt necessary to remind us all of the *scene* of reading, its bodily dimension and context. So, what follows in this chapter is a series of suggestions aimed at thinking about reading as a kind of attentive listening, and while there is a metaphorical leap that draws reading around the figure of listening, there is a subtle reminder that accompanies this metaphorical gesture. Listening stands in here as both metaphor and reference. When I suggest that we think of reading as a kind of listening, I am pointing in two directions at once, simultaneously towards reading 'as if' it were an active and engaged listening, and reading 'as' an active and engaged listening.

Listening-to: Luce Irigaray's way of love

The Way of Love (2002) comes out of Irigaray's careful reading of key texts by Martin Heidegger,[15] an encounter that provokes her, somewhat paradoxically, to outline the possibility of a philosophy that values intersubjectivity, dialogue, difference and attention to present life.[16] Throughout the work, Irigaray returns to the practice of listening, listening-to, and listening-with as a preparation for what she refers to as 'a wisdom of love between us' (Irigaray 2002: vii). While reading is certainly not the focus of her discussion, I nonetheless find her work helpful in pursuing the links I am developing between reading and ethics in this book. Irigaray's insistence on listening provides the ground for an attentive relation, a slow reading I will refer to as the 'present' of reading in this chapter.

Irigaray's work on listening needs to be read – or perhaps 'heard' – in the context of the history that, as we have seen, Jonas points us towards, a history that contextualizes the desire to know within the perceived nobility of sight, the elevation of vision and the concomitant devaluation or silencing of the other senses. This history finds early expression in the opening passage to Book I of Aristotle's *Metaphysics*:

> All men by nature desire to know. An indication of this is the delight we take in our senses; for even apart from their usefulness they are loved for themselves; and above all others the sense of sight. For not only with a view to action, but even when we are not going to do anything, we prefer seeing (one might say) to everything else. The reason is that this, most of all the senses, makes us know and brings to light many differences between things.
> ARISTOTLE 1971 Met A, 980 a25

According to Aristotle, 'we' prefer seeing to everything else, for it makes us know, and brings to light many differences between things.[17] And yet this (largely unconscious) preference or way of thinking covers over the elemental ground of our sensory being, leaving us with a philosophy denuded of its more richly elaborated bodily ground. Philosophy as a love of wisdom and a way of life gives way to philosophy as a determination to calculate and to know. The objectivity and abstraction that follows literally distances us from the world, and our dominant philosophical institutions have tended in varying and complex ways to celebrate this separation. The practices of reading that emerge from this process of separation have diminished capacities to engage in substantial and sustained ways with the real otherness or difference of that world.

Perhaps the kind of abstraction that emerges here is what leads to the 'coercive philosophy' that Robert Nozick identifies in *Philosophical Explanation* (1981). Here Nozick suggests that a certain philosophical training or apprenticeship has the effect of moulding our way of doing philosophy, and thus determining what we believe philosophy to be (Nozick 1981: 5). A philosophy that abstracts itself from what is foreign in the other, a philosophy unable to listen to and engage with the other, is a philosophy that trains us for adversarial battle and argument, rather than one that prepares us for an intersubjective exchange. Following Sigmund Freud, Havi Carel suggests that this kind of argumentative or coercive philosophy is one that is unable to listen to the other, and that a philosophy that consistently cannot listen to the other is one that cannot listen to itself. This 'repetition compulsion' ties the philosopher in a kind of deadness: 'it is the end of listening that signifies the death of dialogue' (Carel 2004: 228).[18] The death of dialogue is a helpful way to consider the excesses of philosophy in its institutional form – where intersubjective exchange no longer has the ability to challenge instituted ways of doing philosophy. In light of this, it is worth examining how contemporary institutional forms pit colleagues against each other in competitive struggles for status, funding and prestige. In this context, the combination of our philosophical training and the competitive frame of our encounters weakens our ability to really listen attentively to those with whom we work.

Irigaray's insistence on listening and its role in a newly imagined philosophy, allows us to think through the heaviness and solidity of the body in relation to work and thought. In addition, it allows us to return philosophy to the domain of non-adversarial, intersubjective exchange – to philosophy as a love of wisdom and a way of life. In the Preface to *The Way of Love*, Irigaray indicates that her objective is to bring philosophy into the present, to 'suggest a concrete, living context and a present situation of dialogue' with the reader (xv). This present is not to be theorized or pointed towards, but is rather to be made; it is to exist *in* the work. To a large extent, this present will come into being through a proximate meeting with the other, or reader; an exchange that will involve both listening and listening-to in order to make something exist. A meaning that does not yet exist emerges out of this listening, and this is where Irigaray celebrates the values of intersubjectivity in her outline of what we can, with Le Dœuff, refer to as a future philosophy. Our ability to listen to the other thus emerges as a key to this intersubjective exchange or sharing that promises to bring such a future into the present 'now'. I am interested to think about Irigaray's work on this present, and its reliance on listening, in the context of my own work on reading, and to this end I explore what she has to say in her book.[19]

While in this chapter I focus on *The Way of Love,* Irigaray's earlier work, positioned between philosophy and psychoanalysis, provides another space from which to think questions of listening and reading. Indeed, I argue that her ethical orientation towards listening comes from her commitment to (and training in) psychoanalytic practice. I have mentioned this briefly in Chapter Three, where I argued that the idea of the unconscious provides Irigaray an attentive way of listening to the repressions and denials of philosophy (and psychoanalytic theory itself). In 'The Power of Discourse and the Subordination of the Feminine' (1975), Irigaray writes:

> This process of . . . rereading has always been a psychoanalytic undertaking . . . That is why we need to pay attention to the way the unconscious works in each philosophy, and perhaps in philosophy in general. We need *to listen* (psycho)analytically to its procedures of repression, to the structuration of language that shores up its repressions, separating the true from the false, the meaningful from the meaningless, and so forth.
> IRIGARAY 1985c: 75, emphasis added[20]

It is interesting that in another of her early essays, 'The Poverty of Psychoanalysis' (1977), Irigaray distinguishes the early psychoanalysts's ability to listen-to and be surprised by what they hear from the Lacanian analysts who know in advance what they will find. Freud and the early analysts proceed without knowing in advance what to expect and, because of this, they are still capable of *listening* and of being surprised. To rephrase Irigaray, we can say that Freud and the early analysts are still capable of wonder in relation to what they hear (Irigaray 1991: 118–32).[21]

Irigaray begins *The Way of Love* by suggesting that we lack a culture of the relation with the other (Irigaray 2002: ix). This statement is significant because it sets the scene for the encounter between self and other that she intends her work to initiate. While we integrate the other, we seldom encounter or meet the other. This robs us of our ability to speak to (and converse with) the other. What we need, she says, is a culture that makes possible a more expansive encounter with the other: '*The Way of Love* proposes ways to approach the other, to prepare a place of proximity: with the other in ourselves and between us. The book is in search of gestures, including gestures in language, which could help on the way to nearness, and in order to cultivate it' (Irigaray 2002: ix).

While we will return to the question of proximity and nearness later in the chapter, it is important at this stage to note that the approach that Irigaray mentions here implies a new and very different relation with language, one that favours the act of speech in the present (ix) over and above a codified or regulated speech. To this end, Irigaray enters into an intimate dialogue with the reader of *The Way of Love*, and it is at this moment that she introduces the idea of listening into her work. In effect, Irigaray asks us to suspend our conventional habits of reading – that is, to judge quickly and without adequate reflection – in order to allow an encounter between us to emerge:

> I ask the reader of the text to accept the invitation to listen-to in the present, to enter into dialogue with a thought, with a way of speaking, and to give up appropriating only a content of discourse in order to integrate it among knowledge already gained. I suggest to the reader, he or she, to let the speaking resonate in themselves and to pay attention to the transformation in their own speech. Reading *The Way of Love*, the reader enters in any case into an interweaving of exchanges ... To limit listening to the text as to a linear message or to codified rules of translation is thus impossible. It would be better to let oneself listen-to without first knowing where and how the reader will be led to correspond to what has been heard.
> IRIGARAY 2002: x

Listening-to comes before knowing. Irigaray clearly privileges listening – or listening-to – as a prerequisite to any encounter or meeting between self and other. Listening enables a meeting in the present, thus opening the possibility of a shared space and time from which dialogue might emerge.[22] This shared space and time does not, however, imply a shared meaning. Difference emerges from the 'interweaving of exchanges' between two – a listening that is not mediated by a single, shared meaning. Enabling this exchange is an attentive listening that orients us bodily towards the other; facing the other, open to communication.[23] Attentive listening provides the necessary interval or hesitation that makes it possible to avoid consuming or integrating the other.[24] The other's speech, for Irigaray, might best be thought of as poetic expression, and the listening that is called forth in response is, similarly, a poetic listening (or listening-to) that does more than simply receive and summarize what the other says. Listening, for Irigaray, is the poetic practice that allows us to suspend singular meaning in favour of an open and more ethical response:

> [S]uch an experience of speech . . . is related to an experience of listening-to. But here, once more, we would not have to listen to what comes back to us from a language or a world already there. We have to listen to the present speaking of the other in its irreducible difference with a view to the way through which we could correspond to it in faithfulness to ourselves.
> IRIGARAY 2002: xi

The focus on the present speaking of the other – the present of speech – is Irigaray's way of capturing the encounter between self and other that is occurring, rather than the encounter that may have already occurred. In the present act of speaking, meaning has not yet congealed into *a* meaning, and thus dialogue is still a possibility. By remaining in the present,[25] in the here and now, Irigaray's elemental philosophers listen to one another with attentive ears, each bringing their own subjectivity to the dialogue that ensues. This listening opens each to a meaning different from its own, and in this difference the rudiments of an effective intersubjectivity is born. In *The Way of Love*, intersubjectivity is framed in terms of a loving encounter that permits a dialogue in difference; a difference which, for Irigaray, rests upon a (prior) sexual difference (Irigaray 2002: xvii).

When, in the introduction to her book, Irigaray asks why only one meaning of the term philosophy has been retained – 'the love of wisdom' – she suggests that a first and perhaps more original meaning might be 'the wisdom of love' (Irigaray 2002: 1). From here she goes on to say that if philosophy as the wisdom of love has been forgotten that this might have something to do with the denial of sexual difference that philosophy effects. This denial goes hand-in-hand with a philosophy that constructs itself as the business of men and their knowledge:

> Why thus has the wisdom of love and, in part, wisdom itself, been forgotten? Due to a taste for games? The arrogance of whoever masters something or someone? A certain contempt for life and for the one who gives it? All that and many other things.

For example, the will or the need to continue to philosophize among men, conversing with men's methods about problems concerning men.

IRIGARAY 2002: 4

Irigaray suggests that the philosopher's speech privileges the object and that this results 'from a fear or an incapacity to enter into relation with the other' (Irigaray 2002: 5). Her very relational philosophy thus offers an alternative to this dominant tradition of philosophy in the West, and it helps us to think about how a desire to know operates within an institutional structure that has historically marginalized women.

Much of what Irigaray says in relation to speech and listening is offered as an alternative to what she sees as the shortcomings of the dominant mode of philosophy in the West (the present imperfect?). This mode of philosophy displays a historical disrespect for the other, and concerns itself more with a rationality that speaks *about* things or objects than one that would speak *with* others. This radical disconnect with the other fails to 'correspond to a human wisdom' and certainly does not lead the philosopher towards happiness (Irigaray 2002: 6–7). For Irigaray, this disconnect results in isolation, 'an exile surrounded by fortifications[26] where man takes shelter ... in language itself' (Irigaray 2002: 7). In entering this fortified world of a certain language and thought, man leaves behind him his significant others: 'the masculine subject has ... left behind him nature, woman, and even children. His culture amounts to a sort of monologue more and more extrapolated from the real, unfolding itself parallel to this real in order to carve it up and thus dominate it' (Irigaray 2002: 6). The language of this kind of philosophy is, accordingly, the language of isolation.

For Irigaray, a philosophy true to the present speech of the other is a philosophy that speaks *with* the other, rather than one that names what the other is. Such a philosophy moves towards the other in wonder,[27] without integrating the other into what it already knows. Language in this sense remains open and attentive, listening to the other's call. 'In this world otherwise lived and illuminated, the language of communication is different, and necessarily poetic: a language that creates, that safeguards its sensible qualities so as to address the body and the soul, a language that lives' (Irigaray 2002: 12).[28] Listening offers a privileged mode of access to the other's speech, and thus cultivating an attentive ear is the ethical task set forth for the elemental philosopher in the present. Distance and isolation give way to relation. 'From a solipsistic love, from a certain reason dominated by logical formalism, philosophy passes to a wisdom of love' (Irigaray 2002: 9). With love returned to its former place, philosophy is free to reinvent itself. 'Philosophy then finds itself radically modified, released from intangible essences and more or less magical ontologies. It may again use certain concepts and notions that had become obsolete or taboo' (Irigaray 2002: 10–11). It becomes (again) elemental, a philosophy worked in and through the body and speech. Indeed, philosophy becomes again instituting: a love of wisdom and a wisdom of love.

Irigaray's present of speech and the attentive listening that allows us to pause and encounter the other resonates strongly with my own desire to hesitate and suspend reading, to slow it down in order that we avoid hasty, definitive and closed readings. Her work on the relation between subjects and the attentive listening so crucial to any intersubjective domain offers me a valuable way of thinking further about reading in a more ethical mode. It allows me to take Irigaray's discussion of the present of speech and rephrase it in terms of the *present of reading* in order to explore listening as a way of thinking differently about how we read.

When Irigaray writes that 'talking to the other has become impossible' (Irigaray 2002: 15), she takes us back to the question of listening. She suggests that philosophers in the West have hardly wondered about the other or our ability to speak with the other. Philosophers have cared little about the relation between subjects, and this is most evident in our hesitance or inability to listen to the other in any profound way. We have developed a language more appropriate for objects than for our intersubjective exchanges of listening and speaking with others. As a consequence, we need to bypass or suspend this mode of philosophy in order to ground a relational bond with the other.[29] For Irigaray, this bond suggests a mode of sharing and exchange – an invitation we extend to the other: 'It is . . . a question of calling for an exchange by making already heard something of what is proposed in sharing, a question of opening some possibility or possibilities leading to sharing . . . It would be nothing but an invitation to share. Not yet closed upon some meaning, but opening from the one to the other – a between-two' (Irigaray 2002: 16).

Irigaray's notion of a 'between-two' focuses on the intersubjectivity and relation between self and other that she believes philosophy, in its more dominant Western mode, has forgotten. Her 'invitation to share' rests upon an attentive listening to the other, establishing the necessary attitude for an ethical reading to occur. Such sharing or exchange comes out of a patient attention to the other; one willing to slow down and to wait for meaning to emerge. In this slower, more attentive mode, philosophy actively listens: 'Is listening from then on changed? Less passive in a way, which is not to say less attentive. Would it be more polysensorial? It is more concerned about communicating with the other – and with oneself – than about discovering the exact and definitive sense of a being, to teach to the other' (Irigaray 2002: 24).[30]

There is a tendency in the West to associate listening – historically and culturally – with both femininity and receptivity – hence its ties, perhaps, with passivity – and Irigaray touches upon this complex association when she indicates that it is the feminine subject who often does the work of relation and communication between two (Irigaray 2002: 24). Is listening historically women's work?[31] If so, then philosophy as an institution in the West has done much to isolate itself from this domain.[32] The work of men, overdetermined as more conceptual and abstract, has historically and culturally been equated with vision and sight – the supposedly more active and intentional domains. Irigaray's call to open philosophy to the present speech of the other, to listen attentively to the other, is one way of bringing the feminine subject to the attention of philosophy and of elevating listening to the work that each of us needs to do.[33] For my own part, the idea of attentive listening reminds me that the philosophical work that we do always involves us bodily,[34] that it always engages us as embodied – and necessarily *sexually* embodied – beings.

Irigaray's call to listen to the other demands of us a receptivity, an openness that draws no prior conclusions concerning what the other might possibly say. It is a call to listen attentively to the other as wholly other, to turn towards the other while simultaneously turning inward in order 'to disappropriate the world' (Irigaray 2002: 36). What Irigaray seems to mean by this is that we each need to loosen the formalized and largely invisible hold that language has on us. We need to challenge a language that works invisibly to orient us in instrumental or appropriative ways towards things as objects, rather than towards others.[35] If successful, this challenge allows us to face the other: 'the subject then comes to a standstill in front of the irreducibility of the other' (Irigaray 2002: 36) and the creation of a new speaking and a new listening begins (Irigaray 2002: 35).[36] Irigaray speaks of a play between appropriation and disappropriation in language, suggesting that different situations call forth different gestures. She speaks, too, of the listening that accompanies these gestures, each specific to the kind of speech enacted:

> Whoever speaks is then confronted with a triple operation of appropriation. One of them concerns their relation to a language in which they are already situated, the other their relation to the world or to the object they have to name, the third their relation to the other. These operations are not practiced in the same direction with regard to appropriation and disappropriation. Sometimes it is a question of inquiring about language, of knowing how to use it, making it one's own with a certain detachment. Sometimes it is necessary rather to take an interest in what is to be designated in order to be able to name it in an appropriate way: a way that is proper to it. Sometimes it is a matter of being attentive to what is proper to the other without wanting to appropriate it. Listening in each of these cases is different, as is the relation to oneself that they presuppose.
> IRIGARAY 2002: 36–7

This turn inward towards the self in order to disappropriate ourselves of appropriative language is work still to be done: 'There does not yet exist an inward return of the subject beyond such a use of language, a return which would allow questioning another possible relation to language, thus modifying the status of language and of oneself as human' (Irigaray 2002: 38). Nomination remains dominant, and the verbal process of creating, linking, bridging and moving towards the other is similarly work yet to be done. 'The verb disappears, fades away, is forgotten in the substantive. Speaking then loses a large part of its creative function in the present' (Irigaray 2002: 39). This is why, for Irigaray, attention to the present of speaking is so crucial. To a large extent, our speech lacks the connectivity that bridges the space between ourselves and the other, and this connection can only be created by an attentive listening to the present of speech, to an awareness that the other speaks in a voice different from our own. Listening is thus crucial, as it makes it possible for us to slow down and to hear traces of a speech that eludes the dominant formalizations of our largely technological communication.[37] Listening allows us to 'discover again astonishment, contemplation, admiration, restored to the ingenuousness of the child' (Irigaray 2002: 45). In a state such as admiration, one is able to be-with the other, to listen-to the other, to exchange with the other, and to be co-present. Being-with the other requires a 'being-with where speech and thought agree to begin radically listening to and not to lie in wait for new denominations' (Irigaray 2002: 48). This radical listening lies at the heart of Irigaray's focus on the present of speech, and it speaks directly to the kind of attention I explore in the 'present of reading'.

Irigaray's radical listening emerges from what she refers to as the state of 'letting be' – a state 'that is open – in oneself and to the other – to a still unknown speech and silence' (Irigaray 2002: 50). One takes shelter in this refuge of letting-be,[38] and the space this provides allows us to work towards creating a dwelling with the other. Such a dwelling relies on the development of a new speech, new words and a new and radical listening, and Irigaray reminds us that these are all yet to be: 'These words do not yet exist, and they could never exist in a definitive way. It is in a new listening to oneself and to the other that they will be discovered, pronounced' (Irigaray 2002: 50).[39] Irigaray's radical listening ensures that the other becomes more than simply a resource for our own projects and preoccupations: 'The other is not at our disposal . . . the other must remain an other, someone different' (Irigaray 2002: 116). Being-with the other helps to protect the other and to lay the ground for a possible coexistence between two, a coexistence that renounces the 'imperatives born from the subjection of the one to the other' (Irigaray 2002: 117). Being-with comes from the refuge of letting-be.[40] This letting-be allows us to step back from our habitual relations with the world and the other, relations that place both world and other at our disposal, favouring making and productivity over connection and speech (Irigaray 2002: 123).[41] In this sense, letting-be provides the ground for a being-with that arises spontaneously with listening.[42]

For Irigaray, our task is the labour of listening; it is the work of being attentive to what the other has to say; the work of being attentive to the infinite possibility that the other is:

How, from then on, to speak about the place where thinking is at work? Listening to the present speaking of the other and to the response to provide assumes a new importance here. It is no longer a matter of receiving, alone or as a people, the gift of a constituted speech but of being attentive to what the other says, or wants to say, including in his, or her, silences.
IRIGARAY 2002: 161–2

This listening amounts to 'a fundamental dimension of thinking' (Irigaray 2002: 162), a dimension that receives without being passive. It involves a bodily dimension of perception that connects us with the other and with what the other is able to say. Listening helps to keep 'alive the astonishment, the questioning, the movement of thinking and of saying' (Irigaray 2002: 164), and this is, I think, how good reading works. The present of reading would then be something like a reading capable of a radical listening, a reading attentive to the presence, proximity and nearness of the other; a transformative openness that offers the world anew.[43] In this, the present of reading re-engages with the transformative potential of philosophy as a love of wisdom and a way of life.

Proximity and nearness characterize much of Irigaray's work on the ethics involved in listening. In *The Way of Love*, we have seen how she describes approaching the other in terms of the letting-be that advances slowly, step-by-step towards the other.[44] Such a slow advance safeguards 'the obscurity and the silence that the other remains for me [and] aids in discovering proximity' (Irigaray 2002: 151). In preparing a proximity between two, Irigaray reminds us to avoid a reduction of the near to 'the measure of a calculation' (Irigaray 2002: 20) as this would leave proximity without any interval or distance: 'Being placed side by side does not suffice for reaching nearness' (Irigaray 2002: 68). It becomes clear that, for Irigaray, attentive listening is a privileged mode of our nearness with the other. Attentive listening provides the possibility for proximity, and is the very possibility of an ethics between two subjects. In the absence of an attentive listening, something else must call us back to an ethical relation with the other. Something else must alert us to the obscurity that the other is: 'Some lightning strike of love will be necessary, some flash or illumination in order to reopen the path of proximity. But such fulguration is not easily shared and it would be less indispensable if the other was listened to every day in their difference' (Irigaray 2002: 158). Blinding love can hope to bring us within the vicinity of the other, reopening the path of proximity, but it is the everyday openness of listening that allows us to be really near.

In his work on a post-Heideggerian hermeneutics of nearness, Krzysztof Ziarek traces the fragile boundaries between poetry and philosophy in order to think through proximity and nearness as the possibility of ethics. Ziarek's mode of reading, and his attentiveness to the ethical dimensions of proximity, come close to Irigaray's work in certain respects, and I mention it here because listening plays a key role in his work as well. In *Inflected Language: Toward a Hermeneutics of Nearness* (1994) Ziarek distinguishes his hermeneutics of nearness from a hermeneutics of knowing, a desire to know:

> [It] does not intend to interpret, understand, or extract meaning but induces language to 'pay attention' to the inscriptions of otherness, of the unsaid, in what it brings to words . . . at stake is not a hermeneutics of knowing or understanding but one of listening, of *Seinlassen*, of letting come into one's own – efforts summed up by the enigmatic sense of nearing. It is a hermeneutics that, rather than simply reading and interpreting, attempts to deliver a message, to let it say itself, without covering or explaining away what remains baffling and other in it.
> ZIAREK 1994: 10

Ziarek's hermeneutics of listening and nearing remind us that the links we are drawing here between reading and attentive listening gesture towards (or summon up) a mode of reading that resists the institutional lure to 'extract meaning' (to mine), or to interpret and to understand in the shallowest sense of those terms. For Ziarek, the openness at work in proximity, nearness and listening is the fragile link with the other that attempts to deliver a message, a possibility that institutional modes of philosophical or theoretical reading unwittingly erase. He calls upon a rethought Heideggerian sense of listening (one specifically indebted to Levinas and Celan)[45] to enable a 'turn toward the other in an attitude of attentiveness' (Ziarek 1994: 185). Such attentiveness orients the specific kind of listening that Ziarek has in mind:

THE PRESENT OF READING: IRIGARAY'S ATTENTIVE LISTENING 121

> [W]hat is at stake in my questioning of listening . . . is an attempt to rethink it otherwise than in metaphysical terms . . . listening is no longer at the subject's discretion . . . Here listening, if it is still the right term to use, has a changed valency: it is a radical expositing, a displacement of the subject. The other is no longer an outside, already turned into the comfort and familiarity of the interior, but instead marks the impossibility of closure, of covering one's ears. In this context, it is not the subject, already constituted as itself, already speaking itself, that decides to listen. Rather, the subject, before it can speak, is already 'all ears'.
>
> ZIAREK 1994: 204, 205

What makes Ziarek's kind of listening ethical is precisely its proximity or nearness to the other, a nearness that nonetheless allows the foreignness of the other to be.[46] The changed valency of this listening displaces the familiarity of the subject's world with an attentiveness to what sounds obscure or strange in the other. This attentive listening provides another way of thinking about reading in ethical terms.

The present of reading: Friedrich Nietzsche and others

The attentive listening that Irigaray and Ziarek both champion in their work has much in common, I think, with Nietszche's slow reading and his habit to 'no longer write anything which does not reduce to despair every sort of man who is "in a hurry"' (Nietzsche 1982: 5).[47] Nietzsche's exhortation 'to go aside, to take time, to become still, to become slow' and to undertake 'delicate' and 'cautious' work that 'achieves nothing if it does not achieve it lento' (ibid.), resonates particularly with Irigaray's attentive listening that arises out of, and simultaneously depends upon, the process of 'letting-be'. 'Letting-be' opens 'a place of resource and of meditative gathering' (Irigaray 2002: 173).

Listening provides us with an attentive attitude towards the other, one that essentially slows us down; this involves a 'letting-be' that places us in no hurry to determine or impose meaning on the other's speech (or on what the other has to say). We pause in front of the other with an almost infinite patience, listening for the present of speech. We suspend our usual inclination to make a judgement, and to decide what the other has said. With this, we simultaneously suspend our immediate decision either to agree or disagree with what we imagine the other has said. Attentive listening is slow because it draws out the process of reading, helping us to register the habitual ways in which we rush to a judgement, without waiting patiently for the other's speech to fully emerge. The kind of patient listening I am referring to here is not, however, opposed to an impatient listening that imposes its own meaning on the other's speech. It is not simply a waiting for and listening to the authority of the other's speech. It is, more importantly, a refusal of this opposition. The patience of attentive listening involves an open exchange where listening is not mediated by shared understanding, but by difference. Attentive listening respects the other's difference.

If we listen carefully to Nietzsche, we learn that philosophy is (or should be) the art of learning to read slowly, to listen attentively to the other's voice. It is, as well, the art of learning how to frustrate an age of 'work' that hurries with 'indecent and perspiring haste' (ibid.). Philosophy slows us, allows us to pause, to consider and reconsider, to listen and engage, to sit patiently and wait for the work of thought to emerge. By reading slowly, or becoming slow, we pause long enough to establish a conversation or dialogue with the other. This has, of course, implications for how the institution of philosophy functions. In response to Nietzsche's way of thinking about what philosophy is, and how we should go about it, Lancelot Fletcher has the following to say about what it means to teach philosophy. Following Nietzsche's cue, he argues for a teaching of slow reading, coupling this with an emphasis on listening:

> The teaching of slow reading ... is an experiment that aims beyond itself. In itself the practice of slow reading intends to create occasions for joining in conversations with ... [others] ... to think with them and learn from them. But the aim of slow reading beyond itself is to consider whether the practice of slow reading might foster the recovery of a certain art of conversation: that in which listening holds at least equal place with speaking.
>
> FLETCHER 2007

Fletcher's way of thinking about what slow reading achieves, or hopes to achieve, reinforces the idea I have been developing here: that slow reading is a kind of listening that fosters conversation, dialogue and intersubjective exchange. In addition, his suggestion that slow reading and listening work to undo the habitual modes of reading[48] that we develop in everyday institutional practice[49] is important because it reminds us of the need to re-engage with the instituting moments of philosophy as a love of wisdom and a way of life. It reminds us, too, to resist the instituted structure of reading reduced purely to the dictates of a limited desire to know:

> The intention of the teaching of slow reading ... is to subvert the customary mode of reading. Its intention is to afford students (i.e. those who make us the gift of their listening) some critical access to their own interpretive activity ... to subvert this mode of reading we do first need to make students aware of what they are doing, aware of the fact that they are in the habit of imposing their own meanings on the text. ...
> the teaching of slow reading is intended to give students some critical access to their own interpretive activity – their own habit of manufacturing meanings. However, this is not the end of slow reading. It is only the beginning ... The purpose of the teaching of slow reading is to allow us to enter into conversations with ... authors whose distinction is that they afford us the opportunity to think things that are worthy of thought.
> FLETCHER 2007[50]

By entering into conversations with authors who afford us the opportunity to think things worthy of thought, Fletcher points us towards the opportunities to encounter the complexity and intensity that we have seen in Hans Ulrich Gumbrecht's work on pedagogy in the Introduction. Teaching slow reading means providing our students with experiences that can transform their often instrumental relations with the world around them. By encouraging our students to listen attentively to what they read, we offer them opportunities to slow their habitual tendencies to read without regard for the intricate possibilities that any text contains. This provides a slowing down that helps each of us to suspend judgement in order to open to the possibility of entering into a conversation with what we read. The slow reading that emerges from this kind of listening begins precisely with the process of becoming slow, of slowing, not with reading itself:

> Slow reading doesn't start with reading. When slow reading begins, you are already reading. You have been reading for a long time. Slow reading starts, not with reading but with slowing. But even that is not quite right. It would be more accurate to say that slow reading starts with stopping, with turning around . . . If one could begin slow reading the first lesson would be: Just be present to the words on the page. Allow the words to simply BE there.
>
> FLETCHER 2007

Fletcher's comments provide, I think, a useful bridge (an arc) between Nietzsche's work on reading slowly and Irigaray's attention to listening. By thinking of reading in terms of pedagogy, he focuses our discussion towards the practical and everyday activities of how we teach (by example) others to read and to respond. This fits well with what Irigaray has written in her own work on pedagogy, where she draws connections between teaching and a careful, attentive listening: 'Western tradition is founded on looking-at rather than on listening-to. In our tradition, listening is at the service of looking, especially with regard to teaching . . . Now this way of teaching is no longer appropriate to our times' (Irigaray 2008: 231). In an effort to transform this relation, Irigaray calls for a teaching that listens-to the other.[51] Such a listening would avoid grasping or containing the other in order to open to the infinite strangeness the other is. This teaching-as-listening would not 'amount to grasping something in order to integrate and order it into our own world, but to opening one's own world to something or someone external and strange to it. Listening-to is a way of opening ourselves to the other and of welcoming this other, its truth and its world as different from us, from ours' (Irigaray 2008: 232). Listening-to preserves the singularity of teacher and of student – or, we might say, of reader and of text – while simultaneously enabling their being-in-relation. Listening-to is both the present of teaching and the present of reading, the keeping open of that dimension between the two. For Irigaray, listening-to allows us to protect our teaching (and our reading) from resentment and revenge, both of which emerge out of our refusal to open ourselves to the other, to welcome the other and to awaken them 'to their present time' (Irigaray 2008: 233).

Resentment, too, thrives under conditions of high time pressure, where teaching is seen to limit the productive work of research and publication. Pitting teaching against research is one of the ways the institution structures resentment, and Simon Critchley's comments in the Introduction are pertinent here, too. Reclaiming pleasure and joy in teaching is one substantial way that we can, as teachers of philosophy, reclaim the instituting moments of philosophy as a love of wisdom and a way of life. In this sense, listening-to fulfils the task of teaching which is, in part, a withdrawing in order that the other be and discover his or her own path.[52] Only in this way, Irigaray claims, can we come close to rethinking what teaching is and what teaching can do: what philosophy is and what philosophy can do:

> [In listening-to and the teaching this calls forth] authority can exist, an authority that results from our becoming human in a more accomplished way. An authority that imposes nothing if not a certain respect, attention and questioning. An authority that can awaken the other(s) to a beyond with respect to their present state and open a way to the future. An authority that calls the other to a transformation of himself or herself, to a becoming with the accomplishment of humanity in view. An authority that does not amount to the exercise of a power that is more or less repressive, but is teaching itself.
> IRIGARAY 2008: 240

This kind of authority reconceived is what is ultimately at stake in any ethical discussion of what it means to do philosophy today.[53] Here Irigaray gestures towards a future philosophy, one that engages in and with the institution in order that pedagogy – our relation with our students – be the ethical centre of a revival of the instituting moments in philosophy that pursue a love of wisdom and a wisdom of love. Such a revival would, of course, be something other than a romantic return to a past age. Rather, it would look towards the future by revising how philosophy can function within the contemporary institution in new and provocative ways.

CHAPTER FIVE

Romance and Authenticity: Beauvoir's Lesson in Reading

> *I began with certainty . . . I ended in doubt, both as to who she was &, even more shockingly, as to who I was.*
> RICHARD FLANAGAN, *GOULD'S BOOK OF FISH*: 307

[She] tries to see with his eyes; she reads the books he reads.[1]

Simone de Beauvoir's distinction between romantic and authentic love in *The Second Sex* (*TSS*) (1949) allows us to continue our coupling of slow reading and love, begun with our earlier work on Irigaray. Not surprisingly, Beauvoir's discussion of love serves a different purpose to Irigaray's, and it is this that allows us to approach the question of reading from an alternative perspective. By distinguishing two types of love, Beauvoir helps us to think of two different approaches to reading and how these are once both opposed and interconnected.[2] By thinking of reading in these terms, we can chart the complex ways in which reading can both resist and reinforce the institution.

By accepting Beauvoir's account of romantic love as a flawed, dependent mode of being, and her suggestion that an authentic love – one that engages maturely with the other – is possible, we can take the risk of thinking of reading in these terms. I argue that a romantic reading demonstrates an immature dependence in relation to the (other) text, or an equally immature expectation of completeness in relation to the text; whereas an authentic reading offers the possibility of a mature and open-ended approach. Such a reading accepts both the text's possibilities and its limitations, leading us towards an open and ongoing reading. Here, I maintain that Beauvoir's notion of authentic love can be reworked in order to develop the idea of an authentic reading as an ethical encounter. Reading Beauvoir's work in the light of this discussion raises the question of what kind of reader she is. Specifically, it allows us to ask how Beauvoir reads Sartre – the Sartre of *Being and Nothingness*. I argue that Michèle Le Dœuff's immensely influential reading of Beauvoir's reading of Sartre (in terms of an operative philosophy) can be rethought in terms of Beauvoir's own categories of romance and authenticity, and it is in this sense that we can think of Beauvoir's work on love as a lesson in what it means to read.

Romantic and authentic love

I am going to take Beauvoir's work on 'The Woman in Love' as my starting point. This chapter appears in Part VI (Justifications) of Book Two in *TSS*. It is here that Beauvoir elaborates her discussion of love and interestingly, she does so by relying quite heavily upon literary and popular cultural references. Although the discussion is punctuated by sporadic references to philosophers (writers) such as Nietzsche and Sartre, the chapter is full of literary passages from Colette, Katherine Mansfield, Cécile Sauvage, Isadora Duncan, Madame d'Agoult, Julie de Lespinasse and Violette Leduc. The chapter focuses on love, and yet this is only part of Beauvoir's exploration of human relationships. Indeed, a good part of Book Two of *TSS* is oriented towards relations in so far as they elucidate the question of woman's life today. Chapters such as 'The Young Girl', 'Sexual Initiation', 'The Lesbian', and 'The Married Woman' precede Beauvoir's chapter on 'The Woman in Love', laying a ground of 'formation' and 'situation' for her observations on love. As I have already suggested, there are two dominant forms of love that emerge throughout Beauvoir's discussions in this chapter. Romantic love, a deeply flawed and somewhat infantile mode of being, where the self is reduced to a slave-like dependence, is discussed in Beauvoir's work alongside authentic love, a potential mode of being in which one maturely and independently engages with another.

For Beauvoir, the most important thing about romantic love is that it is a dependent relation, one in which the self is subject *to* the other. In 'The Woman in Love', she analyses the specific situation of women in this regard, beginning with a passage from Friedrich Nietzsche's *The Gay Science* on the difference between men and women in relation to love:[3]

> The single word love in fact signifies two different things for man and woman. What woman understands by love is clear enough: it is not only devotion, it is a total gift of her body and soul, without reservation, without regard for anything whatever. This unconditional nature of her love is what makes it a *faith*, the only one she has. As for man, if he loves a woman, what he *wants* is that love from her; he is in consequence far from postulating the same sentiment for himself as for woman; if there should be men who also felt that desire for complete abandonment, upon my word, they would not be men.
> FRIEDRICH NIETZSCHE, *The Gay Science*,
> cited in *TSS*: 652

Nietzsche's musings on what we might refer to as the gendered nature of love serve as an ambiguous frame to Beauvoir's following discussion. From here, she goes on to develop an account of romantic love that emphasizes the dangers and moral wrong of assuming a dependent love in relation to a transcendent other. In this account, she depicts romantic love as the type of love that robs us of our transcendence, our sense of self and subjectivity. Ironically, romantic love robs us of our transcendence precisely through the lure or *promise* of transcendence. Beauvoir writes that '[s]hut up in the sphere of the relative, destined to the male from childhood, habituated to seeing in him a superb being whom she cannot possibly equal, the woman who has not repressed her claim to humanity will dream of transcending her being towards one of those superior beings, of *amalgamating* herself with the sovereign subject' (*TSS*: 653, emphasis added).[4] The result of this search for transcendence through romantic love, Beauvoir argues, is that despite our conscious intentions we are robbed of our freedom to live and think independently of a despotic other. Accordingly, the power of romantic love is, she claims, the power to seduce us away from ourselves towards the other as centre of all value, meaning, and sense:[5]

The measure of values, the truth of the world, are in his consciousness; hence it is not enough to serve him. The woman in love tries to see with his eyes; she reads the books he reads, prefers the pictures and the music he prefers; she is interested only in the landscapes she sees with him, in the ideas that come from him; she adopts his friendships, his enmities, his opinions; when she questions herself, it is his reply she tries to hear; she wants to have in her lungs the air he has already breathed; the fruits and flowers that do not come from his hands have no taste and no fragrance. Her idea of location in space, even, is upset: the center of the world is no longer the place where she is, but that occupied by her lover; all roads lead to his home and from it. She uses his words, mimics[6] his gestures, acquires his eccentricities and his tics.

TSS: 663[7]

Although we will have occasion to return to this important passage later in the chapter, I should say that what we are referring to here as 'romantic love' is the love Beauvoir associates with the woman *in* love: *l'amoureuse*.[8] From the outset, we need to distinguish what Beauvoir is saying here about romantic love (as a one-sided love that disables and reduces the woman) from the reciprocated experience of loving passionately or burning with (mutual) desire. The term 'romantic' in this context speaks to the experience of women trapped in the clutches of a kind of love that cripples. Of course, this suggests that we need to ask questions about the various relations between 'romantic love' and 'being in love' in the popular imagination.[9]

Beauvoir's romantic love seems in no sense positive. Her depiction throughout 'The Woman in Love' suggests a love that stands in place of a life of one's own. At times, Beauvoir suggests that romantic love is an almost inevitable response to the restrictions placed on women's lives: 'No other aim in life which seemed worthwhile was open to them, love was their only way out' (*TSS*: 655). Yet this is coupled with an argument that depicts romantic love as the too-easy alternative to a life of responsibility, a 'choice' that women make through laziness and despondency, rather than a reality that is imposed: 'It is agonizing for a woman to assume responsibility for her life … [I]t is woman's misfortune to be surrounded by almost irresistible temptations; everything incites her to follow the easy slopes; instead of being invited to fight her way up, she is told that she has only to let herself slide and she will attain paradises of enchantment' (*TSS*: 655).[10] These two aspects of romantic love circulate throughout Beauvoir's work, and this is perhaps one of the strengths of her analysis. She is sensitive to the complex interplay between what a woman chooses and what she has internalized. In any case, one of Beauvoir's important tasks in this chapter is to lay bare the pitfalls of a love that ends up reducing woman to passive object status.

Much of what Beauvoir has to say about romantic love refers to the unfortunate infantilism of women. In fact, her discussion of romantic love as in part woman's desire to reconstruct a situation of adult protection, anticipates Irigaray's later important work on women and *déréliction* – the state of abandonment where women find themselves outside the symbolic order, devoid of (maternal) protection. Here the unsymbolized bond between mother and daughter results in the daughter's incessant quest to fill herself up with love and things in the place of a nourishing woman-to-woman sociality.[11] Beauvoir's way of thinking about this state is to point to the existential implications of this infantilism: 'What she wants to recover is a roof over her head, walls that prevent her from feeling her abandonment in the wide world, authority that protects her against her liberty. This childish drama haunts the love of many women . . . many women suffer in becoming adults' (*TSS*: 655). Romantic love, seen from this perspective, is not so much a choice, says Beauvoir, as a necessity (*TSS*: 658); a necessity that has woman 'attain supreme existence through losing [herself] in the other' (*TSS*: 659).[12]

Fear and servility overwhelmingly characterize the life of dependency that Beauvoir equates with romantic love: 'For woman, love is a supreme effort to survive by accepting the dependence to which she is condemned; but even with consent a life of dependency can be lived only in fear and servility' (*TSS*: 678).[13] For Beauvoir, as we have seen, this kind of love leads to a deeply flawed mode of being, an inauthentic reduction of self to object status. Romantic love repeats an infantile dependence or uncritical devotion[14] and seeks to avoid the difficulty of human responsibility.[15] It echoes and mimics the superiority of the other in a servile and demeaning way. 'It is', Beauvoir writes, 'one of the loving woman's misfortunes to find that her very love disfigures her, destroys her; she is nothing more than this slave, this servant, this too ready mirror,[16] this too faithful echo' (*TSS*: 675).[17]

As an alternative to the servile and disfiguring character of romantic love, Beauvoir provides us with glimpses of her vision of genuine or authentic love.[18] Her account of this kind of love can be understood, at least in part, as her response to the problem of Jean-Paul Sartre's rather pessimistic depiction of human relations.[19] Sartre's account of self–other relations (Sartre 1956: 221–430) famously depicts 'man's' desire to be 'god' – the *subject-for-itself* or pure transcendence – as a desire that places him in inevitable conflict with others, in amorous contexts and more generally.[20] In another of her works, *The Ethics of Ambiguity* (*TEOA*) (Beauvoir 1962),[21] Beauvoir offers what might be read as a solution to the problem of Sartre's existential combat.[22] She reworks his notion of inevitable conflict between self and other towards a notion of generosity and love.[23] While (diplomatically?) accepting Sartre's negative accounts, she suggests that this is only a 'partial truth', and by doing so offers what is arguably a more balanced and certainly more optimistic account of human love.[24] Beauvoir's discussion of *being-in-relation-with-others* and *being-for-others* provides us with an account that suggests that, while we cannot escape the pain of knowing that we can never be God, we can – and this is important – discover the joy of becoming human and the experiences of intimacy that this entails (Hansen 1979: 341). Indeed, we can strive towards a reciprocal relation between self and other (subject and object) and this seems to be what she means by the terms 'genuine' or 'authentic' love. In so striving, our existence ceases to be Sartre's 'useless passion' and becomes, instead, a 'positive existence'.[25] We move from an immature desire to imitate or be the other (God) towards a process of identification that allows for differentiation. Returning to *TSS*, we see that Beauvoir is quite specific about the reciprocity that love, in general, entails:

> It is possible to rise above this conflict [between self and other] if each individual freely recognizes the other, each regarding himself and the other simultaneously as object and as subject in a reciprocal manner. But friendship and generosity, which alone permit in actuality this recognition of free beings, are not facile virtues; they are assuredly man's highest achievement, and through that achievement he is to be found in his true nature.[26]

For Beauvoir, this reciprocal relation with the other is no easy task. And yet it is a crucial one, for it defines the very outline of our human being, the essentially ambiguous nature of our humanity, caught as we are between subject and object in relation to others in our world.[27] One of the lessons we are to learn is that we must respect the subjectivity of the other who ultimately escapes us. We must love the other in his or her otherness, we must renounce a desire to possess the other and, significantly, we must simultaneously recognize the other as a being of limitations.[28]

While objectification of the other is inevitable (and a total lack of it arguably undesirable), Beauvoir suggests we need to balance this tendency towards the other by treating him or her as he or she is – *both* subject *and* object. 'There is nothing wrong, then, in an objectification of the other, as long as [one] realizes that the other is more than the object he [or she] appears to be . . . The objectification which is wrong is that which seeks to treat [others] *wholly* as objects' (Hansen 1979: 342). In 'Eye for Eye', Beauvoir writes: 'There is no scandal [in the tendency to objectify] until the moment that a man treats his fellows as objects, when by torture, humiliation, slavery, and murder, he denies them their human existence' (Beauvoir 2004: 247).

Looking in the opposite direction, Beauvoir cautions that it is similarly important not to fall into the trap of ascribing a pure subjectivity to the other's being; that is, to see the other 'only in terms of his or her freedom or transcendence, and not to see his or her limitations'. It is wrong (morally, ethically), she suggests, to treat the other as God.[29] Indeed, this trap of ascribing a pure or transcendent subjectivity to the other is precisely the tendency of romantic love. It is arguably the moral or ethical fault that founds romantic love.

Accordingly, Beauvoir offers what Linda Hansen has described as two complementary aspects of authentic love, and these speak to the essential interrelatedness of our subjectivity and objectivity.[30] In the first instance, this authentic love involves our ability to recognize the other as a subjectivity or freedom. In 'Personal Freedom and Others' – in *TEOA* – Beauvoir characterizes this ability in terms that emphasize the distance between ourselves and the other. I think, following Emmanuel Levinas, that her account points towards the infinite nature of the other – towards desire:

> It is only as something strange, forbidden, as something free, that the Other is revealed as an Other. And to love him genuinely is to

love him in his otherness and in that freedom by which he escapes. Love is then renunciation of all possession, of all confusion. One renounces being in order that there may be that being which one is not. Such generosity, moreover, can not be experienced on behalf of any object whatsoever. One can not love a pure thing in its independence and its separation, for the thing does not have positive independence.

BEAUVOIR 'Personal Freedom and Others' in *TEOA*: 67

Authentic or genuine love welcomes the strangeness of the other. Indeed, it exists in and through this strangeness. This independent love denounces possession and the demeaning relations that possession entails. There is a generosity that emerges from this encounter with the strangeness of the other, and this generosity finds further expression in the closing pages to Beauvoir's discussion of 'The Woman in Love'. Here Beauvoir thinks of generosity in terms of the gift of self I make to the other in recognition of our mutual freedoms:

> Genuine love ought to be founded on the mutual recognition of two liberties; the lovers would then experience themselves both as self and as other: neither would give up transcendence, neither would be mutilated; together they would manifest values and aims in the world. For the one and the other, love would be revelation of self by the gift of self and enrichment of the world.
>
> *TSS*: 677[31]

The second aspect of authentic love speaks to the contingency or situation of the other. Beauvoir contends that while encountering the other in his or her strangeness, we ought simultaneously to recognize the other as one *in* situation, as a grounded and limited human being. This 'being-in-situation' arguably brings us closer to – or more proximate with – the other, to some extent undoing the strangeness that is so crucial to an ethical or authentic love. If there is a paradox here, it is the paradox – or ambiguity – of genuine love; the essential interrelatedness of subjectivity and objectivity in the intimate domain. Beauvoir writes: 'An authentic love should accept the contingency of the other with all his idiosyncrasies, his limitations, and his basic gratuitousness. It would not pretend to be a mode of salvation, but a human interrelation' (*TSS*: 664).[32] To see the other as limited – as something more finite than the strange subjectivity and freedom that escapes all our attempts to possess it – is to see the other in what Hansen refers to as his or her objectivity:

> [O]ne must see in the other an object, a being who does exist in a situation. The objectivity of the other is a concrete way for one to see the other as limited, as a finite being. It is crucial to human relationships that man understands that, unless he sees the other in his objectivity, he will not be able to truly appreciate the other's subjectivity. Man's being is finite; his freedom cannot then be understood apart from the situation in and through which it is expressed.
>
> HANSEN 1979: 343

Accordingly, the reciprocity and mutual recognition that characterize Beauvoir's descriptions of authentic love move between subject and object, between self and other, in such a way as to empower us rather than to diminish us. It is then perhaps not so surprising to find Beauvoir concluding 'The Woman in Love' with a powerful coupling of love with life. She writes: 'On the day when it will be possible for woman to love not in her weakness but in her strength, not to escape herself but to find herself, not to abase herself but to assert herself – on that day love will become for her, as for man, a source of life and not of mortal danger' (*TSS*: 679).

Reading and love

Now that we have looked at Beauvoir's categories of romantic and authentic love – categories we may connect with Le Dœuff's distinctions between identification and separation, and fidelity and infidelity – I want to explore exactly how we can use these terms to help us think about our approaches to reading. Let us begin with a notion of romantic reading. What initially strikes me about romantic reading is that it appears in opposition to the kind of reductive reading I have explored in Chapter Two. There I suggested that reductive readings aggressively, impatiently and somewhat prematurely close off the possibilities of the text. Such readings work to reduce the text to a relatively simple statement or position, a position that can ultimately be rejected and left behind. In effect, these readings work to caricature the text in order to make it easy to dismiss.[33] In contrast to reductive readings, the problem with romantic reading is that it demonstrates a high degree of deference to the text. Romantic reading performs an immature dependence in relation to the text or an equally immature expectation of completeness in relation to the text it reads – an overestimation of what the text can realistically achieve. Here the reader operates as a faithful (or even passive) servant in relation to the dominance of the (master) text. It is this notion of romantic reading – as dependent and deferential – that I shall consider in what follows, but it would be interesting in the future to think through the ways in which these two seemingly antagonistic tendencies – reduction and deference – actually work together in complex ways in certain contexts.[34] It is not altogether clear to me that aggressive reduction and excessive deference are in fact oppositional terms. (No doubt psychoanalysts would have much to say on this point.)

Attentive to Beauvoir's account of the dangers of romantic love, my argument is that a reading characterized as romantic risks an uncritical or blind devotion, without reservation, and a faith that too readily becomes a fidelity;[35] an uncritical confusion/fusion of self with text; and a displacement and a disfiguring that enslaves the self in a servile relation with the text. Here as reader we are subject *to* the text, incapable – or unwilling – to think independently of it. Through the lure or false promise of transcendence, the text robs us of our own independence and subjectivity – our own voice. Such a deferential reading positions us in a dependent relation with the other/text.[36] It reduces us to an infantile dependence upon the text – an inauthentic reduction of self to mute object status. In psychoanalytic terms we might say that an uncritical, devotional reading *forecloses* any sense of lack in the other/text and, in doing so, sets up an expectation of completeness, an overestimation the text can never fulfil. As a consequence of such devotion (and fusion) we avoid the responsibility of a distance that allows us to ethically engage the text, to face the text while facing the difficult process of separating from it, in order to experience it anew. To paraphrase Beauvoir: one of the romantic reader's misfortunes is to find that our love for the text disfigures us, destroys us; we are nothing more than this slave, this servant, this too ready mirror, this too faithful echo.

On the other hand, an authentic reading – and I am still following Beauvoir here – would offer a somewhat different approach. As an alternative to this particular depiction of romantic reading, I propose authentic reading as one offering the possibility of a mature and more reflexive approach to the other/text; that is, one that reads in terms of both the subjectivity *and* the objectivity that Beauvoir identifies – the text's infinite possibilities as well as its limitations. An authentic or genuine reading would (maturely, confidently) regard the text as other and independent, and yet it would see itself as connected to and in relation with what it reads in significant ways. It would not confuse the text with itself, and yet it would nonetheless be capable of acknowledging its relations with the text. It would not simply repeat or paraphrase the text.[37] It would open generously towards the text, secure that it would not become the text or fuse with it. An authentic reading would take pleasure in encountering the text as something strange, forbidden, as something free and revealed as other. It would renounce possession (total comprehension?) in order that the text remain open to future or contrary readings. An authentic reading would assume the contingency of the text, its lacks and limitations, its ground.[38] It would not treat the text as authority or God. An authentic reading would attempt to engage (realistically) with what the text knows, and what it does not or cannot know; that is, its failures, shortcomings and oversights.[39] While all readings engage in some manner or other with the text, an authentic reading would differ by not being alienated from its own process; that is, by not falling prey to mystifications concerning its relations with the text. An authentic reading would celebrate the ambiguity of the text, revel in its multiple meanings and wonder at its ability to effortlessly escape us.[40] It would be a reading that would accept both the text's possibilities and its limitations, leading us towards open and repeated readings (rereadings). An authentic reading might, then, provisionally be characterized as an ethical reading, an ethical encounter with the text – ethics in this instance denoting something like mature expectation, appraisal or encounter. To paraphrase Beauvoir: it is only as something strange, forbidden, as something free, that the text is revealed as other. And to read it genuinely is to read it in its otherness and in that freedom by which it escapes us. Reading is then renunciation of all possession, of all coincidence. We renounce total comprehension in order that there be meaning that escapes our sometimes neurotic desire to 'know'. Such is the generosity of an authentic reading.

Authentic reading highlights the productive context of one's own reading practice. In this it differs from a tendency in romantic reading to subordinate one's own reading to the authority of the text. In effect, romantic reading is the disciple's denial of self that simultaneously reifies the author as master/text. In this, romantic reading is an avoidance of ethics, rather than an engagement with it. What makes a reading ethical is the risk it takes in differentiating itself from what it reads – the kind of gracious ingratitude that comes from really engaging with the provocations of the text.

Walter Benjamin's work on aura provides another way of thinking about what distinguishes a romantic from an authentic reading. In his essay on Baudelaire, Benjamin writes:

> [L]ooking at someone carries the implicit expectation that our look will be returned by the object of our gaze. Where this expectation is met (which, in the case of thought processes, can apply equally to the look of the eye of the mind and to a glance pure and simple), there is an experience of the aura to the fullest extent. 'Perceptibility', as Novalis puts it, 'is a kind of attentiveness'. The perceptibility he has in mind is none other than that of aura. Experience of the aura thus rests on the transposition of a response common in human relationships to the relationship between the inanimate or natural object and man. The person we look at, or who feels he is looked at, looks at us in turn. To perceive the aura of an object we look at means to invest it with the ability to look at us in return.
> BENJAMIN 1969: 188

Following Novalis, Benjamin couples aura with 'a kind of attentiveness' that reaches towards the other precisely by looking back or returning the other's gaze. For him, the auratic quality of a work of art, poetry or reading can be thought in terms of its ability to return our gaze. We note, here, the 'transposition of a response common in human relationships to the relationship between the inanimate or natural object and man' or between our reading and the text. Where the expectation of the other returning our gaze is met, Benjamin confirms that 'there is an experience of the aura to the fullest extent' (Benjamin 1969: 188). This auratic quality of an open and attentive orientation towards the other, one that looks back to the other, is characterized in Benjamin's work simultaneously as a gesture of reaching towards. I like to think of this auratic quality in Benjamin's thought as a form of reading – an auratic reading which involves a kind of attentiveness that is capable of hovering between affirmation and critique, temporarily suspending the critical gesture of a purely objective interpretation. This suspension is what authentic reading achieves. The 'looking back' of auratic reading provides us with an ethical space that affords us the distance to contemplate the world and the other in wonder. From this perspective, romantic reading is one that does not have the capacity to look back or to return the gaze of what it reads. Perhaps, more correctly, a romantic reading is one that is not yet able to do so. An authentic reading, on the other hand, has both the distance and maturity (are they the same thing?) to be able to look back – to confidently, though not aggressively, return the gaze. The quality of attention inherent in this looking back is something the authentic reading develops *over time*. Authenticity benefits from the passage of time that opportunities to reread provide. 'Looking back' is another way of thinking about the authenticity that Pierre Hadot identifies when he refers to the profound transformation sought by the Hellenistic and Roman philosophers. The early philosophers undertook a series of spiritual exercises that oriented philosophy towards a way of living and an art of life. This philosophical activity 'raise[d] the individual from an inauthentic condition of life, darkened by unconsciousness and harassed by worry, to an authentic state of life, in which he attain[ed] self-consciousness, an exact vision of the world, inner peace, and freedom'. The spiritual exercises that Hadot explores were aimed towards 'a profound transformation of the individual's mode of seeing and being' (Hadot 1995: 83). With a little help, we can think of slow reading as the impetus to rereading that acts as a modern-day spiritual exercise bringing about a profound transformation from romantic to authentic reading. A slow, careful, and open attentiveness to reading works therapeutically to transform the seeing and being of romantic love into the looking back of the authentic relation. As Hadot points out, the early philosophers understood that it was not easy to undergo such a transformation and this is precisely why the spiritual exercises were undertaken. 'Little by little, [slowly] they make possible the indispensable metamorphosis of our inner self' (Hadot 1995: 83).[41]

It seems to me that the exercise or practice of authentic reading that I am developing from Beauvoir's description of authentic love has something in common with the practice of discernment that Teresa Brennan explores in *The Transmission of Affect* (2004). Discernment, Brennan explains, comes from the meditative tradition in philosophy. It involves a sustained attention that one develops over time. Brennan refers to the effects of discernment in terms of the 'other I', a self not dominated by the anxieties or self-interest of the ego; a part of the self open to the possibility of a loving (unguarded) relation with the other and the world. (We will return to the question of discernment in the conclusion to this work.)

What I have briefly outlined here is that Beauvoir's descriptions of love – romantic and authentic – offer us broad ways of characterizing the approaches to reading many of us either consciously or unconsciously adopt. In this light, authentic reading offers tentative steps towards a practice of reading I would like to term 'ethical': one embodying an open and mature encounter with the text. As such, authentic love holds the promise of a more mature and more ethical encounter with what we choose both to read and reread.[42] We might be tempted from the previous discussion to infer that romantic love – being predominantly the domain of women in a patriarchal context – suggests that romantic reading is a predominantly feminine mode. And while there would be good reason to think that this femininity referred solely to women, I want to suggest that when it comes to reading, the romantic tendency is one that remains perhaps all too familiar to men and women alike. Feminine it may be, but a femininity that is readily adopted by readers of any sex. Simply put, romantic reading is the type of reading that remains slavishly attached to the truth, brilliance (or wrongness) of the text.

While I have suggested that Beauvoir does not herself connect the question of reading with love, there is a sense in which this is not entirely true. In her discussion of male writers, in Book One of *TSS*, Beauvoir explores the way that the myth of woman operates in the work of the writers Montherlant, Lawrence, Claudel, Breton and Stendhal. The question of reading is by no means the focus of her discussion here, which is, ostensibly, writing. And yet I think that what Beauvoir has to say nonetheless has relevance to our discussion. Beauvoir's observations on how these male authors write about women and about love reveals something about their own abilities to read – in this case, their abilities to 'read' women.

Beauvoir's discussion of these particular male authors reveals a series of repetitive instances of woman as myth. She concludes that in almost all cases these men construct women in narrow and reductive terms; that is, they construct women characters through a masculine myth of 'woman' or 'femininity'. This entails positioning woman as other to man. This is not always carried out in the same manner; each of these writers takes a different path, but each inevitably falls prey to the myth of woman, and in so doing loses real women, and the possibility of imagining a real love between men and women in the process. The only exception to this is Stendhal, who Beauvoir praises for being the 'tender friend of woman' who refuses 'to believe in the feminine mystery, precisely because he loves them as they really are' (*TSS*: 268).

In effect, Beauvoir claims – though not in these words – that Stendhal has the ability to 'read' women in a manner that is more authentic (and ethical) than other male writers because he faces them in a proximate and open way. 'What he likes in them is what today we call their authenticity: that is the common trait in all the women he loved or lovingly invented; all are free and true beings' (*TSS*: 271). Stendhal's women are not mythical creatures of passivity and self-sacrifice. They do not embody the mystery of religious or poetic 'Truths'. They do not lose themselves in familial or passionate devotion. They are not passive possessions or immanent flesh. They exist. And Stendhal embraces them in their very existence. Stendhal's women are real. They have strengths and they have weaknesses. And because he accepts their very realness, Stendhal escapes the masculine tendency to 'read' and thus write women as (mythical) other. Stendhal's strength, Beauvoir concludes, comes from his ability to see through the nonsense (and indeed, violence) of the romantic *myth* of woman,[43] a myth that in one way or another circulates in the work of the other writers whom Beauvoir judges so critically.[44] Because Stendhal refuses to be party to this myth, Beauvoir claims that he is able to figure love differently – as an authentic engagement between two – man and woman both subjects together. 'Test, reward, judge, friend – woman truly is in Stendhal what Hegel was for a moment tempted to make of her: that other consciousness which in reciprocal recognition gives to the other subject the same truth that she receives from him. Two who know each other in love make a happy couple' (*TSS*: 277). In what sense, then, might we say that Stendhal's work opens towards an ethical attitude? For Beauvoir, the answer to this question is in the very fact that he refuses to reduce the other either to an absolute Other or to an object of his own subjective being. Ethics here is thus understood in entirely existential terms.

Authenticity as ethics?

Beauvoir's discussion of authenticity has led me to suggest provisionally that an authentic reading is also an ethical one. But on what grounds do I make this claim? In what sense might we say that authenticity and ethics meet? It seems to me that Beauovoir's work answers this question. If we return to *TEOA* we find her descriptions of the moral attitudes or characters that fall short of what she herself considers to be ethical behaviour. Beauvoir describes the serious man, the nihilist, the adventurer, the passionate man and the aesthete, and claims that in complex ways each fails to engage ethically with his world. Although she presents a detailed discussion that is, at least in part, a defence of existentialism against those claims that it has no ethics – that it offers no concrete content for action – what she also does here is to distinguish ethical from non-ethical behaviour. It becomes clear that authenticity is, for Beauvoir, the route to a life ethically lived.

What is interesting for my purposes is that we can see some similarities between Beauvoir's depictions of the serious man and her depictions of the woman in love. Likewise, there are links between her characterization of the ethical man – the man of good will – and authentic love. Beauvoir claims the fault of the serious man is that he 'plays the part of the inessential' (*TEOA*: 46) and that his aim is to 'lose himself in [the object or other]' (*TEOA*: 47). She suggests that women and 'the humble' typically occupy this attitude through 'laziness and timidity in resignation' (*TEOA*: 48). Significantly, Beauvoir suggests the serious man 'puts nothing into question' (*TEOA*: 49). This final point arguably connects the serious man with both the woman in love and romantic reading. It suggests an attitude of deference that accords with our previous discussion. Beauvoir goes on to describe the nihilist, the adventurer, the passionate man and the aesthete, and what is most relevant here for our discussion is her claim that passion, pride and the spirit of adventure all lead in complex ways to tyranny, by which she means a foreclosure of the other in unacceptable ways. This she condemns from the standpoint of existential ethics (*TEOA*: 72).

In contrast to these attitudes, Beauvoir puts forward 'the man of good will' who embodies an authentic and thus ethical approach to the other and his world. This ethical subject acknowledges the freedom of the other and refuses to follow the tyrant whose self-certainty leads him to annul the other's being. According to Beauvoir, the man of good will embodies one of the most important consequences of existential ethics – the rejection of every principle of authority (*TEOA*: 142). Such an ethics 'finds its truth if it considers itself as a free engagement of thought in the given, aiming, at each discovery, not at fusion with the thing, but at the possibility of new discoveries' (*TEOA*: 79). What we have here is Beauvoir's understanding of ethics as a particular and free *engagement* with the other, and I think we can take this model of open engagement and use it to measure what happens (or fails to happen) when we read.

Returning to Beauvoir: how does she read?

While Beauvoir's work on love and authenticity provides us with an interesting way of thinking about reading – about how *we* as philosophers read, and *our* relation with the text – it arguably offers us something else. It offers us a way of thinking more specifically about her own ways of reading. In the light of this, we might think of Beauvoir as one who reads generally (Kant, Hegel and others); as one who reads – more specifically – the work of Jean-Paul Sartre; as one who reads – very specifically – Sartre's *Being and Nothingness*; and, finally, as one who reads – interprets – the 'couple' Beauvoir and Sartre. (In addition to this we might include Beauvoir as one who, famously, reads her own work.)[45] In what follows, I shall briefly explore two of these instances by posing the following questions: what kind of reading does Beauvoir perform in relation to Sartre's *Being and Nothingness*? And how does Beauvoir read (interpret/represent) her (intellectual) relation with Sartre? I shall ask these questions with ideas of authenticity and romance always close at hand.

It is now relatively common to speak of the tensions (or even contradictions) in Beauvoir's relation to Sartre's existential philosophy. For instance, there are references to the dual nature of her analysis, the tension between her feminist analysis and her phenomenological or existential framework. What is suggested here is that the feminist perspective of Beauvoir's analysis sits rather uneasily with the Sartrean (and Hegelian) framework, categories and commitments it purportedly upholds. Indeed, this depiction of Beauvoir's work has led, in certain cases, to a rather uncritical appraisal of her intellectual contribution.[46] Despite this, there remain what I would like to depict as open and generous accounts of Beauvoir's work, attempting to engage with the real complexity of Beauvoir's existential relation – asking questions about the kind of philosophy that Beauvoir ultimately achieves.[47] Among these, Michèle Le Dœuff's readings are exemplary. Over what now amounts to years, Le Dœuff has read Beauvoir and offered us, in turn, critical insight into largely neglected aspects of Beauvoir's philosophical work.[48] Let us now look briefly at just a few of the things Le Dœuff has had to say.

Le Dœuff's rereading of Beauvoir's reading of Sartre: operative philosophy

I have been rereading the Introduction to *The Second Sex*. Incisive, forceful, and wonderfully clear, such a text scarcely calls for the pretensions of an exegesis. 'To be read, and reread' would seem to be the only possible commentary. Instead, I would like to explicate certain impressions prompted by reading it, and simply give voice to these impressions, the signs no doubt of a mute reworking of the text by a reading which progressively rewrites it. I have sought to elucidate my own, contradictory responses to de Beauvoir's discourse, and from this I have embarked on a series of considerations that are more complicated than I might have liked.

LE DŒUFF 1980: 277

In an early paper Le Dœuff (1977: 2–11)[49] is concerned, among other things, to ask questions about Beauvoir's intellectual relation with Sartre, and she does so partly through her notion of the erotico-theoretical transference.[50] This exploration is concerned with the erotics of the pedagogical relation and refers specifically to the transference that develops between the 'one who is presumed to know' and she who wishes to know all he (presumably) knows. In a later version of this work, Le Dœuff raises important questions concerning the historical relation of the female disciple and male master, noting that in each historical case the women involved experienced great passions for their male 'instructors': 'although they lived in very different times, these women had one thing in common: they all experienced great passions, and their relationship with philosophy existed only through their love for a man, a particular philosopher' (Le Dœuff 1989: 104).

From here she moves to Beauvoir and Sartre, claiming this famous couple represents a somewhat modern variation on a traditionally sexist theme: woman's lack of any direct relation to the institution of philosophy or the breadth of philosophical thought. She writes that the erotico-theoretical transference 'is equivalent to an absence of any direct relationship of women to philosophy' (Le Dœuff 1989: 104) and that it is the price women pay for the amateur position to which they are condemned (Le Dœuff 1989: 105).[51] In *The Philosophical Imaginary* Le Dœuff explains her reasons for thinking of Beauvoir and Sartre in terms of the erotico-theoretical relation. In short, she claims Beauvoir was 'confined to the feminine condition, that is to say accepted a ready-made philosophy; or that, in accepting existentialism as a constituted doctrine, she was excluded from the philosophical enterprise' (Le Dœuff 1989: 119).

While Le Dœuff's early discussion highlights the traditionally 'feminine' position that Beauvoir adopts in relation to both Sartre and the institution of philosophy, in a piece written after the initial 1977 publication Le Dœuff moves on, building an altogether more complex analysis of what this relation actually entails. In her influential paper 'Simone de Beauvoir and Existentialism' (Le Dœuff 1980: 277–89), Le Dœuff is more concerned with carefully and openly *re*reading Beauvoir's use of Sartre's existentialism.[52] She is interested in what Beauvoir manages to do with it; that is, the difference that Beauvoir's own reading makes. In this piece, Le Dœuff traces the merging of what we might refer to as fidelity and infidelity in Beauvoir's use of existential philosophy, and goes on to suggest that, on the one hand, Beauvoir works within Sartre's philosophical structure; that is, she works without disrupting his existential philosophy. On the other hand, Beauvoir ultimately produces feminist insights that counter the *individualist* constraints of Sartre's existentialism; that is, her work disrupts and exceeds these individualist existential constraints.⁵³ Le Dœuff writes:

> My intention is to show how the ethic of authenticity functions as a pertinent theoretical lever, an operative viewpoint for exposing the character of women's oppression. Consequently, one cannot, as I confess I am in the habit of doing, dissociate the philosophical substratum of . . . Beauvoir's work from that more empirical dimension, which I see as more relevant today than the conceptual grid via which this feminist investigation is executed. But even if they cannot be divorced, there is still no pre-established harmony between this philosophical position and the results to which it leads in *The Second Sex*.
> LE DŒUFF 1980: 278⁵⁴

Le Dœuff's point is that Beauvoir uses Sartrean existentialism as an *operative viewpoint* for exposing the character and detail of women's oppression. But how exactly does Beauvoir do this? Given the real problems of both the excessive individualism and misogyny of Sartre's early work, the question of how Beauvoir manages to use his existentialism as the basis for a feminist philosophical analysis is, indeed, an interesting one.⁵⁵ If her work remains (as some would claim) a too-faithful account of Sartre's philosophy, then how is it that she is able to develop her feminist critique? Le Dœuff's response to questions such as these is to suggest that Beauvoir transforms the universality of Sartre's existential philosophy into a perspective or point of view; that is, she uses existentialism as a *methodology*, not as a *truth*.⁵⁶ Beauvoir recognizes that external constraints are internalized and accepted as part of one's self-definition. This, Le Dœuff claims, represents a considerable modification of the Sartrean position – of *Being and Nothingness* – because it admits that consciousness needs to be at least partially understood in terms of external forces. There is, Le Dœuff writes,

> this little sentence in the Introduction [to *The Second Sex*]: 'Woman does not assert her demands as a subject because she lacks the concrete means'. In Sartrianism it is above all a question of denying the effect of exteriority as an obstacle, constraint, adversity or alienating cause . . . Beauvoir here poses a displaced problem: it is not enough to be persecuted by exteriority, it is also

necessary for exteriority to furnish the means for one's self-affirmation as a subject. If she insists so heavily in the course of *The Second Sex* on feminine narcissism, this is directly in line with this initial observation. Woman, is, first and foremost, deprived of exteriority; she cannot be 'conquering,' as the problematic of the for-itself demands.

LE DŒUFF 1980: 283[57]

Le Dœuff goes on to suggest that Sartre's existentialism (unwittingly) makes it possible for Beauvoir to formulate a feminist position. More precisely, I would maintain that it is Beauvoir's open and authentic reading of Sartre's existentialism in *TEOA* that allows her to formulate this position. Le Dœuff writes:

The requirement, which assumes that the feminine condition is not a matter of course, could be posed by . . . Beauvoir in its fully radical form only thanks to the ethic of authenticity. The ethic enabled her to sufficiently *distance herself from the lot of women* to be able to describe it as a shocking contingency, a strangeness, something nonnatural to be transformed as rapidly as possible.

LE DŒUFF 1980: 284[58]

Because existentialism rules out the belief in a fixed essence or human nature, Beauvoir is able to reason that women are in no sense naturally subservient to men. Sartre argues for the transcendence of the subject – its ability to free itself of a pre-given human nature – and Beauvoir simply and logically applies this to women. In the end, Beauvoir's analysis in *TSS* leads to different conclusions and observations from Sartre's in *Being and Nothingness*. In essence, she transforms Sartre's existentialist problematic well beyond its original parameters.[59] Beauvoir's work is, I maintain, a mature rereading and reconsideration of Sartre's existential philosophy.

Ultimately, Le Dœuff's reading refuses simply or too quickly to reduce Beauvoir's work to Sartre's philosophical schema. Le Dœuff is successful, I think, in situating Beauvoir as someone other than a faithful or dependent reader of Sartre. And perhaps all the more so because she is willing simultaneously to acknowledge the ambivalent moments in Beauvoir's reading – those moments where Beauvoir appears faithfully (and somewhat surprisingly) to repeat some of Sartre's more problematic statements. I would say that one of the strengths of Le Dœuff's reading is that it allows the tensions in Beauvoir's thought to remain, without attempting to erase these ambiguities in pursuit of the fantasy of a coherent or consistent text.[60]

Rethinking operative philosophy with the help of Beauvoir's own categories of romance and authenticity

Le Dœuff's claim – that Beauvoir's reading works as an operative viewpoint – can be understood in Beauvoir's own terms; that is, as a question concerning love. We can reread Le Dœuff's reading, understanding it anew, by returning to Beauvoir's own categories: romantic and authentic love. Beauvoir's terms help us to further appreciate the important insight that Le Dœuff's work brings – in this case, to the question of how Beauvoir reads. I am suggesting that: (i) Le Dœuff's discussion of the 'erotico-theoretical transference' – or transference in this intellectual sense more generally – brings us back to Beauvoir's question of romance, or more specifically to the stultifying effects of the romantic love characterized so well in *TSS*; and (ii) Le Dœuff's analysis of an 'operative philosophy' makes great sense when we think of it in terms of Beauvoir's understanding of authentic love. To say this is to highlight and support Le Dœuff's claims by 'going back' to Beauvoir. To date, the greater focus has been on Le Dœuff's important claim that Beauvoir reads 'operatively', but we should not forget the fact that Le Dœuff identifies two conflicting tendencies in Beauvoir's reading of Sartre. To remember that Beauvoir is also at times prey to a transferential reading of Sartre is to suggest that we think of this reading in terms of romance. Indeed, Beauvoir's reading hovers between varying moments: at times tentative or romantic, and at other times more authentically engaged.

So, taking Le Dœuff's account a little further – and, as I have suggested, this means 'going back' to Beauvoir – I argue that Beauvoir's reading is, for the most part, a mature and authentic assessment of Sartre's work. Her reading engages with Sartre's philosophy as both 'subject' *and* 'object'; that is, she is able to acknowledge (though perhaps not overtly or consciously)[61] the shortcomings of his thought, replete as it is with masculine frailties, faults, omissions and limitations. She is able to do this, I should add, without objectifying it or rejecting it out of hand. When reading in this mode, Beauvoir remains philosophically connected and yet independent from Sartre's existential position. There is no confusion of her thought with his. She moves in an open and generous manner towards his text, to return to herself and her own independent feminist conclusions. At this moment, Beauvoir establishes what I would refer to as an 'authentic connection' with the strange otherness of the Sartrean text. She does this, as Le Dœuff suggests, by bombarding the existential framework with the detail and minutiae of women's lives.[62]

Yet there are moments when Beauvoir seems to read *Being and Nothingness* faithfully, as if it were a total system.[63] Adopting Beauvoir's own terms, I suggest we think of this faithful rendering of Sartre's existential philosophy as a kind of romantic reading, one that constructs Sartre and his work – albeit momentarily? – as absolute reference: an absolute Subject or subjectivity. Indeed, Beauvoir's faithful and rather uncritical reliance on the dualist structure and terminology of existentialism can be thought of in these terms. For example, her faithful return to the couple of immanence/ transcendence – especially in her discussion of the nomad – brings along with it a whole host of unanalysed assumptions and prejudices, ones that do some considerable injustice to her feminist work.[64] Likewise, Beauvoir's uncritical adoption of Sartre's liberal problematic, and the excessive individualism that at times follows from this, suggests a too ready deference to – or echo of – Sartre's position.[65] Are there grounds here for thinking of these moments in her reading as romantic? Let us return to Beauvoir's own account of what romantic love entails: 'The measure of values, the truth of the world, are in his consciousness' (*TSS*: 724). We would be hard pressed here to demonstrate a purely romantic relation – in Beauvoir's sense of the term. While it might be fair to say that she rather uncritically adopts Sartre's dualist metaphysic and its liberal context, it is probably quite another thing to label this romantic. Or is it?

Beauvoir reading the couple: 'Sartre and Beauvoir'

Let us now move on to ask how these two types of reading – one romantic, one authentic – square with what Beauvoir herself has had to say about her relation to Sartre and his philosophy. It has been said that Beauvoir consistently refused to characterize herself as a philosopher, suggesting that this was rightly Sartre's role.[66] Beauvoir has often been portrayed – in a manner that annoys a good many of us – as Sartre's 'follower' or disciple,[67] and yet what remains perhaps most important is the question of what role, if any, she has played in the circulation of this 'myth'. In her appeal to 'reopen the question of influence' between Beauvoir and Sartre, Margaret Simons suggests that Beauvoir's depiction of herself – in philosophical terms – changes dramatically from the period before meeting Sartre to that afterwards (Simons 1998).[68] From the time she meets Sartre, her own quite personal philosophical questions appear to be absorbed into what many depict as her faithful elaboration of Sartrean themes. According to Simons, 'Beauvoir stated more than once and unequivocally that she was not a philosopher, that she did not do philosophy, and that she could not have influenced Sartre's philosophy'. However, she notes 'this denial is contradicted by Beauvoir's own written words in her recently discovered 1927 diary, written while Beauvoir was a philosophy student at the Sorbonne, two years before her first meeting with Sartre' (Simons 1998: 17–18).[69] In this diary Beauvoir states 'her passionate commitment to doing philosophy, outlines her literary methodology for doing philosophy, acknowledges early philosophical influences, and defines major themes of her own later philosophy and that of Sartre's *Being and Nothingness*' (Simons 1998: 18).[70]

Does Beauvoir's apparent 'retreat' from her identity as philosopher tell us anything about how she reads her (intellectual) relationship with Sartre? And if so, can we draw on the distinction she draws between romantic and authentic love in order to understand her reading of 'the couple'? In *Force of Circumstance*, the third volume of her autobiography, published originally in 1963 (Beauvoir 1968), Beauvoir has the following to say about her relation with Sartre:

> [W]e might almost be said to think in common. We have a common store of memories, knowledge and images behind us; our attempts to grasp the world are undertaken with the same tools, set within the same framework, guided by the same touchstones. Very often one of us begins a sentence and the other finishes it;[71] if someone asks us a question, we have been known

to produce identical answers. The stimulus of a word, a sensation, a shadow, sends us both traveling along the same inner path, and we arrive simultaneously at a conclusion – a memory, an association – completely inexplicable to a third person . . . Our temperaments, our directions, our previous decisions, remain different, and our writings are on the whole almost totally dissimilar. But they have sprung from the same plot of ground.

BEAUVOIR 1968: 643[72]

How are we to read this? Perhaps we can begin to think about what Beauvoir is saying if we recall the passage we cited from *TSS* at the beginning of this chapter:

> The measure of values, the truth of the world, are in his consciousness; hence it is not enough to serve him. The woman in love tries to see with his eyes; she reads the books he reads, prefers the pictures and the music he prefers; she is interested only in the landscapes she sees with him, in the ideas that come from him; she adopts his friendships, his enmities, his opinions; when she questions herself, it is his reply she tries to hear; she wants to have in her lungs the air he has already breathed; the fruits and flowers that do not come from his hands have no taste and no fragrance. Her idea of location in space, even, is upset: the center of the world is no longer the place where she is, but that occupied by her lover; all roads lead to his home and from it. She uses his words, mimics his gestures, acquires his eccentricities and his tics.
>
> *TSS*: 663

In this instance perhaps Beauvoir's relation to Sartre verges on what she elsewhere refers to as romantic love. All paths lead back to Sartre. It is possible to suggest that in this passage Beauvoir 'tries to see with his eyes', that she 'reads the books he reads', that she is interested only 'in the ideas that come from him', that she adopts 'his opinions', that 'when she questions herself, it is his reply she tries to hear': 'if someone asks us a question, we have been known to produce identical answers'. Now, we may protest that what Beauvoir portrays here is something quite other – that she attests to the mutuality and reciprocal nature of their relationship.[73] But it is Beauvoir's own point that the 'fiction' of reciprocity is precisely what makes this unhealthy and somewhat blind fidelity possible for the woman in love.[74] It is the woman in love's 'error' to confuse the mutuality of the 'same inner pathways' with the reality of 'all paths back to him'. Sartre's silence on the question of their relation – and significantly Beauvoir's meaning for him – does not help. When he does comment on the mutuality and reciprocity of his relation with another writer it is, significantly, not Beauvoir he refers to, but his 'intellectual son'.[75] This is a difficult issue and I am more than mindful of the dangers of returning to this most significant of intellectual couples.[76] To paraphrase Beauvoir, of intellectual couples: surely [e]nough ink has been spilled in quarrelling over [this couple] . . . and perhaps we should say no more about it (*TSS*: 13).[77]

With this in mind let me say something briefly about my own reservations in taking this particular path – of the effects of reading Beauvoir in this particular way. In suggesting that we think, albeit momentarily, of Beauvoir's reading of her intellectual relation with Sartre as 'romantic', we risk reducing the complexity and originality of Beauvoir's work to something less than it is. We risk tying her back to Sartre in such a way as to close off more nuanced readings of her work. We risk, too, reinforcing the stereotype of romance as a peculiarly feminine state.[78] So why take this risk? Perhaps to demonstrate the power and pervasiveness of what I am referring to as romantic reading. Although I have shown that Beauvoir is critically aware of the dangers inherent in a romantic inflation of others – indeed, she is the one who does so much to alert us to this danger – she nonetheless falls prey to this same romantic impulse.[79] Not always, and not even often, but perhaps enough to demonstrate the need for vigilance. Beauvoir's romantic lapse suggests this threat remains an ever-present possibility for the less than vigilant reader. We have all found ourselves at this point some time in our own philosophical careers. We have all – at some moment or phase – lovingly inflated the words of our favourite philosophers (or philosophies) and immaturely overestimated their worth. We have imagined them impervious to critical attack and failed to think independently of them. In short, we all – as 'students of philosophy' – retain a tendency, however small, towards a youthful and somewhat romantic relation to the work we read. But perhaps this romance is a phase or moment we need to experience in order that we develop the maturity to move on. If this is the case, then there might well be cause to rethink romance and authenticity sensibly as moments in a continuum or evolution of reading (or love), rather than as opposed or mutually exclusive terms. Le Dœuff's observation that we cannot dissociate the seemingly contradictory moments of Beauvoir's work in relation to Sartre's existentialism may well be confirmation of this. My point is that, in the end, we might discover that the romance of being 'in love' represents a necessary or inevitable moment in the movement towards an authentic, engaged and ethical reading; that it is an immature gesture, or a first, tentative step in the direction of a future relation that, if attained, will ensure the maturity of difference.[80] Perhaps what matters most about romantic reading is not that we avoid it – this might well be unrealistic – but rather that we learn from it and ultimately move beyond it; that our reading matures and in so maturing opens us to the other in more creative and generous ways.

Indeed, it is worth wondering whether generosity – the generosity that follows on from an authentic and engaged reading – actually brings us back in some sense to the question of romance. Is the passion of the devoted reading not itself a kind of generosity? Can we conceive of devotion in other than negative terms? Perhaps generosity is precisely this – the move through and beyond authenticity that allows us to return to the other without fear for the self.[81] Sylvia Walsh touches upon this indirectly when she reads Beauvoir alongside the Danish philosopher Søren Kierkegaard. She claims that, while both are critical of feminine devotedness and self-abandon, each 'reaffirm[s] the validity and importance of these qualities when given expression in appropriate form and in the proper social and/or spiritual context' (Walsh 1998: 28).[82] Surely this suggests a need to rethink our most commonsense views on devotion and romance? Perhaps an abandoned or devoted reading provides us with the ground from which we can – with care – move towards an authentic engagement. Perhaps authenticity and 'philosophy proper' can emerge only from the passionate realms of romance, abandon and devotion. In fact, doesn't Socrates say as much when, in Plato's *Phaedrus* and *Symposium* (for example, *Phaedrus* 245b and *Symposium* 209e), he declares the passion of erotic love *(eros)* as the motivation and ground for the philosopher's journey? Indeed, all of this arguably brings us back to Nietzsche and the peculiar passage we saw Beauvoir quoting at the beginning of 'The Woman in Love'. Nietzsche writes: 'What woman understands by love is clear enough: it is not only devotion, it is a total gift of her body and soul, without reservation, without regard for anything whatever' (Nietzsche, cited in *TSS*: 652). While it would be all too easy to read Nietzsche here in negative terms, what he refers to might in fact be the generosity that emerges from an unreserved and abandoned devotion of self to other. In this case, the gift of self – the excessive generosity of Nietzsche's giving without reserve – might gesture towards another economy of reading, one we will explore in the following chapter in relation to the work of Hélène Cixous.

When all is said and done, where does this leave us in relation to the question of reading? What can we take with us from Beauvoir's discussion of love? What is it that her work gives? In simple terms, my claim has been that Beauvoir's work on romantic love – when translated to the domain of reading – calls attention to the potential dangers of a limited, hurried and immature response wherein the reader passes up the opportunity to engage attentively, slowly and critically with the otherness of the text. A reading that remains romantic robs us of a mature and confident relation with the text, whereas an authentic or generous reading sets the terrain for an engaged and open relation that we might term 'ethics'. This ethical domain exists along a continuum over space and time. Authentic reading resists the excesses of what we have been referring to as institutional forms of reading: professional practices that occur without the time required to allow the dust to settle, or for impressions to be received. Returning to reading by slowly rereading provides us with the discerning quality of attention that allows for a profound transformation from romance to authenticity to unfold. This slow and deliberate process of rereading allows us to encounter the strangeness in what we read. Authentic reading is a slow practice or exercise of attention that builds towards maturity. This maturity does not occur overnight; it will not be hurried. It takes time to establish, and this occurs by building on the spontaneity of the first force of romantic love. As such, authentic reading works through the problems inherent in institutional forms of reading, by re-engaging with the instituting moments of philosophy as a love of wisdom and a way of life.

CHAPTER SIX

Intimate Reading: Cixous's Approach

She seemed to be seeking to exist in defiance of weight, of gravity.
RICHARD FLANAGAN, *GOULD'S BOOK OF FISH*: 306

It's perfectly possible to make a machine out of the text, to treat it like a machine and be treated by it like a machine. The contemporary tendency has been to find theoretical instruments, a reading technique which has bridled the text, mastered it like a wild horse with saddle and bridle, enslaving it.[1]

[S]aving the moment is such a difficult thing, and we never have the necessary time, the slow, sanguineous time, that is the condition of this love, the pensive, tranquil time that has the courage to let last.[2]

The guiding idea of philosophy as a love of wisdom can be the source of a transformative relation, and this idea is evident in Hélène Cixous's practice of intimate reading. In this final chapter I engage with her work in order to consider slow reading as an approach of intimacy, as well as of tenderness and love. By approaching the other in this unhurried way, we are changed – literally, transformed – from one existential state to another. Cixous's approach takes us from the heaviness of the subject who desires at all costs to know, to the weightless, attentive and receptive space of ethical encounter. Just as Le Dœuff's approach to philosophy as 'work' involves shifting thinking from one stage to another, Cixous's intimate approach moves us to unfamiliar terrain.

Cixous's work offers us a unique opportunity to think through the interrelations between reading and writing. In this chapter I explore what is particular in Cixous's readings by first discussing the central place writing holds in her work. As we shall see, Cixous's writing is motivated by a slow and respectful approach towards the other, rather than by any desire for appropriation, mastery or knowledge of the other. This approach guides her reading too, towards close contact with the strangeness of the text. The intimacy of Cixous's reading makes possible an ethical encounter with the other that both opens and transforms. Cixous's intimacy comes from, though is not reducible to, the generous gift of love, one that recalls Friedrich Nietzsche's unconditional gift of body and soul. As we will see, intimacy occupies a space alongside love rather than being reduced to it. In her essay 'Coming to Writing' (1991), Cixous explains the intimate bond between reading and writing in her work. Here she characterizes her writing – and *écriture féminine* more generally[3] – as resting on an attentive reading; a writing by '[s]he who looks with the look that recognizes, that studies, respects, doesn't take, doesn't claw, but attentively, with gentle relentlessness, contemplates and reads, caresses, bathes, makes the other gleam' (Cixous 1991: 51). For Cixous we are on the way to writing, or coming to writing, when we are able to read in this contemplative form. When we take the time, in an unhurried manner, to read with an attentive gaze, or to look back, we have begun the journey towards the kind of engaged writing she describes. Cixous writes: 'I am a reader before I write. Writing for me is born of reading. And I never write without reading. I am always accompanied by reading and furthermore I believe that when I write I am reading, I mean to say that everything that I write is but reading' (Cixous 2010: 22).[4]

A desire resonant with love

Much of what Cixous has to say about writing involves an emptying out of the self that prepares the ground for a passage between the self and the strangeness of the other. As we will see, this emptying has much in common with the attentive reading that prepares the way for writing. In order to effect this emptying, Cixous draws upon the resources of the unconscious and this places her work in relation to psychoanalytic theory. However, this relation is by no means straightforward. While she draws inspiration from Freud's voyage towards the subterranean recesses of unconscious life,[5] she remains ever critical of his fixation on castration and law, arguing that this covers over the trace of an entirely different libidinal relation with the world. Beyond threat, loss and repression exists another mode of being, one that she somewhat provocatively refers to as 'feminine'. This feminine response to law and the symbolic order foregoes submission in favour of an irreverent attitude of indifference. It refers back to the archaic and playful relation with the maternal body prior to the interdiction of Oedipal law. In retracing an alternative libidinal economy, Cixous refuses to accept Freud's depiction of woman as the figure of castration, the mutilated body that threatens man with the loss of his own symbolic power and prestige.[6] Instead she inscribes the feminine as the site of an excessive and overabundant pleasure, a creativity that literally overflows the dams of patriarchal law. The writing that accompanies this feminine economy remains indifferent to the logic of castration which effectively tries to annul difference in the name of a monosexual or phallocentric world-view. Feminine writing, as we will see, involves the exchange of rhythm and gesture in language. It speaks the body's desires in a fully sensual manner without succumbing to 'the fear of expropriation, of separation, of losing the attribute' (Cixous 1986: 80). For Cixous, real writing emerges from an indifference to the logic of castration. It involves an affirmation, a kind of Nietzschean 'yes' that laughs at the meagre desire of lack:

> Their 'symbolic' exists, it holds power – we, the sowers of disorder, know it only too well. But we are in no way obliged to deposit our lives in their banks of lack . . . to reinstate again and again the religion of the father . . . We have no womanly reason to pledge allegiance to the negative. The feminine (as the poets suspected) affirms: '. . And yes,' says Molly, carrying *Ulysses* off beyond any book and toward the new writing: 'I said yes, I will Yes.'
> CIXOUS 1976: 884[7]

In her engagement with the discourse of psychoanalysis, Cixous radically departs from an understanding of desire based on lack.

In effect, she rewrites psychoanalysis towards a desire resonant with love, referring to this as an 'economy of positive lack' (Cixous 1988: 24), a love that approaches rather than appropriates the other. One that moves towards the other in passion and grace: 'an economy of thankfulness' (Cixous 1988: 24). This alternative understanding of love challenges the restrictive and reductive accounts that characterize the law of castration, proposing bridges or links between the self and other, ones that connect rather than separate the two.[8]

For Cixous, writing the self provides the opportunity for that self to encounter the other. It is a way for the self to enter language as a speaking subject who does not obliterate the other. It also provides a space for the other's voice to emerge. In light of this, Cixous characterizes woman as the one whose voice emerges despite phallic or symbolic attempts to repress her specifically feminine mode of speaking otherwise.[9] She calls upon the resources of the unconscious maternal body that provide both a resistance and alternative to paternal law. Cixous is adamant that to transform language, to enter it in an entirely different way, we need the vast resources of the unconscious, for it is only here that we find what we might call the ethical dimension that is necessary to challenge the symbolic code.[10] The subjectivity that emerges in Cixous's account is more proximate, more intimate in its relation with others, than more orthodox Freudian or Lacanian accounts. It carries the body with it, incorporating its rhythms and gestures in the symbolic processes of language and writing.[11]

Cixous writing: *entredeux*

[Writing] is deep in my body, further down, behind thought. Thought comes in front of it and it closes like a door.[12]

Whoever wants to write must be able to reach this lightening region that takes your breath away, where you *instantaneously* feel at sea and where the moorings are severed with the already-written, the already-known.[13]

It is from the body's rhythms and gestures that a certain kind of writing emerges. For Cixous, in order to write one must be body;

sink into the heaviness of the body. The body is the scene of writing, a writing that has the power to subvert traditional cultural forms. The body of Cixous's own writing, her corpus, is a vast and expansive terrain, somewhat like the maternal body she celebrates in defiance of patriarchal law. Her works comprise well over forty books and in excess of a hundred articles, spanning the genres of theory, fiction and drama.[14] Cixous writes about writing, and in fact she often pursues the question of writing even when it appears that she is writing about something else entirely.

It is noteworthy that much of what Cixous has to say concerning writing relates back to the embodied experiences of mourning and loss. She has stated many times that her own writing emerged from the experience of loss she encountered as a young child with the untimely death of her father. For Cixous, mourning throws us into a place we rarely, if ever, inhabit. We are literally displaced, forced to deal with a pain that severs us from the familiar, the familial. Writing from this space makes fear retreat.[15] It does not relieve the pain of loss but opens the possibility of another relation with the world:

> I believe that one can only begin to advance along the path of discovery, the discovery of writing or anything else, from mourning and in the reparation of mourning. In the beginning the gesture of writing is linked to the experience of disappearance, to the feeling of having lost the key to the world, of having been thrown outside. Of having suddenly acquired the precious sense of the rare, of the mortal. Of having urgently to regain the entrance, the breath, to keep the trace.
> CIXOUS 1994: xxvi

Writing weaves itself intricately around the space of loss, both compensating for and inscribing this loss (Sellers 1996: xiii), enabling us to open out to the other, to take the risk of bridging the enormous distance between ourselves and the ultimate other – death. It is by engaging with the otherness of death that we are then able to encounter the other in life, to move towards and affirm life in the other.

Our move towards the other begins in writing through the processes of our own erasure. Cixous contends that we need to undergo a kind of evaporation of the self in order that we become something like pure space.[16] By doing so we literally make space for the other, an intimate terrain or 'between' that allows the other truly to emerge. For Cixous, this evaporation engenders a positive incomprehension that allows the other to be 'very much other', 'so very much not-me' (Cixous in Cixous and Calle-Gruber 1997: 16).[17] This staging of otherness[18] – or *entredeux* – provides a passage between the self and the strangeness of the other. It is an event 'which evicts us from ourselves' (Cixous, cited in Cixous and Calle-Gruber 1997: 9). In this eviction we begin to understand the subversive nature of Cixous's writing. For her, writing is the site of a substantial resistance to the law:[19] 'writing is precisely *the very possibility of change*, the space that can serve as a springboard for subversive thought, the precursor movement of a transformation of social and cultural structures' (Cixous 1976: 879). It is revolutionary in that it summons forth new possibilities, new ways of thinking and saying what we seldom hear.[20] This is perhaps nowhere more evident than in poetic writing, where grammatical subversion devours language from within.[21] Cixous's own writing aims to devour the silence imposed on language and thought by a relentless return to the repressed forces that usher in a new art and a new culture.[22] Such social, political and cultural change is very much tied, for Cixous, to the question of a feminine writing, an *écriture féminine* that challenges the restrictions imposed by a masculine symbolic imaginary. This kind of poetic writing carries the pre-Oedipal body into language, referring back to the undisciplined *jouissance* of the child's relation with the mother's body, its excessive pleasures of play and passion. It inscribes the body in defiance of Oedipal law, drawing directly on the resources of the uncensored unconscious realm. In this sense, Cixous's writing works in defiance of Lacanian attempts to relegate the mother to a pre-symbolic, prelinguistic and silent domain. Here the mother's body writes, and is in turn written. This feminine writing is an intimate discourse that moves towards the other, breaking with the conventions of a patriarchal language structured by distance, separation and denial.

Cixous's discussion of feminine writing refers back to the distinction she draws between masculine and feminine libidinal economies. For her, these represent possible responses to law and authority with different relations to pleasure, rather than fixed biological categories. In addition, they point to different ways of responding to generosity and the gift. A feminine economy finds itself at odds with authority and thus inscribes a language that subverts the existing order. Because it is positioned beyond the threat of castration or castigation, feminine writing is able to delve freely into the depths of unconscious life, drawing upon the resources of the body, its passions and strengths. For Cixous, such a writing is rare, as it is in essence a direct refusal of the social and psychological laws by which most of us live. For this reason she argues that we seldom find writers capable of sustaining such intensity.[23] While in theory the feminine mode is open to both men and women, Cixous argues that women do have a kind of privileged access to its force.[24] The experiences of a woman's body, especially in pregnancy, childbirth and lactation open it to the intimacies of the other in unique and dramatic ways: 'It happens that culturally, women have more of a chance of gaining access to pleasure, because of the cultural and political division of the sexes, which is based on sexual difference, on the way society has used the body and on the fact that it is much easier to inflict on men than on women the horror of the inside. After all women do all virtually or in fact have an experience of the inside, an experience of the capacity for other, an experience of non-negative change brought about by the other, of positive receptivity' (Cixous 1988: 18). It is this positive receptivity that characterizes feminine writing. Here, the body's intimate maternal experiences are inscribed in a writing that aims to bring about new experiences of, and encounters with, the other. Once again, the body's resources are drawn into writing and in effect become the substance of that writing.

Cixous proposes a radically different model for understanding our relations with ourselves, others, and the world in which we live. For her, writing offers the key to this new mode of being, acting as a kind of existential cipher of things yet to be. It is 'the passageway, the entrance, the exit, the dwelling place of the other in me – the other that I am and am not, that I don't know how to be, but that I feel passing, that makes me live – that tears me apart, disturbs me, changes me' (Cixous 1986: 85). Writing opens the world to new meanings and importantly to new bodies capable of sustaining these meanings. For Cixous, the body is primary; it is the place where writing meets the world. '"Writing" seized me, gripped me, around the diaphragm, between the stomach and the chest, a blast dilated my lungs and I stopped breathing ... this "coming" to language is a fusion, a flowing into fusion ... A practice of the greatest passivity' (Cixous 1991: 9, 56–7). Writing orients this newly born body towards life, it 'preserves life' (Sellers 1996: xiii),[25] valorizes it. Indeed, the body that emerges from Cixous's feminine writing is replete with life; it is an excessive body propelled by an economy of giving and spending (*dépense*). Again, Cixous differentiates here between a masculine economy of production, accumulation and profit and a feminine economy of giving, spending and excess. She argues that these represent two possible relations with the other. While the masculine gives only in the certainty of some immediate return, the feminine reaches out towards the other in an excessive gesture of generosity or grace. In feminine writing the text structures itself as gift, opening itself without reserve to the otherness or foreignness of the other.[26] This simultaneous opening and giving infiltrates the text with uncertainty and ambiguity. In essence, it is a poetic form of writing that concerns itself little with law, grammar or established style.

For Cixous the initial gift is the maternal gift of life. This giving disrupts the illusion of an autonomous sense of self. It also disrupts more individualistic notions of ownership and property. The mother's body gives abundantly, without thought of return. It provides an alternative economy that touches lightly upon the other without reducing it back to the self's appropriating demands. For Cixous, this giving is echoed in feminine writing where the excessive resources of the mother's body become the substance of the text.[27] 'How' she asks, 'could the woman, who has experienced the not-me within me, not have a particular relationship to the written? To writing as giving itself away (cutting itself off) from the source?' (Cixous 1986: 90). Cixous's gift here is to make it evident that the authority of paternal law – symbolic law – exists in an always precarious relation with the mother's desire to give. To acknowledge and celebrate this desire is simultaneously to recognize the inherent instability of symbolic law and, by extension, the rigid ego it constitutes.[28]

Writing as gift and generosity

There is another sense in which Cixous's work offers itself as gift. Over time, Cixous has sought not only to theorize the notion of giving but, perhaps more importantly, to inscribe it in her own writing practice.[29] Put simply, we could say that Cixous's writing performs the very giving that she insistently describes. To approach Cixous from this perspective is to a certain extent to refuse those characterizations of her work that reinstate a largely artificial distinction between works of theory and fiction. In *The Book of Promethea*, giving takes the form of a poetics of proximity, an intimate connection between the book and its subject (Cixous 1991a).[30] Love for the female character, Promethea, is enacted here in a writing that refuses to undo her strangeness, her foreignness to the narrator's pen. By remaining just beyond the narrator's powers of representation, Promethea remains alive and thus able to be loved. Cixous's gesture towards a completely foreign other in this text indicates the possibility of a place from which to begin the incredible journey towards the other which, she insists, involves a delicate balance between proximity and distance. 'The most difficult thing to do is to arrive at the most extreme proximity while guarding against the trap of projection, of identification. The other must remain in all its extreme strangeness within the greatest possible proximity' (Cixous 1988: 29). Close and yet not overtaken. Writing here extends towards the other, moves to the other, without deforming her or returning her to its own place. In doing so it leaves the time of the other intact; that is, the time of now. *The Book of Promethea* concerns itself with a writing that speaks the present 'now'; a writing that entwines itself with life in the present moment. Indeed, it poses the question of writing's relation to living, and the possible exchanges between the two.

Performative texts such as Cixous's *The Book of Promethea* echo the disturbance of psychoanalytic theory that we witness in the best of Freud's writing. His case studies, important literary works in their own right, continually resist strict classification as either theory or fiction. In a similar manner, Cixous's writing exceeds the bounds of genres as they are traditionally defined. Her works refuse to be drawn in by the limitations of what we tend to think of as either theory or writing. In place of these they build a rich and elaborate world, and in it they fashion a language that summons the other; a voice simultaneously able to retreat in order to heed the other's call.

Cixous's refusal to limit by defining feminine writing is counterbalanced throughout her œuvre by a commitment to inscribing the resonances of the body's voice and breath.[31] Her writing performs the body's gestures in its very materiality, thereby undoing to some extent the repression that symbolic law rests upon. We can hear in her prose the materiality of the body's weight, its rhythms, its time. Strict grammatical structure and division give way to a poetic prose that opens out towards the other, beckoning the other.

Generosity, love, abandon

In the previous chapter we explored Simone de Beauvoir's work, foregrounding the different types of love – romantic and authentic – she identifies. At the time, we noted a passage that frames, in a rather ambiguous way, Beauvoir's early discussion. It is time to return to that passage now, to reread it in order to explore a dimension of Cixous's work on love that arguably exceeds Beauvoir's account. In *The Gay Science* Nietzsche writes:

> The single word love in fact signifies two different things for man and woman. What woman understands by love is clear enough: it is not only devotion, it is a total gift of her body and soul, without reservation, without regard for anything whatever. This unconditional nature of her love is what makes it a *faith*, the only one she has. As for man, if he loves a woman, what he *wants* is that love from her; he is in consequence far from postulating the same sentiment for himself as for woman; if there should be men who also felt that desire for complete abandonment, upon my word, they would not be men.
> FRIEDRICH NIETZSCHE, *The Gay Science*,
> cited in Beauvoir 1984: 652

Coming as it does at the beginning of Beauvoir's description of romantic love, we might assume that she cites Nietzsche's account as evidence in support of her claim that a devotional romantic love disqualifies woman from any authentic relation with either man or herself. However, although Beauvoir is clearly critical of romantic love it is not altogether clear exactly how she reads Nietzsche's words. Rereading this passage with the help of Cixous's account of masculine and feminine libidinal economies, it is possible to suggest that other than negative meanings emerge. Does Beauvoir sense these possibilities? Nietzsche's man, closed off from the economy of giving that typifies woman's devotion, seeks love in the form of property and appropriation. What he wants is to possess woman's love, incapable, as he seems to be, of giving it (as anything other than an exchange) himself. Nietzsche's woman, on the other hand, gives love without reservation – without keeping back something in reserve for herself. Her devotion is an excessive love; an unconditional giving that gives the total gift of her body and soul. Although Nietzsche undoubtedly has other agendas at play, his account is nonetheless helpful for exploring the dimension of giving that underscores all of Cixous's work.

At the conclusion to our chapter on Beauvoir, I asked whether it was possible to conceive of devotion in other than negative terms. I suggested that under certain conditions it can be thought of – and here Nietzsche helps us – as an act of generosity or giving that moves us through and beyond authenticity, allowing us a proximity with the other without fear for the self. Beauvoir's authenticity demands a certain distance between self and other that allows for subjectivity to emerge. If this distance is too great, however, intimacy becomes compromised. Here generosity – and possibly devotion – can act to bridge the distance between authentic selves. Devotion thought of as self-abandonment, as we see in Søren Kierkegaard's work, does not necessarily imply a loss of self.[32] Rather, it enables an evaporation or erasure of the *dominating* self that otherwise leaves no space or *entredeux* for the other to emerge. Generosity counters this dominating self, leaving us open to the other in important ways.[33]

In 'The Laugh of the Medusa' (1976), Cixous writes that woman 'has constituted herself necessarily as that "person" capable of losing a part of herself without losing her integrity ... she can merge with [the other] without annihilating herself: because she's a giver' (Cixous 1976: 888). Here, the gift of giving permits an abandon that does not equate with annihilation. Devotion, thought in these terms, involves a generosity towards the other without fear for the self. It is this form of generosity that Cixous celebrates in woman's excessive love. She speaks of a desire resonant with love that bridges (without collapsing) the distance between self and other. Love is 'the desire-that-gives' (Cixous 1976: 893):

> Elsewhere, she gives. She doesn't 'know' what she's giving, she doesn't measure it; she gives, though, neither a counterfeit

impression nor something she hasn't got. She gives more, with no assurance that she'll get back even some unexpected profit from what she puts out. She gives that there may be life, thought, transformation. This is an 'economy' that can no longer be put in economic terms. Wherever she loves, all the old concepts of management are left behind. At the end of a more or less conscious computation, she finds not her sum but her differences. I am for you what you want me to be at the moment you look at me in a way you've never seen me before: at every instant. When I write, it's everything that we don't know we can be that is written out of me, without exclusions, without stipulation, and everything we will be calls us to the unflagging, intoxicating, unappeasable search for love. In one another we will never be lacking.

CIXOUS 1976: 893

By embracing this extravagant gesture towards the other, Cixous unsettles Beauvoir's arguably stereotypical depictions of romantic love: with woman as the object or victim of a love that can only benefit man. In Cixous's account, woman emerges as the triumphant subject of love in an excessive and intimate form. Are there implications here for generosity and reading? I think there are. Generosity is central to the open spaces that Cixous establishes in her reading and writing, and this distances her approach from those she depicts as dominated by fear and closure. Again, we can understand these differences in terms of her distinction between masculine and feminine economies.[34] According to Ian Blyth and Susan Sellers:

at the heart of *écriture féminine* lies the desire to set up a non-acquisitional space – a space where the self can explore and experience the non-self (the 'other') in mutual respect, harmony and love. A 'feminine' approach to the other is generous and giving, it avoids the ('masculine') impulse to appropriate or annihilate the other's difference, allowing the other to remain as 'other'.

BLYTH and SELLERS 2004: 15

These 'masculine' and 'feminine' attitudes towards the law, and their implications for our relation with the other, are fundamental for understanding Cixous's refusal of fear – specifically the psychoanalytic fear of castration or loss. Cixous's generosity towards the other opens her and allows her to take the risk of proximity with the strangeness of the other, placing her approach at odds with the masculine economy of accumulation and property, the economy that breeds fear:

> The realm of the proper, culture, functions by the appropriation articulated, set into play, by man's classic fear of seeing himself expropriated, seeing himself deprived ... his refusal to be deprived, in a state of separation, by his fear of losing the prerogative, fear whose response is all of History. Everything must return to the masculine. 'Return': the economy is founded on a system of returns. If a man spends and is spent, it's on condition that his power returns. If a man should go out, if he should go out to the other it's always done according to the Hegelian model, the model of the master–slave dialectic.
> CIXOUS 1981: 50

The fears motivating the so-called masculine libidinal economy are fears underwritten by loss. In Hegelian terms, the other threatens me with loss – whether of property, prestige, freedom or life. My relations with the other are thus determined within this threat of loss. Consequently, they are relations of hostility and distance.[35] According to Cixous, these hostilities are heightened by another form of fear when generosity or giving is introduced into the equation. Obligation and debt generate fear in the masculine subject who has no interest in being indebted to the other: 'the moment you receive something you are effectively "open" to the other, and if you are a man you have only one wish, and that is hastily to return the gift, to break the circuit of an exchange that could have no end' (Cixous 1981: 48). For Cixous – and for Irigaray – the gift of birth is the mother's gift that man does his best to repress because, in a phallocentric economy, he can only understand this gift in terms of indebtedness. Could this be the source of his anxiety in relation to the other? His fear of openness towards the other? What is the status of this unpaid and unacknowledged debt?[36] Whatever the case, Cixous is determined to work beyond the limitations and fears of the masculine libidinal economy, to bring to the fore the art of receiving, respecting and of keeping alive (Cixous 1987: 14–20), so it is not surprising that her open-ended generosity[37] brings us back to the extravagant gesture of Nietzsche's woman who loves without reserve.[38]

Cixous reading: intimacy, giving

The quality of loving without reserve provides Cixous with the courage to approach the other and to read in wholly intimate terms. While intimacy is not the same as love it is, nonetheless, not far from it. For Cixous, intimacy is a cause for celebration, not for fear. The generosity we witness in her writing is inseparable from the intimacy she achieves in her reading. Intimacy is simply openness; openness to the other, openness to what we read, an openness that allows us to be transformed in the act of reading. If Gayatri Spivak is correct and 'the hardest lesson is the impossible intimacy of the ethical', then Cixous's work can be thought of in ethical terms (Spivak 1993: 171).[39] We learn this lesson in her work in and through her reading. Reading is, for Cixous, purely and simply the process of establishing intimacy with the other.

In many senses, the key to Cixous's intimate reading is time. Cixous is adamant that good reading takes time and that it should not be hurried. To read is to linger over the possibilities and ambiguities of the text;[40] to understand the importance of being-with the text – of sharing its space and time.[41] Intimacy takes time, and over time this opens us to the text. Openness is a central feature of Cixous's reading. In 'Conversations' she describes this opening as a slow journey[42] or loving encounter with the other, a movement towards the other: 'reading must be a movement capable of following all the stages of this vast journey from one to the other, to me, to you' (Cixous 1988: 146). This opening is at odds with the institutional reading she identifies, the techniques that reduce the text to an object to be tamed by theoretical instruments: 'It's perfectly possible to make a machine out of the text, to treat it like a machine and be treated by it like a machine. The contemporary tendency has been to find theoretical instruments, a reading technique which has bridled the text, mastered it like a wild horse with saddle and bridle, enslaving it' (Cixous 1988: 147).[43]

Cixous focuses on the foreignness or strangeness of the text, arguing that it is its unfamiliar accents that attract the reader's attention. An attentive relation is a crucial aspect of her reading as it helps to establish a bridge towards the other's strangeness. She sees the danger involved in contacting this strangeness as well worth the risk because the openness that comes from this contact helps her to resist readings that remain limited, closed and fearful of any potential loss. Cixous has for decades taken the risk of preserving foreignness and strangeness through a collaborative practice of reading. Working closely together in her seminars, Cixous and her group embody the future form of collective work we have seen Le Dœuff champion in Chapter One. For Cixous, working collectively ensures that 'the essence of each strangeness is preserved' (Cixous 1988: 146).[44] To contact and to preserve strangeness we need to call forth different approaches to reading. Working collectively is one possible approach. Slowness, however, is the foundation of any fundamentally different relation with the text. Cixous understands this and in *Vivre L'Orange/To Live the Orange* (Cixous 1979) she acknowledges the very real struggle involved in slowing down: 'saving the moment is such a difficult thing, and we never have the necessary time, the slow, sanguineous time, that is the condition of this love, the pensive, tranquil time that has the courage to let last' (Cixous 1979: 18). Slowness, Cixous explains, 'is the essence of tenderness' and love (Cixous 1994: 88) and we find repeated reference to these intertwined terms throughout her œuvre. Cixous claims she learns this slowness, and its accompanying gestures of love and tenderness, in 'the school of sources, in inner Brazil', in the strange and utterly foreign writing of Clarice Lispector (Cixous 1994: 89).

The approach: a slow passage between the self and the strangeness of the other

At the school of Clarice Lispector, we learn the approach.
CIXOUS 1991: 60

Perhaps the most intimate of Cixous's readings are those she undertakes with Lispector – the writer who teaches her slowness and 'the awesome beauty of learning to read' (Cixous 1991: 59).[45] Cixous begins the essay 'Clarice Lispector: The Approach' (1991) by posing the following questions: 'How to "read" Clarice Lispector ... What will we call "reading", when a text overflows all books and comes to meet us, giving itself to be lived? *Was heisst lesen?* (What is called reading?)' (Cixous 1991: 59). The kind of reading Lispector teaches Cixous is the approach – the great lesson of living, slowness. This slowness takes many forms, among these calling, letting ourselves be called, letting come and receiving. With Lispector, Cixous announces: 'There are nothing but ways' (Cixous 1991: 61). Following a decidedly Heideggerian way (*Weg*),[46] Cixous understands Lispector's work as the slow gathering and gleaning of letters that allows us to read:[47]

> Her voice, peopled, wild, listens. *Gives us the lesson of slowness.* Slowness: the slow time that we need to approach, to let everything approach, life, death, time, the thing; all the slowness of time that life must take in order to give itself without hurting us too much, all the time we must put in to reach the thing, the other, to attain it without hurrying it, to come close to it.
>
> CIXOUS 1991: 62

To read is to approach, and to approach is to embrace slowness in all its proximate forms.[48] We cannot avoid it or hurry it, as '[h]urrying annuls' (Cixous 1991: 62).[49] In humility and generosity we embrace the slowness of the approach towards the other:

> We are living in the time of the flat thought-screen, of newspaper-thinking, which does not leave time to think the littlest thing according to its living mode. We must save the approach that opens and leaves space for *the other*. But we live mass-mediatized, pressed, hard-pressed, blackmailed. Acceleration is one of the tricks of intimidation. We rush, throw ourselves upon, seize. And we no longer know how to receive.
>
> CIXOUS 1991: 62

The pathology of receiving Cixous identifies sets us apart from the approach, and thus apart from the world of living things. Only time, and the slowness of the approach, can return the living world to us. Lispector 'teaches us to give ourselves, again, the time not to forget, not to kill' so that we might 'keep the space of waiting open' (Cixous 1991: 62).[50] Cixous speaks of a 'tender attentive slowness'

(Cixous 1991: 65) and a patience that aids in our approach towards reading.[51] Here wonder, astonishment, tenderness, love and contemplation come to the fore, and yet, '[a]ttention is the key' (Cixous 1991: 70)[52] – attention, and proximity.

Cixous's intensely intimate reading of Lispector culminates in what she refers to as a relation of extreme proximity. Again, she encounters this proximity in Lispector's writing. Cixous often refers to her reading as an apprenticeship[53] with Lispector, from whom she learns the lightness of the self in relation to the other: 'Approaching with such an absence of self, with such lightness, without disturbing its proximity' (Cixous 1991: 75). In 'Extreme Fidelity' Cixous writes about learning the lesson of nearness: 'The most difficult thing to do is to arrive at the most extreme proximity while guarding against the trap of projection, of identification. The other must remain in all its extreme strangeness within the greatest possible proximity' (Cixous 1988: 29). This tension between strangeness and proximity is the tension that propels Cixous's reading towards the other in the lightest of ways.[54] Extreme proximity places us near the other while allowing us to preserve the slightest interval that stops us projecting, identifying or incorporating the other. In reading we are close enough to feel the other's breath[55] and yet we refrain from incorporating the other, from taking the other in.[56] This kind of proximity, in distance, is the possibility of reading in the ethical manner that Cixous intends. We are intimately close to the text without ever losing sight of its impossible strangeness.[57]

Cixous and Irigaray: extreme proximity?

Cixous's celebration of extreme proximity has affinities with the nearness Krzysztof Ziarek explores in the space between Heidegger's and Levinas's work. In Chapter Four's discussion of Irigaray's attentive listening, we looked briefly at Ziarek's post-Heideggerian hermeneutics of nearness. From the perspective between Heidegger and Levinas, Ziarek claims that while difference 'can all too readily be identified with the distance between the subject and the object', and hence can be complicit with an erasure of otherness, that differentiation, on the other hand, can find 'the condition of its operation in proximity to the extent that it is the *extreme nearness* to the other that allows difference to unfold' (Ziarek 1994: 11, 12, emphasis added). Like Cixous, Ziarek is determined not to collapse nearness with identity, and to this end he summons a passage from Irigaray's early work in support of an ethically proximate relation. Ziarek reads, in Irigaray's words, a proximity that undoes the distance between self and other, by 'derailing the logic of separation and identity' (Ziarek 1994: 16). In *This Sex Which Is Not One*, Irigaray speaks of a '[n]earness so pronounced that it makes all discrimination of identity, and thus all forms of property, impossible' (Irigaray 1985b: 31, cited in Ziarek 1994: 16). We can think of this nearness in terms of Cixous's extreme proximity. This allows us to explore other moments that link Irigaray's work with Cixous's, though to suggest this is not – of course – to conflate their projects; to do away with the crucial interval between them. It is, simply, to draw attention to those moments where bridges can be built *entredeux*.

We have already seen that proximity plays an important role in establishing the attentive listening that Irigaray urges us to create in our relations with the other, and we have thought about the relevance of this for reading. Irigaray reminds us that her work in *The Way of Love* proposes 'ways to approach the other, to prepare a place of proximity: with the other in ourselves and between us'. Her book is, she claims, 'in search of gestures, including gestures in language, which could help on the way to nearness, and in order to cultivate it' (Irigaray 2002: ix). There are resonances here with Cixous's work and we benefit from bringing these approaches together. In 'Rebuilding the World', Irigaray indicates that 'safeguarding the obscurity and the silence that the other remains for me aids in discovering proximity' (Irigaray 2002: 151), and that the lightning strike of love is necessary to reopen this path (Irigaray 2002: 158). Placing the self and other – or the self and text – alongside one another is not enough to ensure proximity. Being near and close involves something more, and we know from Cixous's work that this something more involves an approach towards the other. Irigaray, too, speaks of the importance of this approach:

> To approach the other ... does not mean to live in the neighborhood of one another ... To approach implies rather becoming aware of the diversity of our worlds and creating paths

which, with respect for this diversity, allow holding dialogues. Being placed side by side does not suffice for reaching nearness. This local, cultural, national proximity can even prevent the approach because the forgetting of the fact that going the path toward the other is never achieved, requires an unceasing effort and not a standing in the same.

IRIGARAY 2002: 68

An unceasing effort is required for the work of the approach to be done, so that the other remains both foreign and strange. Proximity, then, is the most difficult thing to achieve with those closest to us. While Lispector's work may be sufficiently foreign to Cixous's ear, the real challenge – for all of us – is to hear something strange in those works nearby. Is an extreme proximity possible between Irigaray and Cixous? In 'Approaching the other as other', Irigaray explores the difficulty of respecting the interval between ourselves and the other:

> We have been accustomed to reduce the other to ours or ourselves. On the level of consciousness as on the level of feelings, we have been educated to make our own what we approach or what approaches us. Our manner of reasoning, our manner of loving is often an appropriation, either through lack of differentiation, a fusion, or through transformation into an object, an object of knowledge or of love, that we integrate into our world. We act in this way especially towards others who are closest to us, forgetting that they are other, different from us, but also towards the foreigner who is welcomed on the condition that he, or she, agrees to being assimilated to our way of living, our habits, our world.

IRIGARAY 2004: 5

Cixous's encounter with Lispector's writing reminds us how relevant this idea of the approach is in terms of our reading. Something like a lightning strike of love (to return to Irigaray's phrase) is required when we approach the text. This is, perhaps, not far from the wonder we have seen in Descartes's *Passions*. For Cixous, the approach is the work of preparing for the wondrous encounter with the other, the encounter that will cause us to pause in front of the foreignness or strangeness of what we read. Cixous's approach towards this wondrous encounter is the open work of reading, where reading is a kind of attentive listening that draws me to the other in extremely proximate ways. Listening to the text is 'the stringent work on the self' that comes from the 'active receptivity' of the one who hears.[58] 'We listen to a text', writes Cixous, 'with numerous ears' (Cixous 1988: 148); indeed, for reading 'we should have eyes which are [also] ears' (Cixous 2010: 33). And perhaps, recalling Nietzsche, delicate eyes and fingers too.

The gifts of abandon and grace: an ethics of reading

Cixous's approach between self and text sets up a chiastic intertwining that connects the two in unexpected and intimate ways. In Maurice Merleau-Ponty's work we find the figure of the chiasm, the twofold otherness that simultaneously connects and separates self from other.[59] To think the chiasm as a model of reading[60] is to acknowledge the ethical dimension of Cixous's approach. It is to appreciate the extreme proximity and impossible nearness that exists in the *between* of self and other. To read in this mode is to encounter an intimate other who will never be mine. The ethical dimension evident in Cixous's approach to reading is very much grounded in the attentive intimacy she seeks to establish with the other. To read is to be attentive to the trace of the other, and this attention takes time. Additionally, and perhaps paradoxically, it calls for an emptying of the self to prepare a space for the other, an abandon that allows the other to gleam. Accompanying attention is patience, and Cixous demonstrates this in the slow and considered waiting that forms the approach, which is nothing other than the imperceptible movement towards the other in passion and in grace. Grace, as we will see, is the patient work of ethics.

In 'Reaching the Point of Wheat' (1987), Cixous explores the processes of depersonalization or absence of the self Lispector achieves in her writing. What she has to say here helps me to identify an intuition I have in relation to Cixous's work about reading. Her approach to reading is, I think, distinguished by the equanimity or felicity she herself finds in Lispector's difficult attitude towards the self: 'when one is courageous enough to drop the heavy self and open to the other, then everything can happen' (Cixous 1987: 18). In this attentive mode one dispenses with the heavy self in order to reach the greatest exteriorization. This work involves an evaporation of the masterful self, made possible through an economy of attention. It is, to borrow one of Lispector's terms, 'Mansuetude' – a joy that is 'like a hand of grace' (Cixous 1987: 19). We learn from Cixous that grace is a having that circumvents the system of debt, a pure receiving, a pure attention, a looking with beneficent eyes; in short, an enormous effort that overrules 'the ego and the pretense of mastering things and knowing things' (Cixous 1987: 20). Is this what reading can be, the grace of looking with beneficent eyes?

If Cixous's reading is the grace of looking with beneficent eyes it is because it overrules the pretence of mastering things and knowing things; because it resists the instituted structure of philosophy reduced to a desire to know. In place of this desire, Cixous's approach offers us a reading that bypasses the mastery of institutional reading, which is structured by theory and system. The economy of attention and of pure receiving in Cixous's approach transforms us from the heaviness of the subject who needs – at all costs – to know, towards the weightless, attentive and receptive space of reading. As such, it takes us closer to the instituting moments of a love of wisdom and philosophy as a way of life.

Conclusion: The Attentive Work of Grace

> *Even my feverish pen cannot approach my rapture,*
> *an amazement so intense*
> RICHARD FLANAGAN, *GOULD'S BOOK OF FISH*: 2

> Reading – except where there is a certain quality of attention – obeys the law of gravity ... With a higher quality of attention our reading discovers gravity itself, and various systems of possible balance.[1]

In his 1964 film *Bande à Part*, Jean-Luc Godard has the three protagonists run through the Louvre in an attempt to view all the art treasures there in nine minutes and forty-three seconds. It is a marvellous cinematic moment, and one that has been referenced ever since (see also Bertolucci's *The Dreamers*), and yet we hardly think of this flight as a model of engaged art appreciation.[2] This is not how we look at art. (Of course, this is precisely what lends the scene its energy and force.) We understand how much there is to gain and to experience in standing for extended periods in front of major art works. Complex works of philosophy require a similarly committed 'viewing'. Throughout this book I have called for a slow reading of complex philosophical works. What I have meant by the term 'slow' has differed from context to context. Sometimes it has meant returning to texts in order to reread and reconsider them, at whatever speed. Other times it has meant sinking slowly and carefully into the atmosphere, mood, or *Stimmung* that the work creates. And still, in other contexts, it has involved a fine-tuned attention to detail and nuance, the kind that usually escapes our everyday hurried readings fuelled, as they increasingly are, by the corporate nature of much of our institutional work.

In my effort to develop practices of slow reading I have called on various metaphors and images to help us think through the many forms that slow reading may take. For example, I have figured these practices in terms of an openness or open-endedness, an unhurried reception, a meandering, a kind of essayistic mode, a meditative relation, a patience, an intimacy, a loving relation, a wondrous appreciation, a listening-with, a careful engagement, a proximity or nearness, an authentic relation, a generosity, an auratic quality, a careful habit, a receptive attitude, a polite respect, a giving, an approaching and a grace. What ties these different ways of thinking about slow reading together is, I think, the quality of attention. Slow reading is an openness to the other that is made possible through an attentive relation that allows us to sink into the world. The quality of our attention is the key to appreciating how slow reading works.[3]

Why does slow reading matter? In the Introduction we looked at the complex play between the *instituting* moments of philosophy – a love of wisdom and a way of life – and the *instituted* structure of philosophy – a desire to know. I argued that the dynamic, transformative moment and the determinant structure of the disciplinary or institutional norms work together to produce an ambivalent whole. Samuel Weber's notion of the 'intrinsic and violent instability of the institution' (Weber 1987: 17) underpins Wlad Godzich's view that the institution polices and forbids while simultaneously exploring the new. Godzich's point, that the guiding idea belongs with the instituting moment, suggests that, in the case of the institution of philosophy, a love of wisdom is 'both proper to it and yet alien'; present and 'yet curiously irrelevant to immediate concerns' (Godzich 1994: 237). In the light of this, slow reading matters because it develops practices aimed to revive the instituting moments of a love of wisdom and philosophy as a way of life. Slow reading engages the guiding idea in order to restore the transformative potential of philosophy, ensuring that it become something more than curiously irrelevant to immediate concerns.

CONCLUSION: THE ATTENTIVE WORK OF GRACE

In ethical terms, it matters that we engage with the other, with what is foreign and beyond us. It matters because this transforms us from one existential state to another. However, this engagement needs to be open. To engage in limited, protective and hurried ways is barely to engage at all. An ethical engagement with the other or with the text is one that opens us and changes us – transforming us over time. Slow reading is important precisely because it provides us with the attentive quality necessary for openness to occur. We can inquire into the conditions that facilitate open and engaged readings and we can ponder the elements required for an ethical community of readers to emerge. Throughout this book I have argued that the answers to these inquiries are to be found in the quality of attention we bring to our encounters and to the motivations behind this attention. Attention provides the means towards a transformative experience of openness to the other, to strangeness and to the world. Ethics is an approach that literally pays attention to the traces of the other in any such encounter. In terms of reading, we can think of ethics as an approach unburdened by preconceived ideas, ideologies or truths. It is a consent we bring to the text that allows us to encounter the particularity, uniqueness or the strangeness of the other, without immediately reducing this back to what we already know. This is, to return to Spivak, the 'impossible intimacy of the ethical' (Spivak 1993: 171) and the quality of attention is the key to reading well.

Although the quality of attention has been a theme weaving in and out of each of the chapters of this book, it is arguably in our work on Cixous that we have engaged it most wholeheartedly. As we have seen, Cixous's work on the approach allows us to think of reading in terms of an attentive intimacy. Her approach is grounded in an economy of attention, a slow and considered waiting that moves imperceptibly towards the other in passion and in grace. Attention, for Cixous, is accompanied by patience, equanimity and felicity. It involves an abandon that empties or evaporates the masterful self in preparing a space for the other. By dispensing with what Cixous refers to as 'the heavy self', attention allows us to reach the greatest exteriorization – the grace of a pure receiving and a pure attention which, as we have seen, is a wholly transformative rather than a simply passive experience (Cixous 1987: 18). The work of attention in countering the heavy self brings to mind Simone Weil's discussion of gravity and grace and it is worth detouring briefly to consider it here.

Simone Weil: attention to gravity and grace

Weil's work on attention has accompanied me in a silent way throughout the writing of this book. Much of what she works towards can be thought of in terms of the attentive patience that opens us to the other. In this it shares something with the slow reading I have developed here. When Weil writes that '[a]ttention is the rarest and purest form of generosity'[4] she confirms the ethical orientation of the attentive relation. Attention, for Weil, is what counters the weight of the ego-subject. She speaks of an 'attention which is so full that the "I" disappears' (Weil 1995: 118). Attention is heightened in the state she describes as waiting – the habitual form of empty attention that leads, in certain cases, to contemplation and the abandonment of the self. Attention is the work of grace, and Weil positions this against the gravity of self-centred and self-aggrandizing relations. Gravity is the descending movement that consolidates our terrestrial location; it forges the self and continues to offer it an egoistic weight. Gravity enlarges the self. Like Cixous's 'heavy self', gravity is what places a barrier between the self and the other by asserting the self's priority. Weil counterposes the weight of gravity with the weightless being of grace. She writes of the 'descending movement of gravity, the ascending movement of grace and the descending movement of the second degree of grace' (Weil 1995: 3–4). Grace is a falling away or ruin of the heavy self, made possible through detachment and attention. Attention, Weil claims, allows us to de-create, to empty or abandon the heavy self, in preparation for an encounter with the other.[5] We must de-create or destroy the heavy self or ego within ourselves in order to leave this space free. The act of grace is, for Weil, the possibility of ethics and thus the possibility of our encounter with the other: 'I have to deprive all that I call "I" of the light of my attention and turn it on to that which cannot be conceived' (Weil 1995: 118).[6] Attention flows from the heavy self towards the other.

Turning our attention to what cannot be conceived is another way of thinking about reading in ethical terms. Weil's work here, once again, touches lightly against Cixous's economy of pure attention and pure receiving. Weil writes: 'Attention consists of suspending our thought, leaving it detached, empty and

CONCLUSION: THE ATTENTIVE WORK OF GRACE 181

ready ... Above all, our thought should be empty, waiting, not seeking anything, but ready to receive' (Weil 1951: 56).[7] In this passage we hear, too, faint echoes of Virginia Woolf's advice, encountered in our Introduction, to embrace the true complexity of reading by 'receiving impressions' and waiting for 'the dust of reading to settle' (Woolf 1925: 266). In both cases judgement is bypassed or suspended in favour of an attentive sitting-with the world.[8] For although Woolf acknowledges the necessity of a second phase of reading which involves passing judgements and making comparisons, the inevitability of this is significantly lightened by her observation that we must pass judgement, '[b]ut not directly'. Between reading and judgement there lies the space and time of waiting: 'Wait for the dust of reading to settle; for the conflict and questioning to die down; walk, talk, pull the dead petals from a rose, or fall asleep' (Woolf 1925: 266). For Weil, this waiting or attention provides the possibility of a reading that balances the law of gravity: 'Reading', she writes, 'except where there is a certain quality of attention – obeys the law of gravity ... With a higher quality of attention our reading discovers gravity itself, and various systems of possible balance' (Weil 1995: 136).

Weil's higher quality of attention partakes of the slowness that I have been referring to as slow reading – it involves waiting and receiving. In this it reminds us of the profound existential transformation Pierre Hadot describes in relation to the spiritual exercises of the Hellenistic and Roman philosophers. A slow, careful and open attentiveness to the world works therapeutically to transform our relation with the other: 'Little by little, [attentive waiting] make[s] possible the indispensable metamorphosis of our inner self' (Hadot 1995: 83). Reading is an attentive state that allows us to wait for the other to appear. As such, it is a state of grace for it de-creates the weight of the ego or self who believes he or she knows everything concerning the other in advance. In Chapter Five, in our discussion of Beauvoir, we saw how Teresa Brennan grounds her work on discernment within the meditative tradition in philosophy. Brennan's quality of discernment is relevant here. While she makes no connections with Weil's understanding of attention or grace, there are, I think, significant points of contact. Discernment involves a sustained attention that one can develop only over time. From this, an 'other I' emerges, an aspect of the self open to an unguarded relation with the other and the world. Like

Weil's state of grace, Brennan's 'other I' discerns without self-interest or self-aggrandizement: it 'gathers attention together to discern the affects that disrupt concentration and reflection'. The attention so central to discernment accords, Brennan claims, with the life-drive by providing 'an alternative to the subject-centered focus' (Brennan 2004: 129).[9] Discernment falters, however, when it is hurried: 'it makes mistakes when it is rushed to conclude before its time (it is rushed by the ego, which always needs a plan)' (Brennan 2004: 120). In such cases, discernment registers as a feeling and it is here that I think we can connect Brennan's work with the discussion of *Stimmung* we have undertaken in Chapter Two.[10] Hans Ulrich Gumbrecht's work on reading for *Stimmung* makes a case for the attentive work of following 'configurations of atmosphere and mood in order to encounter otherness [and to yield to it] in intense and intimate ways' (Gumbrecht 2012: 12–13).[11] This experimental mode of reading opens thought out, towards feeling, atmosphere, and mood in vital and energetic ways. With what purpose? To transform us 'little by little', making possible 'the indispensable metamorphosis of our inner self' (Hadot 1995: 83).

Martin Heidegger: rapture (*Rausch*) and meditative thinking

We can think of Weil's attention in terms of a discernment or an intense and intimate encounter. In both cases, the question of surrender arises. Whether in discerning or the attentive work of reading for *Stimmung* – or, similarly, Cixous's approach as *entredeux* – we find an evaporation of self, an erasure that makes space for the other. The heavy self of ego and mastery (or even, for that matter, of ideology) makes way for or surrenders to the strangeness of the other. This surrender engenders a positive incomprehension that allows the other, as we have seen Cixous claim, to be 'very much other', 'so very much not-me' (Cixous in Cixous and Calle-Gruber 1997: 16). To empty the self in surrender is to abandon the ego to allow the other to gleam. In terms of reading, what we are talking about here is a slow and careful attention that opens without fear or anxiety. Without these barriers reading takes on an entirely different form. In fact, we can say – with Martin Heidegger – that reading in this attentive and

CONCLUSION: THE ATTENTIVE WORK OF GRACE

receptive state comes close to the rapture (*Rausch*) of aesthetic experience. Rapture, understood as joy or ecstatic wonder, is a pure receiving that manifests as a non-appropriative desire to reach towards the other (Bray 2004: 148). In rapture, subject and object fall away. Heidegger writes:

> Rapture as a state of feeling explodes the very subjectivity of the subject . . . Beauty breaks through the confinement of the 'object' placed at a distance, standing on its own, and brings it into essential and original correlation to the 'subject'. Beauty is no longer objective, no longer an object. The aesthetic state is neither subjective nor objective.
>
> HEIDEGGER 1991: 123

There are links here with the work on wonder we have explored in Luce Irigaray's writing in Chapter Three. Reading in this sense involves an aesthetics of rapture or openness, or even one of receiving. Attention dissolves the heaviness of self and other in an infinite and wondrous engagement with life. This receptive attitude or patient attention towards what we read allows us literally to surrender to the text. Heidegger's concern with rapture comes out of his engagement with Friedrich Nietzsche's work on art and the aesthetic state, focusing on feeling and mood. For Heidegger, moving beyond what he sees as the limitations of Nietzsche's metaphysics, rapture is the state of release from the heavy self that allows us to extend towards the other; it is, most importantly, an 'ascent beyond oneself' (Heidegger 1991: 136). Rapture binds and connects without force or restraint, and opens us to the other. Rapture links us to the meditative thinking that Heidegger urges us to embrace; a 'persistent, courageous thinking' linked to the openness of what he refers to as *Gelassenheit* (Heidegger 1966: 56).[12] From this form of meditative thinking a different reading emerges, one that does more than take notice, one that grows more thoughtful and ponders the question at hand (Heidegger 1966: 52). Without this meditative thinking and the reading that accompanies it, Heidegger warns of the danger of an indifference that could result in 'total thoughtlessness' (Heidegger 1966: 56). Writing in 1955 he speculates: 'the approaching tide of technological revolution in the atomic age could so captivate, bewitch, dazzle, and beguile man that calculative thinking may someday come to be accepted and practiced *as the only* way of thinking' (Heidegger 1966: 56). Calculative thinking ushers in a thoughtlessness: 'For nowadays we take in everything in the quickest and cheapest way, only to forget it just as quickly, instantly' (Heidegger 1966: 45). We are, Heidegger claims, 'in *flight from thinking*' and this flight is 'the ground of thoughtlessness' (Heidegger 1966: 45). The peculiarity of calculative thinking:

> consists in the fact that whenever we plan, research, and organize, we always reckon with conditions that are given. We take them into account with the calculated intention of their serving specific purposes. Thus we can count on definite results. This calculation is the mark of all thinking that plans and investigates. Such thinking remains calculation even if it neither works with numbers nor uses an adding machine or computer. Calculative thinking computes. It computes ever new, ever more promising and at the same time more economical possibilities. Calculative thinking races from one prospect to the next. Calculative thinking never stops, never collects itself. Calculative thinking is not meditative thinking, not thinking which contemplates the meaning which reigns in everything that is.
> HEIDEGGER 1966: 46

Calculative thinking, as Heidegger describes it, is at odds with the quality of attention we have seen in Weil's work. In essence, it is a kind of anti-attention incapable of stopping, pausing, pondering, or collecting itself. Calculative thinking serves specific purposes, counts on definite results, plans and investigates, races from one prospect to the next. There is no meandering, no opening out to an unknown and unknowable path. Given this, meditative thinking and rapture work as antidotes to the thoughtlessness of calculative thinking and are, thus, kin to the slow reading we have been investigating here.[13]

Reading as an aesthetic experience

Our brief glimpse of Heidegger's work on rapture brings to the fore the aesthetic dimension of slow reading. In Chapter Two, in the context of our discussion of Adorno's work on the essay, we looked

CONCLUSION: THE ATTENTIVE WORK OF GRACE

at Luiz Costa Lima's work on criticity, the kind of questioning that he distinguishes from both judging (critique) and criticism. Criticity, as we have seen, is a critical orientation, but one coming out of an openness and a questioning that does its best to resist ideological formulations. Unlike aestheticization, it avoids the limitations of law and systematic order. By engaging with works as unique and strange, criticity preserves the meanderings and the ramblings of the experimental drive. In this, we can say that it shares something of the attentive and receptive attitude of Heidegger's rapture, and certainly of his meditative thinking. For Costa Lima, criticity engages the moment of suspension and expectation that accompanies aesthetic experience (Costa Lima 1996: 129). By transforming the everyday world of nearness into the strange and the surprising, criticity gives us back the world anew: 'This transformation of the proximate into the distant, of the automatized into the surprising, allows the receiver to examine the work also ethically, for this is one of the dimensions of criticity, its "real" world'. This means, for Costa Lima, that criticity is neither identical with nor opposed to the domain of the ethical, but rather that it 'recognizes the ethical from the vantage point of this distanced position' (Costa Lima 1996: 130); this distanced position being art.

What might this mean for our discussion of slow reading? Like Costa Lima's criticity, slow reading inhabits the spaces of suspension and expectation. By pausing, meandering, and bypassing the demands of calculative thought it transforms the everyday world of nearness into the strange and the surprising, thus permitting us both an ethical and aesthetic opening to the other. Slow reading teaches us attention and the patience to wait for the other to emerge. Like Walter Benjamin's art critic [*Kunstkritiker*], slow reading distinguishes itself from the art judge [*Kunstrichter*], the one who, relying on a body of applicable legislation, 'lays down the law and then judges in accordance with it' (Costa Lima 1996: 146). By taking other avenues, by meandering around the systematic demands of law, order, and calculation, slow reading arrives at a very different place. Is this the space where ethics and aesthetics meet? In this sense, slow reading does not finalize debate on what the other (or text) is. On the contrary, it opens and re-opens questions posed. As such, it partakes of the thoughtfulness of Heidegger's meditative thinking because its aim is primarily to continue and to deepen thought. Slow reading counters the institutionalization of thinking – and thus reading – which is more concerned with stabilizing meaning by reducing thought to debatable formulas and identifiable positions. Rather than seeking to reduce and to simplify, slow reading – as we have seen in the case of Gumbrecht's work – is propelled by a desire to embrace complexity. It does not provide answers; rather, by questioning, it quite simply provokes thought.

Hans Ulrich Gumbrecht: reading for intensity

In the Introduction we saw Gumbrecht suggest that in confronting complexity, reading comes close to aesthetic experience. While the negativity of aesthetic experience sits uncomfortably with the corporate nature of the modern institution – starved as it is for 'time' – Gumbrecht makes the case for untimeliness: 'We need institutions of higher education to produce and to protect excess time against the mostly pressing temporalities of the everyday' (Gumbrecht 2003: 87).[14] Such untimeliness provides an important step towards the possibility of an aesthetic response in the institutional domain. By providing our students with complexity and the time to engage with it, slow reading teaches us, in turn, the art of doing philosophy well. And yet what, precisely, is this? In doing philosophy well we engage in thought in order that it transform us, in order that it shift our thinking from one stage to another, little by little. In doing philosophy well, we reconnect with the instituting moments of a love of wisdom and philosophy as a way of life.

Following this line of thought, Gumbrecht returns to the proximity of reading and artistic practice in his discussion of the aesthetic experience of intensity. Here he argues that aesthetic experience offers us moments of intensity that resist our everyday tendencies to interpret and to ascribe meaning. As with complexity, this intensity cannot be read in calculative ways. Reading purely for meaning or for some specific outcome is a way of avoiding the intensity one confronts. The kind of reading Gumbrecht calls forth involves a movement between losing and regaining intellectual control. This type of reading emerges out of stopping; it comes out of our 'being quiet for a moment', and this is only possible when time is not an issue (Gumbrecht 2004: 142–3). Gumbrecht's reading oscillates between moments of meaning and what he refers to as 'presence'. He suggests that the possibility of experiencing meaning and presence simultaneously is Niklas Luhmann's way of thinking about the specificity of art (Gumbrecht 2004: 108). Presence indicates a bodily intensity wherein we sink into the world, open to the epiphany that the aesthetic experience can be. Gumbrecht writes of being lost in focused intensity, where we 'connect with a layer in our existence that simply wants the things of the world close to our skin' (Gumbrecht 2004: 106). He links the oscillation between meaning and presence, and between losing and regaining intellectual control, with Heidegger's notion of *Gelassenheit*. In his version, *Gelassenheit* is itself an oscillation, a movement simultaneously between our openness to the aesthetic experience and the existential state summoned by the aesthetic encounter (Gumbrecht 2004: 116). It is, as well, the state of being simultaneously quiet and wide awake (Gumbrecht 2004: 136). What I think Gumbrecht means by this is that *Gelassenheit* – whether we think of this as serenity, composure, or releasement – is our ability to encounter intensity in such a way that our thinking and our reading open out in more than calculative ways. Reading here hovers between intensity and perfect quietness. Gumbrecht claims that in being close to art, this new form of reading is '*deictic*, rather than interpretive and solution-oriented' (Gumbrecht 2004: 128), because it stages ongoing encounters with both the intense and the complex.[15]

With Gumbrecht's work in mind we can think of slow reading in terms of an aesthetics of reading that promotes encounters with intensity beyond the everyday. Such a reading resists reductive interpretation in order to sit with the aesthetic experience of intensity, much in the manner that we saw, in the Introduction, Stieglitz sit with his land.[16] Thought in this way, the aesthetic dimension of rapture brings us back to the bodily intensity of a pure attention and a pure receiving. Slow reading, framed from this perspective, suspends analysis and judgement – narrowly defined – in order to articulate feelings and intensities. By approaching the work in an unencumbered or uncluttered way, the reader surrenders to the uniqueness of the text. In this, the reading that emerges becomes itself an aesthetic experience or a work of art capable of keeping the question of ethics alive.

Throughout this book I have undertaken a celebration of slow reading, though I have certainly not intended to position it as the only reading we ought to engage with. There are times when other forms of reading are called for. Nonetheless, what I have hoped to show is that slow reading somewhat thematically involves an intensity of reading – a quality of attention – that keeps the question of ethics alive. In

> an age of 'work', that is to say, of hurry, of indecent and perspiring haste, which wants to get 'everything done' at once ... this art does not so easily get anything done, it teaches to read well, that is to say, to read slowly, deeply, looking cautiously before and aft, with reservations, with doors left open, with delicate eyes and fingers.
> NIETZSCHE 1982: 5

Slow reading reminds us to take the time to ponder precisely why slow philosophy is so important in this age of hurry and indecent and perspiring haste. If Heidegger is correct, and we risk falling into an age where calculative thinking is the only mode of thought, then slow reading is the timely reminder that the quality of our attention is what is required in order to stage intense encounters with both the other and the world, in order to be transformed little by little.

The quality of our attention is constantly under threat. In institutional terms, our opportunities to engage in slow and attentive reading have significantly decreased. The worldly and corporate concerns of productivity, speed, and efficiency now haunt the academy, impacting on our ability to do philosophy well. This is why it is so important to re-engage with the sheer pleasure that reading can entail. Somewhat paradoxically, the inspiration for renewing the quality of attention within the institution comes from 'outside' – from non-institutional or non-professional, recreational forms of reading. Throughout the writing of this book many works of fiction have accompanied and sustained me. Above all, they have reminded me of what is possible when we fully engage in reading slowly. One of these many works is Richard Flanagan's *Gould's Book of Fish* (2001), and I have inserted fragments from this book amidst the pages here. Each chapter is prefaced by a passage from Flanagan's rather astonishing work, and I have chosen to do this for several reasons. One of these involves the gesture of importing something of my recreational reading into my professional work in order to restore the aesthetic experience of reading slowly and attentively to the institutional domain. In the Introduction, Woolf urged us to read slowly and unprofessionally, 'reading for the love of reading' (and for the love of wisdom, we might add), refusing the speed and haste of the critic and the circumstances that lead to him having 'only one second in which to load and aim and shoot' (Woolf 1925: 270). Woolf's everyday reader reads outside, beyond, or even in spite of the institution. By importing the intensity of this attentive experience back within the context of the institution we seek to re-engage the instituting moments of a love of wisdom and philosophy as a way of life.

NOTES

Preface: Why Slow Reading Today?

1 Althusser (1979: 15).
2 For a discussion of Althusser's 'guilty reading' see Boulous Walker (1998: 27–49).
3 For a literary approach to this question see Hillis Miller (1987). See also Poole (2002).
4 Could it be that part of our (irrational) desire to smoke in spite of the dangers stems from the fact that it momentarily brackets the speed and productivity of life around us? The cigarette break arguably offers us respite from the technocratic demands of the modern work place. Perhaps, though, as a non-smoker I am romanticizing the situation.

Introduction: On Being Slow and Doing Philosophy

1 In Plato's *Apology* (1877) Socrates famously claims that his aim is to try 'to persuade each of you to concern himself less about what he has than about what he is, so that he may make himself as good and as reasonable as possible' (Plato *Apology* 36b).
2 Hadot claims that a transition is in place and that underneath the literary charm of Plato's dialogues the trace of a more scholarly practice linking the dialogues to the Platonic Academy is underway. Aristotle completes this move by codifying the rules of the dialectic: 'There were well-defined roles for both questioner and respondent in these argumentation exercises, and the rules of this intellectual fencing were rigorously defined' (Hadot 1995: 153).
3 Gilbert Ryle's Presidential Address to the Aristotelian Society, 'Knowing How and Knowing That', raises questions that are

pertinent to our discussion here: 'Philosophers have not done justice to the distinction which is quite familiar to all of us between knowing that something is the case and knowing how to do things. In their theories of knowledge they concentrate on the discovery of truths or facts, and they either ignore the discovery of ways and methods of doing things or else they try to reduce it to the discovery of facts. They assume that intelligence equates with the contemplation of propositions and is exhausted in this contemplation'. And further: 'The uneducated public erroneously equates education with the imparting of knowledge-that. Philosophers have not hitherto made it very clear what its error is' (Ryle 1946: 4, 16).

4   Arendt adds: 'The extent to which this strolling determined the pace of his [Benjamin's] thinking was perhaps most clearly revealed in the peculiarities of his gait, which Max Rychner described as "one advancing and tarrying, a strange mixture of both"' (Arendt in Benjamin 1969: 21–2).

5   Brian Castro writes: 'Slowness is essential to consciousness. Great art slows down time' (Castro 2011: 20).

6   Of course Stieglitz's reference to 'snap shots' here carries a weight of ironic understatement.

7   Paul Cilliers explores the equation of slowness and stupidity in three novels in his insightful philosophical work on the importance of slowness (Cilliers 2006: 110f).

8   *Shorter Oxford English Dictionary*, Vol 2. N-Z (Oxford: Oxford University Press, 2007: 2878). For an excellent discussion of the central role of speed in late capitalist culture, see Brennan (2000).

9   Teresa Brennan notes the popular associations of the deadly sin of sloth with inertia, reaching from medieval times: 'The slothful are inert. They literally cannot move. They are symbolized now by a century that began with hysterical paralysis as a most popular disorder and ended with the syndrome of chronic fatigue'. See Brennan (2004: 101).

10 Lutz Koepnick offers a thoroughly engaging reconceptualization of slowness in his recent work: 'Once denigrated as the tool of conservatives or reactionaries, slowness today serves a crucial function to challenge deterministic fantasies of mindless progression and develop concepts of meaningful progress instead' (Koepnick 2014: 14). He claims that while the core of modernism has almost always been equated with speed, slow movements have always cohabited its space in complex and important ways.

11 Prevarication can be thought of in terms of procrastination, which Anna Della Subin argues has, since the 1950s, been largely pathologized. In 'How to Stop Time' (Della Subin 2014) she makes a case for re-figuring procrastination as an act of resistance. Extending the work of the Egyptian-born novelist Albert Cossery, Della Subin calls for a strict schedule of idleness to counter the canonized value of productivity in contemporary Western culture. Cossery's *Laziness in the Fertile Valley* brings to mind Paul Lafargue's important book *The Right to be Lazy (1880)* (Lafargue 1917). See Cossery (2005).

12 Cilliers underscores the significance of delay in our understanding of complex systems: 'An event in the environment of the system does not have inherent and immediate significance for the system. Its significance is established in time as it is re-enacted in the system and carried over into the future' (Cilliers 2006: 109). See also Cilliers (1998).

13 The argument against an unreflective valuation of speed and for slowness is, Cilliers claims, a political one: 'We should put up some resistance to a culture in which being fast is a virtue in itself. We should say "no" with a little more regularity' (Cilliers 2006: 106).

14 Undoubtedly, one of the most influential of these works is Daniel Kahneman's recent study, *Thinking, Fast and Slow* (Kahneman 2013). In this work, Kahneman takes an existing distinction between 'System 1' and 'System 2' (in contemporary 'dual-process' psychological models of the brain) to develop what he refers to as a 'psychodrama with two characters' (21). He does this in order to explore the fundamentally different ways we relate to the world around us. As the title of the book suggests, Kahneman differentiates these modes of apprehending the world in terms of thinking fast and thinking slow. While in System 1 thinking occurs automatically, in System 2 thinking is accompanied by focused attention and arousal (415). Interestingly, it is only System 2 that he identifies as an attentive mode, a slow and deliberate effort – though this mode is far from central to his discussion throughout the book. It is System 1, with its fast, associative, automatic orientation, which emerges as the focus of his research and as the 'hero' of his book. He writes: 'I describe System 1 as effortlessly originating impressions and feelings that are the main sources of the explicit beliefs and deliberate choices of System 2' (21). The speed of these impressions is, however, often problematic, creating coherence by radically simplifying its engagement with the world: 'When information is scarce, which is a common occurrence, System 1 operates as a machine for jumping to conclusions' (85). Kahneman's mostly positive account of speed remains wedded to largely unexamined

associations between slowness and sloth. At times he makes these prejudices explicit, labelling System 2 as slothful and prone to 'ego-depletion' (42).

15 See also Newkirk (2012) and Miedema (2009).
16 For a discussion of the contemporary implications of doing philosophy 'professionally' see Sayre (2004: 241–55).
17 My thanks to Nick Trakakis for bringing my attention to this aspect of Wittgenstein's work.
18 In *Culture and Value*, Wittgenstein writes: 'In philosophy the winner of the race is the one who can run most slowly. Or: the one who gets there last' (Wittgenstein 1998: 34).
19 McGinn writes: 'Wittgenstein's method is aimed, not at producing new, stateable conclusions, but at working on us in such a way as to change our whole style of thinking or way of approaching problems. The concept of therapy emphasizes that Wittgenstein's philosophical method aims to engage the reader in an active process of work on himself' (McGinn 1997: 23). McGinn's observation is supported by what Pierre Hadot earlier says of Wittgenstein's work: 'What motivates the *Tractatus* is the will to lead the reader to a certain kind of life, and a certain attitude, which, moreover, is fully analogous to the existential options of ancient philosophy: "to live within the present", without regretting, fearing, or hoping for anything' (Hadot 2002: 273).
20 Of course, this call to slowness is hardly new; Hegel criticized Kant for his lack of contemplation.
21 Monk writes: '[O]ne of Wittgenstein's central themes in his later work is the importance of preserving the integrity of a *non-scientific* form of understanding, the kind of understanding characteristic of the arts and the kind of understanding that Goethe, Spengler and Wittgenstein sought to protect from the encroachment of science and scientism' (Monk 2005: 101).
22 Monk is referring here to Wittgenstein's idea of 'imponderable evidence'.
23 Woolf begins this essay by stating that the only advice one should take on the matter of how to read a book is to take no advice at all. She goes on, though, to encourage the reader's independence and to warn against the tyranny of authorities 'heavily furred and gowned' (Woolf 1925: 258). An admirable beginning to any reading, she says, is to 'banish all preconceptions' (259).
24 Woolf writes: 'to open the mind wide to the fast flocking of innumerable impressions' (Woolf 1925: 267).

25 In Chapter Two we will return to the question of judgement, differentiating it from the finality of verdict.

26 In a recent work Siri Hustvedt identifies two modes that parallel, to some extent, Woolf's two phases; these she identifies as reading and reflecting: 'When I read, I engage my capacity for inner speech. I assume the written words of the writer who, for the time being, becomes my own internal narrator, the voice in my head. This new voice has its own rhythms and pauses that I sense and adopt as I read. The text is both outside me and inside me. If I am reading critically, my own words will intervene. I will ask, doubt, and wonder, but I cannot occupy both positions at once. I am either reading a book or pausing to reflect on it' (Hustvedt 2012: 134).

27 'Judgement' is arguably open to change, evolution, reconsideration, while 'verdict' suggests finality.

28 This other reading beyond judgement and its links with slowness are captured in two passages from Michael Ondaatje's novel *The English Patient*: 'To rest was to receive all aspects of the world without judgement' (49), and 'Read him slowly, dear girl, you must read Kipling slowly. Watch carefully where the commas fall so you can discover the natural pauses. He is a writer who used pen and ink. He looked up from the page a lot, I believe, stared through his window and listened to birds, as most writers who are alone do. Some do not know the names of the birds, though he did. Your eye is too quick and North American. Think about the speed of his pen. What an appalling, barnacled old first paragraph it is otherwise' (94). There are numerous references to speed and slowing throughout the novel. See Ondaatje (1992). For an exploration of reading as an act, see Wolfgang Iser's (1978) work on the specificity of reading literature.

29 There is something in Woolf's evocation of time that reminds me of the 'purposeless strolling' that characterizes much of Walter Benjamin's work. Benjamin's figure of the *flâneur*, inspired by Baudelaire's essay 'Le Peintre de la vie moderne' (Baudelaire 1863: 877–83), haunts both the themes and the style of his thought. In her introduction to Benjamin's essays *Illuminations: Essays and Reflections*, Hannah Arendt writes: 'It is to him [the *flâneur*, Benjamin], aimlessly strolling through the crowds in the big cities in studied contrast to their hurried, purposeful activity, that things reveal themselves in their secret meaning: "The true picture of the past *flits* by" ('Philosophy of History'), and only the *flâneur* who idly strolls by receives the message . . . the *flâneur*, through the *gestus* of

purposeless strolling, turns his back to the crowd, even as he is propelled and swept by it' (Arendt in Benjamin 1969: 12, 13). And further: 'The extent to which this strolling determined the pace of his thinking was perhaps most clearly revealed in the peculiarities of his gait, which Max Rychner described as "at once advancing and tarrying, a strange mixture of both"' (Arendt in Benjamin 1969: 21–2). Benjamin's *flâneur* literally embodies the slow and hesitant movement that enables the reader to read against the grain or stand out from the crowd. The act of strolling is a provocation to a system built upon haste and production. Strolling literally allows the dust of reading to settle.

30 In *Moments of Being* Woolf explores those moments of concentrated intensity that we can distinguish from everyday experience, characterizing the former as a 'slow opening up of single and solemn moments of concentrated emotion' (Woolf 1976: 22). These 'moments of being' are depicted throughout both Woolf's novels and memoirs. Jeanne Schulkind suggests, in her 'Introduction' to *Moments of Being*, that Woolf's writing plays between the poles of surface and spreading depths, often (as in the memoir 'A Sketch of the Past') interweaving the two: 'The moments of being, sometimes charged with revelations of astonishing intensity, are threaded among scenes, of typical days' (Schulkind in Woolf 1976: 22). In her own work, Woolf describes the intensity of her moments of being in terms of the openness of intuition or the capacity to receive shock which, she claims, is the capacity that makes her a writer (Woolf 1976: 81, 83). To write is to be open to those privileged moments of being: 'we are sealed vessels afloat on what it is convenient to call reality; and at some moments, the sealing matter cracks; in floods reality' (142). The openness that Woolf the writer embodies can, I think, be adopted, too, in our reading.

31 Woolf's coupling of reading slowly with reading unprofessionally, finds an interesting echo in Helen Garner's amusing coupling of reading slowly with innocence: 'How wonderful it was, the way we read as children . . . [Later] I read much too fast. It's an insane, desperate guzzling. At its worst it gets so that I have to force myself to read each paragraph twice. One morning as I skimmed the news headlines, my stomach knotted with the usual anxiety about whether I would ever, ever be well-informed – *and what if somebody asks me a question about the Republic?* – I noticed an advertisement for a speed reading course. It occurred to me that these courses might make provision for people with the opposite problem. After breakfast I called the number. A pleasant man answered. I outlined my problem and what I needed. His response was an endless, dumb-struck silence.

He must have thought it was a hoax. But surely I can't be the only person who suffers from this malady? There's a niche in the market here. Some smart operator could make a fortune, reconstituting innocence' (Garner 2001: 40–1). Of course, the answer to Garner's quest is to enrol in a suitable philosophy course! (My thanks to Caitlin Goss for this passage).

32 On the disjunction between 'science' and 'reading', and the particular problem of establishing a 'science of reading', Kamuf writes: 'For if reading is on the condition of some alterity, some otherness that cannot be appropriated by the same as sure and certain knowledge – thus, a possible science – then would not a science of reading, if it were one day possible, have to spell the end of reading? To be possible, this science would have somehow to overcome the unknowable, irreducible alterity that is the condition at the heart of reading. It can achieve itself as science only by appropriating to itself the heart of alterity – the other's heart – as knowledge. No doubt the same movement toward appropriation can be discerned at work in all scientific endeavours – it is indeed the very movement of science or philosophy' (Kamuf 2000).

33 Gumbrecht's reference to an 'auratic' concept of reading is interesting. Benjamin, following Novalis, characterizes aura as 'a kind of attentiveness' (Benjamin 1969: 188). I return to reading and its links with attentiveness in the final chapter of this book.

34 See Luhmann (1990).

35 Further: 'I am convinced that it is our preeminent task today to confront students with intellectual complexity, which means that *deictic gestures* – that is, pointing to occasional condensations of such complexity – are what we should really focus on' (Gumbrecht 2004: 95). And: 'good academic teaching is a staging of complexity; it is drawing our students' attention to complex phenomena and problems, rather than prescribing how they have to understand certain problems and how, ultimately, they must deal with them. In other words, good academic teaching should be *deictic*, rather than interpretive and solution-oriented' (Gumbrecht 2004: 128).

36 Gumbrecht qualifies this, insisting on the differences he sees between the domains of institutional learning and aesthetic experience. Following Karl Heinz Bohrer, he notes the incommensurability that exists between the 'negativity' of aesthetic experience and the practices of state-funded universities founded to profess truth (Gumbrecht 2003: 86–7).

37 We can link Gumbrecht's untimeliness with what Gaita has to say about protecting the unworldly space that university teaching should

be: 'When a university provides students with a space that protects them from the pressures of the world – from worldliness . . . and from the pressures that conspire to make them children of their times, then it fulfils its primary public obligation . . . The unworldly connotations of the expression "a community of scholars" should not be a source of embarrassment . . . we must preserve the unworldly space in which university teachers are able to reveal to their students what it means, mostly deeply, to devote one's life to an academic vocation' (Gaita 2012).

38 Gaita argues that a kind of high-flying thoughtlessness thrives in our current institutional context: 'Academics now tend to cut their subjects down to a size that is tractable enough to meet the demands of accountability. Impressive technicality, a kind of high-flying thoughtlessness, can shine in such conditions. This is true even in philosophy that glories, but increasingly without justification, in the fact that radical self-criticism is of its essence' (Gaita 2012).

39 In Chapter Two and the Conclusion I revisit this question of intensity in another of Gumbrecht's books *Atmosphere, Mood, Stimmung* (Gumbrecht 2012).

40 For a discussion of 'riskful thinking' see Gumbrecht (2002: 140–7). Gumbrecht maintains that the image of the 'ivory tower, more often than not a negative reference, provides the distance or interval from the everyday world that makes "riskful thinking" possible' (Gumbrecht 2004: 126).

41 Maurice Merleau-Ponty's course notes on the institution allow us to think of slow reading as an initiative that impacts upon the (academic) institution in new and potentially positive ways. See Merleau-Ponty (2010).

42 Critchley's exploration of pleasure and joy in teaching philosophy resonates with Raimond Gaita's depiction of philosophy in terms of love and joy. See Gaita (2012).

43 Critchley refers to modern universities as 'factories for the production of knowledge' issuing 'degrees, PhD theses, and research' (27); 'an increasingly uniform and pleasureless machine, a kind of knowledge factory at the service of the abstractions of the state and capital' (Critchley 2010: 20).

44 Critchley refers to the fragility of the intellectual ethos which, to his mind, is 'the easiest thing in the world to destroy' (Critchley 2010: 30). He defines 'ethos' as, on the one hand, 'atmosphere, climate, and place', and, on the other, 'a disposition for thinking and thoughtfulness' (29). Critchley's notion of ethos touches up against Gumbrecht's notion of *Stimmung* that we examine in Chapter Two.

45 Critchley draws on Lacan's distinction between knowledge and truth, where the slowness of 'truth' challenges the relentless self-certainty and activity of knowledge: 'truth is something new, something unpredictable and surprising, something with a relation to enjoyment, something that perhaps even *idles* in the relentless activity of knowledge' (Critchley 2010: 27, emphasis added).

46 In the same preface Nietzsche comments on the significance of his own scholarly itinerary, writing: 'It is not for nothing that one has been a philologist, perhaps one is a philologist still, that is to say, a teacher of slow reading' (Nietzsche 1982: 5).

47 On the question of reading as conflict and battle, I suggest that typically 'combative' readings in much contemporary philosophical work function to close down possibilities for thought by containing what is being read in simple statements that reduce the complexity and ambiguity at play. Opposing or criticizing a text all too often becomes an excuse to read poorly (or unethically), glossing over inconvenient ambiguities that may impede a neat and tidy resolution. See Boulous Walker (2006: 237, n. 58). Kelly Oliver suggests that Nietzsche would do well to heed the 'manliness' of his own reading. She argues that there are 'manly' implications (of occupation) that need to be considered in relation to Nietzsche's 'genealogical reading', his 'reading well': 'Genealogy is a way of reading that opens on to the other of the text. Yet within Nietzsche's genealogy, that other is not permitted to be feminine' (Oliver 1995: 20).

48 A 'read' is the stomach of an animal, specifically the abomasum or fourth stomach of a ruminant. *Shorter Oxford English Dictionary*, Vol 2. N-Z (Oxford: Oxford University Press, 2007: 2477).

49 The Free/Slow University of Warsaw has joined the general movement towards slowness. See Gora (2010). See also Parkins (2004: 363–82) and Craig and Parkins (2006).

50 Emmanuel Levinas has something to say indirectly about eating in his work on understanding. While he explores Western conceptual thought through the metaphors of seizure and grasping, he also talks about the relation of totality characterized by a 'living from' or 'absorption and incorporation of the other'. Here the *bonne conscience* is something of a *bonne vivant*, eating well and taking the world into itself – incorporating the other. This consumption is at odds with Levinas's depiction of the relation of infinity or desire, where the other remains at an ethical distance, not digested or assimilated as 'good soup'. Levinas writes: 'The other arrests the rhythm of my life by its ability to disrupt the familiarity of "living from" the world, from nourishing myself and attending to my daily

needs'. Ethics is the distance that stops me from assimilating the world to myself (Levinas 1969). For an excellent discussion of Levinas and eating, see Hirst (2004). In a recent book, David Mikics links slow reading with appetite. He writes: 'The great English Romantic critic William Hazlitt advocated reading with gusto. To read well requires appetite. My primary advice to you, always, is to be hearty in your desire for the written word, and to keep your sense of fun' (Mikics 2013: 6). Mikics's book is a practical how-to guide for slow reading, which 'will teach any interested person how to be a good and careful reader, a slow reader, even in the age of the Internet' (3). To this end, Mikics offers fourteen *rules* for reading: patience, asking the right questions, identifying the voice, getting a sense of style, noticing beginnings and endings, identifying signposts, using a dictionary, tracking key words, finding the author's basic thought, being suspicious, finding the parts, writing it down, and, finally, finding another book. While I am pleased to see the publication of works devoted to slow reading, I am somewhat concerned about approaching this in terms of 'rules'. Perhaps Mikics means something more like 'guides', 'starting points' or 'suggestions'.

51 What is ethical, in Reading's terms, is that this practice of reading does not ask what the text means but rather what demand the text makes or how one is addressed by the text (Readings 1991: xxv). In Lyotard's work, reading 'instantiates a "space-time" or a "universe" alien to that of either interpretation or theory'; it 'shares a temporality and a positioning with aesthetic and ethical judgment' (Readings 1991: xix). Readings observes that 'The time of reading as site of resistance is to be opposed to both the timelessness of theory and the accountable, teleologically unified and organized "time of extraction" that characterizes the process of hermeneutic interpretation' (xix). Reading is a 'resistance to the rule of understanding as conceptual reduction ... that rule by concept is the function of both capitalism and state bureaucratic totalitarianism' (xx).

52 For a discussion of Lyotard's work in terms of 'paralogical experimentation' see Readings (1991: 123).

53 Readings (1991: 107): 'We must try to judge without importing criteria from other genres – such as that of theory'.

54 For a discussion of how indeterminate judgement links with Lyotard's notion of injustice and the *differend*, see Boulous Walker (1998: 68–84).

55 Costa Lima uses the term '*criticidade*' (criticity) in order to distinguish the act of questioning from both judging (critique) and

criticism, (see also translator's note: ix in Costa Lima 1996). In this work, he follows Georg Lukács's argument in *Soul and Form* (Lukács 1911), speaking of a 'judgment but not a verdict' (as in the case with a system). The emphasis here is on the process of judgement rather than a final resolution or verdict (Costa Lima 1996: 62). The issue of judgement arises again in his *Control of the Imaginary: Reason and Imagination in Modern Times* (Costa Lima 1988: 6).

56 For an edited collection of Costa Lima's works in English, see Lamb (2008).

57 See Matthew Lamb's introduction to Costa Lima's work: Lamb (2008a: 3–7).

58 Irigaray writes: 'And doesn't the machine unceasingly threaten to destroy us through the speed of its acceleration?' (Irigaray 1993: 74). We might think of this in terms of a juxtaposition of 'speed reading' with a 'wondrous' or 'slow' reading. We will return to Irigaray's reading of Descartes's *Passions* in Chapter Three.

59 Irigaray writes: 'Could Nietzsche's *Beyond Good and Evil* signify something of a return to wonder? . . . Of losing one's gravity . . . In which the stake is to wonder again and again without ever stopping. To steer incessantly toward the unpublished. Also to turn over everything that has already been impressed, printed, in order to liberate its impact and find its impetus on this side and beyond' (Irigaray 1993: 80, 81).

60 For a discussion of Irigaray's work on wonder see Boulous Walker (1998a: 44–7) and Boulous Walker (2009: 45–52).

61 To this list we could add Sigmund Freud, whose psychoanalytic interpretation – a slow process if ever there was one – gestures towards a reading that admits only partial and open-ended truths.

62 I thank Matthew Lamb for helping me to make this connection. See Lamb (2010).

63 Hadot suggests that aspects of the work of Montaigne, Descartes and Kant remain 'ancient', and how – in certain regards – the work of others might also be included in this list, e.g. Schopenhauer, Emerson, Thoreau, Kierkegaard, Marx, Nietzsche, Bergson, Wittgenstein and Merleau-Ponty (Hadot 1995: 270). 'Throughout the history of Western philosophy, we note a certain permanence and survival of the ancient notion. From the Middle Ages to today, some philosophers have remained faithful to the vital, existential dimension of ancient philosophy' (261). Hadot claims that Montaigne's *Essays* 'show the philosopher trying to practice various modes of life proposed by ancient philosophy: "My trade and my

art is living"' (263). The quote from Montaigne comes from his *Essais* (Montaigne 1962: 359).

64 However, Hadot qualifies this characterization of Descartes, pointing to those aspects of the *Meditations* that retain a link with ancient spiritual practice. See Hadot (2002: 263–5), where he distances himself from Michel Foucault's claim that Descartes initiates the 'theoreticizing' of philosophy.

65 Hadot notes: 'To use the Stoic model and the Epicurean model – successively or alternately – was a way of achieving a certain balance in life for Nietzsche' (Hadot 2002: 277). In this context, Hadot cites the following passage from Nietzsche: 'So far as praxis is concerned, I view the various moral schools as experimental laboratories in which a considerable number of recipes for the art of living have been thoroughly practiced and lived to the hilt. The results of all their experiments belong to us, as our legitimate property' (Nietzsche, cited in Hadot 2002: 277). This passage comes from Nietzsche's *Werke* (1988 vol. 5, part 2: 552–3).

66 Links between attention, contemplation and mindfulness ought be explored here in order to discern their suitability for practices of slow reading. Jon Kabat-Zinn's brief description of mindfulness in contemporary meditative practice is suggestive of links to be made: 'Mindfulness can be thought of as moment-to-moment, non-judgmental awareness, cultivated by paying attention in a specific way, that is, in the present moment, and as non-reactively, as non-judgmentally, and as openheartedly as possible' (Kabat-Zinn 2005: 108).

67 Philosophy practised as a way of life is the theme of an edition of the popular German *Philosophie Magazin*, which in 2013 featured a series of short articles around the question *Leben wir zu schnell?* (Are we living too fast?) In his editorial to the collection Wolfram Eilenberger notes that in 1929 the English philosopher Alfred North Whitehead proposed the following to the question of what our existential goals ought to include: to live, to live well, and to live better. For Whitehead, the key to living well was to exercise and care for the faculty of reason, which he thought only possible in the context of time, quietness and patience (Eilenberger 2013: 3).

68 The kind of close or deconstructive reading we have come to associate with Jacques Derrida's work is at odds with the kind of systematic version of close reading I am referring to here.

69 See Gumbrecht (2004: 133–52) for strategies on how this might be done.

NOTES

70 This brings to mind Simone Weil's work on attention, waiting and grace. Weil writes: 'Attention consists of suspending our thought, leaving it detached, empty . . . Above all our thought should be empty, waiting, not seeking anything' (See Weil 1951: 56). My thanks to Carole Ramsey for this passage from Weil. For a discussion of ethics in the work of Weil and Levinas, see Boulous Walker (2002: 295–320). Alongside meditation and attention, we can also place surrender. In a book devoted to reading the work of the poet Rainer Maria Rilke, Stephanie Dowrick speaks of a surrendered reading as an uncluttered, unencumbered reading; a reading that requires us to be both present and still. Poetry demands such a reading, and it is well worth thinking about what benefits such a surrendered reading might bring to philosophy as well. See Dowrick (2010).

71 Ute Guzzoni uses these terms in relation to her discussion of Adorno's thought. See Guzzoni (1997: 37).

72 Teresa Brennan's work on 'discernment' offers a thoughtful reconnection with the largely overlooked meditative tradition in Western philosophy, and this has much to offer to the exploration of slow reading I am developing here. Brennan figures discernment as a sustaining attention or concentration that challenges judgement and its 'ego-bound I'. The 'other I' of discernment is the way Brennan thinks of a receptive and open attitude towards the world. Discernment is slow and careful; it can't be rushed. It is a contemplative orientation that connects us bodily to the world, bridging sensation and feeling. Indeed, she notes that discernment registers as a feeling when it doubts the ego's judgement (Brennan 2004: 120). The evenly suspended attention of discernment, a technique Brennan borrows from Freud's psychoanalytic practice, helps us to avoid 'confirming what one already knows' (197). We will return to the connection between discernment and feeling briefly in Chapter Two when we look at Hans Ulrich Gumbrecht's work on *Stimmung*.

73 Perhaps this is akin to Gumbrecht's reference to *redemption* as the 'intense quietness of presence' or the ecstatic stare of unmediated being-in-the-world that relieves us of 'the permanent obligation to move and to change' (Gumbrecht 2004: 138).

74 In the English translation of Goethe's work that Hadot cites, John Oxenford has Goethe saying that he has been working at his reading for eighteen years. In the German original, Goethe indicates that it is, indeed, eighty years (*achtzig Jahre*)! See Eckermann (1925: 564) and Eckermann (1913: 428).

75 To read also means to guess, to construct a meaning from a range of possible meanings, and while this guessing often occurs quickly, we might think of slow reading as a practice of slow guessing that retains more of the ambivalence or possible range of meanings in the original text. *Shorter Oxford English Dictionary*, Vol 2. N–Z (Oxford: Oxford University Press, 2007: 2477).

76 Jacques Lacan refers to the 'Aha-Erlebnis' in his famous essay 'The Mirror-stage as Formative of the I' (Lacan 1977: 1–7). Lacan refers to Wolfgang Köhler's work where he discusses the 'ah-ha' moment in which the elements of a task or problem come together and emerge as a gestalt. See Köhler (1969).

77 Simon Critchley points to the real dangers of internalizing our institutional structures: 'At some point in the 1980s, an ideological mist descended, making academics obsessed with research, cutting the fragile bonds of solidarity with their colleagues (and collegiality is *so* important to academia and *so* fragile), and introducing an obsession with measuring and the ranking of institutions. Academics have almost entirely conspired with this process and are completely culpable. We have shifted from a model of oppositional politics in the Marxist sense, where there was a sort of war or class struggle between academics and the state that required strong unions, to a Foucaultian model, where university academics learn to discipline themselves and govern themselves in terms of structures and criteria handed down to them by university management and state departments of education' (Critchley 2010: 23).

Chapter 1: Habits of Reading: Le Dœuff's Future Philosophy

1 For a discussion of the paradoxical relation of an externalized other as internal enemy in Le Dœuff's account see Boulous Walker (1998: 9–26).

2 Are there links between the fidelity of this reading and the romantic reading that we identify in relation to Beauvoir's work in Chapter Five?

3 An example of this reading as work, or this active endeavour that allows what we read to come to life again, is Jane Gallop's seminal work *Reading Lacan*. See Gallop (1985).

4 Le Dœuff urges us to orient our philosophical work towards contemporary issues. See Le Dœuff (2000a).

5   For a discussion of these dangers – permissiveness, amateurism and fidelity – see Boulous Walker (1998: 20–3).

6   In the French context Pierre Macherey writes: 'All authentic reading is in its own way violent, or it is nothing but the complaisance of a paraphrase', cited in Sharp (2011: 117).

7   We can link the experience of Le Dœuff's vestal or faithful reader with what she has to say in 'Long Hair, Short Ideas' concerning the erotico-theoretical transference circulating between a female disciple and a male philosopher. While commentary is usually produced with the benefit of an institutional context to absorb the direct erotics of an intimate pedagogical relation, the faithful nature of commentary means that transference between a reader and a great man can nonetheless structure the intellectual relation. See Le Dœuff (1989: 104–5).

8   Meaghan Morris highlights the institutional implications of Le Dœuff's observations, noting that woman's access to philosophy 'implies a complex confrontation with both institutions and modes of writing . . . breaking out of the vestal syndrome requires an unsettling of the hierarchies of philosophical discourse. The problem (or the trap) of commentary, for example, lies in the ways in which it has been represented – in an oscillation between acts of creative violation (original, "masculine" readings) and of scrupulous fidelity (subordinate, "feminine" ones)'. The vestal is an attentive listener 'charged with giving philosophers and philosophy a sense of fullness, completion. It is only a discourse able to assume its own incompleteness, Le Dœuff suggests, which might be able to disengage from the dynamics of subordination' (Morris 1988: 76, 77).

9   Diana Fuss asks the question of what it means to read as a woman or a man. In doing so she engages with three texts that have been influential in Western feminist debates – Robert Scholes's 'Reading Like a Man' (1987), Tania Modleski's 'Feminism and the Power of Interpretation' (1986) and Gayatri Spivak's 'Subaltern Studies: Deconstructing Historiography' (1987). See Fuss (1989: 23–37).

10 Is it possible to recuperate the loving and faithful commentaries of careful women philosophers in the past, i.e. to appreciate something of great worth that we too easily overlook in our haste to find the definitive interpretation by the latest, greatest and most fashionable philosopher? Clearly, the French tradition does value these commentaries, and this is, of course, Le Dœuff's point. However, such commentaries or readings arguably support existing philosophical values, reinforcing the hegemony of great texts by great men. If, however, we return carefully to these commentaries, and read them anew, we might discover something beyond fidelity

and respect. Are we guilty of having under-read these works? Of finding within them little other than what our expectations (and prejudices) predict?

11 We will return to the question of the relation between reading and writing in Chapter Six on Cixous.

12 Le Dœuff writes 'Sartre corrects everyone. Simone de Beauvoir excuses practically everybody. Could this be another effect of their respective experiences of themselves in society? Whatever the case, this change also has philosophical effects' (Le Dœuff 1991: 93).

13 Having a degree of distance can be a positive thing. In this context, Le Dœuff notes approvingly that the seventeenth-century philosopher Gabrielle Suchon, acknowledging women's exclusion from institutional learning, calls women to work outside schools, first alone by reading, and then collaboratively by forming 'societies for the purpose of thinking, arguing, and debating with one another' (Le Dœuff 2003: 36). 'This collaborative work' counters the fact that women are kept in ignorance 'by depriving them of everything that might nourish their intelligence' (36). See also Le Dœuff (2000: 243–55).

14 Le Dœuff reports that receptive readings are more likely to fail than their authoritative counterparts: 'The question is whether it is because this kind of reading is not highly valued that the women fail, or whether it is not highly valued just because it is evidently feminine. I prefer the second hypothesis, and would add that the feminine is excluded because it is associated with the idea of lack of authority' (Le Dœuff 1989: 124).

15 Timidity is associated with what Le Dœuff identifies as women's tendency to underestimate their capabilities: 'men overevaluate their capabilities, whilst women underestimate theirs' (Le Dœuff 1989: 123).

16 Given the rather undiagnosed equation of masculinity with overview and femininity with detail, we might reassess the question of reading by focusing on the ethical qualities of an attentiveness to detail. See Boulous Walker (1993a: 79–91). See also Schor (1987). Additionally, we should recall the importance of Beauvoir's inclusion of the detail of women's lives and the difference this inclusion makes to the schema of Sartrean existentialism.

17 For a reference to Le Dœuff's notion of 'institutional analysis' see Le Dœuff (1991: 236), and Penelope Deutcher's interview with Le Dœuff in *Hypatia* (Deutscher 2000a: 236–42).

18 Janice Moulton analyses the dominance of the 'adversary method' in philosophy, referring to the 'unhappy conflation of aggression with

success' (Moulton 1983: 149). She writes: 'Under the Adversary Paradigm, it is assumed that the only, or at any rate, the best, way of evaluating work in philosophy is to subject it to the strongest or most extreme opposition' (153).

19 In *Hipparchia's Choice* Le Dœuff (speaking of Beauvoir's responses to others) explores alternatives to authoritative readings that do not fall prey to either diatribe or excessive kindness. Le Dœuff argues for a golden mean between the two, and we can think of this as the necessary interval that makes ethics possible (Le Dœuff 1991: 94).

20 Le Dœuff acknowledges the importance of commentaries by Marie Delcourt, Geneviève Rodis-Lewis and Cornelia de Vogel (Le Dœuff 1989: 125).

21 It might be productive to think of Catherine Malabou's work on Hegel as a contemporary example of commentary that provokes. If so, what does Malabou's relation to Hegel's works tell us about the fidelity – or otherwise – of her approach? In a brief introduction to an early English translation of Malabou's work in *Hypatia* she is framed in the following terms: 'Malabou is a canny and faithful reader, and allows her classic "maître" to speak, if not against his own grain, at least against a tradition too attached to closure and system'. In an accompanying article Lisabeth During characterizes Malabou's reading as both scrupulous and inventive – committed to a 'plastic' reading that follows Hegel's own instruction. Malabou's 'generous reading' tells us less about Hegel's meaning than undertaking a Hegelian reading of its own. Malabou's fidelity is the fidelity of transformation – a plastic reading that explodes in ways that Hegel could only applaud. Malabou's reading performs the plasticity of speculative thought by being a 'movement that dissolves and restores, fractures and reweaves, in the same way that plasticity allows the organ to regain its resilience or the work of art to make and remake the possibilities of its material' (During 2000: 193). See Malabou (1996) and Malabou (2000: 196–220).

22 Le Dœuff understands Pascal's position as 'the only psychotheoretical attitude which makes collective work possible and necessary – a "collectivity" whose scope obviously extends beyond the "group" of people working together' (Le Dœuff 1989: 128).

23 In the Introduction I mentioned a report that focuses on teaching the group identified as 'screenagers' (those teenagers whose everyday learning experiences are becoming dominated by Internet research). In this paper Mark Bauerlein argues for regular engagements with complex reading tasks: 'This is not to say that schools should go Luddite. We should continue to experiment with educational

technology, but we should also preserve a crucial place for unwired, unplugged, and unconnected learning. One hour a day of slow reading with print matter, an occasional research assignment completed without Google – any such practices that slow down and intensify the reading of complex texts will help. The more high school teachers place complex texts on the syllabus and concoct slow, deliberate reading exercises for students to complete, the more they will inculcate the habit. The key is to regularize the instruction and make slow reading exercises a standard part of the curriculum. Such practices may do more to boost college readiness than 300 shiny laptops down the hall – and for a fraction of the price' (Bauerlein 2011: 33).

24 Hustvedt writes: 'reading is a particular human experience of collaboration with the words of another person, the writer . . . books are literally animated by the people who read them because reading is an embodied act' (Hustvedt 2012: 134).

25 This is Meaghan Morris's phrase. She writes: 'The methods of reading employed by Michèle Le Dœuff have not been chosen for their intrinsic value (whether "value" is calculated in terms of progressiveness, scientificity, transgressive potential, or novelty-and-shock), but for their *sufficiency to their tasks* – which are, from the very beginning, circumscribed by the project of analyzing a particular discourse in its self-determination and in its social functioning' (Morris 1988: 73–4). For a discussion of Le Dœuff's approach to philosophy as 'work' see La Caze (2003: 244–56).

26 Steven Maras distinguishes Le Dœuff's work of reading from Derrida's deconstruction on the basis of what he refers to as her interest in a particularism that avoids the generality of attacks on an entire tradition (Maras 2000: 100). See also Barker (2000: 127–46).

27 Hustvedt writes: 'But no reading experience, even of an identical text, is the same . . . [In rereading] [t]he text is the same, but I am not. And this is crucial. Books are either unleashed or occluded by the reader' (Hustvedt 2012: 137).

28 For a discussion of Le Dœuff at home with us see Boulous Walker (2000: 163–86).

29 In 'Women, Reason, Etc.' Le Dœuff notes Rousseau's ethical point in emphasizing 'the incompleteness of the theoretical' (Le Dœuff 1990: 10).

30 Le Dœuff explores the idea of a philosophy without borders in 'Ants and Women, or Philosophy without Borders' (Le Dœuff 1987: 41–54).

31 Max Deutscher summarizes the strengths of Le Dœuff's open-ended incomplete philosophy: 'vitality, economy, lightness, sharpness, thoroughness, and wit and irony in the service of a still serious attention to the issue' (Deutscher 2000: 10).

32 Le Dœuff prefaces the Third Notebook to *Hipparchia's Choice* with the following overview: 'attempts to define the conditions necessary for an unbegun and unfinished work' recognizing that philosophy remains an 'undiscipline' (Le Dœuff 1991: 135).

33 For a discussion of the ethical values inherent in 'looking back' see Boulous Walker (2009).

Chapter 2: Reading Essayistically: Levinas and Adorno

1 *Shorter Oxford English Dictionary: On Historical Principles* Sixth Edition Vol 1. A–M (Oxford: Oxford University Press, 2007: 864).

2 For a more general discussion of Levinas's work on ethical response and obligation to the other, see Boulous Walker (2002: 295–320).

3 For Levinas's discussion of ethics as patience, see Levinas (1996: 46–7).

4 And further: 'In the realm of truth, being, as the *other* of thought becomes the characteristic *property* of thought as knowledge' (Levinas 1989: 76). There are links here with our discussion of Heidegger's critique in the Preface.

5 Paul Carter juxtaposes 'light writing' – writing concerned with reason, conclusions and straight lines – with 'dark writing' – an underwriting found in traces connected with sleep, dreams, shadows, and the unconscious. I'm curious about the possibility of a 'dark reading': one that shuns the 'light of reason'. See Carter (2009).

6 The concrete or embodied expression of understanding is typical in the German language. *Fassen* suggests to seize, grasp, take, (lay) hold of, catch, apprehend, and figuratively: to seize (mentally), grasp, conceive, understand. To form or conceive an idea is *einen Gedanken fassen*, while to compose takes the reflexive form *sich fassen*. In English I think that we hear this *fassen* as something akin to 'fashion': as in 'to fashion an argument'. *Auffassen* has the figurative meaning of to conceive (mentally), understand, comprehend, grasp, interpret, construe, and also to read! To be quick of understanding is *leicht auffassen* and to be slow (in the uptake) is

schwer auffassen – 'heavy' or 'difficult' understanding to our ears. In addition, *fassen* can be linked with *das Fass*, which refers to a cask, keg or barrel – something that contains – and *die Fassung* refers to the frame, another form of containment. The verb *einfassen* means to frame. So understanding, with its myriad links to grasping and containment in the German language, would be juxtaposed with reading, in my work, as an open, receptive and open-ended practice.

7 Anxiety motivates much of the move to reduce, calculate and to know, i.e. to diminish the impact, meanings and possibilities of the text – perhaps even to diminish the troubling ambiguity of life. Philosophy, seen from a psychoanalytic perspective, is something of a neurotic discourse of mastery. In *Die Zukunft einer Illusion* (1927), Freud characterizes philosophy in terms of the neurotic structure of its thought, i.e. the neurotic imposition of rationality in order to displace uncertainty or lack of control. The psychoanalytic notion of the 'unconscious' challenges any philosophical certainty or truth about the human condition and encourages us to open 'truth' to a more open-ended engagement and inquiry. Truths are at best perhaps partial truths, rather than absolute ones. This suggests the validity of partial readings or conditional ones. See Freud (1961).

8 In Chapter Three, I provide an example of this kind of reductive (unethical) reading.

9 For a discussion of knowledge as an act, rather than as food for consumption, see Le Dœuff (2003: 34–9).

10 Other translations have the philosopher stuffing the incoherence of the dream/other with his pyjamas.

11 On the aggressive nature of certain philosophical approaches see Moulton (1983: 149–64).

12 Steven Smith describes *le Dit* as 'the structurally coherent text created by language' and *le Dire* as 'the primordially generous, nonthematic upsurge of communication'. He goes on: '"Saying" belongs to the horizon of sociality that is incommensurable with the text of the "Said" but is its origin and presupposition' (Smith 1986: 61 and also 53–72).

13 Levinas has the following to say in relation to his 'Saying': 'This passivity of passivity and this dedication to the Other, this sincerity, is Saying – not as a communication of something Said, which would be immediately recovered and absorbed or extinguished in the Said, but Saying holding its opening open, without excuse, without evasion or alibi, giving itself without saying anything of the Said – "Saying" saying "saying" itself (Dire disant le dire meme), without thematizing it, but still expositing it' (Levinas 1998: 142–3).

NOTES

14 Rosalyn Diprose's work on ethics and vulnerability is relevant here. See Diprose (2013). See also Drichel (2013).

15 To do so is to think of reading differently from the reading that (by its very nature) loses sight of the ethical. See Greisch (1991).

16 For an excellent discussion of how a 'slow' reading seeks to resist 'the temptation to erase . . . signs of struggle and incompleteness' in the text, see Clarke (2005: 131–58 (especially 132)).

17 For my discussion of what Robert Bernasconi and Simon Critchley refer to as a Levinasian hermeneutics, 'defined by its readiness for re-reading', see Boulous Walker (2006: 225). See also Bernasconi and Critchley (1991: xi (xi–xvii)). For a further discussion of Levinas and reading ethically see Champagne (1998). In her impressive study of Levinas, Oona Ajzenstat looks carefully at both how and what Levinas reads. She writes: 'All his readings are . . . strong readings; they alter the surface of the text at issue – but the intent is to preserve and convey the text's meaning, which always bears on the necessity of asking the ethical question. Levinas is aware of the conditions under which his readers read and address them, partly simply by drawing us back through his hermeneutical anamnesis – by responding, for instance, to questions about Hegel with answers about the Talmud – in order to pave the way for an existential anamnesis, and partly by offering a strong clear critique of modern sacred groves, a critique that is already a turn to the other on his part and can be subsequently adopted as a turn to the other on the part of his readers. Levinas's writing, both hortative and critical, is an ethical and a political act' (Ajzenstat 2001: 18). See also Davis (2006), Eaglestone (1997), Robbins (1999), Sikka (1999: 195–206).

18 Positioning himself between Levinas's work on proximity (*proximité*) and Heidegger's work on nearness (*Nähe*), and how these terms allow us to rethink and re-figure otherness, Krzysztof Ziarek develops what he calls a hermeneutics of nearness that 'induces language to "pay attention" to the inscriptions of otherness, of the unsaid' (Ziarek 1994: 10). Ziarek's approach is helpful for thinking through the ethical dimension of what I am referring to here as slow reading. I look at Ziarek's work in relation to Irigaray's attentive listening in Chapter Four.

19 Michèle Le Dœuff's writing on philosophical work as open-ended is also crucial here. I have addressed her important concerns in Chapter One. See Le Dœuff (1989: 126–8).

20 Propositional and assertive modes, while valuable for certain philosophical work, arguably restrict the open-ended inquiry that the essay permits.

21 The essay 'draws the fullest consequences from the critique of the system' (Adorno 2000: 98).

22 In 'The Essay as Form', Adorno mentions that in Germany the essay is 'decried as a hybrid; that it is lacking a convincing tradition . . . the academic guild only has patience for philosophy that dresses itself up with the nobility of the universal, the everlasting' (Adorno 2000: 92). He goes on to give his own positive description of the essay as something open, unfinished and contingent, although he acknowledges that historically there exist many examples of failed or journalistic essays (Adorno 2000: 94–5). Compare this to Virginia Woolf's depiction of the essay guided by the principle that everything in it should be subdued to the end that it gives pleasure. See Woolf (1925a: 267).

23 In 'The Actuality of Philosophy', Adorno's 1931 inaugural lecture at the University of Frankfurt, he speaks against a totalizing philosophy, proposing his own version of *interpretation* as an alternative philosophical style. Here we can read this early work alongside 'The Essay as Form' (written in 1958) in order to chart the movement of Adorno's thought in relation to the essay. He writes: 'The English empiricists called their philosophic writings essays, as did Leibniz, because the power of freshly disclosed reality, upon which their thinking struck, continuously forced upon them the risk of experimentation. Not until the post-Kantian century was the risk of experimentation lost, along with the power of reality. Thus from a form of great philosophy the essay became an insignificant form of aesthetics . . . If, with the disintegration of all security within great philosophy, experiment makes its entry; if it thereby ties onto the limited, contoured and unsymbolic interpretations of aesthetic essays, then that does not appear to be condemnable, provided that the objects are chosen correctly, that they are real. For the mind (*Geist*) is indeed not capable of producing or grasping the totality of the real, but it may be possible to penetrate the detail, to explode in miniature the mass of merely existing reality' (Adorno 2000a: 38). In this same piece, Adorno hints towards remarks he makes later in 'The Essay as Form' when he says that seeing philosophy as interpretation means thinking of it in terms of riddle-solving, where the practice of placing elements in configuration produces a kind of compelling illumination whereby the non-conceptual other can be articulated. He refers to this configuration as a 'constellation'.

24 We need to consider Adorno's complex relation with Walter Benjamin's work on the fragment.

25 As we have seen in the Introduction, Adorno's friend Walter Benjamin cultivates the 'purposeless strolling' of the *flâneur* and we might liken this to the meandering of the essay. In the faltering gesture of starting, stopping and standing still, Benjamin's thought establishes an open-ended philosophy that arguably develops its own ethical gesture. In *The Origins of German Tragic Drama* (*Trauerspiel*) Benjamin describes his approach in terms of return and irregularity, noting his need to pause for breath 'proper to the process of contemplation' (Benjamin 1977: 27). He writes: 'For by pursuing different levels of meaning in its examination of one single object it receives both the incentive to begin again and the justification for its irregular rhythm' (28). See Michelle Boulous Walker, 'Walter Benjamin: The Art of Critical Thought' (unpublished essay).

26 We can think of Virginia Woolf's memoir 'A Sketch of the Past' (published in *Moments of Being*) as embodying the essay form as Adorno describes it. Indeed, in her introduction to the work, Jeanne Schulkind picks up on the slow, ruminative meanderings of Woolf's piece: 'The memoir is characterized by a flowing ruminative expansiveness; it presents a consciousness which follows its own peculiar byways rather than a pre-ordained route as it ponders the meaning of reality and the mystery of identity' (Jeanne Schulkind in Woolf 1976: 19 and Woolf 1976: 71–162).

27 In the context of his discussion of the affinity between philosophy and music in Adorno's thought, especially in relation to Adorno's *Negative Dialectics* (Adorno 1979), Jarvis notes Adorno's dismissal of extracting (mining for?) 'founding arguments' as the basis for effective criticism of philosophical texts: 'Criticism of philosophical texts often proceeds by extracting for discussion what are taken to be the founding arguments in them, in the belief that everything else follows from these. Adorno argues that such a procedure is no more adequate to understanding a philosophical text than an attempt to interpret a musical composition by summarizing the key-changes in it' (Jarvis 1998: 128).

28 This image of elements crystallizing into a configuration resonates with Simone Weil's work on waiting and attention. The slow process of crystallization (crystal formation) shares something with Weil's attentive, meditative thought, and I think we can borrow this as an image for slow reading. We look, briefly, at Weil's work in the Conclusion.

29 In Chapter Three we explore Descartes's four principles (*A Discourse on Method*) alongside his work on wonder (*The Passions of the Soul*).

30 It is interesting to note the importance both Hadot (see our discussion in the Introduction) and Adorno place on Descartes in their respective analyses. While Hadot's initial portrayal of Descartes's work has something in common with Adorno's account of the Descartes that emerges in *A Discourse on Method*, Hadot's later discussion of the *Meditations* indicates an entirely different aspect of Descartes's philosophical approach – one linking him back to the ancients. Indeed, Hadot finishes this discussion by suggesting that *A Discourse on Method* has, in part, a recognizably Stoic orientation. He concludes: 'The extent to which the ancient conception of philosophy is present in Descartes is not always adequately measured' (Hadot 2002: 265).

31 Adorno writes: 'The essay comes to no final conclusions and makes explicit its inability to do so by parodying its own *a priori*; it is then saddled with the guilt that is actually incurred by those forms that erase every trace of arbitrariness' (Adorno 2000: 105).

32 Albert Camus's essay 'The Myth of Sisyphus' (Camus 1955) provides a good example of the kind of essay Adorno has in mind. See Chapter Four of Matthew Lamb's doctoral thesis for a discussion of the role of questioning in Camus's lyrical essay (Lamb 2010).

33 Samuel Weber investigates Adorno's thoughts on how to read (and reading's relation to interpretation) in an essay that looks at the problem that emerges for Adorno in relation to reading Hegel. Adorno refers to his reading of Hegel as an 'art' where one discerns the 'new' as something other than the 'machine' of the 'Hegelian' dialectic. Two conditions are necessary for this kind of reading as art: First '"immersion" (*Versenkung*) in the text's most minute details' and second 'the ability to retain one's freedom and "distance" from them, despite the "immersion"' (Weber 2002: 384). A play or tension between immersion and distance allows Adorno's art of reading to avoid what he elsewhere refers to as the reified and ritualized practices typical of mass culture that reduce reading to 'a "deciphering" of a fixed code of isolated, abstract "graphic signs" (*Schriftzeichen*), *as a more or less mechanical effort to reduce the strange and alien to the known and familiar*' (Weber 2002: 386, emphasis added).

34 Chris Marker's cinematic work has been described by André Bazin and others as essay films: '[films] setting out to depict the process of thinking around a given subject, with all its attendant messiness, hesitations, and sudden insights intact'. Marked by meandering digressions and free of commercial obligations, Marker's elegant

films (*La Jetée* 1963 and *Sans Soleil* 1983) voice the unsayable. See Lupton (2007: 6–13).

35 Following Nietzsche, we can think of slow reading (as we have in the Introduction) as a kind of rumination, and this brings to mind the slow digestion and thinking-over of thought. We ruminate and in doing so allow ourselves time to think over what we read. We might think of slow reading in terms of the slow movement generally, which acknowledges that 'speed has helped to remake our world in ways that are wonderful and liberating', but that our current addiction to haste is now verging on the catastrophic (Honoré 2004: 4). The Slow Food Movement promotes the very rumination that I am celebrating here, and to juxtapose these two – slow reading with slow food – is to bring reading and eating into an interesting dialogue.

36 These are terms used by Ute Guzzoni in her useful discussion of Adorno on reason. Here she addresses the 'character of passivity and receptivity' that might challenge traditional modes of reason. 'A reason capable of evading the modern tendency toward calculation and mastery would neither stand over its object, nor try to embody and manifest itself through it. It would instead move with its object, listening to it and remaining open to the other's speaking and asking; i.e. the receptive attitude of a patient attention and an acceptance of the other's attitude and action' (Guzzoni 1997: 33–4).

37 Guzzoni links Adorno's work here with Sloterdijk's more Asian-inspired 'ascendance to silence in force' and Heidegger's *Gelassenheit*. She writes: 'This passivity is a letting-be and letting-happen, more exactly a letting-come-forth, a giving-birth and a transgression from a mode of being prepared to do anything to one that is calm and collected, that is *gelassen*' (Guzzoni 1997: 37).

38 For a careful discussion of Adorno's work as contemplative see Seel (2004: 259–69).

39 Paulo Henriques Britto, 'Translator's Note' in Costa Lima 1996: ix. He continues: 'The questioning, non-normative function is certainly already present in Kantian criticism, but the distinction was never captured by a contrasting pair of words, in English or in Portuguese'. For a broader contextualization of Costa Lima's work see Boulous Walker (2013: 194–208).

40 Costa Lima relates these terms to Walter Benjamin's distinction between 'art critic' [*Kunstkritiker*] and 'art judge' [*Kunstrichter*]. While the art judge relies on a body of applicable legislation, and sometimes legislates himself, the art critic takes other avenues,

producing theory instead of applying existing rules (Costa Lima 1996: 146). See Benjamin (1974: 52).

41 Costa Lima is referring here to the method developed in the early work of Friedrich von Schlegel, who he depicts as the main practitioner (with Schiller) of criticity in the early German Romantic era. He limits this critical phase of Schlegel's work (when he develops a genuine theory of literature) to the years 1797 to 1800, arguing that an opposing force in Schlegel's work – a conservative religion of art – ultimately overtakes this criticity in order to establish the end point or goal of an 'aristocracy of artists, understood as the indispensible condition for becoming a member of an "alternative church"' (Costa Lima 1996: 175). In opposition to this conservatism, Schlegel's earlier criticity is marked by its 'progressive, experimental drive that does not aim at a predetermined point of arrival' (Costa Lima 1996: 176).

42 For example: 'Despite the weighty perspicacity that Simmel and the young Lukács, Kassner and Benjamin entrusted to the essay, to the speculative investigation of specific, culturally predetermined objects, the academic guild only has patience for philosophy that dresses itself up with the nobility of the universal, the everlasting, and today' (Adorno 2000: 92).

43 However, this resemblance is simply that – resemblance rather than identity. The essay differs from literature (from art) in adopting its critical mode. Costa Lima summarizes Lukács's point: 'The essayist's situation is quite different [from the poet's]: his work does not place him in immediate contact with destiny, nor does he give shape to destiny; his task is to speak of objects that have already been made into form . . . In poetry, the question asked of destiny is solved in form. In the essay, instead, the questions burn so brightly that there is no space for them to resolve into form' (Costa Lima 1996: 61).

44 Costa Lima (1996: 62). (Costa Lima is paraphrasing Lukács).

45 In the second chapter of *The Limits of Voice*, Costa Lima returns to the questions of the essay and the fragment in his reading of Schlegel's 'Critical Fragments'. He contends that Schlegel's critical work (his criticity) avoids system and finality by playing the interval between the fragment and the essay: 'To Schlegel, then, criticism operates along the axis whose opposite poles are the fragment and the essay. Criticism remains essayistic as long as it does not become associated with a systematic aesthetics' (Costa Lima 1996: 166). Further: 'The fragment, as the minimal form of the essay, suggests what is the territory open to criticism: criticism is a mode of the essay. As such, it is a quintessentially modern genre' (Costa Lima

1996: 157). And finally: 'the fragment is the minimal seminal form of the essay. By this we mean both that the fragment-essay is a modern form, rooted in the experience of a self, and that it is of the nature of a search that is never concluded – that is, its nature is incompleteness' (Costa Lima 1996: 153). In addition, Costa Lima reproduces the following noteworthy passage from Lacoue-Labarthe and Nancy: 'The fragment is a statement that does not aim at exhaustiveness and corresponds to the idea – no doubt a properly modern one – that what is unfinished may or even should be published (or also to the idea that what is published is never actually finished)'. See Lacoue-Labarthe and Nancy (1978: 62).

46 See also Deleuze's depiction of reading in terms of laws, codes and regulations in 'Nomad Thought' (Deleuze and Guattari 1986: 142).

47 In his discussion of Montaigne, Costa Lima makes several references to the rambling or meandering pace of his essays (Costa Lima 1996: 37, 40, 55), noting that Montaigne searched for a new flexible form (the essay) to bear witness (56), one that accommodated his condemnation of fixed positions, codification, and 'the exultation of the factual as an index of truth' (52). Montaigne invents 'a floating, unsystematic punctual, personalized meditation . . . [which addresses] the strangeness of what is unknown to reason' (Costa Lima 1996: 34). On Montaigne and the essay see also Auerbach (2003) and Merleau-Ponty (1964: 198–210).

48 See Montaigne (2003). In her biography of Montaigne, Sarah Bakewell argues that his slow, meandering style provides an ideal role model for the contemporary Slow Movement: 'Like Montaigne, its adherents make slow speed into a moral principle . . . [For him] slowness opened the way to wisdom' (Bakewell 2010: 72, 73). In the Introduction (n. 63) we noted Hadot's inclusion of Montaigne along with the 'Ancients' due to his fidelity to 'the vital, existential dimension of ancient philosophy' (Hadot 1995: 261).

49 In *The Differend*, Lyotard describes his project of indeterminate judgement in terms of a slow searching for new rules and new idioms for forming and linking phrases in the hope that justice is to be done: 'A lot of searching must be done to find new rules for forming and linking phrases' (Lyotard 1988: 13).

50 Costa Lima accuses Adorno of being against method. He writes: 'If our intention were to discuss Adorno's problem in particular, we would have to refuse the opposition between essay writing and the order of method, which Adorno reiterates. The essay is not against method, but against its totalizing pretension' (Costa Lima 1996: 63).

I do not agree with Costa Lima's depiction of Adorno here. The following passages from Adorno's essay indicate, I think, Adorno's more nuanced understanding of method. He writes: 'The essay simultaneously suspends the traditional concept of method' (Adorno 2000: 99); the essay 'proceeds, so to speak, methodically unmethodically' (101); 'In this the very method of the essay expresses the utopian intention' (101); and 'the essay struggles aesthetically against that narrow-minded method that will leave nothing out' (104). For Adorno, the essay resists the pretensions of *a certain kind of method*, but it does so by developing its own 'unmethodical' method. In the light of this discussion (and in consideration of Nietzsche's aphoristic style), it is interesting to note Francis Bacon's distinction between aphorism (growth) and method (standstill). In *The Advancement of Learning* (1605) he writes: 'in aphorisms and observations, [knowledge] is in growth; but when it once is comprehended in exact methods, it may, perchance, be further polished, and illustrate and accommodated for use and practice, but it increaseth no more in bulk and substance' (Bacon 1901: 37); 'the writing in aphorisms hath many excellent virtues, whereto the writing in method doth not approach' (125); and finally 'aphorisms, representing a knowledge broken, do invite men to inquire further; whereas methods, carrying the show of a total, do secure men, as if they were at furthest' (150). It is worth pointing out that Bacon published this work thirty-two years before Descartes published *A Discourse on Method*. The many differences between English empiricism and French rationalism find expression in this distinction between method and its other.

51 Gumbrecht describes the layered meanings of *Stimmung* (atmosphere, mood) in German, noting connections with *Stimme* (voice), *stimmen* (to tune an instrument) and *stimmen* (to be correct). His aim is to point out the connections between moods, atmospheres and listening and hearing: 'I am most interested in the component of meaning that connects *Stimmung* with music and the hearing of sounds. As is well known, we do not hear with our inner and outer ear alone. Hearing is a complex form of behavior that involves the entire body. Skin and haptic modalities of perception play an important role. Every tone we perceive is, of course, a form of physical reality (if an invisible one) that "happens" to our body and, at the same time, "surrounds" it' (Gumbrecht 2012: 4). In Chapter Four we take up the question of attentive listening.

52 I think there are productive links to be made here with Teresa Brennan's work on discernment. Brennan writes: 'Discernment, when it doubts the ego's judgment, registers as a feeling' (Brennan 2004: 120).

53 '"Reading for *Stimmung*" always means paying attention to the textual dimension of forms that envelop us and our bodies as a physical reality' (Gumbrecht 2012: 5).

54 Gumbrecht's approach is an experimental mode rather than a method or theory. In this, we can link his work with Nietzsche's, and with moments of Deleuze's and Guattari's, where they call for us to 'experiment, never interpret!' (Deleuze and Guattari 1983: 62). Gumbrecht writes: 'I am skeptical about the power of "theories" to explain atmospheres and moods, and I doubt the viability of "methods" to identify them' (Gumbrecht 2012: 17).

55 Gumbrecht repeatedly distances this approach from interpretation and truth narrowly defined: 'Lukács's distinction between "truth" and "life" sets his objectives apart from matters of "interpretation" – that is, the task of laying bare the "truth" (i.e., the propositional content) that works are presumed to contain. An essay that concentrates on atmospheres and moods will never arrive at the truth located within a text; instead, it seizes the work as a part of life in the present' (Gumbrecht 2012: 18). See also Gumbrecht (2004).

56 Gumbrecht outlines a brief history of *Stimmung* and its earlier relation with mediation and harmony, noting that *Stimmung* no longer implies any form of reconciliation or harmony (Gumbrecht 2012: 10). He refers to David Wellbery's work on reconstructing a history of the concept of *Stimmung*, 'exploring its many historical and semantic layers' (Gumbrecht 2012: 7). See Wellbery (2003).

57 We need to guard against a too-simple opposition of openness and closure. Closure might not always suggest reduction. As Martyn Lloyd suggests, a eulogy may well provide closure in ethical terms. Is the open-ended in all circumstances ethical?

58 See Irigaray (1991a: 178–89) and (1993: 85–217). Might Irigaray's readings of Levinas be something like the necessary ingratitude that Derrida refers to in his own reading of Levinas, i.e. the ethical interruption sought and elicited by Levinas's own work? See Derrida (1991: 11–48).

Chapter 3: Rereading: Irigaray on Love and Wonder

1 Irigaray 2002: 122.
2 We can think of this open and attentive mode to the other in terms of Teresa Brennan's exploration of the gift of attentiveness or 'living

attention' as an energetic force that, like love, enhances life. See Brennan (2004: 31).

3 For an excellent discussion of the particular mode of interpretive analysis coming out of the geography of the psychoanalytic setting (the 'practicable'), one that unsettles the binary arrangement of subject and object and its links to attentive listening, see Kelso (2007: 68–109). Kelso explains that the geography of the analytic encounter sets up a body-to-body relation distinct from Levinas's face-to-face encounter, and that this relation establishes a dialectically open and incomplete structure of analysis. She notes Irigaray's appreciation of the efficacy of the psychoanalytic setting over and against any orthodox adherence to psychoanalytic theory. See also Irigaray (2002a: 193–204) and Hirsch (1994: 285–315).

4 It is interesting that in another of her early essays, 'The Poverty of Psychoanalysis' (written in 1977), Irigaray distinguishes the early psychoanalyst's ability to listen to and be surprised by what they heard from the Lacanian analysts who 'know' in advance what they will find. Freud and the early analysts proceed without 'knowing' in advance what to expect and, because of this, are still capable of *listening* and of being surprised. We might say that Freud and the early analysts are still capable of wonder in relation to the other (Irigaray 1991: 79–104).

5 In Chapter Four we undertake an extended discussion of Irigaray's work in relation to reading as an attentive listening.

6 Irigaray urges us to 'listen with another ear' (Irigaray 1985b: 29).

7 In another early piece Irigaray writes: 'When the pscho-analyst . . . listens, there ought not to exist, strictly speaking, *a priori* truths. The discourse/statement of the person being analysed, its transfer, cannot be forced, in advance, into a unique and definitive interpretation' (Irigaray 1977: 70).

8 For an example of Irigaray's attentive reading, one that avoids the 'inattentive', 'predatory' or 'speculatve' gaze, see 'Introducing . . . Love Between Us' in Irigaray (1996: 24–5).

9 For a discussion of these two modes of reading see Whitford (1991: 23). Whitford offers a concise introduction to Irigaray's relation to psychoanalysis in Chapter Two of her book (29–52, especially pages 31–8). On the two kinds of reading outlined above, see also Felman (1977: 5–10) and Gallop (1985: 22–30). In another piece, Whitford addresses the transferential possibilities of reading Irigaray and contends that engaging with Irigaray calls for a 'dynamic reading strategy' that brings both interpretive and transferential readings together, somewhat in the manner of Irigaray's 'amorous exchange'

(Whitford 1994: 23). Earlier, Whitford writes: 'The transference of the reader is not a more or less accidental, "emotional" or subjective response which can be set aside to get at the "theory," but in fact gives a clue to what is at stake. If, as a reader, you "resist," then this resistance itself is worth analyzing and exploring further' (Whitford 1986: 8).

10 Judith Still differentiates Irigaray's approach ('poetic nuptials') from a purely critical reading: 'poetic nuptials are an alternative to ways of reading such as critique which demand a particular distance between what becomes subject and object' (Still 2002: 7).

11 The slow progress of analysis leads Freud to the related question of whether 'there is such a thing as a natural end to analysis?' (Freud 1974: 219). He goes on to list the factors responsible for interminable analyses, arguing that lengthy treatments occur, in large part, as a wish to analyse negative transference. We might ask: is there such a thing as a natural end to slow reading?

12 For a discussion of psychoanalysis and reading in relation to Plato's *Symposium* see Brenkman (1982: 396–456).

13 It is this opening paragraph that motivates Andrea Nye to respond to Irigaray's reading in a manner that I find troubling. I outline my discomfort with Nye's reading in the final section of this chapter.

14 We might ask whether Irigaray's depiction of Hegel's dialectic here is fair. If not, then we would need to ask what it means for Irigaray to present a 'straw' Hegel in support of what I am calling her 'ethical' reading to Diotima.

15 Irigaray contends that this form of love is the form of Diotima's own teaching; i.e. that her theme and the enactment of her theme are one and the same – love. 'This mediating role is indicated as part of the theme, but it is also perpetually at issue, on stage, in the exposition of the theme' (21). This is precisely what Irigaray's own reading achieves; i.e. it is simultaneously a discussion and an enactment of the theme of love as intermediary – a *loving* reading. Compare Irigaray's notion of love as intermediary with Julia Kristeva's in her discussion of Eros in the *Symposium*: 'Diotima's love is a daemon, but contrary to the Christian demon, and more peacefully than in *Phaedrus*, it is above all a unifying go-between, an agent of synthesis' (Kristeva 1987: 72).

16 Tina Chanter suggests that Diotima is, for Irigaray, an intermediary, 'one of those mythical figures of the spirit, an "angel" who mediates between immortality and mortality?' See Chanter (1995: 159).

17 Socrates learns about love and how to question simultaneously from Diotima. In the introduction to a contemporary translation of Plato's works, Reeve observes: 'Socrates knows about the art of love in that

he knows how to ask questions' (Reeve 2006: xx). He notes, too, that the noun *erôs* (love) and the verb *erôtan* (to ask questions) appear to be etymologically related. Additionally Cratylus (398c5–e5): 'the name hero (*hērōs*) is only a slightly altered form of the word "love" (*erôs*) – the very thing from which the heroes sprang. [Heroes were] skilled questioners . . . heroes turn out to be speech-makers and questioners' (Reeve 2006: xix).

18 The philosophical significance of Diotima's laughter should be noted here. Rather than opposing or contradicting Socrates, Diotima responds with a laughter that unsettles the usual pedagogic relation between master and disciple. Diotima's laughter is arguably an ethical bridge that sets a relation between herself and Socrates. In this case, laughter invites the other in, to participate. Laughter is halfway (mid-way) between knowing and not knowing, truth and ignorance, right and wrong, and in this shares something with the demonic character of love. See Plato (1967: 80 *Symposium* 202a). In response to Diotima's laughter, Irigaray writes: 'Her retort is not at all angry, the effect of hesitating between contradictory positions; it is laughter based on other grounds' (Irigaray 1993: 22).

19 See also Plato, *Symposium* 203b (Plato 1967: 81). Here Diotima explains: '"[Love] is a great spirit, Socrates; everything that is of the nature of a spirit is half-god and half-man." "And what is the function of such a being?" "To interpret and convey messages to the gods from men and to men from the gods, prayers and sacrifices from the one, and commands and rewards from the other. Being of an intermediate nature, a spirit bridges the gap between them, and prevents the universe from falling into two separate halves . . . God does not deal directly with man; it is by means of spirits that all the intercourse and communication of gods with men, both in waking life and in sleep, is carried on . . ."' (203b, Plato 1967: 81). For a discussion of the daemonic as the bridge between the secular and the divine, see Nicholls (2000: 62–70).

20 Diotima contends that love is the child of need (poverty) and abundance (plenty). Chanter notes that the ambiguous nature of love's parentage is crucial for Levinas's depiction of eros throughout his works: 'Levinas characterizes eros as essentially ambiguous . . . On the one hand, eros is situated on the plane of economic need – the lover lacks what it loves, and, according to a simple structure, in order to be satisfied, the object of love must be obtained. "Need," says Levinas, "a happy dependence, is capable of satisfaction, like a void, which gets filled". On the other hand, eros is situated on the plane of a desire that cannot in principle be satiated, a desire that transcends the structure of needs that can be met. Levinas

expresses the difference between eros as need and eros as desire in these terms: "in need I can sink my teeth into the real and satisfy myself in assimilating the other; in Desire there is no sinking one's teeth into being, no satiety, but an uncharted future before me"' (Chanter 1995: 160). For Levinas, need equates with the attitude that devours or appropriates, while desire marks the beginning of the ethical encounter. Chanter goes on to suggest that when Irigaray responds to Levinas's work on eros and ethics she does so by recalling 'the formulation of love that she borrowed from Diotima, who sees eros as some kind of rebirth of the self and the other. The lovers, says Irigaray, "bestow on each other – life"' (Chanter 1995: 214). Eros, for Irigaray, is the totally ambiguous state on the 'threshold' between need and desire that recasts 'the subject who has learned to control its world, who has achieved mastery of itself, back into a state of flux where the borders of self and other, between the I and the world, are no longer so clear, where the gap between the I and the other is not so well-defined, nor so easily grasped' (Chanter 1995: 215).

21 *Symposium* 204 (Plato 1967: 83). Earlier, Diotima asks Socrates the following: '"Do you think . . . anything that is not wisdom is ignorance? Don't you know that there is a state of mind half-way between wisdom and ignorance?" "What do you mean?" "Having true convictions without being able to give reasons for them", she replied. "Surely you see that such a state of mind cannot be called understanding, because nothing irrational deserves the name; but it would be equally wrong to call it ignorance; how can one call a state of mind ignorance which hits upon the truth? The fact is that having true convictions is what I called it just now, a condition half-way between knowledge and ignorance"' (*Symposium* 202a, Plato 1967: 79–80). This is clearly important if we are to think of philosophy as a movement towards understanding rather than its completion.

22 It is noteworthy that Irigaray adds that the philosopher (eros) is a philosopher through his mother: 'He inherits this endless quest from his mother. He is a philosopher through his mother and skilled in art through his father. But his passion for love, for beauty, for wisdom comes to him from his mother, and from the date that he is conceived. Desired and wanted, moreover, by his mother' (Irigaray 1993: 24).

23 Compare Hamilton's translation of this passage from the *Symposium,* line 206: 'There is something divine about the whole matter; in procreation and bringing to birth the mortal creature is endowed with a touch of immortality' (Plato 1967: 86).

24 Chanter writes: 'That Diotima is said to miscarry could be due to Diotima's inability to bring to fruition the thought that, on Irigaray's account, she had begun to bear. Or again, it could be due to the incompetence of the midwife, Socrates, the one who acts as a mediator on behalf of Diotima, carrying her words both to the other participants of Plato's dialogue, and to us, the readers of Irigaray's commentary on Plato' (Chanter 1995: 161). On metaphors of birth and miscarriage in Plato's work see also Caverero (1995: 91–120).

25 In later works Irigaray returns to the question of love in order to radically rethink our entire legacy of love in the West. Here she calls for a relation of indirection between the lovers, not one of appropriation or of product. See Irigaray (1996, 2000, 2002). We look at *The Way of Love* (Irigaray 2002) in the following chapter of this book.

26 Irigaray notes, without further comment, the following: 'Of course, once again, *she is not there. Socrates relates her words.* Perhaps he distorts them unwittingly or unknowingly' (Irigaray 1993: 27).

27 *Symposium* 208b (Plato 1967: 89).

28 Plato writes: 'When by divine inspiration a man finds himself from his youth up spiritually fraught with these qualities, as soon as he comes of due age he desires to procreate and to have children, and goes in search of a beautiful object in which to satisfy his desire; for he can never bring his children to birth in ugliness. In this condition physical beauty is more pleasing to him than ugliness, and if in a beautiful body he finds also a beautiful and noble and gracious soul, he welcomes the combination warmly, and finds much to say to such a one about virtue and the qualities and actions which mark a good man, and takes his education in hand. By intimate association with beauty embodied in his friend, and by keeping him always before his mind, he succeeds in bringing to birth the children he has long desired to have, and once they are born he shares their upbringing with his friend; the partnership between them will be far closer and the bond of affection far stronger than between ordinary parents, because the children that they share surpass human children by being immortal as well as more beautiful. Everyone would prefer children such as these to children after the flesh' *Symposium* 208c–209e (Plato 1967: 90–1).

29 See also Fox Keller 1985: 21–32, especially 24.

30 For an excellent and nuanced account of Diotima's 'identity' see Halperin (1990: 91–120). See also Waithe (1987: 16) and Caverero (1995: 93). Chanter notes that Irigaray is only too aware of the way in which Diotima has been historically reduced to Platonism, and

that her response to this is to emphasize 'the uncertainty that surrounds not only Diotima's words, but her very existence'. The importance of this gesture is to ground the larger question informing much of Irigaray's work: 'How can we begin to ask about sexual difference, when the inclusion of women is not yet, still not, assured in discourse? When their very existence as women is in question, still a contested site?' (Chanter 1995: 162).

31 And further: 'Thus love passes imperceptibly into love of works. The passion for beautiful bodies is transmuted into the discovery of the beauty found in knowledge . . . *"which is eternal, not growing up or perishing, increasing or decreasing"*' (Irigaray 1993: 31–2).

32 For Irigaray's work on the sensible transcendental see 'An Ethics of Sexual Difference' in Irigaray (1993: 116–29). Irigaray writes: 'This creation would be our opportunity, from the humblest detail of everyday life to the "grandest", by means of the opening of a *sensible transcendental* that comes into being through us, of which *we would be* the mediators and bridges. Not only in mourning for the dead God of Nietzsche, not waiting passively for the god to come, but by conjuring him up among us, within us, as resurrection and transfiguration of blood, of flesh, through a language and an ethics that is ours' (Irigaray 1993: 129).

33 The fugue is a style of musical composition in at least two voices with a recurring theme, where the final entry of the theme returns to the opening key. The closing element is usually referred to as the coda.

34 What does Irigaray's ethical reading of Diotima's speech mean for her reading of Plato?

35 Of course, we should ask whether reading and being read are the same. As Tuan Nuyen has suggested, the question of how we wish to be read might problematize this open willingness to rereading.

36 For a different discussion of Nye's reading of Irigaray, one that celebrates her recuperation of Diotima for feminist scholarship, see Boulous Walker (1998: 13–14).

37 The following description of Descartes's work draws on Cottingham's discussion and all further page references to his book are found in parentheses in the text.

38 It is tempting to offer a psychoanalytic or, more specifically, object-relations reading of the bits and pieces of Descartes's 'many parts as possible'.

39 The entire passage reads: 'the intellectual conscience that should, in Descartes's philosophy, keep watch over the necessity of knowledge is

transformed into the arbitrariness of a "frame of reference". In order to satisfy a methodological need and to support the plausibility of the whole, *it becomes an axiomatic doctrine that is being set up as the gateway to thought* while no longer being able to demonstrate its own validity or proof' (Adorno 2000: 103, emphasis added).

40 For a discussion of art and wonder, see Boulous Walker (1998a: 44–7).

41 *L'admiration* carries a sense of 'wonderment'. In *Genre and Void* Max Deutscher notes that in the *Petit Robert* wonder also takes the idiomatic sense of *sentiment d'épanouissement* – 'a feeling of opening out, or blossoming' (Deutscher 2003: 199, n. 2).

42 Perhaps Descartes's interest in wonder comes from Aristotle who, in Book One of the *Metaphysics*, writes: 'For it is owing to their wonder that men both now begin and at first began to philosophize; they wondered originally at the obvious difficulties, then advanced little by little and stated difficulties about the greater matters, e.g. about the phenomena of the moon and those of the sun, and about the stars and about the genesis of the universe. And a man who is puzzled and wonders thinks himself ignorant (whence even the lover of myth is in a sense a lover of Wisdom, for the myth is composed of wonders); therefore since they philosophized in order to escape from ignorance, evidently they were pursuing science in order to know, and not for any utilitarian end' (Aristotle 1971: 981b). See also Schaeffer (1999: 641–56).

43 Merleau-Ponty connects wonder to the phenomenological reduction when he writes: 'The best formulation of the reduction is probably that given by Eugene Fink, Husserl's assistant, when he spoke of "wonder" in the face of the world'. Merleau-Ponty (1962: xv, viii). See also Kingwell (2000: 85–107), Parsons (1969: 84–101), Rubenstein (2011), La Caze (2013), and Plumwood's evocation of wonder in relation to the non-human in Plumwood (2007: 17–36).

44 Is wonder the point of revelation, where Descartes's radical doubt breaks down?

45 Irigaray's reading of Levinas also appears in this book. It is worth noting that Levinas claims that 'I' fail to consume the other because the mode of desire is a mode of *a kind of wonder* – a wonder at the other's existence that disrupts the familiarity of my 'living from' (i.e. need/enjoyment). This distinction between need and enjoyment, on the one hand, and desire (wonder) on the other, provides a background that Irigaray takes with her to her reading of Descartes.

46 Is this reference to rereading Descartes 'a little' a clue to Irigaray's reading? A selective reading? A strategic reading? Or is it reference to Descartes's later distinction between wonder as great or small?
47 Irigaray writes: 'all philosophers – except for the most recent ones? And why is this so? – have always been physicists and have always supported or accompanied their metaphysical research with cosmological researching . . . It is only lately that this ground of research has been abandoned' (Irigaray 1993: 72).
48 Is it wonder that made the early philosophers physicists?
49 And further: 'Attracting me toward, wonder keeps me from taking and assimilating directly to myself' (Irigaray 1993: 74,75).
50 Descartes positions love as secondary to wonder, the first of the passions. According to Irigaray, wonder comes both before and after love; wonder 'inaugurates' love which, unlike wonder, is an enveloping: 'Wonder is not an enveloping. It corresponds to time, to space-time before and after that which can delimit, go round, encircle. It constitutes an *opening* prior to and following that which surrounds, enlaces. It is the passion of that which is already born and not yet reenveloped in love' (81–2).
51 My exploration of Irigaray's reading of Descartes on wonder has benefited enormously from my conversations with Caitlin Goss, Emma Wilson, Rebecca Young, Darcy Burgin, Bryanna Moore, Joshua Keller, Emma Davies, Thomas Ryan, Leah Carr, Joshua Keyes-Liley, Liam Miller, Patrick Begley, Joanne Brennan, Sam Burch and Bart Mearus. My warm thanks to each of them.
52 We can think of wonder as a counter to the scalding objectification of the Sartrean gaze. In fact, Max Deutscher sees Irigaray reconstructing the Sartrean grammar of domination: 'If each person can "wonder" at the other, there will be "two-way predication"' (Deutscher 2003: 202).
53 This instrumental reduction of wonder to knowledge can arguably be seen earlier when Descartes applauds the fact that wonder 'causes us to learn and retain in our memory things of which we were formerly ignorant' (Descartes 1931: art. LXXV, 364). An ethical or slow reading would seek to resist this kind of instrumental reduction.
54 Carolyn Bynum Walker captures this ethical dimension of attentive wonder when she writes: 'our research is better when we move only cautiously to understanding, when fear that we may appropriate the "other" leads us not so much to writing about ourselves and our fears as to crafting our stories with attentive, wondering care' (Bynum Walker 1997: 25).

Chapter 4: The Present of Reading: Irigaray's Attentive Listening

1. Carel (2004: 225).
2. Nancy (2007: 1). Nancy's work resonates with Derrida's early text 'Tympan' in *Margins of Philosophy* where he evokes Nietzsche: 'To philosophize with a hammer. Zarathustra begins by asking himself if he will have to puncture them, batter their ears (*Muss man ihnen erst die Ohren zerschlagen*), with the sound of cymbals or tympani, the instruments, always, of some Dionysianism. In order to teach them "to hear with their eyes" too' (Derrida 1982: xii–xiii). See also Derrida (1985).
3. Irigaray (2002: x).
4. Hustvedt (2012: 140).
5. The question of the remaining senses could, of course, be raised in this context. Hearing and listening are my focus here, but what might we discover if we explore smell, touch, etc. The link I have drawn, however tentatively, between listening and ethics would no doubt be suspect from the perspectives of those inhabiting deaf communities – and rightly so. What is important here is to think through the many possible connections between listening and touching and smelling. Indeed, Walter Ong points to the intimate links between hearing and touch when he writes: 'sound, both in speaking and in hearing, is closely linked with touch and kinaesthesia. One "mouths" words quite literally, and our hearing is partly a "feeling"' (Ong 1991: 25). For a discussion of the ethical possibilities of looking, a looking that potentially partakes of the proximity of touch, see Mazis (1979: 321–8). See also my discussion of 'looking back' and the 'loving regard' in Boulous Walker (2009: 45–52) for an alternative, more ethical way of thinking about looking. For her part, Irigaray acknowledges the possibility of an attentive or contemplative regard, one that is neither an inattentive nor a predatory gaze (Irigaray 1996: 24).
6. For a discussion of the ethical and political implications of listening, see Bickford (1996) and Macnamara (2015).
7. Jonas refers to 'the unique distinction of sight' – simultaneity, neutralization and distance (Jonas 1953: 136–7).
8. Objectivity emerges out of 'distance' – sight's quality *par excellence*: 'perceptual distance may turn into mental distance, and the phenomenon of disinterested beholding may emerge, this essential ingredient [is] what we call "objectivity"' (Jonas 1953: 151–2).

9   Jonas claims that via the faculty of imagination theoretical truth is converted to abstract and free thought (Jonas 1953: 147).

10 Jonas distinguishes hearing and touch from sight in the following way: hearing involves the 'presentation of sequence through sequence'; touch involves the 'presentation of simultaneity through sequence'; and sight involves the 'presentation of simultaneity through simultaneity' (Jonas 1953: 142).

11 In an anthropological discussion of the development of the senses in the child, Walter Ong points to the interdependence of vision and touch: 'Sight, at first perhaps less informative, soon becomes in many ways the most informative of the senses, commonly in connection with kinaesthesia and other senses of touch, for the tactile senses combine with sight to register depth and distance when these are presented in the visual field' (Ong 1991: 25).

12 For an excellent discussion of Arendt's problematizing of the division between 'theory' and 'practice' see Taminiaux (1996: 215–32).

13 Angelica Nuzzo challenges what she sees as those too reductive readings of Kant in her comprehensive reconstruction of his theory of sensibility across the three Critiques. Nuzzo develops an idea of 'transcendental embodiment' to rethink Kant's views. See Nuzzo (2008).

14 Why might this be so? Is there something peculiar to reading that makes us less aware of our bodies? Is this true of listening as well? What kinds of listening might remind us of our embodiment?

15 In the Preface to *The Way of Love*, Irigaray writes: 'The text proposed to the readers is thus written with three voices [Irigaray's and those of the two translators], and even four, the fourth being that of Martin Heidegger with whom *The Way of Love* converses' (Irigaray 2002: ix). In a later note, she identifies the French translation of Heidegger's *Unterwegs zur Sprache* (Pfullingen: Verlag Günter Neske, 1959) as the main source of her engagement with his thought. See Heidegger (1971). In this collection of essays Heidegger's 'The Way to Language' (111–36) arguably serves as a starting or counterpoint to Irigaray's work in *The Way of Love*. Irigaray's other important response to Heidegger's work is Irigaray (1999).

16 Irigaray characterizes this as 'a philosophy in the feminine' (Irigaray 2002: vii).

17 Walter Ong explores the distinction drawn between the Greeks, for whom understanding is primarily a seeing, and the Hebrews, for whom understanding is primarily a hearing. While the Greeks are historically and culturally identified with this focus on seeing, Ong points out that they are far less exclusively so than post-Cartesian

NOTES

Western 'man'. He points to the work of Thorlief Boman (1961) in gathering considerable evidence in support of a Greek–Hebrew contrast. See Ong (1991: 25–30) and Boman (1961). The Hebrew association with hearing can be linked to later Christian cultures as those who listen for the word of God. Are there associations between looking/knowledge and listening/faith to be drawn here? If so, what implications might this hold for the kind of philosophy that Irigaray brings into being? Ong addresses the questions of cultural and historical specificity in his work, arguing, for example, that 'the world of sound itself does not have always the same importance in all cultures with relation to the worlds of other senses' (Ong 1991: 26). And further: 'Cultures vary greatly in their exploitation of the various senses and in the way in which they relate their conceptual apparatus to the various senses' (26). In the light of this, Ong urges us to think of cultures in terms of 'the organisation of the sensorium'; i.e. the culturally and historically specific ways that cultures organize the 'entire [sensory] apparatus as an operational complex'. Differences in cultures can, he claims, be thought of as differences in this sensorium, 'the organisation of which is in part determined by culture while at the same time it makes culture' (28).

18 And further: '[The] movement from the *subjective* experience of speaking to the *intersubjective* experience of being listened to allows us to shift our view, and it is this shift that makes it transformative, makes it a learning experience' (Carel 2004: 231); 'we must listen *and* be listened to in order to do philosophy. Philosophy cannot be done completely alone, because it is essentially an *intersubjective* practice constituted through reciprocal listening and speaking . . . Like politics and sex, philosophy is an inherently communal activity' (234–5).

19 Listening is a theme that runs in and out of all of Irigaray's work. In the Preface to *Between East and West*, Irigaray speaks of the importance of: 'the negative, the step back, listening and silence, the necessary alternation of doing and letting be, toward self and other, in the relation to a different subject', see Irigaray (2002c: xi). In *I Love to You*, Irigaray writes: 'Thus: how am I to speak to you? And: how am I to listen to you?' (Irigaray 1996: 113). See also Irigaray (2002b). There is important work on listening in the following publications: Irigaray (2010: 3–23) and Irigaray (2013: 217–26). My thanks to Laura Roberts for her help with these references.

20 And further: 'We need to proceed in such a way that linear reading is no longer possible' (Irigaray 1985c: 80). Julie Kelso discusses the

centrality of listening to Irigaray's reading, noting the importance Irigaray places on the 'efficacy of the psychoanalytic setting' over and above any uncritical adherence to psychoanalytic theory. Kelso emphasizes 'the mode of attentive listening that enables the silences of discourse to be not only accounted for, or critically interpreted, but to be *heard differently*' (Kelso 2007: 69).

21 See Chapter Two for a discussion of Irigaray's work on love and wonder. The practical centrality of listening to psychoanalytic practice means that it provides an excellent apprenticeship in attentive reading. Indeed, Havi Carel has something to say about this when, in her work, she indicates that philosophy can benefit from the lessons of psychoanalysis, in the sense that listening is central to the analytic experience. Such an attentive listening can help to rejuvenate the intersubjective heart of philosophical practice (Carel 2004: 226). Similarly, Michael Guy Thompson, in his discussion of Heidegger's notion of poetic dwelling, characterizes psychoanalysis as the space of listening that allows us to collect ourselves and our thoughts. In psychoanalytic practice, as in Heidegger's philosophy, 'words call us to hear' (Thompson 1997: 64); 'what is important is that we take the time to measure what our life is about in the first place – and that we listen to what we have to say, and hear it' (65). What is important is that we dwell. However, Thompson's discussion of Heidegger's attentive dwelling arguably reproduces the problem Irigaray ultimately sees with Heidegger's work; i.e. its orientation towards language at the expense of an orientation towards the other.

22 Carel writes: 'listening to the other and being listened to converge . . . both depend on the capacity to risk oneself, on the ability to open oneself up to the other or to the other in me' (Carel 2004: 229).

23 Irigaray's discussion of the 'practicable' is helpful here – the ethics of listening in the psychoanalytic context; i.e. the 'staging' of listening; the positioning of bodies, etc (not 'facing', but 'listening'). For a discussion of the feminist significance of Irigaray's practicable see Kelso (2007: 76–80). It is worth thinking about how this differs from Levinas's discussion of the *face-to-face* relation.

24 For a discussion of active listening in relation to the non-human world see Deborah Bird Rose's engagement with Val Plumwood's philosophical animism in Rose (2013).

25 In his discussion of spiritual exercises in the philosophical tradition of Greco-Roman antiquity, Pierre Hadot notes the centrality of attention to present life. Attention (*prosoche*) and meditation (*meletai*) are both nourished by the intellectual exercises, and two

of these include listening (*akroasis*) and reading (*anagnosis*). Spiritual exercises, in the Epicurean tradition, are therapeutic and aim to prepare the soul for relaxation and serenity. We might think of these as slow and careful ways of being in the world. See Hadot (1995: 84).

26 Irigaray's description, here, brings to mind Lacan's powerfully visual description of the ego in his famous mirror stage essay: Lacan 1977: 1–7.

27 In Chapter Three we explored the ethical qualities of Irigaray's work on wonder.

28 Irigaray asks at this stage whether it is 'necessary for all that to destroy the existing philosophical corpus? Or rather to modify its perspective? To accept that we have, for centuries and centuries, confused a truth of specialists with that of the human itself' (Irigaray 2002: 12).

29 Irigaray depicts our potential subjectivity as relational, writing: 'Whoever is capable of providing in oneself a place not only for the other but for the relation with the other is human' (Irigaray 2002: 80). In order for this humanity to come into being, 'An interior reserve is indispensable, a kind of availability to thinking which permits listening, welcoming, and a response respecting the two subjects and their relation' (80–1).

30 Irigaray's suggestion that this listening would be less passive, though not less attentive, is important, and brings us back to Hans Jonas who, in his work, focuses exclusively on 'hearing' without any consideration of 'listening'. Jonas thinks of hearing (and touch) as fully passive, and he contrasts this with seeing, which he characterizes as active and intentional. 'In hearing, it is true, there is also no doing on my part, but all the more on the part of the object . . . Thus hearing, bound to succession and not presenting a simultaneous coordinated manifold of objects, falls short of sight in respect of the freedom which it confers upon its possessor' (Jonas 1953: 146, 137). If Jonas had considered listening as a special instance of hearing then he may have rethought his distinction, marking the active and intentional character of listening. Listening can be thought of as a selective form of hearing, one that chooses either to hear or not to hear. One can opt not to listen or be open to the other. One can close down rather than open up or out to the other. The fact that one can choose – or learn – to listen to the other, and thus hear the other, is perhaps what makes listening, rather than hearing, 'ethical'. If so, this suggests that an active, intentional relation of openness is what counts as ethical.

31 Is it possible that women's work starts out as the work of the child? While there are good reasons to claim a cultural association between women and receptive listening, it is interesting to think of what is for many the earliest experience with reading; i.e. listening to the voice of the mother who reads aloud. Such an association positions the child as the attentive listener to the mother's voice, and this intimate relation of listening-between-two might be another way of thinking about the attentive listening or invitation to share that Irigaray discusses. In 'The End of Reading', Peggy Kamuf agrees that the child (in the West?) learns to read by first listening to the mother's voice: 'before the child's invention of silent reading, it is the mother's voice that has been made to echo with the letters taking shape on the page' (Kamuf 2000). This suggests another reason to explore the idea of reading as a kind of listening: one that importantly begins with the mother's voice.

32 Do men hear and leave listening to women? If so, is this why Jean-Luc Nancy depicts the philosopher (a man?) as 'someone who always hears (and who hears everything), but who cannot listen'? Do women do the work of 'straining' to listen that Nancy differentiates from hearing? (Nancy 2007: 1).

33 Meaghan Morris points to the cultural stereotypes linking women with the work of listening: 'For the lovers of high-speed iconoclasm, the lowly labour of listening carefully to a text connotes the fussiness of housewife's psychosis' (Morris 1998: 95–6). She draws our attention to those situations in which women are simply not listened to. This is linked to what she refers to as 'the woman's complaint'. Nagging can be thought of as speech that is (for a variety of reasons) simply not listened to. Morris describes nagging in the following manner: 'One of the defining generic rules of "nagging" is unsuccessful repetition of the same statements' (Morris 1998: 15). She has some important things to say about the problems associated with nagging, and we need to consider these in the absence of a relation that supports attentive listening between a woman and a man. See also Boulous Walker (1993a: 79–91).

34 In his work on *Stimmung* (atmosphere, mood) as a contemporary way in to reading literature, Hans Ulrich Gumbrecht has the following to say in relation to the physicality of listening and hearing: 'I am most interested in the component of meaning that connects *Stimmung* with music and the hearing of sounds. As is well known, we do not hear with our inner and outer ear alone. Hearing is a complex form of behavior that involves the entire body. Skin and haptic modalities of perception play an important role. Every tone we perceive is, of course, a form of physical reality (if an

invisible one) that "happens" to our body and, at the same time, "surrounds" it . . . Being affected by sound . . . physically, [is] a concrete encounter (in the literal sense of *en-countering*: meeting up) with our physical environment' (Gumbrecht 2012: 4). Gumbrecht's focus on *Stimmung* aims to follow 'configurations of atmosphere and mood' in literary texts in order to 'encounter otherness in intense and intimate ways' (13). In this sense, I think that his work sits well beside Irigaray's more obviously philosophical aim to do the same; i.e. to encounter the other in intense and intimate ways. In Chapter Two, we engage with Gumbrecht's work on *Stimmung*.

35 Irigaray states: 'In our tradition, the highest and most disinterested intention of language would be naming the world and its objects. It is a matter of grasping them in a saying through words corresponding to the Western logos with its conceptual predominance, or of designating them while letting them be, which is nearer to the eastern language that the Western poet sometimes approaches. Language is the tool, the *techné*, which the speaking subject uses in order to exist in a world, to dwell in it and to continue to construct it as human' (Irigaray 2002: 38).

36 Irigaray writes: 'It is not possible to learn once and for all how to speak – at each moment the creative work of inventing a speaking is imposed. And if it is necessary here to listen to someone or to something, it is to ourselves and to the one, him or her, with whom we want to dialogue in the present that we have to lend an ear' (Irigaray 2002: 64).

37 Irigaray refers to a kind of technological stage of communication that she sees as dominant today: 'That stage of communication – which is related to a kind of information that the techniques of formalization can grasp and make their domain – becomes obsolete and appears as corresponding to a need to communicate tied to the seizure of the world but not to a saying that lets it and us be' (Irigaray 2002: 38).

38 Irigaray's reference to 'letting-be' connects with her earlier reference to relinquishing, recognition and gratitude, all of which flow from a mindfulness that Irigaray describes in the following manner: 'The highest rule of the word would consist in not appropriating the thing but letting it be as thing. What is sought here is beyond: how to let be the other as other while speaking, speaking to them. Moreover: how to encourage the other to be and to remain other. How to let the other come into presence, even to lead them there, without claiming to be their foundation' (Irigaray 2002: 29). In

addition, letting-be 'opens a place of resource and of meditative gathering' (173).

39 And further, in relation to listening: 'How to listen to the other, to open oneself, horizontally, to the other's sense, without preventing the return to oneself, to one's proper way? What words, not common a priori, will be able to assist, even mark out a path?' (Irigaray 2002: 58–9). And: 'we still have to invent the words while continuing to listen to those of the other' (65).

40 For a discussion of 'letting-be' as creation in Christian theology in the work of one of Heidegger's translators, see Macquarrie (1977). See also Macquarrie (1994).

41 In the context of his exploration of Irigaray's new economy of relations, Krzysztof Ziarek discusses her strategy to identify and then unsettle any distinction between making and letting-be: 'It would be a mistake to assume that Irigaray disparages or underestimates the importance of making and production, for making, as she remarks several times, is indispensable to human development. Rather, what Irigaray wants to question is the predominance of making over letting-be, which has led to a certain inability to let be and, more important, to the prevalent disregard for letting be, misunderstood as a symptom of powerlessness and inaction' (Ziarek 2007: 72). Ziarek examines the importance Irigaray places on cultivating 'invisibility' as a counter to productive modern relations, and in so doing outlines the positive inscriptions of looking and seeing that her new economy can imagine. For a discussion of the Heideggerian terms *machen* (making) and *lassen* (letting-be) in terms of producing and enabling, see also Ziarek (2001: 355–71).

42 At the beginning of this chapter I mentioned that *The Way of Love* comes out of Irigaray's reading of key texts by Martin Heidegger. To the attentive reader the echo of Heidegger's voice in Irigaray's work will be evident. Irigaray's talk of technological communication, dwelling, letting-be and being-with will seem familiar to those who have read Heidegger themselves. Let us look briefly at some of the key moments in Heidegger's *œuvre* where listening and hearing frame the philosophical work that he does. In ¶ 34 of *Being and Time*, in a brief discussion devoted to hearing, Heidegger positions listening and listening-to as central to Dasein's openness. He writes: 'Listening to . . . is Dasein's existential way of Being-open as Being-with for Others. Indeed, hearing constitutes the primary and authentic way in which Dasein is open for its ownmost potentiality-for-Being – as in hearing the voice of a friend whom every Dasein carries with it . . . Being-with develops in listening to

one another [*Aufeinander-hören*]' (Heidegger 1962: [¶ 34.] 206). Hearing or, more precisely, listening-to is central to Heidegger's understanding of the openness of Being, and the potential for hearing provides the possibility for a 'hearkening' (*Horchen*) which is an altogether more attentive form of listening: 'It is on the basis of this potentiality for hearing, which is existentially primary, that anything like *hearkening* [*Horchen*] becomes possible. Hearkening is phenomenally still more primordial than what is defined "in the first instance" as "hearing"' (Heidegger 1962 [¶ 34.] 163 – English translation, 207). The attentive listening (*Horchen*) that he identifies in his early work will stay with Heidegger and accompany, in a silent way, what he will later have to say in relation to dwelling, where he will call us to remain open to the things of the world, to resist the technological pull of Enframing that serves only to close down our relation with the world and, if we listen to Irigaray, our relation to the other. The significance Heidegger attributes to listening and to hearing is evident in his later essay, 'The Question Concerning Technology', where he writes: 'For man becomes truly free only insofar as he belongs to the realm of destining and so becomes one who listens and hears [*Hörender*], and not one who is simply constrained to obey [*Höriger*]'. And: 'Man . . . fails to see himself as the one spoken to, and hence also fails in every way to hear in what respect he ek-sists. . .' (Heidegger 1977: 25, 27). In 'The Nature of Language', he writes: 'the true stance of thinking cannot be to put questions, but must be to listen to that which our questioning vouchsafes' (Heidegger 1971: 72).

43 For a poetic perspective on the link between reading and listening that we are developing here, see Engler (1982). Engler discusses the limitations of a teaching devoted exclusively to close reading, arguing that the horizontal dimension (of rhythm, sound and intonation) are neglected resulting in a 'predominance of explanation and textual interpretation' that only listening and reciting can hope to remedy (Engler 1982: 109).

44 In Chapter Six we explore Hélène Cixous's slow approach to the other through her reading of Clarice Lispector's work.

45 In *The Way of Love*, Irigaray admonishes Heidegger for seeking proximity with language, rather than with the other: 'The proximity sought by the philosopher is proximity with language or thanks to it, and not with the other and thanks to him, to her' (Irigaray 2002: 32). In keeping with this, she suggests that Heidegger listens to language rather than to the other: 'He is on the way toward the call of speech, not toward the call of another subject' and asks, 'Does he not subjugate not only looking but all the senses, in particular hearing, to

the power of language?' (31). In short, Irigaray admonishes Heidegger for his orientation towards language at the expense of an orientation towards the other. This is interesting, because Ziarek goes to great length to demonstrate another way of reading Heidegger on this point. Indeed, he claims that it is through a careful return to the question of listening and hearing in Heidegger's work that we can find a listening to language that turns towards the other in an attitude of attentiveness. From *Being and Time* through to the later works on poetry, Heidegger characterizes thinking as a listening to others, and claims that listening to others 'marks the way in which *Dasein* turns and opens itself to the world' (Ziarek 1994: 193). Listening 'turns thinking into *Mitdenken*, into thinking-with, which thinks to the extent that it has already been listening' (194). Time and time again, Ziarek claims, Heidegger 'underscores the listening character of poetry, listening that "transpires only in conversation, in an exchange or a turn toward the other"' (198). And further: 'all that happens bears the mark of the turn of thinking toward others. This turn does not simply come after a reflection, as an acknowledgment of the binding power of the rules for ethical behaviour, but instead makes possible and affects any such articulations. Language, poetry, and thinking are always turned towards others; they can approach and think the world, things, and the other (human beings), only as they listen to others. To that extent, it is possible to claim that, in the last count, Heidegger's view of language is determined by his notion of friendship: it is open-ness to others, a linguistic listening figured as friendship, that allows language, thinking, writing, to be in any sense ethical' (Ziarek 1994: 199). Is Ziarek right to hear this in Heidegger's work? If so, how attentively has Irigaray listened to Heidegger?

46 Of course, not all proximity or nearness allows the other to be. Max Deutscher rightly reminds us that sexual and other forms of physical abuse enforce 'proximity rather than creating a bond'. He refers to this kind of proximity as contact without 'wonderment' or 'respect for difference, without reference to *interiority* – that irrecoverable distance which intimacy recognises between those who are most close' (Deutscher 2003: 208).

47 Eric Blondel writes: 'Nietzsche's concepts are . . . worked in a way that releases an imaginary polysemy – ideas – provided one agrees to ruminate'. It is precisely this rumination that takes time. See Blondel (1991: 254).

48 In the Introduction we looked at Mark Bauerlein's work on slow reading as a way of breaking (rather than changing) the habits of poor reading resulting from a lack of encounter with complex texts

in an age dominated by online scanning. Bauerlein calls for changes to current high school practices in order to better prepare students for the rigours of university research: 'One hour a day of slow reading with print matter, an occasional research assignment completed without Google – any such practices that slow down and intensify the reading of complex texts will help' (Bauerlein 2011: 33).

49 Fletcher writes: 'we generally do not pause to take note of what the sentences we read actually SAY. This rush to interpretation and judgment is strongly encouraged by most of our educational practices' (Fletcher 2007).

50 While Fletcher champions a kind of slow reading and slow philosophy that fits well with Irigaray's work on the importance of attentive listening, there are some differences in their aims. Fletcher aims to recover intact pure authorial intention, while I understand Irigaray to be more concerned with the poetic process of a meaning that emerges creatively between self and other (reader and text) once attentive listening has occurred. Irigaray's listening is a creative listening that takes responsibility for co-creating any meanings that emerge.

51 In a similar vein, Simon Critchley links good teaching with listening and the deflation of self-certainty: 'We should be trying to cultivate the conditions under which such an event [truth as that which bores a hole in the self-certainty of knowledge] might happen, in our teaching, our listening to students, and our collaborative being-with others' (Critchley 2010: 27).

52 For a discussion of philosophical listening in the context of education in schools, see Haynes and Murris (2012: 185–230).

53 This brings us back to Michèle Le Dœuff, who reminds us in the most convincing way that teaching reading really matters. In 'Red Ink in the Margin', she draws our attention to the listening and hearing involved in reading, and what this means for young and aspiring philosophers. Le Dœuff asks how, in reading, we 'hear' philosophical works. She convinces us that we should not decide too hastily the certitude of meaning in any given philosophical work; that we 'might learn a good deal by giving a hearing' to those readings by students suggesting possibilities other than those traditionally entertained (Le Dœuff 1989: 99). In response to Le Dœuff's advice, Daniel Nicholls writes: 'for Le Dœuff, there is a special quality involved in "hearing". To *stand before* is to hear, to *stand in for* is to block. To hear is to be a person among people: We don't hear a "univocalization" but a multiplicity of voices. If one student

hears [when reading Descartes] "provisional morality" where the master thinks he should hear "morality by provision," then these are both meanings/sounds (thoughts/images) that emanate from the text. Every reading is at least a *sound* reading in that way. That a consistent sound might not be reproduced by the reader does not indicate that the student has incorrectly heard. A need for this consistency is perhaps a feature of the master who may have heard his own various voices (political, pedagogical, philosophical): the voices of his own "imaginary"' (Nicholls 2000: 158).

Chapter 5: Romance and Authenticity: Beauvoir's Lesson in Reading

1   Beauvoir 1984: 663.

2   Having made this suggestion – that we think about reading and love together – I need to say that such a coupling is by no means straightforward. There are, of course, many senses (practical, corporeal) in which a romantic relation with another (body) differs dramatically from what we might call a romantic relation with the text. Exactly how far can the analogy be taken? For example, the spatial/corporeal/material relation between the reader and the text (page/screen) naturally differs from that between two bodies. Whether it does so emotionally, psychologically or intellectually is, perhaps, another question entirely.

3   I say interestingly, because Beauvoir virtually opens 'The Woman in Love' with this statement from Nietzsche. In total, she cites Nietzsche three times throughout this chapter, and each time we remain somewhat uncertain about her relation to his 'intertexts'. Indeed, I would go so far as to suggest that we need to pay careful attention to each instance of Nietzsche's appearance in this chapter, for these coincide with interesting moves in Beauvoir's textual argument. Further references to Nietzsche include: 'For the loving woman who asks her lover to be a hero, a giant, a demigod, also is asking not to be all the world to him, even though she cannot have happiness unless she possesses him completely'. Says Nietzsche in *The Gay Science (le Gai Savoir)*: 'Woman's passion, a total renunciation of all rights of her own, postulates precisely that the same feeling, the same desire for renunciation, does exist also in the other sex, for if both severally made this renunciation for love, there would result, on my word I do not know just what, shall we say, perhaps, the horror of nothingness? The woman wishes to be taken . . . she demands,

therefore, someone to *take* her, someone who does not give himself, who does not abandon himself, but who wishes, on the contrary, to enrich his ego through love . . . The woman gives herself, the man adds to himself by taking her', cited in *TSS*: 668. I will return to the question of giving and the gift later in the chapter in order to rethink Beauvoir's notion of romantic love in terms of generosity. What follows is the third and final reference to Nietzsche in Beauvoir's 'The Woman in Love': 'Men have vied with one another in proclaiming that love is woman's supreme accomplishment. "A woman who loves as a woman becomes only the more feminine," says Nietzsche' (*TSS*: 678).

4   The passage continues: 'There is no other way out for her than to lose herself, body and soul, in him who is represented to her as the absolute, as the essential . . . She chooses to desire her enslavement so ardently that it will seem to her the expression of her liberty, she will try to rise above her situation as inessential object by fully accepting it; through her flesh, her feelings, her behaviour, she will enthrone him as supreme value and reality' (*TSS*: 653).

5   One way of thinking of the other as the centre of all value, meaning, and sense is the role played by the other or lover in the narcissistic experience of the woman in love. Beauvoir notes that one of the tendencies of romantic love is the importance of the lover as 'witness' to one's life. In *TSS* she writes: 'The woman in love feels endowed with a high and undeniable value; she is at last allowed to idolize herself through the love she inspires. She is overjoyed to find in her lover a witness' (*TSS*: 656). In support of her claim, Beauvoir cites a passage from Colette's *Vagabonde*: 'I admit I yielded, in permitting this man to come back the next day, to the desire to keep in him not a lover, not a friend, but an eager spectator to my life and my person . . . One must be terribly old, Margot said to me one day, to renounce the vanity of living under someone's gaze' (Collette, *Vagabonde*, cited in *TSS*: 657). Thus, the act of 'witness' provided by the lover is a function of the narcissism which a woman is able to enjoy in romantic love. If a woman's lover has become a universal value, then it is under his gaze – his witness – that the contingencies of her life ('her childhood memories, her former tears, her gowns, her accustomed ways, her universe, everything she is, all that belongs to her') become 'essential'.

6   It is worth noting that Beauvoir's negative description of mimicry here seems at odds with Irigaray's work on mimesis and mimicry. While Beauvoir depicts the woman in love's mimicry as a simple repetition of masculine values and a subsequent fall from self, Irigaray teases the complex gestures involved in the strategies of mimicry open to women in phallocentric contexts. For Irigaray, mimicry involves

woman's deliberate attempt to avoid (simply) taking on the position of masculinity: 'To play with mimesis is thus, for a woman, to try to recover the place of her exploitation by discourse, without allowing herself to be simply reduced to it' (Irigaray 1985c: 76). Mimicry 'caricatures and deforms' masculine language in order to prevent it simply being reproduced (Irigaray 1985d: 137).

7 Earlier, Beauvoir writes: 'to justify her future she puts it in the hands of one who possesses all values. Thus she gives up her transcendence, subordinating it to that of the essential other, to whom she makes herself vassal and slave . . . little by little she does lose herself in him wholly; for her the whole of reality is in the other' (*TSS*: 661).

8 In H.M. Pashley's translation of *TSS*, *l'amoureuse* has been translated as 'the woman in love'.

9 In her discussion of Beauvoir's analysis of romantic love, Kathryn Pauly Morgan points out that Beauvoir's perspective on romantic love is inseparable from her existential philosophical work. What would it mean to think about romantic love from a different starting point? 'The question then arises: Does the negative moral assessment of romantic love proceed through the value system of existentialist ethics alone? Suppose we leave aside the lofty language of transcendence and immanence and the model of human nature which depends upon a theory of objectifying self-deception as a universal human desire. What moral assessment should we make of romantic love? Beauvoir's moral condemnation of romantic love is powerful and clear. But what of those individuals who do not operate within an existentialist conceptual and moral universe of discourse? They might maintain that a life of romantic love is either morally neutral or, like Balzac, claim that it is the unique source of woman's genuine equality with man' (Morgan 1986: 136).

10 Here, romantic love is a particular form of 'being-for-the-other' that offers one a way of avoiding the hard work and responsibility of forming the self.

11 See also Irigaray 1981. What Beauvoir has to say in *TSS* about women and rivalry, supports – and indeed anticipates – Irigaray's later analysis: 'In a state of uncertainty, every woman is a rival, a danger. Love destroys the possibility of friendship with other women' (*TSS*: 674).

12 In the following discussion, Beauvoir points out that this denial of self or 'losing of oneself in the other' can take the form of making oneself indispensable to the other: 'She reads the papers, clips out articles, classifies letters and notes, copies manuscripts, for him' (*TSS*: 660).

13 And just prior to this: 'most often woman knows herself only as different, relative; her *pour-autrui*, relation to others, is confused with her very being; for her, love is not an intermediary "between herself and herself" because she does not attain her subjective existence; she remains engulfed in this loving woman whom man has not only revealed, but created. Her salvation depends on this despotic free being that has made her and can instantly destroy her. She lives in fear and trembling before this man who holds her destiny in his hands' (*TSS*: 678). It is noteworthy that a discussion of servility and dependence emerges early in Beauvoir's work, and finds considerable expression in *The Ethics of Ambiguity (TEOA)*. She argues: 'There are beings whose life slips by in an infantile world because, having been kept in a state of servitude and ignorance, they have no means of breaking the ceiling which is stretched over their heads. Like the child, they can exercise their freedom, but only within this universe which has been set up before them, without them ... This is also the situation of women in many civilizations; they can only submit to the laws, the gods, the customs and the truths created by males' (Beauvoir 1962: 37). Beauvoir does not, however, view this condition as unavoidable: 'It is then that we discover the difference which distinguishes them from an actual child: the child's situation is imposed upon him, whereas the woman (I mean the Western woman of today) chooses it or at least consents to it' (*TEOA*: 38). In relation to this infantilism, Beauvoir notes in *TSS* that even where independence is available, it is the other path which seems 'the most attractive to a majority of women: it is agonizing for a woman to assume responsibility of her life' (*TSS*: 655).

14 For an insightful discussion of the themes of devotion and self-abandonment in Simone de Beauvoir and Søren Kierkegaard, see Walsh (1998: 35–40). Walsh writes: 'Perhaps the most interesting similarity to emerge ... is the degree to which both, in spite of their strong and similar critiques of feminine devotedness and self-abandonment, reaffirm the validity and importance of these qualities when given expression in appropriate form and in the proper social and/or spiritual context' (38).

15 On the question of why women 'choose' or 'opt for' romantic love, over and against accepting their existential responsibility, Morgan's discussion of Beauvoir's work is instructive. Morgan emphasizes Beauvoir's observation that women are discouraged from transcendence and propelled towards a life of immanence, with the result that 'their' (our?) lives are barely 'human' (Morgan 1986: 125). As Beauvoir famously notes, women's lives traditionally and

typically engage with the simple replication of everyday life and are, as such, not 'genuinely creative' or 'properly human' (120). According to Morgan, this existential analysis makes it easy for Beauvoir to make sense of why many women desire romantic love. This desire, she says, is tied up with: '(1) the general human desire to avoid a life of responsible self-determination (the phenomenon of bad faith or *mauvaise foi*); (2) the concrete social and economic circumstances of many women; and (3) romantic ideology which is carefully inculcated in girls and women from an early age' (125), plus (4) the desire to gain an identity in and through their association with 'a superior male' (126). Morgan goes on in her article to explore the paradoxes experienced by the woman in love in her pursuit of love as a form of liberation. See Morgan (1986: 117–48). The distinction I am drawing in this chapter between romantic and authentic love to some extent resonates with a distinction Meryl Altman uncovers in her work on Beauvoir. Altman cites a passage from Beauvoir where she refers to dependence and responsibility. Beauvoir makes this distinction in the context of her own relation to Hegel's work. In *La Force de l'Age*, Beauvoir writes: 'The more I went along, the more I separated from Hegel, without ceasing to admire him. Now I knew that I was linked to my contemporaries, to the marrow of my bones; I discovered the other side of the coin of this dependence, my responsibility' (Altman 2007: 537). We might say that romantic love (dependence) and authentic love (responsibility) operate here in a non-oppositional manner. I will return to this possibility – non-opposed terms – later in the chapter. What is crucial in Altman's paper, and relevant for my work here, is that she underlines the necessity of thinking through Beauvoir's work in relation to philosophers other than Sartre – in her case, Hegel. Beauvoir's *La Force de l'Age* is translated as Simone de Beauvoir, *The Prime of Life: The Autobiography of Simone De Beauvoir* (1992).

For further discussion of Beauvoir's independent philosophical position, and her connections with philosophers other than Sartre, see Bauer (2006: 65–91), Lundgren-Gothlin (1996), Kruks (1990), Heinämaa (1996) and Bergoffen (1997). For an excellent collection of essays placing Beauvoir in dialogue with Husserl, Merleau-Ponty, Heidegger, Foucault, Levinas and others, see Simons (2006).

16   Irigaray's reworking of Jacques Lacan's 'mirror stage' is apt here. Irigaray claims that the phallocentric process of specularization, man's projection of himself and his ego on to the world, occurs through the appropriation of woman's body as mirror (or tain). This

process robs woman of her own self-representation. See Irigaray (1985a).

17 Beauvoir's scathing conclusion to the chapter reads: '[L]ove represents in its most touching form the curse that lies heavily upon woman confined in the feminine universe, woman mutilated, insufficient unto her self. The innumerable martyrs to love bear witness against the injustice of a fate that offers a sterile hell as ultimate salvation' (*TSS*: 679). Morgan comments on the intense nature of Beauvoir's criticisms of romantic love, emphasizing that Beauvoir's analysis demands a harsh response: 'Beauvoir's critique is so ruthless [because] she is committed to exposing romantic love as an existential fraud. Whereas the woman in love sees in her love a form of transcendence, a form of genuine liberation, Beauvoir sees it as an inevitable downward spiral into abject servility incompatible with any surviving remnant of self-respect' (Morgan 1986: 131). We will return to the question of Beauvoir's phrase, 'this too faithful echo', in the latter part of this chapter. For the moment, though, it is worth noting Beauvoir's own strategy of 'othering' here; i.e. the clearly negative identification she draws with 'the woman in love'.

18 Morgan refers to authentic love as 'genuinely reciprocated human love' and points out that this would 'preserve both self-respect and autonomy' (Morgan 1986: 146).

19 See Vintges (1996: 46–66) and Deutscher (2003: 250).

20 In *Being and Nothingness* Sartre writes: 'I shall never touch the Other save in his being-as-object' (Sartre 1956: 410). And further: 'The *essence* of the relations between consciousnesses is not the *Mitsein*: it is conflict' (429). Ursula Tidd (1999) notes that 'For Sartre, the Other transcends me and places restrictions on my freedom, and I must therefore negate and transcend the Other by making him or her into an object' (164). She goes on to say that Sartre's conflictual view of self–other relations is also evident 'in his theatre and fiction of this period, notably *Huis clos* (Sartre 1945) and *L'Age de raison* (Sartre 1949). In these texts, the Other constitutes an obstacle to the protagonists' transcendence' (Tidd 1999: 172, n.1). Nancy Bauer takes up the question of *Mitsein* in Beauvoir's work, suggesting that she associates it almost exclusively with inauthenticity, thus overlooking the potential for reciprocal recognition it brings: 'My being with others leaves open the possibility that I may invite them to judge me freely: not as I wish to be reified, but as they genuinely – in their own assumed freedom – are inclined to experience me' (Bauer 2001: 144).

21 For a discussion of the importance of reclaiming this book as one of Beauvoir's major philosophical works see Langer (1994: 181–90).

22 We find this as well in *TSS* where Beauvoir depicts the erotic encounter in the positive terms of an ambiguous and reciprocal experience: 'The erotic experience is one that most poignantly discloses to human beings the ambiguity of their condition; in it they are aware of themselves as flesh and as spirit, as the other and as subject' (*TSS*: 423). See also Diprose (1998: 1–20).

23 Deutscher 2003: 250. See also Lundgren-Gothlin (1996: 149, 217–18) and Vintges (1996: 46–66).

24 Towards the end of *Being and Nothingness*, Sartre briefly suggests that by ceasing to value the goal of being God, and valuing, in this place, freedom, 'man' might encounter the other. However, as Linda Hansen, Max Deutscher and others have pointed out, Sartre fails to pursue this insight. In her paper, Hansen contends that Beauvoir takes this insight and develops it, making it possible to think of Sartre's conflictual account as merely a partial truth. See Hansen (1979: 338–46). In a sense, we could say that Beauvoir does the philosophical 'work' on relationships, love and intimacy that Sartre himself never undertakes. Does this suggest a 'sexual division of labour', with the male philosopher working on conflict, combat and self, while the female philosopher works on love, generosity and relation?

25 Hansen writes: 'If man is willing to assume his failure to be God, and freely place value instead on his free disclosure of being, his existence ceases to be a "useless passion" as in Sartre's description, and becomes, as de Beauvoir says, a "positive existence"' (Hansen 1979: 340).

26 Beauvoir *TSS*, Book One, Part III, Chapter IX: 'Dreams, Fears, Idols', 172. For a discussion of reciprocity and friendship in Beauvoir's work see Ward (1999: 36–49). Ward suggests that in this passage Beauvoir makes it clear that the Hegelian master–slave relation can be overcome (43).

27 Beauvoir's focus on ambiguity suggests the need for us to return to her work, in dialogue with philosophers such as Maurice Merleau-Ponty and Emmanuel Levinas in order to think through the complexity of her positions. This would also do something towards correcting the tendency to think through Beauvoir's work only in terms of how it accords – or not – with Sartre's philosophy. In this chapter, I am aware that in the final sections my coupling of Beauvoir with Sartre does, to some extent, repeat this gesture. I have misgivings about reading Beauvoir exclusively in relation to Sartre. As I have already mentioned, we need to read her in terms of the complexity of her many intellectual 'intertexts' or 'influences'; for

example, Kant, Hegel, Levinas, Merleau-Ponty, Levinas and Camus. However, having said this, the great wealth of material that Beauvoir writes on Sartre provides us with a particular instance of Beauvoir, herself, as reader. And it is Beauvoir the reader that I shall address in these final sections. For a collection of excellent texts addressing Beavoir's relation with a variety of philosophers, see my suggestions in n.15.

28 For a further discussion of authentic love through the categories of ambiguity and appeal, see Gothlin (1999: 83–95). Gothlin asks what cost authentic love might have for a man; might there be cause for reluctance. In relation to this, she cites Beauvoir: 'To recognize in woman a human being is not to impoverish man's experience: this would lose none of its diversity, its richness, or its intensity if it were to occur between two subjectivities . . . It is simply to ask that behavior, sentiment, passion be founded upon the truth' (*TSS*: 291, cited in Gothlin 1999: 88). Gothlin goes on to cite Beauvoir's work on authentic love in 'Sexual Initiation' in support of her own discussion which envisages an authentic sexual act: 'alterity has no longer a hostile implication, and indeed this sense of the union of separate bodies is what gives its moving character to the sexual act; and it is the more overwhelming as the two beings, who together in passion deny and assert their boundaries; are alike (equals) and yet different' (Beauvoir *TSS*: 422, cited in Gothlin 1999: 89, translation modified).

29 Hansen summarizes Beauvoir's position thus: 'Just as it is wrong to objectify someone, so is it wrong to totally "subjectify" someone, to see that person only in terms of his freedom, his transcendence, and not to see his limitations, his being in a situation. That would be to attempt to treat another as God. One who is seeking God in another person is naturally going to be disappointed, because human beings are limited beings. But more importantly, one who looks for God in another may miss seeing the human good that there is' (Hansen 1979: 342).

30 See Hansen (1979: 342–3). Hansen writes: 'These are not opposed versions of the nature of authentic love, but rather complementary ones. Neither is really complete without the other' (342). It is worth pointing out that Beauvoir herself does not combine these discussions in one unified statement on love, but rather that we can find these elements throughout the corpus of her work.

31 Gothlin writes that Beauvoir's authentic love is 'founded upon reciprocal recognition, friendship, generosity, and understanding' (Gothlin 1999: 88).

32 Beauvoir continues: 'Idolatrous love attributes an absolute value to the loved one, a first falsity that is brilliantly apparent to all outsiders ... It is a searing disappointment to the woman to discover the faults, the mediocrity of her idol'.

33 When we think of reductive readings it might be instructive to look again at what Harold Bloom has to say about the motivations that lie behind what he refers to as 'the anxiety of influence'. See Bloom (1973). Here Bloom finds instances of what I am referring to as reductive or aggressive readings in the writing of (young) men. Another way to think of this kind of reductive reading is the desire to reduce the text to oneself, and in discussion Fred D'Agostino has characterized this gesture as typical of the hyberbolic extension of the Davidsonian project of interpretation.

34 At first glance, we might think of reductionist readings and devotional readings as quite opposed; however, if we think of both of these as immature gestures, then it becomes easier to hypothesize a relation between the two. When we belittle another (reduce him or her) we are arguably acting as immaturely as one who exhibits a sycophantic (devotional?) attitude. Indeed, a colleague tells of having worked in an institutional context where the teaching staff were famous for belittling others, with the result that their graduate students not only repeated this belittling but coupled this with an overwhelming devotion to authority, thus exhibiting both signs of immaturity in quite exaggerated ways.

35 The question of transference seems relevant here. Luce Irigaray's work on the transferential relation (see Kelso 2007) and Michèle Le Dœuff's elaboration of the erotico-theoretical relation are useful for thinking through these connections. Might romantic reading be, in part, an attempt to deny the complex processes of transference and counter-transference? I refer briefly to Le Dœuff's work on transference in the following chapter.

36 While it may seem that I am overstating the case for a blind devotional reading, we need only think of certain neo-Kantians, neo-Marxists and others whose devotion to the orthodoxy of the text blinds them to critical failures, problems, tensions or silences inherent in these texts. Here, blind devotion or romantic reading characterizes those readings that demonstrate an inability to engage maturely with both the text's shortcomings and its strengths. I would suggest that this type of reading is more prevalent than we think, and thus the issue of romantic reading is more important than it might at first seem. We might go on to ask the difficult and complex question of whether romantic reading is grounded in a specifically Christian

tradition and training. Is there something peculiar to the Christian tradition (biblical hermeneutics?) that orients us culturally towards devotional readings? Does the need to assimilate oneself *to* the text bind a certain practice of reading in the West to an unproductive sincerity and fidelity? Recall that Nietzsche refers to woman's romantic love as 'a *faith*, the only one she has', cited in *TSS*: 652. Is romantic reading, as I am characterizing it here, a religious reading vaguely analogous to religious fundamentalism; i.e. an uncritical *submission* to what we believe another's interpretation to be?

37 Pierre Macherey has a somewhat aggressive way of differentiating this kind of reading from paraphrase. He writes: 'All authentic reading is in its own way violent, or it is nothing but the complaisance of a paraphrase', cited in Sharp (2011: 117).

38 To paraphrase Beauvoir: an authentic reading should accept the contingency of the text with all its idiosyncrasies, its limitations and its basic gratuitousness. It would not pretend to be a mode of salvation but an interrelation.

39 The question of what a text knows, what it does not know and what it cannot know brings to mind Louis Althusser's exemplary practice of symptomatic reading. For Althusser, the non-vision of a text (its silences) is a function of its vision (what it voices). Oversight, non-vision, silence are all absences that concern what is present (i.e. sight, vision, voice). 'Non-vision is therefore inside vision, it is a form of vision and hence has a necessary relationship with vision' (Althusser 1979: 21). When we read symptomatically, then, we compare a text with itself: its non-vision or silence with its vision or voice. In Althusser's words, we attempt: 'To understand this necessary and paradoxical identity of non-vision and vision with vision itself . . . [in order] to make us see what the . . . text itself says while not saying it, does not say while saying it' (21–2). This complex notion of reading leads us in the direction of what I am here referring to as an authentic reading. See also Boulous Walker (1998: 27–49).

The relation between vision and reading, while seemingly an obvious one, brings to mind the interesting phenomenological work of Hans Jonas. Jonas's 'Nobility of Sight' (which we looked at in Chapter Four) brings the very corporeality of reading into play. By thinking of reading exclusively in terms of vision and sight we 'overlook' or miss the possibility of thinking of reading as a relation with much in common with listening. In the end, it may be the case that 'listening' – rather than looking – best describes what remains ethical (or otherwise) in reading. See Jonas (1953: 135–55).

40 In *TEOA* Beauvoir talks about our individual abilities to grasp the ambiguity of life, and juxtaposes this with the work of the majority of philosophers whose project it has been to mask this ambiguity – a project as inauthentic as it is impossible. The implications of this passage, for the manner in which philosophers read, is important for my discussion here. Beauvoir seems to be saying that the philosophical impulse is to mask the world's ambiguity by striving to forge a single condition or understanding of existence. Implicit in her discussion is a sense in which what I am calling authentic reading is a primary or 'instinctual' human response, one lost in the successive layers of philosophical thought. Beauvoir writes: 'As long as there have been men and they have lived, they have all felt this tragic ambiguity of their condition, but as long as there have been philosophers and they have thought, most of them have tried to mask it. They have striven to reduce mind to matter, or to reabsorb matter into mind, or to merge them within a single substance ... Let us try to assume our fundamental ambiguity ... From the very beginning, existentialism defined itself as a philosophy of ambiguity. It was by affirming the irreducible character of ambiguity that Kierkegaard opposed himself to Hegel, and it is by ambiguity that ... [Sartre elaborated his ontology]' (Beauvoir *TEOA*: 7–10).

41 As we have seen in the Introduction, the spiritual exercises include reading, listening, attention and meditation.

42 I have referred to authentic reading as 'mature' on a number of occasions. While this seems an almost 'natural' association to make, in the light of my discussion, it is worth thinking about the inexperienced or younger reader; for example, the child. The child who has only recently learnt to read arguably reads in an open and wondrous manner – totally ethical under the circumstances, and yet immature in other respects. Perhaps the issue here is not so much a fixed opposition between maturity and immaturity, but rather the problems of immaturity in older readers. Having said this, I nonetheless think that we could revisit the question of maturity/immaturity in and through Luce Irigaray's work on wonder. My thanks to Julie Kelso for raising this question. For a detailed discussion of Irigaray's work on wonder, see Chapter Three.

43 Beauvoir writes: 'No essence defines women once and for all' (*TSS*: 268).

44 'The others – and this is the most important point – pose as transcendents but feel themselves prisoners of a dark presence in their own hearts. They project this "unbreakable core of night" upon woman' (*TSS*: 280).

45 In developing a practice of authentic reading, the question naturally arises: what does it mean for writers to read their *own* work? Without sidestepping too far into the dangerous field of authorial intention, it is worth considering the readings that writers – such as Beauvoir – provide of their own works. Beauvoir herself is notable for attempting to provide readers with what might be termed authorized readings of her work, via texts such as the autobiographical *All Said and Done*. In this 1974 book, Beauvoir observes that '[i]t is dangerous to ask the public to read between the lines. Yet I did so again'. She is referring to the publication of her 1968 novella, *The Woman Destroyed*, in which the protagonist Monique begins to write a journal when it becomes apparent that her husband has betrayed her. Published in *Elle* magazine, the novella was largely dismissed by contemporary critics as a romance story, and renounced by feminists who believed that Beauvoir had betrayed them. The majority of Beauvoir's (largely female) readers, however, identified with the heroine as she struggled to retain her lifeless marriage, and cheating husband. 'Submerged' with letters from real 'women destroyed' following the novella's publication, Beauvoir described her readers' view that the heroine was a virtuous woman married to an unworthy man as an 'immense incomprehension' (Beauvoir, *All Said and Done*, 126). Beauvoir's conscious intention in writing *The Woman Destroyed* was a polemic one, and she describes it as a detective story in which 'here and there [she] scattered clues that would allow the reader to find the key to the mystery – but only if he tracked Monique as one tracks down the guilty character' (125). Monique's 'crime', then, is bad faith – she refuses to accept that her life has changed and that time passes. Now, we might say that Beauvoir's dismissal of her readers' readings (as an 'immense incomprehension') disallows a rereading which takes into account the depth and subtext of the story: in this instance her own philosophy. Given this, her responses to these readers give us some clue as to how she – at least in this case – reads her own work. It also brings us back to the question of Beauvoir's relation to 'the woman in love' – here symbolized by Monique. For a detailed account of Beauvoir's reading of *The Woman Destroyed*, see Goss (2006). See also Beauvoir (1974, 1969a).

46 It is important that we continue to analyse our relations and transferences (both critical and otherwise) to Beauvoir, given her significance as symbolic maternal figure for several generations of feminist philosophers and theorists. For a detailed discussion of the theoretical significance of the mother–daughter relation, especially in the context of philosophical thought, see Boulous Walker (1998).

For references to 'contemptuous dismissal and cavalier mistranslation and misrepresentation of Beauvoir's work' see Simons (1998: 17). It is perhaps interesting to note that in the late 1990s many feminist philosophers were concerned to challenge the negative analyses that seemed to dominate work on Beauvoir prior to this time. It is my feeling that the positive or recuperative readings of Beauvoir now significantly outweigh the negative ones; i.e. there appears to be a significant transferential shift *towards* or *back to* Beauvoir. Again, I think that these developments warrant further critical comment. For a critical and engaged discussion of 'our' relations with Beauvoir – and what this means for our readings – see Le Dœuff (2006: 11–19).

47 The plethora of excellent critical work on Beauvoir over the past years (e.g. Simons 1998, Bergoffen 1997, Vintges 1996, Lundgren-Gothlin 1996, Heinämaa 1996, Diprose 1998) is testimony to the engaged readings that have emerged (partially) in response to earlier reductive and less 'ethical' accounts. Indeed, the special edition of *Hypatia* devoted to Beauvoir's work in autumn 1999 provides an excellent example of the careful and nuanced readings that characterize these accounts. Another example of an engaged reading of Beauvoir's work is Simons (2006).

48 Le Dœuff points to the complexity at play in what is ultimately, for her, a valuable analysis in *TSS*: 'For a feminist reader, that is to say, for an *interested* reading by one principally concerned with finding elements of reflection that might underpin a possible practice, this book has today the appearance of a curious mixture. And thus I feel tempted to try and separate out the elements in the book that I evaluate now as "positive"' (Le Dœuff 1980: 277). A later and much revised version of this work can be found in Le Dœuff 1991: 55–133.

49 Later published in revised form as 'Long Hair, Short Ideas' (Le Dœuff 1989: 100–28).

50 For a discussion of Le Dœuff's notion of the erotico-theoretical transference, in relation to permissiveness, amateurism and fidelity, see Boulous Walker (1998: 20–4).

51 And further: 'Only an institutional relationship, with a place and meaning in an organized framework, can avoid the hypertrophy of the personal relationship between master and disciple' (Le Dœuff 1989: 105).

52 In relation to 'use' and the (feminist) difference that it can make, Anne Freadman has the following to say: '"use" can always do something a little different from merely repeating "usage". In an

attempt to do something towards specifying "women's writing", I shall suppose that it is in the business of transforming discursive material that, in its untransformed state, leaves a woman no place from which to speak, or nothing to say'. See Freadman (1983: 162).

53 In 'The Woman in Love', Beauvoir says that woman longs 'to reconstruct a situation: that which she experienced as a little girl, under adult protection. She was deeply integrated with home and family, she knew the peace of quasi-passivity. Love will give her back her mother as well as her father, it will give her back her childhood. What she wants to recover is a roof over her head, walls that prevent her from feeling her abandonment in the wide world, *authority that protects her against her liberty*' (TSS: 655, emphasis added). We might think of Beauvoir's relation to Sartre's broad ontology (his philosophical system) as the 'authority that protects her against her liberty'. Given Le Dœuff's reading, though, we could add that the authority or structure that Sartre's ontology provides paradoxically frees Beauvoir to reread, reinterpret and refine the conclusions that he draws. The adult protection that Sartre's pre-formulated system symbolizes is thus only a 'moment' in Beauvoir's (philosophical) formation.

54 See also Le Dœuff (1991: 111–12).

55 Le Dœuff writes: 'To confirm this, it is enough to single out two aspects of Sartrianism as of 1943: no oppression can be thematized as such in the existentialist system, women's oppression no more than any other; and at the same time, the terrifying relation of men with women's bodies, expressed in this system grounds an ontological-carnal hierarchy of "the masculine" and the "feminine". Hence de Beauvoir's utilization of this viewpoint emerges as a tour de force deserving of recognition' (Le Dœuff 1980: 280). And further: 'If the doctrine of authenticity leads to such a miscomprehension of every form of constraint, using it to describe the oppression of women must already seem paradoxical' (281). In the 'Second Notebook' in *Hipparchia's Choice*, Le Dœuff spends considerable time addressing and analyzing Sartre's misogyny (Le Dœuff 1991).

56 Le Dœuff writes: 'De Beauvoir operates a series of transformations on the existential problematic. The primary transformation seems to be transposing this *Weltanschauung* from the status of *system* (necessarily turning back on itself) to that of a *point of view* oriented to a theoretical intent by being trained on a determinate and partial field of experience' (Le Dœuff 1980: 283). See also Le Dœuff (1991: 89–9), where she contends that Beauvoir's 'point of view' approach frees her from the circularity and closure of Sartre's existential

system, which leads inevitably towards dissolution (92). In contrast, Beauvoir's operative viewpoint leaves her free to create 'an investigation "in progress"' (91): 'No destiny of repetition, no need for a "sugary death" in Beauvoir's work' (92).

57 Le Dœuff claims that the consequence of Beauvoir's transformation of the universality of Sartre's work into a point of view, and her acknowledgement of external constraint, is that she declines to endorse Sartre's belief in 'bad faith' and the arrogant assumptions it supports: 'To the extent that "bad faith" always refers to the bad faith of the other, this concept seemed to us a macho concept: the macho always also tells us how to think . . . The fact that Simone de Beauvoir does not endorse this category, even when she is adopting the existentialist perspective, seems to me to be of vital importance in reopening a certain number of debates [concerning her relation to Sartre's work]' (Le Dœuff 1991: 95). Further on, Le Dœuff refers to Beauvoir's particular *métis*: her 'technique of reintroduction which undermines the structure' of Sartre's existentialism (Le Dœuff 1991: 108). In this instance what Beauvoir reintroduces is the concept of 'reciprocity' between self and other.

58 And further: 'This perspective enables de Beauvoir to escape essentialism: There is no such thing as an "eternal feminine" nor a "Dark soul," because there is no such thing as "human nature" freedom being the only character of human condition. It is no longer possible to justify a given state of things by reference to a psychological nature that would be fulfilled by a state of things. In other words, it is too easy for the dominant male ideology to say that women *are* such and such' (Le Dœuff 1980: 284).

59 Beauvoir offers us the following non-Sartrean analysis: Woman is from the start constituted as inessential by patriarchal society; however she experiences herself as essential, as subject, and hence lives a dilemma. Beauvoir, unlike Sartre, sees this not as woman's own *moral error* (bad faith or inauthenticity), but as the effect of women's *oppression*. Her 'ethic of authenticity' enables her to distance woman's oppression from woman's so-called 'natural' state and, as a consequence, she escapes essentialism. This provides the starting point for voicing woman's subjectivity in a way that Sartre's existential analysis simply cannot. She argues: 'One is not born, but rather becomes a woman' ('The Formative Years: Childhood' in *TSS*: 296).

60 Linnell Secomb raises some interesting points in relation to Le Dœuff's reading of Beauvoir. She suggests that Le Dœuff positions Beauvoir as a 'point-of-view' philosopher, rather than a more

conventional 'system building' philosopher: 'Le Dœuff interprets Beauvoir's philosophical project as distinct from dominant models of philosophical work. Whereas philosophers are in general system builders, Le Dœuff argues, Beauvoir elaborates a perspective or point of view. This description of the distinction between system-building philosophy and Beauvoir's point-of-view philosophy places Beauvoir outside of philosophy [which is] precisely the creation of concepts' (Secomb 1999: 105). Secomb goes on to point out that Le Dœuff portrays Beauvoir's approach as 'a legitimate philosophical enterprise' (106). However, she contends that in depicting Beauvoir's work in terms of 'point-of-view' analysis and as 'social analysis', Le Dœuff is 'unable to unearth the specificity of the complex though nascent concept-creations within Beauvoir's philosophy' (106). In essence, Le Dœuff's reading overlooks or minimizes the 'concept-creations' at work in Beauvoir's thought (112). Secomb goes on to appeal to Gilles Deleuze and Felix Guattari's work on minor literature in order to argue a case for Beauvoir's non-conventional conceptual work. She contends that Beauvoir writes as 'writer' rather than 'philosopher' in order to deflect antagonism: 'Beauvoir's work gradually develops a conceptual persona of the woman philosopher masquerading as writer. To deflect antagonism towards a woman doing philosophy and to overcome the attacks on her groundbreaking reinvention of femininity, Beauvoir writes philosophy (in her philosophical texts as well as in her novels) under the guise of writer' (107). Hers is 'an accessible and collaborative mode of philosophizing' (96). Beauvoir transforms fixed concepts and develops a 'hybrid philosophy . . . accessible at different levels' (108). Le Dœuff's own work, ethics and reading is the subject of Chapter One. I am interested in the movement of Le Dœuff's reading over time, towards an ethics that encompasses return, revision, re-enactment and reconsideration. In a preliminary sense, we can see some of this at play in her reading of Beauvoir. Le Dœuff's initial reading of Beauvoir arguably frames her through the explanatory work of the *erotico-theoretical transference*, and thus her (dependent?) relation with Sartre, while her subsequent readings – oriented as they are around her notion of an operative philosophy – exceed this frame, allowing us to engage authentically with the real difference that Beauvoir's work makes.

61 In *Hipparchia's Choice* (Le Dœuff 1991) Le Dœuff writes: 'Before trying to see what transformations Simone de Beauvoir carried out on existentialism's formulation of the problems, we need to stress that these transformations were not thought out as such: nowhere does Beauvoir give a critique of Sartre's categories,

nowhere does she state her intention to displace or modify them. Rather what we find is that they are remodeled "in the heat of the moment"' (88).

62 Le Dœuff writes of this attention to detail: 'one finds in this work a host of observations, descriptions, and analyses which I, for my part, can only endorse. When Simone de Beauvoir describes the repetitive nature of housework, when she analyzes the censorious treatment of aggressiveness in little girls, when she sets out notions on female frigidity, when she examines the prevailing conception of women's wages as "salaire d'appoint" supplementing the husband's earnings, she provides essential elements of a *detailed* and *precise* consciousness of women's oppression. And this attention to detail is certainly what gives the book its greatest utility because oppression always also exists where it is least expected and where there is the danger that it will not even be noticed' (Le Dœuff 1980: 277). For a discussion of the merit of detail in feminist work see Boulous Walker (1993a: 79–91). In 'Interpretation and Retrieval: Rereading Beauvoir', Linda Singer alludes to the 'detail' of women's lives when she writes: 'In Beauvoir's work, female existence, and the values emergent from it no longer remain contained within a discourse of domination but are freed for the purpose of becoming ethical, and thus changing the world, and the lives of human subjects who must make their ways there' (Singer 1985: 238).

63 At the beginning of her paper, Le Dœuff notes that Beauvoir remains strangely committed to 'a whole conceptual apparatus that is now a trifle obsolete' (Le Dœuff 1980: 277–8).

64 For a critical discussion of this aspect of Beauvoir's work, see Boulous Walker (1998: 159–75), especially 163–70.

65 On the question of Beauvoir's liberal individualism, Le Dœuff admits that 'this is one stumbling block, politically this time, for me' (Le Dœuff 1980: 287). In *Hipparchia's Choice* (Le Dœuff 1991), Le Dœuff extends this point, suggesting that Beauvoir's focus on relations between individuals – rather than institutions – means that the problem of the contradiction that structures women's lives effectively remains unanalysed (Le Dœuff 1991: 130). While there are grounds for Le Dœuff's objections here, it is worth considering that the *effect* of Beauvoir's work – largely in relation to *TSS* – has been precisely that women throughout the world have made connections between their own personal experience and the institutions that structure their lives. Another way of saying this might be to suggest that the work of reading Beauvoir is the work of making these very connections.

66 For a discussion of Beauvoir's complex and deliberate depiction of herself as a philosopher masquerading as a writer, see Secomb (1999). Secomb suggests that Beauvoir strategically adopts the persona of the woman philosopher masquerading as a writer in order to allow her the space to do things that a more conventional persona of the philosopher would have disallowed: 'By insisting that she is not a philosopher, Beauvoir is able to take liberties with the concept-creations of her philosophical fraternity and so creates a pastiche plane of thought amenable to variation and transformation. However, this disguise of writer also arguably disguises the philosophical import of Beauvoir's work and has limited interpretations of her philosophy to a confused and deformed reformulation of existing concepts. I propose that the difficulty of Beauvoir's work results in part from her invention of a more complex persona. As a woman philosopher masquerading as a writer, she creates concepts within a pastiche plane of thought comprised of counterfeit concepts appropriated from her philosophical milieu' (Secomb 1999: 106).

67 For a detailed discussion of this point, see Simons (1998: 17). For an alternative depiction see Max Deutscher's account of Beauvoir and Sartre in Deutscher (2003). For a relatively early discussion of Beauvoir's absence from the philosophical canon, and the importance of reading her work beyond Sartre's see Singer (1985: 231–8).

68 See also Daigle and Golomb (2009).

69 See Beauvoir (2006). Hazel Barnes, the translator of Sartre's *Being and Nothingness*, has analysed Beauvoir's diaries and journals, and says 'I do not at all preclude the possibility that de Beauvoir has contributed to the formation of Sartre's philosophy. I suspect that *his debt to her* is considerable. All I mean in the present instances is that the novel [in question] serves as documentation for the theory, regardless of who had which idea first' (emphasis added, cited in Simons (1998: 17); originally in Barnes (1959: 121–2). For more on Beauvoir's denials see Simons and Benjamin (1979). For more on Beauvoir's 1927 diary, see Ward (1999: 39f).

70 Simons concludes her discussion of Beauvoir's influence on Sartre with the following words: 'prior to her first meeting with Sartre, Beauvoir had described experiences at the center of the existential phenomenology that she would later share with Sartre: the frustrated pursuit of being, the sense of one's uselessness, the lack of external absolutes to justify one's actions, the temptations of bad faith, the concept of self as a construct of consciousness, a commitment to doing original philosophy, a technique for combining philosophy and

literature, a descriptive philosophical methodology influenced by Bergson and Husserlian phenomenology, and a central philosophical theme of the opposition of self and other' (Simons 1998: 23). Two years before she met Sartre, Beauvoir mused in her journal that 'I know myself that there is only one problem and that it does not have a solution, because perhaps it has no sense; it is the one posed by Pascal, nearer to me Marcel Arland: I would like to believe in something – to encounter total exigency – to justify life; in brief, I would like God' (Beauvoir's 1927 Diary, cited in Simons (1998: 18)). Thus, she recognized in herself, in the absence of Sartre, and two decades before *TSS*, the universal tendency to seek transcendence through an external, universal value. Simons argues that other writings in this early journal seem to anticipate the Sartrean notion of 'useless passion', looking forward to 'nothingness' via reference to the 'daily void' (Simons 1998: 18).

71 We might think of this as an almost psychotic identification that moves from independence towards a disturbing kind of ventriloquy. This passage is perhaps even more disturbing when we discover that Sartre has written the following lines: 'a thought could exist really formed by you and me at the same time'. Why disturbing? Because here Sartre is referring to his desired collaboration with Benni Levi (who Alice Jardine describes as Sartre's 'intellectual son'), not with Beauvoir. This 'ideal' collaboration with Sartre's 'other' remained incomplete at the time of Sartre's death. These words appear in Simone de Beauvoir, 'Entretiens avec Jean-Paul Sartre' in *La Cérémonie des adieux* (1981: 126). See also Jardine (1986: 91).

72 While Beauvoir's account here points to a communion between herself and Sartre, Ward points out that in *TSS* Beauvoir indicates the two barriers to mutual reciprocity or communion between man and woman: (i) reciprocity is not possible without prior equality; and (ii) woman is disadvantaged by her particular history, with the consequence that women experience difficulty seeking relations of mutual recognition with men (Ward 1999: 43). According to Ward, Beauvoir goes on to say that we must, nonetheless, strive for mutual recognition, not individual sovereignty. From here Beauvoir goes into the dangers for the girl/woman who risks becoming object to the other and object to herself. Given this, the question remains: can women go beyond this? (44) Ward argues that Beauvoir gestures in the direction of female–female relations, i.e. woman–woman reciprocity: 'woman's subjectivity is not blocked or negated, but is preserved in the loving gaze of her female friend, her other self' (47). We might ask what this suggests for her own relation with Sartre.

73 Ward has some insightful things to say in this regard. She notes that while Beauvoir claims – in regard to Sartre – that 'We were two of a kind, and our relationship would endure as long as we did' . . . that a careful reading of Beauvoir's *œuvre* reveals fault lines between this statement and Beauvoir's discussions of what actually constitutes, for her, a relation of reciprocity. Ward's reading is detailed and nuanced, but its significant aspect, for our purposes here, is that it places in question Beauvoir's account of her relation with Sartre, and it does so by referring to what Beauvoir, herself, has to say on the matter: 'while Beauvoir claims that she found in Sartre the basis for mutual recognition and reciprocity, it seems she owes her conception of the relation, at least as experienced, to her young female friend, Zaza, and to Hélène, her sister' (Ward 1999: 47). While Beauvoir dreams of a relation of reciprocal recognition with Sartre, her own account of her relation with him reveals something quite other. Ward draws our attention to the episode of the trapped cat in *La Force de l'âge/The Prime of Life*, in order to suggest that it reveals a real difference in Beauvoir's and Sartre's 'conceptions of relation to the other and ideas about reciprocity' (Ward 1999: 36). Ward continues: 'Beauvoir manifests herself as the other who perceives the response of another to need, and in so doing, she participates in that same response to the other. In this respect, she presents a mode of being to others that stands in contrast to the self-absorbed presence of Sartre' (37). Ward goes on to suggest that, in addition to revealing this difference in response, Beauvoir's account of the trapped cat leaves open the possibility of reading this in terms of a metaphor for Beauvoir herself: 'while she writes in *La Force de l'âge (*Beauvoir 1992: 27–8) that she welcomed Sartre's presence, finding in his companionship complete security, freedom, and happiness, the cat episode indicates, perhaps in inchoate form, something to the contrary. For it is not Sartre but an anonymous woman who sees the need and rescues the cat; therefore, the unexpressed thought is that Sartre, who she spares no superlatives in describing, is in some sense a bystander who does not know how to respond to need. Whether the trapped cat is a metaphor for Beauvoir herself or whether she simply participates, by extension, in the response of the woman to the cat remains undetermined; what matters is that the figure who does respond is not Sartre but another woman' (Ward 1999: 39).

74 Beauvoir writes: 'Even in mutual love there is fundamental difference in the feelings of the lovers, which the woman tries to hide' (*TSS*: 670). And further: 'she must either suffer or lie to herself. Most often she clutches at the straw of falsehood. She fancies that the man's love is the exact counterpart of the love she brings to him' (*TSS*: 669).

75 While Beauvoir's statements concerning Sartre – during his lifetime – are on the whole positive ones, Alice Jardine has done some interesting work reading Beauvoir's account of Sartre's death and dying, published in *La Cérémoinie des adieux* in 1981. Jardine begins by alluding to the 'passion, despair and rage' that quietly litter the pages of Beauvoir's earlier writing, suggesting that these emotions (in relation to Sartre) are always negated in 'last capping sentences' that work to dissolve and negate the real instances of her historical suffering (Jardine 1986: 88). This changes, however, when, after Sartre's death, Beauvoir publishes an excruciating account of his bodily and mental demise. Jardine's claim is that in the pages of *Adieux* we find an answer to the question of what Beauvoir had done with her anger and rage: 'this body named Sartre is cut up by the violence of [Beauvoir's] discourse – an explosion of words with razor edges' (91). While Jardine reports that in Paris many considered this book Beauvoir's 'revenge', she goes on to ask the important question of 'revenge for what?' (93). Jardine's analysis of this question is complex and made all the more intriguing when she reads Beauvoir's other farewell book alongside this one. In the pages of Beauvoir's farewell to her own mother, *Une Mort très douce* (Beauvoir 1969b), Jardine finds intriguing parallels with her account of Sartre. While I think that Jardine has unearthed an intriguing relation here – Sartre's decaying body as repressed maternal body – I want to go back a few steps and suggest reading Beauvoir's *Adieux* to Sartre alongside her own account of anger in 'The Woman in Love'. One of the things that Beauvoir says in this chapter is that when the woman in love becomes aware of her overestimation, and is confronted with the inescapable truth of her lover's limitations, romance turns to anguish and sometimes aggression: 'It is a searing disappointment to the woman to discover the faults, the mediocrity of her idol. Novelists, like Colette, have often depicted this bitter anguish. The disillusion is still more cruel than that of the child who sees the father's prestige crumble, because the woman has herself selected the one to whom she has given over her entire being' (*TSS*: 664). 'A fallen god is not a man: he is a fraud ... If he is no longer adored, he must be trampled on' (*TSS*: 665). 'The god must not sleep lest he become clay, flesh; he must not cease to be present, lest his creature sink into nothingness' (*TSS*: 667). And when Sartre finally falls, becomes flesh and sinks into the nothingness of old age and decay, Beauvoir's repressed anger arguably finds expression in the multitude of razor-sharp sentences that chronicle his demise. Jardine draws our attention to the 'unrelenting stream of words' evoking the horror of Sartre's physical decline (Jardine 1986: 92) – references to an abscess in the mouth (91); problems with his teeth (92); problems with eating

and swallowing (92); 'hands that can no longer grip, perform, act on the material world' (92); ruining his clothes (92); losing his eyes (92); finally going blind (92); a body 'out of control' (92). Might we read Beauvoir's public account here as anguished and angry responses to Sartre?

76 In relation to the difficult issue of addressing Beauvoir's relation with Sartre in the context of philosophical inquiry, Tina Chanter's words seem pertinent: 'Whether intended to, or not, her life and relationship to Sartre took on an exemplary status for a whole generation of feminists. Her personal life, as represented both by herself and by others, therefore had enormous influence on feminism' (Chanter 1995: 52). Max Deutscher refers to Le Dœuff's 'risky procedure of considering what they [Beauvoir and Sartre] wrote to each other in letters on the same page as what they wrote in novels or theoretical books' (Deutscher 2009: 95).

77 Beauvoir refers here to women and to feminism, and she continues: 'It is still talked about, however, for the voluminous nonsense uttered during the last century seems to have done little to illuminate the problem' (*TSS*: 13).

78 While it may be convenient to think of romantic reading as a peculiarly feminine affair, we need only think of the devotional readings of our own male students, i.e. their Kantian or Nietszchean or Deleuzian readings, as evidence in support of the claim that romance is an all-pervasive threat. In regard to this question of the gendered nature of romantic reading, it is worth returning to Le Dœuff, who has some important things to say about how men and women traditionally read. She claims that in philosophy men have historically made their marks by disrespectful or distorted readings, ones that bear little resemblance or fidelity to the original text. And that, perhaps as a corollary to this, the few women who have made (minor) careers as philosophers have done so almost exclusively through their respectful and faithful commentary on the great male texts: 'Who better than a woman to show fidelity, respect and remembrance? A woman can be trusted to perpetuate the words of the Great Discourse: she will add none of her own . . . Everyone knows that the more of a philosopher one is, the more distorted one's reading of other philosophers. Think of Leibniz's reading of Malebranche, or Hegel's reading of Kant! They cannot respect the thought of the other: they are too engrossed in their own . . . How could a woman manhandle a text, or violate a discourse? The vestal of a discourse which time threatens to eclipse, the nurse of dismembered texts, the healer of works battered by false editions, the housewife whom one hopes will dust off the grey film that

successive readings have left on the fine object, she takes on the upkeep of the monuments, the forms which the mind has deserted. A god's priestess, dedicated to a great dead man' (Le Dœuff 1989: 125). The implication here? Perhaps that we reward romantic reading in women and expect something much more in men. What is also of interest in Le Dœuff's account is that she acknowledges that *young* men, like women, are indeed prey to the erotico-theoretical transference (and, presumably, the romantic readings this transference induces), and yet that what distinguishes their situation from that of women is that these men grow out of their intellectual infatuations, with the assumption that they go on to develop mature (and faithless?) relations with the philosophers and texts that have so captivated them. Le Dœuff's point here is an important one, in that she claims that the historical relation men enjoy with the institution of philosophy ultimately provides a counter (sublimation) to the infatuations of youth, and that historically women have been denied this institutional context and thus have lacked a structure that can counter (sublimate) the confusion of the amorous with the didactic: 'In fact, you – Tom, Dick and Harry – who were at the Sorbonne or prepared the *aggregation* with me, did you really act any differently from Hipparchia? Was it not only too easy sometimes to sense – in the knotting of a tie, in a hairstyle or some such fad – the symbol of allegiance to some cult figure? One could even tell, just by hearing you talk about your student career, that there was always – at the *lycée*, the university or, most commonly, at the preparatory courses for the *Écoles Normales Supérieres* – some teacher around whom there crystallized something similar to the theoretico-amorous admiration which we have been discussing here. Not only women experience it, then. One thing I am sure of is that this privileged teacher was the one who finally seduced you to philosophy, who captured your desire and turned it into a desire for philosophy . . . But there is a considerable difference between these student companions and Elizabeth or Sophie Volland. In general, the "god–father" relationship has opened up the whole field of philosophy to the disciple's desire, whilst women's transference relationships to the theoretical have opened up to them only the field of their idol's own philosophy. I say "in general" because there are also "failures" with men, and disciples may remain philosophers of particular schools (read "cliques") and never get beyond a repetitious discourse . . . The reason why men (both now and in the past) can go beyond initial transference, and why the love component of their transference is sublimated or inflected from the very beginning, so that it can return to the theoretical, is that the institutional framework in which the relationship is played out provides the third factor which is always necessary for the breaking of the personal relationship; the women amateurs, however, have been bound to the dual relationship, because a dual relationship does not produce the dynamics that enable one to leave I' (Le Dœuff 1989: 105–7).

79 Might anger or disappointment accompany our need to chastise Beauvoir? Perhaps the feminist 'daughter' of Beauvoir finds it intolerable that her (phallic) mother is susceptible to a romance that seems inappropriate in the context? Our responses to Beauvoir's statements on her relation with Sartre are complex and need further consideration. For a discussion of the (unconscious) complexity of Beauvoir's own pronouncements on Sartre, see Jardine (1986: 84–96). For a discussion of the complexity of our own readings of Beauvoir, see Le Dœuff (2006: 11–19). While anger and disappointment might operate in conscious or less than conscious ways in our appraisal of Beauvoir, there might also be something of spite involved. Beauvoir occupies such a magisterial position as *the* woman philosopher for many women in philosophy that our analyses might be involved in unconscious attempts to displace her from this throne. Irigaray's work on aggressive rivalry amongst women, as an effect of the patriarchal social contract, is no doubt relevant here. In 'Commodities amongst Themselves', Irigaray explores the mechanism whereby women are forced, by this economy, into substitution and hate for the 'mother', with the effect that what is actually sacrificed is women's relations with one another. See Irigaray (1985e: 192–7).

80 Perhaps romantic love is only a problem from the perspective of the existential ontology (transcendence/immanence) that Beauvoir works within. Probably not, but this need not stop us thinking of how romantic love might 'evolve' from devotion, through authenticity, towards generosity. Indeed, Kathryn Pauly Morgan acknowledges that Beauvoir's ontology largely determines her condemnation of romantic love when she writes: 'Does the negative moral assessment of romantic love proceed through the value system of existentialist ethics alone? Suppose we leave aside the lofty language of transcendence and immanence and the model of human nature which depends upon a theory of objectifying self-deception as a universal human desire. What moral assessment should we make of romantic love? Beauvoir's moral condemnation of romantic love is powerful and clear. But what of those individuals who do not operate within an existentialist conceptual and moral universe of discourse?' (Morgan 1986: 136).

81 Rosalyn Diprose distinguishes between the destructive generosity that Beauvoir describes in 'The Woman in Love' and a more positive

generosity 'born of flesh'. She admits that this second kind of generosity is not fully elaborated in Beauvoir's account, but argues that we can sketch out its potential from traces scattered throughout Beauvoir's thought. The context for this model of generosity is the erotic experience and the ambiguity it discloses, and Diprose speaks of the potential for 'erotic generosity' in Beauvoir's work: 'For Beauvoir, the erotic encounter and its "freedom" are not about self-control or bodily integrity. On the contrary, they are about the "body at risk" as Debra Bergoffen puts it. Taking this risk through eroticism is generous because it involves opening the lived body to the other and because it is, by virtue of this, creative in transforming the other's embodied situation and hence existence through a self-metamorphosis which, if we set aside Beauvoir's motif of unity, does not reduce the other to the self. Becoming flesh is a project directed toward and beyond the other, a giving without calculation' (Diprose 1998: 10). See also Bergoffen (1997: 158).

82 Walsh refers to Kierkegaard's work on devotion (*Hengivenhed*) and self-giving (*Hengivelse*) in *The Sickness unto Death* (Kierkegaard 1980) and *Works of Love* (Kierkegaard 1995). Walsh goes on to say that while Beauvoir and Kierkegaard have something in common here, they diverge on the question of reciprocity. While Beauvoir believes that reciprocity founds a loving relation, Kiekegaard does not. He sees the 'demand for reciprocity [as] an expression of self-love or selfishness that needs to be rooted out in the transformation of erotic love into unselfish, unconditional love of the other as a neighbor' (Walsh 1998: 39). On the question of the relation between devotion and despair in Kiekegaard's work Walsh writes that 'devotedness does not, in itself, constitute despair for Kierkegaard; rather, despair results from the loss of oneself in, or identification with, the object of one's devotion in such a way as to lose oneself or have no independent self' (37). True love, devotion and self-abandonment 'come to expression only in loving God, which is to say "the neighbor" – a category that includes all human beings, not just one other person. Since, for Kierkegaard, God is love and love is God, God or love constitutes "the middle term" in every love relation' (37).

Chapter 6: Intimate Reading: Cixous's Approach

1 Cixous (1988: 147).
2 Cixous (1979: 18).

3   For a discussion of Cixous's work in the context of *écriture féminine* see Boulous Walker (1998: 134–58).

4   Cixous writes she 'was born a reader-writer' (Cixous 2010: 34); she refers to herself as an 'archreader' for whom 'everything began through reading' (22).

5   Cixous writes: 'I began to write in the regions of the unconscious. I had tremendous and clandestine relations with dreams . . . Putting oneself in relation to the unconscious is delicate, since we can't master the comings and goings, the gushings from the source'. From 'The School of Dreams' in Cixous (1993: 102, 103). For Cixous's positive account of Freud's unconscious, see: 'Conversations' in Cixous (1988: 144–5).

6   For her early and much celebrated discussion of this point see Cixous, 'The Laugh of the Medusa' in Cixous (1976: 875–93).

7   Cixous speaks elsewhere of masculine writing as an economy of reduction at the mercy of castration, giving rise to 'forms which are dry, stripped bare, marked by the negative'. See 'Extreme Fidelity' in Cixous (1988: 25).

8   Verena Andermatt Conley argues that Cixous distinguishes herself from most of her (masculine) contemporaries by imagining 'a desire not based on lack but for a love that lets the other live, that does not incorporate, but lets the other be other'. See her introduction to Cixous (1990: xiii).

9   Ann Wilson provides a good summary of the more orthodox psychoanalytic account of woman's vulnerability in the symbolic order due to castration. She notes that while an investment in the father 'yields a higher return than that in the mother' that a woman pays an inordinately high price for this voice. 'If woman speaks through this language, then she places herself in an irresolvable contradiction because the speech-act, which seems to evince her subjectivity, simultaneously denies it by denying her body' (Wilson 1994: 77, 81). In 'The Laugh of the Medusa' Cixous writes: 'It is by writing, from and toward women, and by taking up the challenge of speech which has been governed by the phallus, that women will confirm women in a place other than that which is reserved in and by the symbolic, that is, in a place other than silence' (Cixous 1976: 881).

10 Cixous writes: 'It is possible to begin transforming a discourse only when the unconscious is taken into account. Where it is negated, where psychoanalysis does not exist, nothing changes and history goes on', cited in Juncker (1988: 426).

11 Susan Sellers puts it well when she describes Cixous's 'I' as that 'which refuses the glorifications available to the self in writing and which seeks, instead, to encounter and inscribe the other' (Sellers 1996: xv).
12 Cixous (1993: 118).
13 Ibid.: 59.
14 For a discussion of the breadth of Cixous's work see Susan Sellers's 'Introduction' to Cixous (1994: xxvi). See also Susan Rubin Suleiman, 'Writing Past the Wall: or the Passion According to H.C.', introductory essay to Cixous (1991: xi).
15 See Cixous and Calle-Gruber (1997: 26).
16 Cixous refers to 'a self that has almost evaporated, that has transformed itself into space'. And further, '[The self] will consent to erase itself and to make space, to become, not the hero of the scene, but the scene itself: the site, the occasion of the other'. See 'From the Scene of the Unconscious to the Scene of History', cited by Sellers (1996), *Hélène Cixous: Authorship, Autobiography and Love*, xiv, xv. This particular discussion of the self has a direct relevance for Cixous's theatrical works.
17 In her discussion of Cixous's *Le Livre de Promethea*, Sarah Cornell writes: 'This process of dispossession, of "de-egoization" ("démoisation"), of distancing from the self-centred ego, creates room for the other. As a result, the author can become the place of the other's inscription' (Cornell in Cixous 1998: 133).
18 Mireille Calle-Gruber in Cixous and Calle-Gruber (1997: 8).
19 There are links here with Luiz Costa Lima's work on writing as a resistance to law. We discuss this in Chapter Two.
20 Pierre Salesne contends that for Cixous writing 'struggles against the mortal muteness which threatens everyone who feels forbidden to speak. Writing is also a liberation, the surging up of all forbidden words' (Salesne in Cixous 1988: 118).
21 Cixous (1988: 14). In her discussion of the process of reading the work of the Brazilian writer Clarice Lispector, Cixous writes: 'One of the efforts we make is to be transgrammatical, the way one could say transgressive. It is not that we despise grammar, but we do not have to obey it absolutely; and we have to work to some degree on degrammaticalization. From this point of view, it is good to work on foreign texts – Clarice Lispector's, James Joyce's and others' – because they displace our relation to grammar' ('"Sunday, before falling asleep": A primal Scene' in Cixous 1990: 4).

22 Verena Andermatt Conley argues that Cixous 'inserts herself in a tradition that, with the German romantics and Nietzsche, adapted recently by some French writers and thinkers, believes in the creative forces contained in the archaic and in the necessity of their unleashing. This tradition from Schiller and Schlegel to Nietzsche and others shapes Cixous's thinking, both in its insistence on untying bound forces and in its belief in the importance of art for social change' (Andermatt Conley in Cixous 1990: xiv–xv).

23 Cixous has for many years argued that the Brazilian writer Clarice Lispector embodies the most complete example to date of feminine writing. Others that she has at various times referred to include, Shakespeare, Kleist, Genêt, Kafka, Tsvetaeva, Bachmann, Rilke and Joyce. While discussions of Lispector's writing can be found throughout Cixous's work, a good place to begin is Cixous (1990). See also Armbruster (1983: 145–57).

24 Cixous writes: 'The relationship to pleasure and the law, the individual's response to this strange, antagonistic relationship indicates, whether we are men or women, different paths through life. It is not anatomical sex that determines anything here' ('Extreme Fidelity' in Cixous [1988]: 18).

25 Pierre Salesne writes: '[For Cixous] [w]riting is the ambivalent place which allows life at its extreme limit to be described, perceived, reflected on, and yet which at the same time is always suspected of being incapable of a close rendering of the aliveness of reality'. See Salesne in Cixous (1988: 115).

26 Morag Shiach points out that Cixous's economy of the gift carries with it an implicit critique of mass or consumer society. See Shiach (1991: 21). Alan Schrift suggests that we might read Cixous's work on giving as the repressed feminine side of Nietzsche's noble economy. He points out that while Nietzsche's economy is one centred on giving, that Cixous opens this up to one of reception as well. Cixous 'provides an account of generosity that does not require *übermenschliche* strength to enact . . . she substitutes maternal compassion for the masterly indifference to one's parasites affirmed by Nietzsche' (Schrift 1995: 101).

27 See also Cixous's description of mother's milk as 'white ink' (Cixous 1976: 881).

28 For an excellent discussion of this point see Wilson (1994: 85–6).

29 Susan Sellers suggests that while Cixous's earlier works technically perform this feminine mode of giving, that nonetheless reading them can be, after Cixous's own 'inspirational descriptions' of

feminine writing, 'a disappointing experience'. Sellers is referring here to what she sees as the alienating effect of Cixous's early 'relentless, claustrophobic exploration of the fragmented "I"' (Sellers 1996: 5). Sellers seems more enthusiastic about Cixous's more recent works, which draw on her writing for theatre in order to produce works capable of transposing us towards the other's situation (see also Sellers 1996: 94–107). Here she refers to works such as *Manna: for the Mandelstams for the Mandelas* (Cixous 1994a).

30 H. Jill Scott describes the book as a gift that alludes to the Promethean gift of fire, 'both the warm glow and the powerful blaze, overflowing the limits of the myth in an expression of a supplemental libidinal economy, one that is continuous, overabundant, and generous' (Scott 1995: 31).

31 Cixous writes: 'The breath "wants" a form. "Write me!" One day it begs me, another day it threatens' (Cixous 1991: 10). For Mireille Calle-Gruber, Cixous's task 'consists in restoring to language its fabulous disposition, and all its vocal cords; carefully handling the echo chamber, the sound boxes, the metaphorical journeys; burrowing between words, between-letters, between-strokes in order to deconstruct our dead language habits' (in Cixous 1994: 210).

32 See Walsh (1998).

33 In 'Sorties', Cixous couples possession with a dispossession of self: 'Being possessed is not desirable for a masculine Imaginary, which would interpret it as passivity – a dangerous feminine position ... A woman, by her opening up, is open to being "possessed", which is to say, dispossessed of herself' (Cixous 1986: 86).

34 Although Cixous prefers to think of the bisexuality of each subject – a combination of both masculine and feminine libidinal economies – she retains these sexually differentiated terms in order to underline the cultural complexity of sexual inscriptions of power: 'The (political) economy of the masculine and the feminine is organized by different demands and constraints, which, as they become socialized and metaphorized, produce signs, relations of power, relationships of production and reproduction, a whole huge system of cultural inscription that is legible as masculine or feminine ... I make a point of using the *qualifiers* of sexual difference here to avoid the confusion man/masculine, woman/feminine' (Cixous 1986: 80–1). According to Lisa Guenther, Cixous's 'Masculine and feminine economies account for different ways of living the body, different modalities of fleshly existence – and different relations to the gift' (Guenther 2006: 53).

35 Relations of love, on the other hand, are open and receptive to the strangeness of the other.
36 For a discussion of these questions in relation to the tradition of Western philosophy, see Boulous Walker (1998).
37 For a discussion of two types of generosity in Beauvoir's work, one destructive and one positive, see Diprose (1998: 1–20).
38 Alan Schrift argues that Cixous's work provides us with a new way to read and think about Nietzsche's work on the gift: 'by making it possible to see the gendered dimension of gift-giving that Nietzsche too quickly discarded, Cixous articulates more clearly an alternative logic of the gift, one with several advantages over more classical exchangist logics that imprison gift-giving within the constraints of the economic assumptions of commodity trading. Cixous shows generosity and non-proprietary relations of cooperative ownership to have always been options of which, for complex social and historical reasons, men have not sufficiently availed themselves' (Schrift 1995: 101).
39 Elsewhere, Spivak claims, in relation to Cixous's work, that the ethical relation with the other implies 'the universalization of singularity' (Spivak 1992: 65–81).
40 Cixous speaks of a reading 'more aligned with incantation, similar to prayer' where the reader can attend to 'everything that is normally neglected, everything that is ambiguous, undecidable' (Cixous 2010: 31, 34).
41 Cixous claims that we need to read in two times, fast and then slow, in order to meditate on the 'poetically beyond' of the other that traditionally escapes philosophy: 'We need to go quicker to begin with in order to go more slowly later on, to be able to take time to meditate on the "poetically beyond"' ('Conversations' in Cixous 1988: 145). Elsewhere she refers to radically different readings, or the double impulse of reading: 'It is as if I were studying a cathedral with a magnifying glass. You need long-distance vision but you also need the magnifying glass on the cathedral, always' (Cixous 2010: 33).
42 Momentarily close to Adorno's meandering, Cixous mentions that in our reading '[w]e need not be afraid of wandering' (Cixous 1992: 3).
43 Elsewhere, Cixous writes: 'Either we tame a text, we ride on it, we roll over it, or we are swallowed up by it, as by a whale. There are thousands of possible relations to a text, and if we are in a nondefensive, nonresisting relationship, we are carried off by the text' (Cixous 1990: 3).

NOTES

44 For an introduction to the collective work carried out in Cixous's seminar see Cixous (1988). In her discussion of what guides the approach to reading in Cixous's seminar, Jennifer Birkett identifies the following: the reader as the guardian of the text, the group as the primary unit of organization, the common focus on the nature of the relationship with the other, a questioning of the role of theory in reading and how this ensures a preservation of strangeness in the text, and the necessity of a 'poetic' encounter between reader and text (Birkett 1990: 206–7).

45 In this chapter, Cixous reads Lispector's *A Paixao Segundo C.L.* [*The Passion According to C.L.*] (Rio de Janeiro: José Olympio, 1974). Cixous claims that in Lispector's writing 'one never arrives at a place, one always strives toward it' (Cixous 1990: 63).

46 There are links between Cixous's work here and aspects of Heidegger's work. See, for example, Heidegger (1971).

47 In the context of her reading of Lispector's 'The Foreign Legion', Cixous speaks of Lispector's skill of gathering without linking, a skill that ensures that the text 'trembles and is always about to disappear' (Cixous 1992: 76).

48 Proximity is inseparable from slowing down, and Cixous suggests this in her account of the experience of reading Lispector: 'One has to reread [Lispector's work] . . . What can happen, by chance, is the moment of encounter between oneself, a space capable of thought and something else. It produces a vibration. If one has been receptive, that is where one can begin to work, at the very point of impact. And it opens up an inexhaustible font, an interminable labyrinth . . . [culminating in] an extreme slowing down' (Cixous 1990: 162–3).

49 Morag Shiach argues that slowness for Cixous is a force opposing the reductive properties of modernity and mass culture, 'the antithesis of dominant political and cultural discourses, which offer volume and speed of communication at the expense of knowledge and understanding' (Shiach 1991: 62).

50 And further: 'What is open is time: not to absorb the thing, the other, but to let the thing present itself' (Cixous 1991: 63).

51 'We need the time of presences, to approach things until they are close to us, us with them, before them, giving each to each other' (Cixous 1991: 67).

52 '[A]ttention is a magical matter. The soul is the magic of attention' and 'attentions move like fish in slowness' (Cixous 1991: 70, 71).

53 Verena Andermatt Conley distinguishes the apprenticeship of lessons to be learned in Cixous's work from any constituted morality. See her introduction to Cixous (1992: xi).

54 Cixous calls for the need to improvise in relation to the play between distance and proximity. Each text will require a different approach: 'If one looks at a thing too closely, it disappears; if one is too far, it also disappears until the moment when it reappears. There is a constant passage to the infinite through proximity of distance. The infinite of proximity and the infinite of distance rejoin and are interchangeable' (Cixous 1990: 112). For a different slant on the relation of proximity between Cixous and Lispector, see Klobucka (1994: 41–62).

55 Cixous concludes 'Extreme Fidelity' with the following words: 'Sometimes one has to go very far./ Sometimes the right distance is extreme remoteness./ Sometimes it is in extreme proximity that it breathes' (Cixous 1988: 35).

56 Cixous mentions the famous encounter between the woman and the cockroach in Lispector's story, *The Passion According to G.H.*: 'the greatest tension is situated between the human subject and the non-human subject . . . the subject with whom Clarice does this work, the love partner, is sufficiently strange for the work to be done in a way that is more obvious to us than if the other were an ordinary human subject . . . But Clarice's ultimate project is to make the other human subject appear equal to – and this is positive – the cockroach' (Cixous 1988: 29, 30). Abigail Bray refers to this as an ethics of approaching the liminal (Bray 2004: 134).

57 In 'Sorties', Cixous writes: 'she comes out of herself to go to the other, a traveler in unexplored places; she does not refuse, she approaches, *not to do away with the space between*, but to see it, to experience what she is not, what she is, what she can be' (Cixous 1986: 86, emphasis added).

58 This is Susan Sellers's description of what Cixous has to say about her way of reading in 'Conversations'. (Sellers's Introduction to Cixous [1988]: 7). Sellers continues: 'a reading which "opens" itself in this way will, Cixous believes, lead the reader to awareness of other possible threads, enabling the reader to advance further on the path of textual and self-understanding' (7).

59 Merleau-Ponty (1968). See Luce Irigaray's, 'The Invisible of the Flesh: A Reading of Merleau-Ponty, *The Visible and the Invisible,* "The Intertwining – The Chiasm"' in Irigaray (1993: 151–84). In the context of his encounter with the poetry of Paul Celan, Ziarek characterizes the *chiasm* in terms of a twofold otherness – of

ontological otherness and ethical alterity (Ziarek 1994: 151). See also Mattéi (1995: 39–150) and Margaroni (2009: 107–25).
60 One way of thinking about a chiasmatic model of reading is to place unexpected texts in proximity, with the aim of encouraging encounters of otherness to take place. The idea here is to construct an ethical space of response between texts; see also Boulous Walker (1997: 432–45), and Boulous Walker (2002: 295–320). Cixous's own juxtaposed readings offer intimate encounters between very different texts, e.g. Joyce/Lispector and Blanchot/Lispector. See Cixous (1992).

Conclusion: The Attentive Work of Grace

1 Weil (1995: 136).
2 Jean-Luc Godard, *Band à Part* (1964) and Bernardo Bertolucci, *The Dreamers* (2003). A counter to Godard's hurried reading can be seen in Richard Linklater's remarkable film *Boyhood* (2014). Linklater creates a fictionalized drama involving the same actors over a twelve-year period (2002–2013). I think of this as an instance of slow film or slow cinema, one that supports the ethical and aesthetic qualities I have been exploring here.
3 For a phenomenological account of attention that touches upon some of our concerns here, see Steinbock (2004).
4 Simone Weil, cited in Veto (1994: 45, n. 15).
5 Weil acknowledges other forms of attention, ones not directed towards the other in open ways. For example, in her discussion of the dehumanizing effects of factory work she claims that the specific kind of attention demanded by repetitive manual work is incompatible with a living attention because it empties the soul of everything except for the concern for speed (Weil 2002).
6 For a discussion of Weil's categories of gravity and grace see Boulous Walker (2002).
7 We could say that for Weil poor readings 'are due to the fact that thought has seized upon some idea too hastily' (Weil 1951: 56).
8 Weil writes: 'Judgment; perspective. In this sense all judgment judges him who forms it. Not to judge. This is not indifference or abstention, it is transcendent judgment, the imitation of that divine judgment which is not possible for us' (Weil 1995: 136).
9 Brennan claims that attention is affiliated with love and the life-drive through their shared processes of connection and that 'the tendency

to bind and bring together, to make things cohere, follows the logic of the life drive' (Brennan 2004: 131, 132). She points out that for Freud 'the life drive operates at all levels from the cellular to the sexual as a principle of union and organization. The affinity and assumed identity between the life drive and the libido is evident not only in the sexual drives, but linked as well to the "attention" used in intellectual concentration' (Brennan 2004: 36). Building on the post-Kleinian object relations theory of Wilfred Bion, Brennan is adamant that 'living attention' is love, an energetic force enhancing life in all dyadic relations (Brennan 2004: 31). Brennan distinguishes between attention and affect, arguing that while attention is other-directed, affect is directed towards another carrying 'a message of self-interest along with the attention it rides on' (Brennan 2004: 41).

10 By registering as a feeling, we are reminded, at the same time, of Jean-François Lyotard's notion of the *différend* when he describes the feeling that registers that a wrong has been committed (Lyotard 1988).

11 Gumbrecht refers to reading in terms of 'discovering sources of energy in artifacts and giving oneself over to them affectively and bodily – yielding to them and gesturing toward them' (Gumbrecht 2012: 18).

12 The translators note that while *Gelassenheit* carries the modern connotations of composure, calmness and unconcern, earlier senses of 'letting the world go' (from German mysticism) also accompany the complex meanings Heidegger introduces in this piece (54, n. 4). *Gelassenheit* is translated in this edition as 'Releasement'.

13 In 'Conversation on a Country Path about Thinking', the second part of *Discourse on Thinking* (Heidegger 1966), Heidegger explores his idiosyncratic notion of *Gelassenheit* through repeated references to slowing down, waiting, resting, listening and opening. The recent publication in Germany of volumes 94–96 (written between 1931 and 1941) of Heidegger's *Gesamtausgabe* (known as the *Schwarze Hefte* – Black Notebooks) has been accompanied by a renewed discussion of Heidegger's involvement with National Socialism, linking his philosophy of place (*Bodenständigkeit* – rootedness in soil) to fundamentally anti-Semitic views. In a recent article Richard Wolin revisits Heidegger's association of Jews with cosmopolitanism; i.e. as a people lacking a capacity for the kind of belonging that is predicated on rootedness in Being. The state of being 'rootless' positions Jews as a global people lacking resolute allegiance to their adoptive lands, unable to appreciate the existential qualities of

German 'space' (*Raum*). See Wolin (2014). In a somewhat more ambivalent response to the recently published Notebooks, Gregory Fried charts the challenges and pitfalls Heidegger's thought pose for us today. His discussion of Heidegger's work on 'machination' (*Machenschaft*) – an orientation that results in the total domination of nature – reminds us that alongside the difficult and unsavoury discussion of Heidegger's political decisions, we nonetheless face the urgent task of asking, with Heidegger, 'who we *are*, and who we are *going to be* as human beings in a newly global world' (Fried 2014). See also Heidegger (2014).

14 Gumbrecht reclaims the expression 'ivory tower' as a counter to the corporate institutionalization of the university arguing that the distance it implies opens up the possibility of riskful thinking: 'If adequately understood, the ivory tower-status of the academic world enables us to dwell precisely on such topics, problems, and questions, without cutting off any possible feedback into society. For to stay with the metaphor for a moment, this tower is remote from society and very different from it, but it certainly has windows and doors. That we can analyze riskful topics thanks to the tower's distance from society, and that we can work them through under conditions of low time-pressure, means that, rather than being obliged to reduce their complexity (as we invariably have to do in everyday situations because we have to come up with quick solutions), we may expose ourselves to their complexity and even increase it)' (Gumbrecht 2004: 127).

15 'But how', he asks, 'will such a deictic teaching style not end in silence and, worse perhaps, in a quasi-mystical contemplation and admiration of so much complexity?' (Gumbrecht 2004: 128).

16 We can think of Geoff Dyer's reading of Andrei Tarkovsky's film *Stalker* as such a reading. Dyer offers a slow reading that gathers feelings in response to the intensity of Tarkovsky's art (Dyer 2012).

REFERENCES

Adorno, Theodor W. ([1951] 1974), *Minima Moralia: Reflections from Damaged Life*, trans. E.F.N. Jephcott, London: New Left Books.
Adorno, Theodor W. ([1973] 1979), *Negative Dialectics*, trans. E.B. Ashton, New York: Seabury Press.
Adorno, Theodor W. (1986), *Aesthetic Theory*, trans. C. Lenhardt, London: Routledge and Kegan Paul.
Adorno, Theodor W. ([1958] 2000), 'The Essay as Form' in Brian O'Connor (ed.), *The Adorno Reader*, 91–111, Oxford: Blackwell.
Adorno, Theodor W. (2000a), 'The Actuality of Philosophy', trans. Benjamin Snow, in Brian O'Conner (ed.), *The Adorno Reader*, 23–38, Oxford: Blackwell.
Adorno, Theodor W. and Horkheimer, Max. ([1944] 1979), *Dialectic of Enlightenment*, trans. John Cumming, London: Verso.
Ajzenstat, Oona. (2001), *Driven Back to the Text: The Premodern Sources of Levinas's Postmodernism*, Pittsburgh: Duquesne University Press.
Althusser, Louis. ([1968] 1979), 'From "Capital" to Marx's Philosophy' in Louis Althusser, Étienne Balibar et al., *Reading Capital*, trans. B. Brewster, 13–63, London: Verso.
Altman, Meryl. (2007), 'Beauvoir, Hegel, War', *Hypatia*, 22 (3): 66–91.
Arendt, Hannah. (1963), *Eichmann in Jerusalem: A Report on the Banality of Evil*, New York: Viking Press.
Arendt, Hannah. (1969), 'Walter Benjamin: 1892–1940' in Hannah Arendt (ed.), *Walter Benjamin, Illuminations: Essays and Reflections*, trans. Harry Zohn, 12–13, New York: Schocken Books.
Aristotle. (1971), *Metaphysics* Book 1, Chapter II, trans. Christopher Kirwan, Oxford: Clarendon Press.
Armbruster, Carol. (1983), 'Hélène-Clarice: Nouvelle Voix', *Contemporary Literature*, XXIV (2): 145–57.
Auerbach, Erich. ([1957] 2003), *Mimesis*, trans. Willard R. Trask, Princeton: Princeton University Press.
Bacon, Francis. (1901), *The Advancement of Learning* [1605], Joseph Devey (ed.), New York: P.F. Collier and Son.
Bakewell, Sarah. (2010), *How to Live: Or a Life of Montaigne in One Question and Twenty Attempts at an Answer*, London: Vintage Books.

REFERENCES

Bande à Part (1964), [Film] Dir. Jean-Luc Godard.
Barker, Victoria. (2000), 'Duplicitous Idolatry of the Philosophical Imaginary' in Max Deutscher (ed.), *Michèle Le Dœuff: Operative Philosophy and Imaginary Practice*, 127–46, Amherst: Humanity Books.
Barnes, Hazel. (1959), *Humanistic Existentialism: The Literature of Philosophy*, Lincoln: University of Nebraska Press.
Barnhart, Robert K. (ed.) (2010), *Chambers Dictionary of Etymology*, London: Chambers Harrap.
Baudelaire, Charles. (1863), *Le Peintre de la vie moderne*, Paris: Editions de Pléiade.
Bauer, Nancy. (2001), *Simone de Beauvoir, Philosophy and Feminism*, New York: Columbia University Press.
Bauer, Nancy. (2006), 'Beauvoir's Heideggerian Ontology' in Margaret A. Simons (ed.), *The Philosophy of Simone de Beauvoir: Critical Essays*, 65–91, Bloomington: Indiana University Press.
Bauerlein, Mark. (2011), 'Too Dumb for Complex Texts?', *Educational Leadership*, 68 (5): 28–33.
Beauvoir, Simone de. ([1947] 1962), *The Ethics of Ambiguity*, trans. Bernard Frechtman, New York: Citadel Press.
Beauvoir, Simone de. ([1963] 1968), *Force of Circumstance*, trans. R. Howard, Harmondsworth: Penguin.
Beauvoir, Simone de. ([1967] 1969a), *The Woman Destroyed*, trans. Patrick O'Brien, London: Collins.
Beauvoir, Simone de. ([1964] 1969b), *A Very Easy Death*, trans. Patrick O'Brien, Harmondsworth: Penguin.
Beauvoir, Simone de. ([1972] 1974), *All Said and Done*, trans. Patrick O'Brien, London: Deutsch and Weidenfeld and Nicolson.
Beauvoir, Simone de. (1981), 'Entretiens avec Jean-Paul Sartre' in *La Cérémonie des adieux*, Paris: Gallimard.
Beauvoir, Simone de. ([1949] 1984), 'The Woman in Love' in *The Second Sex*, trans. H.M. Pashley, 652–79, Harmondsworth: Penguin.
Beauvoir, Simone de. ([1960] 1992), *The Prime of Life: The Autobiography of Simone De Beauvoir*, trans. Peter Green, New York: Paragon House.
Beauvoir, Simone de. ([1946] 2004), 'Eye for Eye', trans. Kristana Arp, in Margaret A. Simons (ed.), *Simone de Beauvoir: Philosophical Writings*, 245–60, Urbana: University of Illinois Press.
Beauvoir, Simone de. (2006), *Simone de Beauvoir: Diary of a Philosophy Student: Vol 1, 1926–27*, Barbara Klaw, Sylvie Le Bon de Beauvoir and Margaret A. Simons (eds), Urbana: University of Illinois Press.
Benjamin, Walter. ([1955] 1969), *Illuminations: Essays and Reflections*, trans. Harry Zone, New York: Schocken Books.
Benjamin, W. ([1919] 1974), 'Der Begriff der Kunstkritik in der deutschen Romantik', in Rolf Tiedermann and H. Schweppenhäuser (eds), *Gessamelte Schriften* Vol. 1, Bk.1, Frankfurt: Suhrkamp Verlag.

Benjamin, Walter. ([1972] 1977), *The Origin of German Tragic Drama*, trans. John Osborne, London: New Left Books.
Benjamin, Walter. (1978), 'On the Mimetic Faculty' in *Reflections: Essays, Aphorisms, Autobiographical Writings*, trans. Edmund Jephcott, 333–6, New York: Harcourt Brace Jovanovich.
Benjamin, Walter. ([1977] 1979), 'Doctrine of the Similar', trans. Knut Tarnowski, *New German Critique*, 17 Spring: 65–80.
Bergoffen, Debra B. (1997), *The Philosophy of Simone de Beauvoir: Gendered Phenomenologies, Erotic Generosities*, New York: SUNY Press.
Bernasconi, Robert. and Critchley, Simon. (eds) (1991), *Re-Reading Levinas*, Bloomington: Indiana University Press.
Bickford, Susan. (1996), *The Dissonance of Democracy: Listening, Conflict, and Citizenship*, Ithaca and London: Cornell University Press.
Birkett, Jennifer. (1990), 'The Implications of *Etudes Féminines* for Teaching' in Helen Wilcox et al, *The Body and the Text: Hélène Cixous, Reading and Teaching*, 204–13, London: Harvester Wheatsheaf.
Blondel, Eric. (1991), *Nietzsche: The Body and Culture: Philosophy as a Philological Genealogy*, trans. Seán Hand, Stanford: Stanford University Press.
Bloom, Harold. (1973), *The Anxiety of Influence: A Theory of Poetry*, New York: Oxford University Press.
Blyth, Ian. and Sellers, Susan. (2004), *Hélène Cixous: Live Theory*, New York and London: Continuum.
Boman, Thorlief. (1961), *Hebrew Thought Compared with Greek*, London: SCM.
Boulous Walker, Michelle. (1993a), 'The Aesthetics of Detail' in Wayne Hudson (ed.), *Aesthetics after Historicism*, 79–91, Brisbane: Institute of Modern Art.
Boulous Walker, Michelle. (1993b), 'Reason, Identity and the Body: Reading Adorno with Irigaray' in Dieter Freundlieb and Wayne Hudson (eds), *Reason and Its Other: Rationality in Modern German Philosophy and Culture*, 199–228, Providence and Oxford: Berg.
Boulous Walker, Michelle. (1997), 'A Short Story about Reason: The Strange Case of Habermas and Poe', *Philosophy Today*, 41 (3): 132–15.
Boulous Walker, Michelle. (1998), *Philosophy and the Maternal Body: Reading Silence*, London and New York: Routledge.
Boulous Walker, Michelle. (1998a), 'Wonder: Coupling Art with Sexual Difference' in Judith Wright (ed.), *Veil – Judith Wright*, 44–7, Brisbane: Institute of Modern Art.
Boulous Walker, Michelle. (2000), 'Bringing Le Dœuff Back Home' in Max Deutscher (ed.), *Michèle Le Dœuff: Operative Philosophy and Imaginary Practice*, 163–86, Amherst: Humanity Books.

Boulous Walker, Michelle. (2002), 'Eating Ethically: Emmanuel Levinas and Simone Weil', *American Catholic Philosophical Quarterly*, 76 (2): 295–320.
Boulous Walker, Michelle. (2006), 'An Ethics of Reading: Adorno, Levinas and Irigaray', *Philosophy Today*, 50 (2): 223–38.
Boulous Walker, Michelle. (2009), 'Writing Couples: Reading Deutscher on Sartre and Beauvoir', *Crossroads: An Interdisciplinary Journal for the Study of History, Philosophy, Religion and Classics*, 4 (1): 45–52.
Boulous Walker, Michelle. (2010), 'Love, Ethics and Authenticity: Beauvoir's Lesson in What it Means to Read', *Hypatia*, 25 (2): 334–56.
Boulous Walker, Michelle. (2013), 'Imagining Happiness: Literature and the Essay', *Culture, Theory and Critique*, 54 (2): 194–208.
Boulous Walker, Michelle. (n.d.) 'Walter Benjamin: The Art of Critical Thought', (unpublished essay).
Boyhood (2014), [Film] Dir. Richard Linklater.
Bray, Abigail. (2004), *Hélène Cixous: Writing and Sexual Difference*, Basingstoke: Palgrave Macmillan.
Brenkman, John. (1982), 'The Other and the One: Psychoanalysis, Reading, *The Symposium*' in Shoshana Felman (ed.), *Literature and Psychoanalysis: The Question of Reading: Otherwise*, 396–456, Baltimore and London: The Johns Hopkins University Press.
Brennan, Teresa. (2000), *Exhausting Modernity: Grounds for a New Economy*, London and New York: Routledge.
Brennan, Teresa. (2004), *The Transmission of Affect,* Ithaca and London: Cornell University Press.
Burke, Carolyn., Schor, Naomi. and Whitford, Margaret. (eds) (1994), *Engaging with Irigaray: Feminist Philosophy and Modern European Thought,* New York: Columbia University Press.
Bynum Walker, Carolyn. (1997), 'Wonder', *The American Historical Review*, 102 (1): 1–26.
Camus, Albert. ([1942] 1955), *The Myth of Sisyphus: And Other Essays*, trans. Justin O'Brien, New York: Knopf.
Carel, Havi. (2004), 'Philosophy as Listening: The Lessons of Psychoanalysis' in Havi Carel and David Gamez (eds), *What Philosophy Is*, 225–35, London and New York: Continuum.
Carel, Havi. and Gamez, David. (eds) (2004), *What Philosophy Is*, London and New York: Continuum.
Carter, Paul. (2009), *Dark Writing: Geography, Performance, Design*, Honolulu: University of Hawaii Press.
Castro, Brian. (2011), 'Slow Boat to Culture', *The Australian Literary Review*, 5 October: 20.
Caverero, Adriana. (1995), 'Diotima' in *In Spite of Plato: A Feminist Rewriting of Ancient Philosophy*, trans. Serena Anderlini-D'Onofrio and Áine O'Healy, 91–120, Oxford: Polity Press.

Champagne, Roland A. (1998), *The Ethics of Reading According to Emmanuel Levinas*, Amsterdam: Rodopi.
Chanter, Tina. (1995), *Ethics of Eros: Irigaray's Re-Writing of the Philosophers*, London and New York: Routledge.
Cilliers, Paul. (2006), 'On the Importance of a Certain Slowness', *E:CO*, 8 (3): 106–13.
Cixous, Hélène. (1976), 'The Laugh of the Medusa', trans. Keith Cohen and Paula Cohen, *Signs: Journal of Women in Culture and Society*, 1 (4): 875–93.
Cixous, Hélène. (1979), *Vivre l'orange/To Live the Orange*, Paris: des femmes.
Cixous, Hélène. (1981), 'Castration or Decapitation?', trans. Annette Kuhn, *Signs: Journal of Women in Culture and Society*, 7 (1): 41–55.
Cixous, Hélène. ([1975] 1986), *The Newly Born Woman*, with Cathérine Clément, trans. Betsy Wing, Minneapolis: University of Minnesota Press.
Cixous, Hélène. (1987), 'Reaching the Point of Wheat, or A Portrait of the Artist as a Maturing Woman', *New Literary History*, 19 (1): 1–21.
Cixous, Hélène. (1988), *Writing Differences: Readings from the Seminar of Hélène Cixous*, Susan Sellers (ed.), Milton Keynes: Open University Press.
Cixous, Hélène. (1990), *Reading with Clarice Lispector*, Verena Andermatt Conley (ed., trans.), Minneapolis: University of Minnesota Press.
Cixous, Hélène. (1991), *'Coming to Writing' and Other Essays*, trans. Sarah Cornell et al., Deborah Jenson (ed.), Cambridge: Harvard University Press.
Cixous, Hélène. ([1983] 1991a), *The Book of Promethea*, trans. Betsy Wing, Lincoln: University of Nebraska Press.
Cixous, Hélène. (1992), *Readings: The Poetics of Blanchot, Joyce, Kafka, Kleist, Lispector, and Tsvetayeva*, trans. Verena Andermatt Conley, Hemel Hempstead: Harvester Wheatsheaf.
Cixous, Hélène. (1993), *Three Steps on the Ladder of Writing*, trans. Sarah Cornell and Susan Sellers, New York: Columbia University Press.
Cixous, Hélène. (1994), *The Cixous Reader*, S. Sellers (ed.), London and New York: Routledge.
Cixous, Hélène. ([1988] 1994a), *Manna: for the Mandelstams for the Mandelas*, trans. Catherine MacGillvray, Minneapolis: University of Minnesota Press.
Cixous, Hélène. (2010), 'B. "I Am an Archreader": Hélène Cixous', Interview with Daniel Ferrer in *The Origins of Deconstruction*, Ika Willis and Martin McQuillan (eds), 22–38, Basingstoke: Palgrave Macmillan.
Cixous, Hélène. and Calle Gruber, Mireille. ([1994] 1997), *Hélène Cixous, Rootprints: Memory and Life Writing*, trans. Eric Prenowitz, London and New York: Routledge.

Clarke, David L. (2005), 'The Last Temptation of Marion Woodman: The Anorexic Remainder in *Bone: Dying Into Life*', *Spring: A Journal of Archetype and Culture*, 72 (1): 131–58.

Conrad, Peter. (2010), 'The Alchemist: Alfred Stieglitz's Lake George Years', *The Monthly: Australian Politics, Society & Culture*, May: 66–9.

Cossery, Albert. ([1964] 2005), 'Les Fainéants dans la vallée fertile' in *Œuvres completes,* Vol 2, 8–170, Paris: Éditions Gallimard.

Costa Lima, Luiz. (1988), *Control of the Imaginary: Reason and Imagination in Modern Times*, trans. Ronald W. Sousa, Minneapolis: University of Minnesota Press.

Costa Lima, Luiz. ([1993] 1996), *The Limits of Voice: Montaigne, Schlegel, Kafka*, trans. Paulo Henriques Britto, Stanford: Stanford University Press.

Cottingham, J. (1995), 'Descartes' in Ted Honderich (ed.), *The Oxford Companion to Philosophy*, 188–92, Oxford: Oxford University Press.

Craig, Geoffrey. and Parkins, Wendy. (2006), *Slow Living*, Oxford: Berg.

Critchley, Simon. (1989), '*The Chiasmus*: Levinas, Derrida and the Ethical Demand for Deconstruction', *Textual Practice,* 3 (1): 91–106.

Critchley, Simon. (2010), 'What is the Institutional Form for Thinking?', *differences: A Journal of Feminist Cultural Studies,* 21 (1): 19–31.

Daigle, Christine. and Golomb, Jacob. (eds). (2009), *Beauvoir and Sartre: The Riddle of Influence,* Bloomington: Indiana University Press.

Davis, Colin. (2006), 'Levinas and the Phenomenology of Reading' in *Studia Phaenomenologia* vol. 6: *A Century with Levinas: Notes on the Margins of His Legacy,* 275–92, Bucharest: Romanian Society for Phenomenology and Humanitas.

Deleuze, Gilles. and Guattari, Felix. ([1972] 1983), *Anti-Oedipus: Capitalism and Schizophrenia*, trans. Robert Hurley, Mark Seem and Helen R. Lane, Minneapolis: University of Minnesota Press.

Deleuze, Gilles. and Guattari, Felix. ([1980] 1986), *Nomadology: The War Machine*, trans. Brian Massumi, New York: Semiotexte.

Della Subin, Anna. (2014), 'How to Stop Time', *The New York Times,* 28 September. Available online: http://nyti.ms/1ndjvUX

Derrida, Jacques. ([1972] 1982), *Margins of Philosophy*, trans. Alan Bass, Chicago: Chicago University Press.

Derrida, Jacques. (1985), *The Ear of the Other: Otobiography, Transference, Translation*, trans. Peggy Kamuf, New York: Schocken Books.

Derrida, Jacques. (1991), 'At This Very Moment in This Work Here I Am', in Robert Bernasconi and Simon Critchley (eds), *Re-Reading Levinas,* trans. Rubin Berezdivin, 11–48, Bloomington: Indiana University Press.

Descartes, René. ([1637] 1912), *A Discourse on Method*, trans. John Veitch, London: J.M. Dent and Sons.

Descartes, René. (1931), *The Passions of the Soul* in *The Philosophical Works of Descartes*, Vol.1, trans. E.S. Haldane and G.R.T Ross, Cambridge: Cambridge University Press.

Deutscher, Max. (ed.) (2000), *Michèle Le Dœuff: Operative Philosophy and Imaginary Practice*, Amherst: Humanity Books.
Deutscher, Max. (2003), *Genre and Void: Looking back at Sartre and Beauvoir*, Aldershot: Ashgate.
Deutscher, Max. (2009), 'In Response', *Crossroads: An Interdisciplinary Journal for the Study of History, Philosophy, Religion and Classics*, Special Issue – Max Deutscher, IV (1): 92–8.
Deutscher, Penelope. (2000), 'At Home in Philosophy' in Max Deutscher (ed.), *Michèle Le Dœuff: Operative Philosophy and Imaginary Practice*, 199–220, Amherst: Humanity Books.
Deutscher, Penelope. (2000a), Interview with Michèle Le Dœuff in *Hypatia: A Journal of Feminist Philosophy*, 15 (4): 236–42.
Diprose, Rosalyn. (1998), 'Generosity: Between Love and Desire', *Hypatia*, 13 (1): 1–20.
Diprose, Rosalyn. (2013), 'Corporeal Interdependence: From Vulnerability to Dwelling in Ethical Community', *SubStance 132*, 42 (3): 185–204.
Dowrick, Stephanie. (2010), *In the Company of Rilke*, Sydney: Allen and Unwin.
Drichel, Simone. (2013), 'Reframing Vulnerability: "So Obviously the Problem . . ."', *SubStance 132*, 42 (3): 3–27.
During, Lisabeth. (2000), 'Catherine Malabou and the Currency of Hegelianism', *Hypatia*, 15 (4): 190–5.
Dyer, Geoff. (2012), *Zona: A Book about a Film about a Journey to a Room*, New York: Pantheon Books.
Eaglestone, Robert. (1997), *Ethical Criticism: Reading after Levinas*, Edinburgh: Edinburgh University Press.
Eckermann, Johann Peter. (1913), *Conversations of Goethe*, trans. John Oxenford, London: G. Bell and Sons.
Eckermann, Johann Peter. (1925), *Geßpräche mit Goethe: in den lezten Jahren seines Lebens*, Leipzig: F.U. Brockhaus.
Eilenberger, Wolfram. (2013), 'Vernünftig entschleunigen?', *Philosophie Magazin*, February/March. 2: 3.
Engler, Balz. (1982), *Reading and Listening: The Modes of Communicating Poetry and their Influence on the Texts*, Bern: Francke Verlag.
Felman, Shoshana. (1977), 'To Open the Question', *Yale French Studies*, 55 (6): 5–10.
Flanagan, Richard. (2012), *Gould's Book of Fish*, Sydney: Vintage.
Fletcher, Lancelot R. (2007), 'Slow Reading: The Affirmation of Authorial Intent' Available online: http://freelance-academy.org/slowread.htm.
Fox Keller, Evelyn. (1985), 'Love and Sex in Plato's Epistemology' in *Reflections on Gender and Science*, 21–32, New Haven and London: Yale University Press.
Freadman, Anne. (1983), 'Sandpaper', *Southern Review*, 16 (1): 162.

Freud, Sigmund. ([1927] 1961), *The Future of an Illusion*, trans. W.D. Robsob-Scott, New York: Doubleday.

Freud, Sigmund. ([1900] 1965), *The Interpretation of Dreams*, trans. James Strachey, New York: Basic Books.

Freud, Sigmund. ([1937] 1974), 'Analysis Terminable and Interminable (1937)', trans. James Strachey in *The Standard Edition of the Complete Psychological Works of Sigmund Freud* Vol. 23, 209–53, London: Hogarth Press.

Fried, Gregory. (2014), 'The King is Dead: Heidegger's *Black Notebooks*', *LA Review of Books*, September 13. Available online: https://lareviewofbooks.org/review/king-dead-heideggers-black-notebooks/?print=1&fulltext=1

Fuss, Diana. (1989), 'Reading Like a Feminist' in *Essentially Speaking: Feminism, Nature and Difference,* 23–37, New York: Routledge.

Gaita, Raimond. (2011), 'To Civilise the City?', *Meanjin*. Available online. http://meanjin.com.au/articles/post/to-civilise-the-city/ (accessed 21 March 2014).

Gallop, Jane. (1985), *Reading Lacan*, Ithaca and London: Cornell University Press.

Garner, Helen. (2001), *The Feel of Steel*, Sydney: Picador.

Godzich, Wlad. (1994), *The Culture of Literacy*, Cambridge: Harvard University Press.

Gora, Joseph. (2010), 'It's Great to Be a Slow Learner', *The Australian*, 27 October. Available online: http:www.theaustralian.com.au/higher-education/opinion-analysis/its-great-to-be-a-slow-learner.

Goss, Caitlin. (2006), 'Beauvoir Reading Herself' (unpublished paper).

Gothlin, Eva. (1999), 'Simone de Beauvoir's Notions of Appeal, Desire, and Ambiguity and their Relationship to Jean-Paul Sartre's Notions of Appeal and Desire', *Hypatia*, 14 (4): 83–95.

Greisch, Jean. (1991), 'The Face and Reading: Immediacy and Mediation' in Robert Bernasconi and Simon Critchley (eds), *Re-Reading Levinas*, 67–82, Bloomington: Indiana University Press.

Guenther, Lisa. (2006), *The Gift of the Other: Levinas and the Politics of Reproduction*, Albany: SUNY Press.

Gumbrecht, Hans Ulrich. (2002), 'Riskantes Denken. Intellektuelle als Katalysatoren von Komplexität' in Uwe Justus Wenzel (ed.), *Der kritische Blick: Intellektuelle Tätigkeiten und Tugenden*, 140–7, Frankfurt am Main.

Gumbrecht, Hans Ulrich. (2003), *The Powers of Philology: Dynamics of Textual Scholarship*, Urbana: University of Illinois Press.

Gumbrecht, Hans Ulrich. (2004), *Production of Presence: What Meaning Cannot Convey*, Stanford: Stanford University Press.

Gumbrecht, Hans Ulrich. (2012), *Atmosphere, Mood, Stimmung: On a Hidden Potential of Literature*, trans. Erik Butler, Stanford: Stanford University Press.

Gumbrecht, Hans Ulrich. (2014), *Our Broad Present: Time and Contemporary Culture*, New York: Columbia University Press.
Guzzoni, Ute. (1997), 'Reason – A Different Reason – Something Different than Reason? Wondering about the Concept of a Different Reason in Adorno, Lyotard, and Sloterdijk' in Max Pensky (ed.), *The Actuality of Adorno: Critical Essays on Adorno and the Postmodern*, Albany: SUNY Press.
Hadot, Pierre. ([1987] 1995), *Philosophy as a Way of Life: Spiritual Exercises from Socrates to Foucault*, trans. Michael Chase, Oxford: Blackwell Publishing.
Hadot, Pierre. ([1995] 2002), *What is Ancient Philosophy*, trans. Michael Chase, Cambridge, MA: Harvard University Press.
Halperin, David. (1990), 'Why is Diotima a Woman?' in *One Hundred Years of Homosexuality: And Other Essays on Greek Love*, 91–120, London and New York: Routledge.
Hannah Arendt (2012), [Film] Dir. Margarethe von Trotta.
Hansen, Linda. (1979), 'Pain and Joy in Human Relationships: Jean-Paul Sartre and Simone de Beauvoir', *Philosophy Today*, Winter: 338–46.
Haynes, Joanna. and Murris, Karin. (2012), *Picturebooks, Pedagogy and Philosophy*, New York: Routledge.
Hegel, Georg Wilhelm Friedrich. ([1807] 1977), *Phenomenology of Spirit*, trans. A.V. Miller, Oxford: Clarendon Press.
Heidegger, Martin. (1962), *Being and Time*, trans. John Macquarrie and Edward Robinson, New York: Harper and Row.
Heidegger, Martin. ([1959] 1966), 'Memorial Address' in *Discourse on Thinking*, trans. John M. Anderson and E. Hans Freund, New York: Harper & Row.
Heidegger, Martin. (1971), *Poetry, Language, Thought*, trans. Albert Hofstadter, New York: Harper and Row.
Heidegger, Martin. ([1959] 1971a), *On the Way to Language*, trans. Peter D. Hertz, New York: Harper & Row.
Heidegger, Martin. (1977), 'The Question Concerning Technology' and 'The Turning' in *The Question Concerning Technology and Other Essays*, trans. William Lovitt, 3–35, 36–49, New York: Harper & Row.
Heidegger, Martin. (1991), *Nietzsche*, Vol. 1: *The Will to Power as Art* and Vol. II: *The Eternal Recurrence of the Same*, trans. David Farrell Krell, New York: Harper & Row.
Heidegger, Martin. [1971] (2013), 'Building Dwelling Thinking' in *Poetry, Language, Thought*, trans. Albert Hofstadter, 141–59, New York: Harper Perennial.
Heidegger, Martin. (2014), *Schwarze Hefte. Gesamtausgabe Vols 94–96*, Frankfurt am Main: Vittorio Klosterman.
Heinämaa, Sara. (1996), 'Woman – Nature, Product, Style? Rethinking the Foundations of Feminist Philosophy of Science' in L. H. Nelson

and J. Nelson (eds), *Feminism, Science, and the Philosophy of Science*, 289–308, Dordrecht: Kluwer Academic Publishers.

Hillis Miller, J. (1987), *The Ethics of Reading: Kant, de Man, Eliot, Trollope, James, and Benjamin,* New York: Columbia University Press.

Hirsch, Elizabeth. (1994), 'Back in Analysis: How to Do Things with Irigaray' in Carolyn Burke, Naomi Schor and Margaret Whitford (eds), *Engaging with Irigaray: Feminist Philosophy and Modern European Thought,* 285–315, New York: Columbia University Press.

Hirst, Angela. (2004), *Eating the Other: Levinas's Ethical Encounter*, PhD thesis, St Lucia: University of Queensland.

Honoré, Carl. (2004), *In Praise of Slow: How a Worldwide Movement Is Changing the Cult of Speed,* London: Orion.

Hustvedt, Siri. (2012), 'On Reading' in *Living, Thinking, Looking*, 133–40, New York: Picador.

Irigaray, Luce. (1977), 'Women's Exile', *Ideology and Consciousness*, 1: 62–76.

Irigaray, Luce. (1981), *Le Corps-à-corps avec la mere*, Montreal: Editions de la Pleine Lune.

Irigaray, Luce. ([1974] 1985a), *Speculum of the Other Woman*, trans. Gillian C. Gill, Ithaca: Cornell University Press.

Irigaray, Luce. (1985b), *This Sex Which Is Not One*, trans. Catherine Porter, Ithaca: Cornell University Press.

Irigaray, Luce. (1985c), 'The Power of Discourse and the Subordination of the Feminine' in *This Sex Which Is Not One*, trans. Catherine Porter, 68–85, Ithaca: Cornell University Press.

Irigaray, Luce. (1985d), 'Questions' in *This Sex Which Is Not One*, trans. Catherine Porter, 119–69, Ithaca: Cornell University Press.

Irigaray, Luce. (1985e), 'Commodities amongst Themselves' in *This Sex Which Is Not One*, trans. Catherine Porter, 192–7, Ithaca: Cornell University Press.

Irigaray, Luce. ([1977] 1991), 'The Poverty of Psychoanalysis' in *The Irigaray Reader*, Margaret Whitford (ed.), 79–104, Oxford: Basil Blackwell.

Irigaray, Luce. (1991a), 'Questions to Emmanuel Levinas', trans. Margaret Whitford, in *The Irigaray Reader*, Margaret Whitford (ed.), 178–89, Oxford: Basil Blackwell.

Irigaray, Luce. (1992), 'Sorcerer Love: A Reading of Plato, *Symposium*, "Diotima's Speech"', trans. Eleanor H. Kuykendall, in Nancy Fraser and Sandra Lee Bartky (eds), *Revaluing French Feminism: Critical Essays on Difference, Agency, and Culture*, 64–76, Bloomington: Indiana University Press.

Irigaray, Luce. ([1984] 1993), *An Ethics of Sexual Difference*, trans. Carolyn Burke and Gillian C. Gill, Ithaca: Cornell University Press.

Irigaray, Luce. (1996), *I Love to You: Sketch of a Possible Felicity in History,* trans. Alison Martin, London and New York: Routledge.

Irigaray, Luce. (1977), *Entre Deux*, Paris: Grasset.
Irigaray, Luce. ([1983] 1999), *The Forgetting of Air in Martin Heidegger*, trans. Mary Beth Mader, Austin: University of Texas Press.
Irigaray, Luce. ([1994] 2000), *To Be Two*, trans. Monique M. Rhodes and Marco F. Cocito-Monoc, London and New Brunswick: Athlone Press.
Irigaray, Luce. (2002), *The Way of Love*, trans. Heidi Bostic and Stephen Pluhácek, London: Continuum.
Irigaray, Luce. (2002a), 'The Setting in Psychoanalysis' in *To Speak is Never Neutral*, trans. Gail Schwab, 193–204, New York: Routledge.
Irigaray, Luce. ([1985] 2002b), *To Speak is Never Neutral*, trans. Gail Schwab, New York, Routledge.
Irigaray, Luce. ([1999] 2002c), *Between East and West: From Singularity to Community*, trans. Stephen Pluhácek, New York: Columbia University Press.
Irigaray, Luce. (2002d), 'Being Two, How Many Eyes Have We?', trans. Luce Irigaray et al., *Paragraph*, 25 (3): 143–151.
Irigaray, Luce. (2004), *Key Writings*, London and New York: Continuum.
Irigaray, Luce. (2008), 'Listening, Thinking, Teaching' in Luce Irigaray and Mary Green (eds), *Luce Irigaray: Teaching*, 231–40, London: Continuum.
Irigaray, Luce. (2010), 'Ethical Gestures toward the Other', *Poligrafi*, 57 (15): 3–23.
Irigaray, Luce. (2013), 'To Begin with Breathing Anew' in Lenart Škof and Emily A. Holmes (eds), *Breathing with Luce Irigaray*, 217–26, London: Bloomsbury.
Iser, Wolfgang. (1978), *The Act of Reading: A Theory of Aesthetic Response*, Baltimore and London: The Johns Hopkins University Press.
Jardine, Alice A. (1986), 'Death Sentences: Writing Couples and Ideology' in Susan Rubin Suleiman (ed.), *The Female Body in Western Culture: Contemporary Perspectives*, 84–96, Cambridge: Harvard University Press.
Jarvis, Simon. (1998), *Adorno: A Critical Introduction*, Oxford: Polity Press.
Jonas, Hans. (1953), 'The Nobility of Sight' in *The Phenomenon of Life*, 135–55, New York: Harpers Row. Reprinted: Alexander, Christopher. (ed.) (2002), *The Nature of Order: An Essay on the Art of Building and the Nature of the Universe*, Berkley: Centre for Environmental Structure.
Juncker, Clara. (1988), 'Writing (with) Cixous', *College English*, 50 (4): 424–436.
Kabat-Zinn, Jon. (2005), *Coming to Our Senses*, New York: Hyperion.
Kahneman, Daniel. (2013), *Thinking, Fast and Slow*, New York: Farrar, Straus and Giroux.
Kamuf, Peggy. (2000), 'The End of Reading', Lecture delivered at the conference 'Book/Ends', University of Albany, 12 October 2000. Available online: http://www-ref.usc.edu/~kamuf/text.html.

Kelso, Julie. (2007), *O Mother, Where Art Thou?: An Irigarayan Reading of the Book of Chronicles*, London: Equinox.
Kierkegaard, Søren. (1980), *The Sickness unto Death*, trans. Howard V. Hong and Edna H. Hong, Princeton: Princeton University Press.
Kierkegaard, Søren. (1995), *Works of Love*, trans. Howard V. Hong and Edna H. Hong, Princeton: Princeton University Press.
Kingwell, Mark. (2000), 'Husserl's Sense of Wonder', *Philosophical Forum*, 31 (1): 85–107.
Klobucka, Anna. (1994), 'Hélène Cixous and the Hour of Clarice Lispector', *SubStance*, 23 (1) Issue 73: 41–62.
Koepnick, Lutz. (2014), *On Slowness: Toward an Aesthetic of the Contemporary*, New York: Columbia University Press.
Köhler, Wolfgang. (1969), *The Task of Gestalt Psychology*, Princeton: Princeton University Press.
Kristeva, Julia. ([1983] 1987), 'Manic Eros, Sublime Eros: On Male Sexuality' in *Tales of Love*, trans. Leon S. Roudiez, 59–82, New York: Columbia University Press.
Kruks, Sonia. (1990), *Situation and Human Existence: Freedom, Subjectivity and Society*, London: Unwin Hyman.
Kundera, Milan. ([1995] 1996), *Slowness*, trans. Linda Asher, New York: Harper Collins.
La Caze, Marguerite. (2003), 'Michèle Le Dœuff and the Work of Philosophy', *Australian Journal of French Studies*, 40 (3): 244–56.
La Caze, Marguerite. (2013), *Wonder and Generosity: Their Role in Ethics and Politics*, Albany: SUNY Press.
Lacan, Jacques. (1977), 'The Mirror Stage As Formative of the Function of the I' in *Ecrits: A Selection*, trans. Alan Sheridan, 1–7, New York: W.W. Norton.
Lacoue-Labarthe, P. and Nancy, J-L. (1978), *L'Absolu littéraire: théorie de la literature du romantisme allemande*, Paris: Seuil.
Lafargue, Paul. (1917), *The Right to be Lazy (1880)*, trans. Charles H. Kerr, Chicago: C.H. Kerr.
Lamb, Matthew. (ed.) (2008), 'Special Issue – Luiz Costa Lima', *Crossroads: An Interdisciplinary Journal for the Study of History, Philosophy, Religion and Classics*, II (II).
Lamb, Matthew. (2008a), 'Introducing Costa Lima: Sailing against the Wind', in Special Issue – Luiz Costa Lima, *Crossroads: An Interdisciplinary Journal for the Study of History, Philosophy, Religion and Classics*, II (II): 3–7.
Lamb, Matthew. (2010), *The Role of Askēsis in the Life and Work of Albert Camus*, PhD thesis, St Lucia: University of Queensland.
Langer, Moniker. (1994), 'A Philosophical Retrieval of Simone de Beauvoir's *Pour Une Morale De L'Ambiguité*', *Philosophy Today*, 38 (2): 181–90.

Le Dœuff, Michèle. (1977), 'Women and Philosophy', *Radical Philosophy*, 17: 2–11.
Le Dœuff, Michèle. ([1979] 1980), 'Simone de Beauvoir and Existentialism', *Feminist Studies*, 6 (2): 277–89.
Le Dœuff, Michèle. (1987), 'Ants and Women, or Philosophy without Borders' in A. Phillips Griffiths (ed.), *Contemporary French Philosophy*, 41–54, Cambridge: Cambridge University Press.
Le Dœuff, Michèle. ([1980] 1989), 'Long Hair, Short Ideas' in *The Philosophical Imaginary*, trans. Colin Gordon, 100–28, Stanford: Stanford University Press.
Le Dœuff, Michèle. (1990), 'Women, Reason, Etc.', *differences*, 2 (3): 1–13.
Le Dœuff, Michèle. (1991), *Hipparchia's Choice: An Essay Concerning Women, Philosophy*, etc, trans. Trista Selous, Oxford: Basil Blackwell.
Le Dœuff, Michèle. (2000), 'Feminism Is Back in France – Or Is It?', *Hypatia*, 15 (4): 243–55.
Le Dœuff, Michèle. (2000a), 'A Little Learning: Women and (Intellectual) Work' in Colin Blakemore and Susan Iversen (eds), *Gender and Society: Essays Based on Herbert Spencer Lectures*, 97–115, Oxford: Oxford University Press.
Le Dœuff, Michèle. ([1998] 2003), *The Sex of Knowing*, trans. Kathryn Hamer and Lorraine Code, London: Routledge.
Le Dœuff, Michèle. (2006), 'Engaging with Simone de Beauvoir', trans. Nancy Bauer, in Margaret A. Simons (ed.), *The Philosophy of Simone de Beauvoir: Critical Essays*, 11–19, Bloomington: Indiana University Press.
Levinas, Emmanuel. ([1961] 1969), *Totality and Infinity: An Essay on Exteriority*, trans. Alphonso Lingis, Pittsburgh: Duquesne University Press.
Levinas, Emmanuel. (1989), 'Ethics as First Philosophy' in Seán Hand (ed.), *The Levinas Reader*, 75–87, Oxford: Basil Blackwell.
Levinas, Emmanuel. (1996), 'Meaning and Sense' in Adriaan T. Peperzak, Simon Critchley and Robert Bernasconi (eds), *Emmanuel Levinas: Basic Philosophical Writings*, 33–64, Bloomington: Indiana University Press.
Levinas, Emmanuel. ([1974] 1998), *Otherwise than Being, or Beyond Essence*, trans. Alphonso Lingis, Pittsburgh: Duquesne University Press.
Lispector, Clarice. ([1964] 1988), *The Passion According to G.H.*, trans. Ronald W. Sousa, Minneapolis: University of Minnesota Press.
Lloyd, Genevieve. (2000), 'Le Dœuff and the History of Philosophy' in Max Deutscher (ed.), *Michèle Le Dœuff: Operative Philosophy and Imaginary Practice*, 33–44, Amherst: Humanity Books.
Lourau, René. (1970), *L'Analyse institutionelle*, Paris: Editions de Minuit.
Luhmann, Niklas. (1990), *Die Wissenschaft der Gesellschaft*, Frankfurt am Main: Surhkamp.

Lukács, Georg. ([1910] (1974), *Soul and Form*, trans. Anna Bostock, London: Merlin Press.
Lundgren-Gothlin, Eva. (1996), *Sex and Existence: Simone de Beauvoir's 'The Second Sex'*, London: Athlone Press.
Lupton, Catherine. (2007), 'Memory's Apostle: Chris Marker, *La Jetée*, and *Sans Soleil*' in *La Jetée/Sans Soleil: Two Films by Chris Marker*, Criterion Edition DVD.
Lyotard, Jean-François. (1984), *Driftworks*, trans. Roger McKeon, New York: Semiotext (e).
Lyotard, Jean-François. ([1983] 1988), *The Différend: Phrases in Dispute*, trans. Georges Van Den Abbeele, Minneapolis: University of Minnesota Press.
Lyotard, Jean-François. (1993), *Libidinal Economy*, trans. I. Hamilton Grant, Bloomington: Indiana Press.
Lyotard, Jean-François. and Thebaud, Jean-Loup. (1985), *Just Gaming*, trans. Wlad Godzich, Minneapolis: University of Minnesota Press.
McGilchrist, Iain. (2009), *The Master and His Emissary: The Divided Brain and the Making of the Western World*, Yale: Yale University Press.
McGinn, Marie. (1997), *Routledge Philosophy Guidebook to Wittgenstein and the Philosophical*, Abingdon and New York: Routledge.
Macnamara, Jim. (2015), 'The Work and "Architecture": Requisites for Ethical Organization-Public Communication', *International Journal of Communication Ethics*, 12 (2): 29–37.
Macquarrie, John. (1977), *Principles of Christian Theology*, New York: SCM Press.
Macquarrie, John. (1994), *Heidegger and Christianity: The Hensley Henson Lectures, 1993–94*, London: SCM Press.
Malabou, Catherine. (1996), *L'Avenir de Hegel: Plasticité, temporalité, dialectique*, Paris: Vrin.
Malabou, Catherine. (2000), 'The Future of Hegel: Plasticity, Temporality, Dialectic', trans. Lisabeth During, *Hypatia*, 15 (4): 196–220.
Maras, Steven. (2000), 'Translating Michèle Le Dœuff's Analytics' in Max Deutscher (ed.), *Michèle Le Dœuff: Operative Philosophy and Imaginary Practice*, 83–104, Amherst: Humanity Books.
Margaroni, Maria. (2009), 'Julia Kristeva's Chiasmatic Journeys' in Kelly Oliver and S.K. Keltner (eds), *Psychoanalysis, Aesthetics, and Politics in the Work of Kristeva*, 107–25, New York: SUNY Press.
Marker, Chris. (2007), *La Jetée 1963/Sans Soleil 1983: Two Films by Chris Marker*, Criterion Edition DVD.
Mattéi, Jean-François. ([1983] 1995), 'The Heideggerian Chiasmus or the Setting Apart of Philosophy' in Dominique Janicaud and Jean-François Mattéi, *Heidegger from Metaphysics to Thought*, trans. Michael Gendre, 39–150, Albany: SUNY Press.

Mazis, Glen A. (1979), 'Touch and Vision: Rethinking with Merleau-Ponty and Sartre on the Caress', *Philosophy Today,* 23: 321–8.
Merleau-Ponty, Maurice. ([1945] 1962), *The Phenomenology of Perception,* trans. C. Smith, London: Routldge & Kegan Paul.
Merleau-Ponty, Maurice. (1964), 'Reading Montaigne' in *Signs,* trans. Richard C. McCleary, 198–210, Evanston: Northwestern University Press.
Merleau-Ponty, Maurice. (1968), 'The Intertwining – The Chiasm' in *The Visible and the Invisible,* trans. Alphonso Lingis, 130–55, Evanston: Northwestern University Press.
Merleau-Ponty, Maurice. (2010), *Institution and Passivity: Course Notes from the Collège de France (1954–1955),* trans. Leonard Lawlor and Heath Massey, Evanston: Northwestern University Press.
Miedema, John. (2009), *Slow Reading,* Duluth: Litwin Books.
Mikics, David. (2013), *Slow Reading in a Hurried Age,* Cambridge: Harvard University Press.
Monk, Ray. (2005), *How to Read Wittgenstein,* New York and London: W.W. Norton & Co.
Montaigne, Michel. (1962), *Essais,* II, 6, A. Thibaudet (ed.), Paris: Gallimard, Pléiade.
Montaigne, Michel. (2003), *Michel de Montaigne: The Complete Works,* trans. Donald M. Frame, New York and London: Knopf.
Morgan, Kathryn Pauly. (1986), 'Romantic Love, Altruism, and Self-respect: An Analysis of Simone De Beauvoir', *Hypatia,* 1 (1): 117–48.
Morris, Meaghan. (1981), 'Import Rhetoric: "Semiotics in/and Australia"' in *The Foreign Bodies Papers,* 122–39, Surry Hills: Local Consumption.
Morris, Meaghan. (1988), *The Pirate's Fiancée: Feminism, Reading, Postmodernism,* London: Verso.
Moulton, Janice. (1983), 'A Paradigm of Philosophy: The Adversary Method', in Sandra Harding and Merill B. Hintikka (eds), *Discovering Reality: Feminist Perspectives on Epistemology, Metaphysics, Methodology, and Philosophy of Science,* 149–64, Dordrecht: D. Reidel.
Musil, Robert. ([1914] 1990), 'On the Essay' in *Precision and Soul: Essays and Addresses,* trans. Burton Pike and David S. Luft, 48–51, Chicago: Chicago University Press.
Nadolny, Sten. ([1983] 2005), *The Discovery of Slowness,* trans. Ralph Freedman, Philadelphia: Paul dry Books.
Nancy, Jean-Luc. ([2002] 2007), *Listening,* trans. Charlotte Mandell, New York: Fordham University Press.
Newkirk, Thomas. (2012), *The Art of Slow Reading: Six Time-Honored Practices for Engagement,* Portsmouth: Heinemann.
Nicholls, Angus. (2000), 'The Secularization of Revelation from Plato to Freud', *Contretemps,* 1: 62–70.

Nicholls, Daniel. (2000), 'The Vision of Morality' in Max Deutscher (ed.), *Michèle Le Dœuff: Operative Philosophy and Imaginary Practice*, 147–60, Amherst: Humanity Books.
Nietzsche, Friedrich. ([1895] 1965), *On the Geneology of Morals*, trans. Walter Kaufmann and R.J. Hollingdale, New York: Viking Press.
Nietzsche, Friedrich. ([1882] 1974), *The Gay Science*, trans. Walter Kaufman, New York: Random House.
Nietzsche, Friedrich. ([1881] 1982), *Daybreak: Thoughts on the Prejudices of Morality*, trans. R.J. Hollingdale, New York: Cambridge University Press.
Nietzsche, Friedrich. (1988), *Werke*, Giorgio Colli and Mazzino Montinari (eds), Berlin: Walter de Gruyter.
Nietzsche, Friedrich. (1996), *Human, All Too Human*, trans. R.J. Hollingdale, Cambridge: Cambridge University Press.
Nozick, Robert. (1981), *Philosophical Explanation*, Cambridge: Belknap Press.
Nuzzo, Angelica. (2008), *Ideal Embodiment: Kant's Theory of Sensibility*, Bloomington: Indiana University Press.
Nye, Andrea. (1990), 'The Subject of Love: Diotima and Her Critics', *Journal of Value Inquiry*, 24 (1): 135–53.
Nye, Andrea. (1992), 'The Hidden Host: Irigaray and Diotima at Plato's Symposium' in Nancy Fraser and Sandra Lee Bartky (eds), *Revaluing French Feminism: Critical Essays on Difference, Agency, and Culture,* 77–93, Bloomington and Indianapolis: Indiana University Press.
Oliver, Kelly. (1995), *Womanizing Nietzsche: Philosophy's Relation to the 'Feminine',* New York and London: Routledge.
Ondaatje, Michael. (1992), *The English Patient*, New York: Vintage International.
Ong, Walter J. (1991), 'The Shifting Sensorium' in David Howes (ed.), *The Varieties of Sensory Experience: A Sourcebook in the Anthropology of the Senses*, 25–30, Toronto: University of Toronto Press.
Parkins, Wendy. (2004), 'Out of Time: Fast Subjects and Slow Living', *Time and Society,* 13 (2/3): 363–82.
Parsons, Howard L. (1969), 'A Philosophy of Wonder', *Philosophy and Phenomnological Research*, 30 (1): 84–101.
Pensky, Max. (ed.) (1997), *The Actuality of Adorno: Critical Essays on Adorno and the Postmodern*, Albany: SUNY Press.
Plato. (1877), *The Apology*, trans. James Riddell, Oxford: Oxford University Press.
Plato. (1967), *The Symposium*, trans. Walter Hamilton, Harmondsworth: Penguin.
Plumwood, Val. (2007), 'Journey to the Heart of Stone', *Nature, Culture, and Literature*, 5: 17–36.

Poole, Roger. (2002), 'Towards a Theory of Responsible Reading' in Niels Jørgen Cappelørn, Hermann Deuser and Jon Steward (eds), *Kieregaard Studies: Yearbook 2002*, 395–442, Berlin: Walter de Gruyter.
Readings, Bill. (1991), *Introducing Lyotard: Art and Politics*, London: Routledge.
Reeve, C.D.C. (ed.) (2006), *Plato on Love*, trans. Alexander Nehamas and Paul Woodruff, Indianapolis and Cambridge: Hackett Publishing Co.
Robbins, Jill. (1999), *Altered Reading: Levinas and Literature*, Chicago: University of Chicago Press.
Rose, Deborah Bird. (2013), 'Val Plumwood's Philosophical Animism: Attentive Interactions in the Sentient World', *Environmental Humanities*, 3: 93–109.
Rosenwald, Michael S. (2014), 'Serious Reading Takes a Hit from Online Scanning and Skimming, Researchers Say', *Washington Post*, 6 April. Available online: http://www.washingtonpost.com/local/serious-reading-takes-a-hit-from-online-scanning-and-skimming-researchers-say/2014/04/06/088028d2-b5d2–11e3-b899–20667de76985_story.html (accessed 28 May 2014).
Rubenstein, Mary-Jane. (2011), *Strange Wonder: The Closure of Metaphysics and the Opening of Awe*, New York: Columbia University Press.
Ryle, Gilbert. (1946), 'Knowing How and Knowing That', *Proceedings of the Aristotelian Society*, New Series, Vol. 46: 1–16.
Sartre, Jean-Paul. (1945), *Huis clos*, Paris: Éditions Gallimard.
Sartre, Jean-Paul. (1949), *L'Age de raison*, Paris: Éditions Gallimard.
Sartre, Jean-Paul. ([1943] 1956), 'Being-for-Others' in *Being and Nothingness*, trans. Hazel Barnes, 221–430, New York: Philosophical Library.
Sayre, Patricia. (2004), 'Philosophy as Profession' in Havi Carel and David Gamez (eds), *What Philosophy Is: Contemprary Philosophy in Action*, 241–55, London and New York: Continuum.
Schaeffer, Denise. (1999), 'Wisdom and Wonder in "Metaphysics" A:1–2', *The Review of Metaphysics*, 52 (3): 641–56.
Schor, Naomi. (1987), *Reading in Detail: Aesthetics and the Feminine*, New York: Methuen Press.
Schrift, Alan. (1995), 'Cixous: on the Gift-Giving Virtue as Feminine Economy' in *Nietzsche's French Legacy: A Genealogy of Poststructuralism*, London: Routledge.
Scott, H. Jill. (1995), 'Loving the Other: Subjectivities of Proximity in Hélène Cixous's *Book of Promethea*', *World Literature Today*, 69 (1): 29–34.
Secomb, Linnell. (1999), 'Beauvoir's Minoritarian Philosophy', *Hypatia*, 14 (4): 96–113.
Seel, Martin. (2004), 'Adorno's Contemplative Ethics', *Critical Horizons: Journal of Social & Critical Theory*, 5 (1): 259–69.

Sellers, Susan. (1996), *Hélène Cixous: Authorship, Autobiography and Love*, Oxford: Polity Press.
Sharp, Hasana. (2011), *Spinoza and the Politics of Renaturalization*, Chicago: Chicago University Press.
Shiach, Morag. (1991), *Hélène Cixous: A Politics of Writing*, London and New York: Routledge.
Shorter Oxford English Dictionary: On Historical Principles (2007), Sixth Edition Vol 1. A–M, Oxford: Oxford University Press.
Shorter Oxford English Dictionary (2007), Vol 2. N–Z, Oxford: Oxford University Press.
Sikka, Sonia. (1999), 'How Not to Read the Other: "All the Rest Can Be Translated" (Emmanuel Levinas)', *Philosophy Today*, 43 (2): 195–206.
Sim, Stuart. (ed.) (1998), *Post-Marxism: A Reader*, Edinburgh: Edinburgh University Press.
Simons, Margaret A. (1998), 'An Appeal to Reopen the Question of Influence', *Philosophy Today*, 42: 17–24.
Simons. Margaret A. (2006), *The Philosophy of Simone de Beauvoir: Critical Essays*, Margaret A. Simons (ed.), Bloomington: Indiana University Press.
Simons, Margaret A. and Benjamin, Jessica. (1979), 'Beauvoir Interview (1979)' in *Beauvoir and the Second Sex: Feminism, Race, and the Origins of Existentialism*, 1–21, Lanham: Rowman & Littlefield.
Singer, Linda. (1985), 'Interpretation and Retrieval: Rereading Beauvoir', *Women's Studies International Forum*, 8 (3): 231–38.
Smith, Steven G. (1986), 'Reason as One for Another: Moral and Theoretical Argument' in Richard A. Cohen (ed.), *Face to Face With Levinas*, 53–72, New York: SUNY Press.
Spivak, Gayatri Chakravorty. (1992), 'Cixous sans Frontièrs' in Mireille Calle-Gruber (ed.), *Du féminin*, 65–81, Grenoble: Publications de l'Université de Grenoble.
Spivak, Gayatri Chakravorty. (1993), *Outside in the Teaching Machine*, New York: Routledge.
Stalker (1979), [Film] Dir. Andrei Tarkovsky.
Steinbock, Anthony J. (2004), 'Affection and Attention: On the Phenomenology of Becoming Aware', *Continental Philosophy Review*, 37 (1): 21–43.
Still, Judith. (2002), 'Poetic Nuptials', *Paragraph*, 25 (3): 7–21.
Suleiman, Susan Rubin. (1991), 'Writing Past the Wall: Or the Passion According to H.C.', introductory essay to Hélène Cixous, '*Coming to Writing' and Other Essays*, Deborah Jenson (ed.), vii–xxii, Cambridge: Harvard University Press.
Taminiaux, Jacques. (1996), '*Bios politikos* and *bios theoretikos* in the Phenomenology of Hannah Arendt', trans. Dermot Moran, *International Journal of Philosophical Studies*, 4 (2): 215–32.

The Dreamers (2003), [Film] Dir. Bernardo Bertolucci.
Thompson, Michael Guy. (1997), 'Logos, Poetry and Heidegger's Conception of Creativity', *Psychotherapy in Australia*, 3 (4): 60–5.
Tidd, Ursula. (1999), 'The Self–Other Relation in Beauvoir's Ethics and Autobiography', *Hypatia*, 14 (4): 163–74.
Veto, Miklos. (1994), *The Religious Metaphysics of Simone Weil*, trans. Joan Dargan, Albany: SUNY Press.
Vintges, Karen. (1996), 'A Place for Love' in *Philosophy as Passion: The Thinking of Simone de Beauvoir*, 46–66, Bloomington: Indiana University Press.
Waithe, Mary Ellen. (1987), 'Diotima of Mantinea' in Mary Ellen Waithe (ed.), *A History of Women Philosophers: Vol. 1 Ancient Women Philosophers 600 B.C.–500 A.D.*, 83–116, Dordrecht: Martinus Nijhoff.
Walsh, Sylvia. (1998), 'Feminine Devotion and Self-abandonment: Simone de Beauvoir and Søren Kierkegaard, on the Woman in Love', *Philosophy Today*, 42: 35–40.
Ward, Julie K. (1999), 'Reciprocity and Friendship in Beauvoir's Thought', *Hypatia*, 14 (4): 36–49.
Weber, Samuel. (1987), *Institution and Interpretation*, Minneapolis: University of Minnesota Press.
Weber, Samuel. (2002), '"As Though the End of the World Had Come and Gone" or *Allemal ist nicht immergleich* – Critical Theory and the Task of Reading' in Nigel Gibson and Andrew Rubin (eds), *Adorno: A Critical Reader*, 379–99, Malden: Blackwell.
Weil, Simone. ([1950] 1951), *Waiting on God*, trans. Emma Craufurd, London: Routledge and Kegan Paul.
Weil, Simone. ([1947] 1995), *Gravity and Grace*, trans. Emma Craufurd, London: Routledge.
Weil, Simone. (2002), *The Need for Roots: Prelude to a Declaration of Duties Toward Mankind*, trans. Arthur Willis, New York: Routledge.
Wellbery, David. (2003), 'Stimmung' in Karlheinz Barck et al. (eds), *Historisches Wörterbuch Ästhetischer Grundbegriffe*, Bd. 5: *Postmoderne-Synästhesie*, Stuttgart und Weimar: Metzler.
Whitford, Margaret. (1986), 'Speaking as a Woman: Luce Irigaray and the Female Imaginary', *Radical Philosophy*, 43: 3–8
Whitford, Margaret. (1991), *Luce Irigaray: Philosophy in the Feminine*, London and New York: Routledge.
Whitford, Margaret. (1994), 'Reading Irigaray in the Nineties' in Carolyn Burke, Naomi Schor and Margaret Whitford (eds), *Engaging with Irigaray: Feminist Philosophy and Modern European Thought*, 15–33, New York: Columbia University Press.
Wilson, Ann. (1989), 'History and Hysteria: Writing the Body in *Portrait of Dora* and *Signs of Life*', *Modern Drama*, 32 (1): 73–88.

Wittgenstein, Ludwig. (1967), *Zettel*, trans. G.E.M. Anscombe, G.H. von Wright and G.E.M. Anscombe (eds), Berkeley: University of California Press.
Wittgenstein, Ludwig. (1976), *Wittgenstein's Lectures on the Foundations of Mathematics, Cambridge 1939*, Cora Diamond (ed.), Hassocks: Harvester Press.
Wittgenstein, Ludwig. (1984), *Über Gewissheit* – on Certainty, Frankfurt: Suhrkamp.
Wittgenstein, Ludwig. (1998), *Culture and Value*, trans. Peter Winch, Georg Henrik von Wright (ed.), Oxford: Blackwell.
Wolf, Maryanne. (2007), *Proust and the Squid: The Story and Science of the Reading Brain*, New York: Harper.
Wolin, Richard. (2014), 'National Socialism, World Jewry, and the History of Being: Heidegger's Black Notebooks', *Jewish Review of Books*. Available online: http://jewishreviewofbooks.com/articles/993/national-socialism-world-jewry-and-the-history-of-being-heideggers-black-notebooks/
Woolf, Virginia. (1925), 'How Should One Read a Book?' in *The Common Reader* Vol. I, 258–70, London: Harcourt.
Woolf, Virginia. (1925a), 'The Modern Essay' in *The Common Reader* Vol. I, 211–22, London: Harcourt.
Woolf, Virginia. (1976), *Moments of Being: Unpublished Autobiographical Writings*, Jeanne Schulkind (ed.), Reading: Chatto & Windus.
Ziarek, Krzysztof. (1994), *Inflected Language: Toward a Hermeneutics of Nearness – Heidegger, Levinas, Stevens, Celan*, Albany: SUNY Press.
Ziarek, Krzysztof. (2001), 'Art as Forcework', *Existentia*, 11 (3–4): 355–71.
Ziarek, Krzysztof. (2007), 'A New Economy of Relations' in Maria C. Cimitile and Elaine P. Miller (eds), *Returning to Irigaray: Feminist Philosophy, Politics, and the Question of Unicy*, 51–75, Albany: SUNY Press.

INDEX

abandon 164–8, 174–5, 179, 180, 242 n.14
acceleration 170
acedia 10
Adorno, Theodor W. xvi, xix, xx, 4, 56, 61–6, 67, 70, 71, 73, 75, 90, 92, 184, 217–18 n.50, 268 n.41
adversary paradigm 207 n.18
aesthetics/aesthetic experience xv, xx, xxiv, 20–1, 66, 71–3, 183, 184–6, 189
Aha-Erlrbnis 31, 204 n.76
Ajzenstat, Oona 211 n.17
Althusser, Louis xii, 191 n.1–2, 248 n.39
ambiguity xx, 4, 33, 48, 65, 80, 82, 86, 87, 88, 92, 132, 133, 134, 137, 162, 168, 249 n.40, 262–3 n.81
ancient philosophy 27–29
Andermatt Conley, Verena 264 n.8, 266 n.22, 270 n.53
Anderson, Sherwood 9
anxiety xxi, 4, 24, 52, 56, 58, 61, 78, 98, 99, 100–1, 140, 167, 182, 210 n.7
approach xxiii, 69, 73, 111–12, 156, 166, 169–71, 172–3, 174–5
Arendt, Hannah xii, 8, 192 n.4, 195–6 n.29, 229 n.12
Aristotle 3, 109, 226 n.42

art 9, 20, 67, 71, 138, 160, 177, 183, 185, 186, 187, 188, 214 n.33, 216 n.43
atmosphere xiv, 33, 70–1, 178, 182, 233–4 n.34
attention/attentiveness xv–xvi, xxii–xxiii, xxiv, 12, 14, 34, 47, 49, 53, 76–7, 87, 94, 97, 98, 103–25, 105, 112, 115–16, 118–19, 120–1, 138–9, 140, 154, 169–71, 175, 177–89, 219–20 n.2, 269 n.52, 271 n.3, 271–2 n.9
Auerbach, Erich 217 n.47
aura 138–9
awe xxi, 99–100

Bacon, Francis 217–18 n.50
Bakewell, Sarah 217 n.48
Barker, Victoria 208 n.26
Baudelaire, Charles 138
Bauer, Nancy 244 n.20
Bauerlinc, Mark xviii, 13–14, 208 n.23, 237–8 n.48
Beauvoir, Simone de xvi, xxii, 50, 127–54, 164–5, 181, 204 n.2, 206 n.12, 206 n.16
Benjamin, Walter 9, 138–9, 185, 191 n.4, 195 n.29, 212 n.24, 213 n.25, 215–16 n.40, 216 n.42
Bergson, Henri 40, 201 n.63

Bernasconi, Robert xx, 211 n.17
Bertolucci, Bernardo 177, 271 n.2
between-two 115–16
Bickford, Susan 228 n.6
Bildung 20, 48
Blondel, Eric 237 n.47
Bloom, Harold 247 n.33
Blyth, Ian 166
body xxi, 32, 70, 78, 85, 91, 93, 95, 100, 104, 107–8, 109, 110, 112, 115–16, 119, 129, 158–9, 160–2, 163–4, 187, 218 n.51, 219 n.53, 229 n.14, 233–4 n.34, 264 n.9
book 18, 42, 157, 163, 170
Boman, Thorlief 229–30 n.17
borders of philosophy 36, 40
Boulous Walker, Michelle 62, 191 n.2, 199 n.47, 200 n.54, 201 n.60, 203 n.70, 204 n.1, 205 n.5, 206 n.16, 208 n.28, 209 n.33, 209 n.2, 211 n.17, 213 n.25, 215 n.39, 225 n.36, 226 n.40, 228 n.5, 233 n.33, 248 n.39, 250–1 n.46, 251 n.50, 255 n.64, 264 n.3, 268 n.36, 271 n.60
Bray, Abigail 270 n.56
breath 158, 159, 161, 163
Brennan, Teresa xvi, xxiv, 140, 181–2, 192 n.8–9, 203 n.72, 218 n.52, 219–20 n.2, 271–2 n.9
Britto, Paulo Henriques 215 n.39

Calle-Gruber, Mireille 160, 182, 267 n.31
Camus, Albert 214 n.32, 245–6 n.27

Carel, Havi 110, 228 n.1, 231 n.21–2
Carter, Paul 209 n.5
Cartesianism 90–1, 94–5
Castro, Brian 192 n.5
Celan, Paul 120
Champagne, Roland 211 n.17
Chanter, Tina 221 n.16, 222–3 n.20, 224 n.24, 224–5 n.30, 260 n.76
chiasm 174, 270–1 n.59–60
Cilliers, Paul 11, 192 n.7, 193 n.12–13
cinema 13
Cixous, Héléne xvi, xxiii, 154, 155–75, 179, 180, 182
Clarke, David L. 211 n.16
collaborative thinking/relation/work 22, 39, 46, 47, 50, 169, 206 n.13, 238 n.52
collegiality 34, 204 n.77
complexity xiii, xiv, xiv, xvii, xviii, 8, 11, 19–20, 31, 37, 48, 58, 65, 80, 86, 92, 123, 152, 177, 181, 186, 273 n.14, 273 n.15
configuration 63, 64, 212 n.23, 213 n.28
contemplation xvii, xx, 4, 21, 66, 95–6, 98–99, 118, 171, 180, 184, 274 n.15
control 36
Cornell, Sarah 265 n.17
Cossery, Albert 193 n.11
Costa Lima, Luiz xvi, xx, 26, 27, 66–9, 70, 71, 73, 185, 200–1 n.55–7, 265 n.19
Cottingham, J 225 n.37
Craig, Geoffrey 199 n.49
Critchley, Simon xvi, xviii, xx, 22–23, 47–8, 58, 125, 198–9 n.43–5, 204 n.77, 211 n.17, 238 n.51

criticity xx, 26, 66–9, 73, 185,
    200–1 n.55

D'Agostino, Fred 247 n.33
Davies, Emma 227 n.51
debt/indebtedness 167, 175
Deleuze, Gilles 40, 217 n.46,
    253–4 n.60, 260 n.78
Della Subin, Anna 193 n.11
Democritus 40
Derrida, Jacques 89–90, 202 n.68,
    208 n.26, 219 n.58, 228 n.2
Descartes, René 3–4, 26, 28, 63,
    73, 76, 90–98, 173,
    201 n.63, 202 n.64,
    214 n.30, 217–18 n.50
desire 96–7, 99, 133, 156–8, 162,
    165, 183, 186
  neurotic xix,
  to know xvi, xvii, xix, 1f, 35,
    46, 59, 91, 96, 99, 104, 105,
    109, 114, 120, 123, 137,
    175, 178
detail 206 n.16, 255 n.62
Deutscher, Max 49, 209 n.31,
    226 n.41, 227 n.52,
    237 n.46, 244 n.19,
    245 n.23–4, 256 n.67,
    260 n.76
Deutscher, Penelope 43, 206 n.17
devotion 129, 131, 136, 141,
    153–4, 164–5, 242 n.14,
    247 n.34, 247–8 n.36,
    260 n.78, 262 n.80,
    263 n.82
Diotima 76, 78–90, 221 n.15,
    222–3 n.18–21, 224–5 n.30
Diprose, Rosalyn 211 n.14,
    251 n.47, 262–3 n.81
discernment xxiv, 140, 154, 181,
    182, 203 n.72, 218 n.52
discipline of philosophy xviii,
    36–7, 49
Dowrick, Stephanie 203 n.70

dream-work 59
Drichel, Simone 211 n.14
During, Lisabeth 207 n.21
dwelling xv, 9, 118, 161
Dyer, Geoff 273 n.16

écriture feminine 160, 166
efficiency xiii, xiv–xvi, 5, 11, 188
Eichmann, Adolf xiii
Eilenberger, Wolfram 202 n.67
entredeux 33, 158–62, 165, 172,
    182
eros 2, 153
erotico-theoretical transference
    144–8, 251 n.50,
    253–4 n.60
essay xix, xx, 51, 55–73, 184
essayistic reading xix, xx, 33,
    55–73, 75, 178
ethical
  approach 174
  community of readers xvii, 179
  domain xvi, xxii
  encounter 128, 137, 156, 179
  movement toward the other
    80, 98, 143, 179
  openness to the world 52, 66
  space 60
ethics
  and aesthetics 185
  as authenticity 142–3
  and criticity 185
  as generosity 180
  as grace 180
  as intimacy 168, 179
  of reading vii, xvi–ii, xxi, 60,
    73, 92, 98, 138, 140, 154,
    168, 171, 174–5, 180, 188
  of response xx, 57
  of the trade 37
  as work 174
exclusion
  philosophy as 36, 40
  of women xix, 41, 51, 206 n.13

felicity 174, 179
fiction 68, 151, 159, 163, 188
Flanagan, Richard xii, 1, 35, 55, 75, 103, 127, 155, 177, 188–9
flâneur 8, 9, 195–6 n.29, 213 n.25
Fletcher, Lancelot 122–4, 238 n.49–50
form 62, 67–8, 69, 71, 75
Foucault, Michel 202 n.64, 204 n.77
fragment/fragmentary 63, 68, 212 n.24, 216–17 n.45
Freadman, Anne 251–2 n.52
Freud, Sigmund 15, 59, 77, 94, 110, 157–8, 163, 201 n.61, 203 n.72, 210 n.7, 220 n.4, 221 n.11, 264 n.5, 271–2 n.9
fusion 173
Fuss, Diana 205 n.9
future philosophy xix, xx, xxi, 33, 36, 37, 40, 46, 47, 49, 50, 52–3, 56, 60, 62, 69, 88, 110, 125

Gaita, Raimond 15, 197–8 n.37–8
Gallop, Jane 204 n.3, 220 n.9
Garner, Helen 196–7 n.31
gift/giving 119, 154, 160, 162–4, 165–6, 168–9, 174–5, 178, 268 n.38
Godard, Jean-Luc 177, 271 n.2
Godzich, Wlad xvii, 6, 178
Goethe, Johann Wolfgang 30, 31, 203 n.74
goodness 60
Google 14
Gora, Joseph 199 n.49
Goss, Caitlin 196–7 n.31, 227 n.51, 250 n.45
Gothlin, Eva 246 n.28, 246 n.31
grace xxiii, xxiv, 33, 75, 158, 162, 174–5, 177–89

gravity xxiv, 29, 33, 177, 179–82, 201 n.59
Greisch, Jean 211 n.15
Guenther, Lisa 267 n.34
guiding idea of philosophy xvii, 7–8, 178
Gumbrecht, Hans Ulrich xvi, xviii, xx, xxiv, 19–22, 30, 32, 48, 69–71, 73, 95, 123, 182, 186–7, 197 n.33, 197–8 n.35–37, 198 n.39–40, 202 n.69, 203 n.72–3, 233–4 n.34
Guzzoni, Ute 203 n.70, 215 n.36–7

habit xvi, xviii, 35–41, 46, 48–50, 52–3, 112, 118, 123, 178
habitation 1
Hadot, Pierre xvii, 2, 27–30, 139, 181, 182, 191 n.2, 194 n.19, 201 n.63, 202 n.64–5, 214 n.30, 217 n.48, 231–2 n.25
Halperin, David 224–5 n.30
Hansen, Linda 133, 135, 245 n.24–5, 246 n.29–30
happiness 114
Hegel, GWF 42, 79, 107, 141, 143, 144, 167, 194 n.20, 211 n.17, 214 n.33, 221 n.14, 245 n.26, 245–6 n.27, 249 n.40
Heidegger, Martin xiv–xv, 108, 120, 170, 171, 209 n.4, 229 n.15, 236–7 n.45, 269 n.46
art, philosophy and time 9
being-in-the-world xv
calculative thinking and thoughtlessness 4, 183–4, 185, 188
dwelling xv, 9, 231 n.21

INDEX

Gelassenheit 183, 187, 272 n.12, 272–3 n.13
hermeneutics of nearness 171
listening and hearing 235–6 n.42
rapture and meditative thinking 182–4, 185
resource xiv–xvi
thing xvi
Heinämaa, Sara 242–3 n.15
heresy 64, 65
Hillis Miller, J 191 n.3
Hirsch, Elizabeth 220 n.3
Hölderlin, Friedrich 9
Honoré, Carl 24, 215 n.35
Horkheimer, Max 61
human resources xiv
Hustvedt, Siri 48–9, 195 n.26, 208 n.24, 208 n.27, 228 n.4
Hyppolite, Jean 42

identity thinking 61–2
imaginary 41, 160
imagination 25, 33, 39, 53, 65, 72
incompleteness xix, 51, 63, 216–17 n.45
institution xiii, xiv, xvi, xviii, 1f, 49, 61–2, 93, 110, 122, 123, 125, 127, 188, 189
  corporate nature of 18, 178, 186, 188
  instituted structure xvi, 35, 60, 175, 178
  instituting moment xvi, xvii, xix, xxii, xxiii, xxiv, 35, 48, 60, 72, 75, 125, 154, 178, 186, 189
institutionalization of thinking and reading 186
'intrinsic and violent instability' 178
instrumental
  reading xv
  reason 4, 61–2, 65

intensity xiii, xvi, xviii, xx, xxiv, 10, 21, 48, 70–1, 73, 123, 161, 177, 182, 186–7
interchangeability xiv
interval 68, 92, 93, 95, 112, 119, 171, 172, 173
intimacy xxiii, 70, 132, 134, 155, 158, 160, 161, 165, 166, 168–9, 171, 174, 178, 179, 182, 237 n.46
Irigaray, Luce xvi, xx, xxi, 26–7, 73, 75–101, 103–25, 127, 131, 167, 171–3, 183, 201 n.58–60, 219 n.58, 241 n.11, 247 n.35, 270–1 n.59
Iser, Wolfgang 195 n.28
Ivory tower 20

Jardine, Alice 259 n.75, 262 n.79
Jarvis, Simon 213 n.27
Jonas, Hans xxi, 104–8, 109, 232 n.30, 248 n.39
judgement xiii, 8, 16–17, 18, 25, 32, 33, 66, 67, 69, 71, 91, 93–4, 97, 99, 112, 122, 123, 181, 185, 187, 195 n.25, 195 n.27, 217 n.49, 218 n.52, 271 n.8
justice 2

Kabat-Zinn, John 202 n.66
Kahnemann, Daniel xvii, 193 n.14
Kamuf, Peggy xviii, 18–19, 197 n.32, 233 n.31
Kant, Immanuel 42, 66, 107, 143, 194 n.20, 201, n.63, 215 n.39, 229 n.13, 245–6 n.27, 247–8 n.36, 260 n.78
Kelso, Julie 220 n.3, 230–1 n.20, 231 n.23, 247 n.35, 249 n.42

INDEX

Kierkegaard, Søren 153, 165, 201 n.63, 249 n.40, 263 n.82
Koepnick, Lutz 192 n.10
Köhler, Wolfgang 204 n.76
Kristeva, Julia 221 n.15

Lacan, Jacques 111, 158, 160, 204 n.76, 204 n.3, 232 n.26, 243–4 n.16
La Caze, Marguerite 208 n.25, 226 n.43
Lacoue-Labarthe, Philippe 216–17 n.45
Lamb, Matthew 201 n.56–7, 201 n.62, 214 n.32
laughter 222 n.18
law 67–8, 157, 160, 162, 164, 166, 181, 185, 265 n.19, 266 n.24
Le Dœuff, Michèle xvi, xviii, xix, xxiii, 35–53, 56, 60, 110, 128, 135, 144–9, 169, 204 n.1, 204 n.4, 205 n.7–8, 211 n.19, 238–9 n.53, 247 n.35, 250–1 n.46
Leibniz, Gottfried Wilhelm 42, 212 n.23
letting-be 118, 119, 121, 234–5 n.38, 235 n.40–2
Levinas, Emmanuel xvi, xix–xx, 4, 56–61, 62, 73, 75, 120, 133, 171, 199–200 n.50, 219 n.58, 222–3 n.20, 226 n.45, 231 n.23, 245–6 n.27
Linklater, Richard 271 n.2
Lispector, Clarice 169–71, 173, 174–5
listening xii, xxi, xxii, 76–7, 89, 112, 174, 215 n.36, 220 n.4–7, 229–30 n.17
associations with femininity and receptivity 116
attentive 33, 103–25
listening-to xxi, xxii, 103, 108, 110, 112, 118, 124–5
listening-with xxi, 108, 178
literature 69, 70, 163, 216 n.43, 256–7 n.70
Lloyd, Genevieve 38–9
Lloyd, Martyn 219 n.57
Lourau, René 6
love xx, xxi, 71, 73, 75–90, 98–101, 119–20, 155, 163, 164–8, 172–3, 178
  authentic xxii, 127–54
  daimonic 81, 82, 83
  romantic xxii, 127–54, 164
  of wisdom xvi, xvii, xx, xxiv, 1f, 34, 35, 39, 48, 53, 81, 113, 119, 154, 155, 175, 178, 186, 189
Luhmann, Niklas 19, 187, 197 n.34
Lukács, Georg 67–8, 70, 71, 201 n.55, 216 n.42, 219 n.55
Lupton, Catherine 214–15 n.34
Lyotard, Jean-François 25–6, 69, 200 n.51–4, 217 n.49, 272 n.10

McGilchrist, Iain xvii, 12–13
McGinn, Marie 194 n.19
Macherey, Pierre 205 n.6, 248 n.37
Malabou, Catherine 207 n.21
Malebranche, Nicolas 41
Mansuetude 175
Maras, Steven 208 n.26
Marker, Chris 214–15 n.34
Marx, Karl xii, 201 n.63, 204 n.77, 247–8 n.36
mass culture 214 n.33
meditation/meditative xxiv, 5, 9, 30, 33, 66, 69, 121, 140,

178, 181, 182–4, 202 n.66, 234–5 n.38
Merleau-Ponty, Maurice 5–6, 48, 174, 198 n.41, 201 n.63, 217 n.47, 226 n.43, 245–6 n.27, 270–1 n.59
Miedema, John 194 n.15
Miller, Liam 227 n.51
Mikics, David 200 n.50
Mimicry 240–1 n.6
mindfulness 202 n.66
Mitsein 76, 244 n.20
Monk, Ray 15–16, 194 n.21–2
Montaigne, Michel de 69, 201–2 n.63, 217 n.47–8
mood xiv, 33, 70–1, 86, 95, 178, 182, 183, 233–4 n.34
Morgan, Kathryn Pauly 241 n.9, 242–3 n.15, 244 n.17, 262 n.80
Morris, Meaghan 205 n.8, 208 n.25, 233 n.33
Moulton, Janet 206–7 n.18, 210 n.11
mourning 159
Musil, Robert xvi, xx, 71–3

Nancy, Jean-Luc 216–17 n.45, 228 n.2, 233 n.32
narcissism 147, 240 n.5
nature 61
nearness xxi, 60, 104, 111–12, 119–21, 171–3, 174, 178, 185
neuroscience xvii, 12–13
neurosis 40, 53, 58, 137
Newkirk, Thomas 194 n.15
Nicholls, Angus 222 n.19
Nicholls, Daniel 238–9 n.53
Nietzsche, Friedrich xvi, xviii, xxiv, 23–32, 39, 42, 71, 72, 78, 100, 121–4, 128, 129, 153–4, 157, 164–5, 168, 174, 183, 188, 199 n.46–7, 201 n.59, 201 n.63, 202 n.65, 215 n.35, 219 n.54, 239 n.3, 260–1 n.78, 266 n.22, 266 n.26, 268 n.38
Novalis 138
Nozick, Robert 109
Nuyen, Tuan 225 n.35
Nuzzo, Angelica 229 n.13
Nye, Andrea 88–90, 221 n.13

Oliver, Kelly 199 n.47
Ondaatje, Michael 195 n.28
Ong, Walter 229 n.11, 229–30 n.17
open-endedness xix, xx, 29, 40–1, 51, 56, 60, 62, 64, 65, 66, 75, 77, 80, 88, 178, 201 n.61
openness 20, 29, 31, 50, 53, 63, 66, 98, 167, 168–9, 178–9, 183, 185, 219 n.57, 235–6 n.42
operative philosophy 50, 128, 144–9
other xxi, 57, 65, 96, 99, 109, 111, 112–13, 114–15, 117, 119, 121, 125, 133, 136, 138, 158–61, 163, 170, 174–5, 178, 180–1, 182, 185, 270 n.56
otherness 31, 36, 53, 57, 70, 72–3, 92, 134, 149, 162, 171, 182

Parkins, Wendy 199 n.49
Pascal, Blaise 207 n.22
passion/s xxi, 94, 95–6, 99, 132, 141, 142, 145, 153, 158, 160, 161, 173, 174, 179, 225 n.31
passivity 5, 65, 96, 141, 162, 179, 215 n.36

patience xix, 8, 57, 61, 65, 122, 171, 174, 178, 179–80, 183, 209 n.3
pedagogy xvii, xxii, 22, 46, 123–5, 144, 222 n.18, 238–9 n.53
philosophy as way of life xvi, xx, 20, 48, 53, 66, 75, 81, 101, 104, 175, 178, 186, 189
Plato 73, 76, 78, 84, 85, 89, 153, 191 n.1–2, 221 n.12, 221–3 n.17–21, 224 n.28, 225 n.34
Platonism 88–90, 95
Plumwood, Val 226 n.43, 231 n.24
poetry/poetic writing 68, 71, 112–13, 114, 120, 138, 141, 157, 160, 162, 163–4, 216 n.43, 236 n.43, 268 n.41, 270–1 n.59
politics xv
Poole, Roger 191 n.3
productivity xiii
proximity xxi, 29, 33, 60, 61, 68, 73, 75, 96, 99, 104, 110, 111–12, 119–21, 134, 141, 158, 163, 165, 167, 171–4, 178, 185, 186, 237 n.46, 269 n.48, 270 n.54–5
psychoanalysis 76–8, 110–11, 136, 157–8, 163, 167, 201 n.61, 203 n.72, 210 n.7, 220 n.3, 220 n.7, 220 n.9, 221 n.12, 225 n.38, 230–1 n.20–1, 264 n.10
psychology xvii, 12

questioning 33, 52, 62, 66, 67–8, 72, 80, 83, 95, 98, 119, 125, 185, 186
quiet/quietness 187

Ramsey, Carole 203 n.70
rapture (*Rausch*) 33, 177, 182–4
reader 103, 112
  attentive xx
  professional xiii
reading xii, 19, 103, 122, 175, 179, 182
  adversarial 33, 39
  as aesthetic experience 184–6
  ahistorical 38
  as auratic 139, 178
  authentic xxii, 127–54, 178
  authoritative xix, 43, 206 n.14
  as caring for 31
  as chiasm 174
  close 29
  combative 24
  as commentary 38, 41–6, 49, 205–6 n.10
  as deciphering 19
  definitions of 30, 204 n.75
  dust of 16, 24, 154, 181
  engaged 10
  as fidelity 38, 135, 145
  and gender xviii
  and generosity 49, 178
  as gift 168–9, 178
  as grace 175, 178
  guilty xii
  hierarchy of 47
  and imagery 38
  as incomplete 51, 80
  as information extraction xviii, 18, 23, 33, 52
  innocent xii
  institutional xv, 32–3, 154, 168, 175
  as interpretation 34
  as looking back 53
  loving and wondrous xx, 10, 75–101
  meandering xix, 33, 56, 63–5, 75, 178, 185

as nomadic 50, 52
non-authoratative 45
non-institutional 17, 65, 188
non-linear 13
open xvii
and pleasure 17, 188
as polite receptivity 43, 49, 178
professionally 18, 154, 189
receptive xix, 61, 65, 77, 178, 183, 215 n.36
recreationally 189
rereading xv, xxii, 11, 17, 53, 61, 73, 75, 86, 87, 98, 137, 140, 144, 145, 178
revelatory 10
romantic xxii, 45, 127–54
as seizing/grasping 57–8, 61, 124, 209–10 n.6
skimming techniques 13
and space 31–2
unfinished 10
unprofessionally 17, 188–9
as verdict 8, 17, 25, 33, 67, 79
Readings, Bill 25, 200 n.51–2
reciprocity 73, 132, 135, 151–2
Reeve, CDC 221–2 n.17
resentment 124–5
responsibility xx, 12, 57, 73, 131, 136, 242–3 n.15
Rilke, Rainer Maria 203 n.70, 266 n.23
riskful thinking 21, 198 n.40, 273 n.14
Roberts, Laura 230 n.19
Rose, Deborah Bird 231 n.24
Rosenwald, Michael 13
Rousseau, Jean-Jacques 208 n.29
rumination xix, 17, 24, 30, 31, 33, 65, 75, 98, 199 n.48, 213 n.26, 215 n.35, 237 n.48
Ryle, Gilbert 191–2 n.3

sadism 46–8
Same 59
Sartre, Jean-Paul xxiii, 128, 132, 143–53, 206 n.12, 206 n.16, 244 n.20, 245 n.25, 257 n.71, 259–60 n.75, 262 n.79
Sayre, Patricia 194 n.16
Schlegel, Friedrich von 216 n.41, 216 n.45
Scholastic tradition 27–9
Schopenhauer 27
Schor, Naomi 206 n.16
Schrift, Alan 266 n.26, 268 n.38
screenagers 13, 207–8 n.23
Secombe, Linnell 253–4 n.60, 256 n.66
secondary revision 59
seeing xii, 105–6
looking xxii, 9
sight xxi, 104–8, 109
Seel, Martin 66, 215 n.38
Sellers, Susan 159, 162, 166, 265 n.11, 265 n.14, 265 n.16, 266–7 n.29, 270 n.58
senses xxi, 104, 106–7, 109, 228 n.5
sensible transcendental 86, 95, 225 n.32
sexual difference 73, 94, 97, 113, 116, 161, 224–5 n.30, 267 n.34
Sharp, Hasana 205 n.6
Shiach, Morag 266 n.26, 269 n.49
Simons, Margaret 150, 250–1 n.46, 256–7 n.70
sitting with xv, 8, 181
slow 10
art 21
cure 14, 19
food movement 24, 215 n.35
work xiii

slowing down 9, 124, 169, 269 n.48
slowness xiii, xvii, 11, 31, 61, 169, 170, 181
　in musical notation and tempo 31
Smith, Steven 210 n.12
Socrates 2–3, 4, 34, 85, 153, 191 n.1, 221–2 n.17, 224 n.26
speaking xii, 103
speed xiii, xv, xvi, xix, 5, 10, 11, 14, 17, 26, 33, 34, 65, 72, 96, 178, 188, 189, 193 n.14
spiritual exercises 2, 139, 181, 231–2 n.25, 249 n.41
Spivak, Gayatri 168, 179, 205 n.9, 268 n.39
standing reserve xiv
Steinbock, Anthony 271 n.3
Stendhal 141
Stieglitz, Alfred 9, 20, 30, 31, 187, 192 n.6
Still, Judith 221 n.10
Stimmung xiv, xx, 69–71, 72, 73, 95, 178, 182, 203 n.72, 218 n.51, 219 n.53, 219 n.56, 233–4 n.34
strangeness xx, 4, 27, 31, 40, 57, 60, 65, 73, 92–3, 98, 133–5, 137, 147, 149, 154, 163, 167, 168–71, 173, 179, 182, 185
stress xiv
surrender 182, 183, 187

Tarkovsky, Andrei 273 n.16
teacher xxii, 43, 47, 124
teaching xviii, 22, 46–8, 88, 122–5, 221 n.15
technology xiv, 11, 18, 118, 183, 234 n.35, 234 n.37
tenderness 66, 169, 170–1

The New Yorker xiii
Thompson, Michael Guy 231 n.21
time 9, 19, 33, 72, 77, 105, 139, 140, 154, 155, 163, 168, 169, 170, 174, 187, 269 n.50–1
　pressure xiv, 48, 52, 125
　starved 186
temporality xiii, xx, 6, 20, 186
Trakakis, Nick 194 n.17
transference 77, 144, 148, 220 n.7, 220–1 n.9, 221 n.11
transformation xvii, xviii, xx, xxiii, xxiv, 2f, 34, 35, 50, 52–3, 60, 66, 72, 77, 79, 83, 92, 112, 119, 123, 125, 139, 154, 155, 160, 166, 168, 173, 178–9, 181, 182, 185, 186, 188

unconscious 59, 76, 111, 139, 157–8, 160–1, 210 n.7, 264 n.5
university xiii–xiv, 19, 20, 22, 24, 28, 33, 43–4, 47, 186, 197–8 n.36–8, 204 n.77, 212 n.23
untimeliness 20, 65, 186

voice 79, 88, 158, 218 n.51, 229 n.15
von Trotta, Margarethe xii

Waithe, Mary Ellen 224–5 n.30
waiting xv, 122, 170, 174, 180–1
Walker, Carolyn Bynum 227 n.54
Walsh, Sylvia 153, 242 n.14, 263 n.82, 267 n.32
Ward, Julie K 257 n.72, 258 n.73
Weber, Samuel 5, 6, 178, 214 n.33,
Weil, Simone xvi, xxiv, 179–81, 184, 203 n.70, 213 n.28

Wellbery, David 219 n.56
Whitford, Margaret 77,
 220–1 n.9
Wilson, Ann 264 n.9
Wilson, Emma 227 n.51
Wittgenstein, Ludwig xvi, xviii,
 14–16, 17, 18–19, 23,
 26, 32, 194 n.18–19,
 194 n.21–2, 201 n.63
Wolf, Marianne xvii, 13
wonder xx, xxi, 26–7, 62, 75,
 90–101, 111, 114, 115, 137,
 171, 173–4, 178, 183,
 226 n.42, 227 n.54,
 237 n.46

Woolf, Virgina xv, xviii, xxii,
 16–17, 181, 189,
 194 n.23–4, 195 n.29,
 196 n.30–1, 212 n.22,
 213 n.26
work xviii, xxiv, 24, 35, 38, 40,
 49, 50, 51–2, 72, 78, 110,
 116, 122, 156, 173, 174,
 188, 206 n.13, 233 n.32,
 235 n.42
writing 103, 156–68, 174

Ziarek, Kristof xvi, 120–1, 171–2,
 211 n.18, 235 n.41,
 236–7 n.45, 270–1 n.59